The Pragmatic Leader

THE PRAGMATIC LEADER

A GUIDE TO MASTERING KEY MANAGEMENT CONCEPTS

KENNETH D MCILROY

iUniverse, Inc.
New York Lincoln Shanghai

The Pragmatic Leader
A Guide to Mastering Key Management Concepts

All Rights Reserved © 2004 by KENNETH D. MCILROY

No part of this book may be reproduced or transmitted in any form or by any means, graphic, electronic, or mechanical, including photocopying, recording, taping, or by any information storage retrieval system, without the written permission of the publisher.

iUniverse, Inc.

For information address:
iUniverse, Inc.
2021 Pine Lake Road, Suite 100
Lincoln, NE 68512
www.iuniverse.com

ISBN: 0-595-31053-2 (Pbk)
ISBN: 0-595-66252-8 (Cloth)

Printed in the United States of America

Contents

List of Diagrams ix
Preface xi

Part I: BASIC ASSUMPTIONS 1
          1 Knowing But Not Doing 3
          2 Assumptions about Business 6
          3 Corporate Life Cycle 10
          4 Business Operations Model 19
          5 Virtual Corporation 22
          6 Personal Operations Model 26

Part II: COMPANY DIRECTION 31
          7 Business Success 33
          8 Choosing a Course 36
          9 The Mission 47
          10 Deployment of Resources 52
          11 Changes in Direction 57

Part III: LEADERSHIP 69
          12 What Is a Leader? 71
          13 Leadership in Action 77
          14 Company Cultures 86
          15 The Entrepreneur 89

Part IV: ATTITUDES AND EMOTIONS 93
          16 Change 95
          17 Work Attitudes 102
          18 Trust 105
          19 Emotions 108
          20 Personal Stability 111
          21 Fear 115

Part V:	SUCCESS	119
	22 Personal Mastery	121
	23 Controlling Time	133
	24 Being Successful	142
	25 Power and Influence	153
	26 Making Things Happen	159
	27 Problem Resolution	164
Part VI:	COMMUNICATION	171
	28 Communication Basics	173
	29 Organizational Communications—Special Situations	178
	30 Negotiations	187
Part VII:	MANAGEMENT	201
	31 Management Fundamentals	203
	32 The Best People	211
	33 Hiring Process	220
	34 Keeping Employees	237
	35 Developing Subordinates	244
	36 Training	251
	37 Employee Exits	262
	38 Meetings	268
	39 Board of Directors	271
	40 Miscellaneous Management Notes	273
Part VIII:	COMPANY OPERATIONS	281
	41 Business Focus	283
	42 Product/Service Delivery	286
	43 Internal Functions	291
	44 Consultants, Friends and Foes	295
Part IX:	SALES AND MARKETING	303
	45 The Sales Cycle	305
	46 Marketing Factors	307
	47 Selling	316
Part X:	CUSTOMERS	327
	48 Enthusiastic Customers	329
	49 Managing Customers	333

Part XI:	INFORMATION TECHNOLOGY	339
	50 Information Technology and Business	341
	51 The Internet	349
	52 Website Considerations	353
	53 IT Projects	362
Part XII:	FINANCES AND EXPENDITURES	367
	54 Financial Reporting	369
	55 Expenditures	372
	56 Managing Shareholder Value	375

CLOSING COMMENTS 377

Recommended Books and Tapes 379
Index 385

List of Diagrams

Chapter	Diagram	Page
3	Corporate Life Cycle	10
4	Business Operations Model	19
5	Virtual Corporation	23
6	Personal Operations Model	26
7	Business Success	34
8	Choosing a Course	37
8	Windows of Opportunity	41
10	Core vs. Support Functions	53
11	Changes in Direction	57
12	Leadership	71
12	Passion	75
13	Employee Motivation	80
15	The Entrepreneur	89
16	Change	96
22	Personal Mastery	122
23	Time Theft	134
24	New Executive Position	147
25	Politics	155
26	Closure	159
27	Modern Brainstorming	166
27	Solving the Problem	167
29	Team Interactions	180
29	Debriefings	182
29	Executive Dashboard	184
30	Power Negotiating	188
32	Best Bosses and Best Employees	211
33	Hiring Employees	222
33	New Hire Productivity	235
36	Training Needs	253
36	Professional Training	256

37	Firing People	263
37	Good Employee Losses	266
38	Meetings	268
41	Five Areas of Business Focus	284
42	Product/Service Delivery	286
44	Consulting Engagement Parameters	301
45	Sales Cycle	305
46	Product Training Schools	314
47	Selling a Solution	316
47	Cross-Selling	320
47	Internet Channel Conflict	322
48	Enthusiastic Customers	329

Preface

The Pragmatic Leader: A Guide to Mastering Key Management Concepts is a presentation of key executive leadership and management concepts in a concise way. It also addresses concepts in the area of self-evaluation and self-mastery, since a business leader must become a master of his or her own self before becoming an effective master of others.

It is often a challenge for busy executives to take a time-out, to clear their heads, and to take notice of where they and their companies are in corporate life. It is too easy to get into a rut—especially the rut of success—and ignore the tornado approaching from the rear. The weather looks clear toward the front, but that can be just a habitual perspective—the wrong perspective. This book helps the beleaguered executive look around and see what is going on—from various perspectives, hopefully some of which are new.

The targeted audience for this book includes executives, middle management, supervisors, and management wannabes. The book is a compilation of some of the best ideas in executive leadership and management, both new ones and old ones. The book is a succinct reminder of the key concepts that executives should be constantly reminding themselves not to forget nor ignore. The overall objective of the book is to make an executive or manager more successful than he or she already is. Successful executives lead their organizations to success after success.

The book's topics address concepts that apply personally to the executive (e.g., personal mastery) and other concepts that apply to the whole organization (e.g., core competencies). After laying out some basic assumptions about business and the executive, the book talks about deciding a company's direction, followed by an enumeration of the leadership principles needed to get to the intended destination. Then, the book lays down a foundation of the attributes needed to achieve success; the areas touched upon include attitude, emotion, self-control, and communication. With that underpinning in place, management practices are explored. Next, business operations, marketing, sales, customer relations, information technology, and finances are covered, before ending the book with some closing remarks.

This book is designed as a review, a chance for the leader to be reminded of things he or she has forgotten or has let get buried in the subconscious. It is expected that the reader, in the course of reading the book, will at times say, "Oh, I remember that!" Since many of the ideas have been gleaned from modern leaders of business thought, there may even be some ideas he or she never considered before.

There are many sources of good ideas. Many great ideas have come from great minds, people with more insight than most of us. Peter F. Drucker comes to mind. Agile, probing minds, if allowed, can lead us into new, wonderful territory. Most of us have received pointed instruction from the school of hard knocks, i.e., the lessons learned from terrible experiences and overwhelming pressures. In this case, the great idea comes from a falling brick that hits you square on the top of the head. After you pull yourself up from the sidewalk of life, you painfully realize you did get the point. Catastrophes change perspective. They shake up the status quo. They are a reality check.

To help reinforce concepts, a number of quotes from insightful people, ancient and modern, have been inserted strategically throughout the book. The selected quotes are short and to the point. Oftentimes, a poignant thought gets a point across much better than a whole paragraph of sentences. Think of the quotes as nuggets of wisdom imparted by people who took some time out to think. They had great ideas.

So, if there are great ideas out there—and there are plenty—why not take advantage of them? This book is full of great ideas—in condensed form—that have been assembled from many books and tapes. But some of the ideas come from the author's own experiences in business life.

> "I not only use all the brains that I have, but all that I can borrow."
> —Woodrow Wilson

I have been a student of business since first working for my father in his grocery store and his new car dealership. Following that, I worked in many different industries over the years and learned much—sometimes too late. My experiences have been many and varied. Much of what I learned from the school of hard knocks is represented here, tempered by the thinking of greater minds than myself. I love great ideas and soak them up like a sponge. In some cases, they are presented with new twists.

This book is sprinkled with many age-old truths—basic truths that have not really changed that much over the years, but are just being applied in new ways. What is the old saying, "There is nothing new under the sun." However, the book will attempt to present those old truths in new contexts—as provided by the constantly changing world of modern commerce.

But basic common sense still prevails in the long run. In the recent past, dot.coms and their investors got caught up in the rush to capture market share, while ignoring profits. Cash ran out. They were finally reminded that businesses must have earnings to survive.

> "Common sense is the knack of seeing things as they are, and doing things as they ought to be done."
>
> —Harriet Beecher Stowe

Executives know what needs to be done—if they will just let their logical mind get in the driver's seat, instead of succumbing to pride, prejudice, fear, or complacency. The frustrating part is that most of the best ideas of today have been known for years—even if left unused by many executives. Occasionally, new ideas will crop up; but for the most part, the best business principles have been known in basic form for a long time.

Connectivity and speed of communications have changed the relative applicability of the ideas, but there are few ideas that are completely new. The interesting part is that the new thinkers in the business world often apply the old ideas in ways never dreamed of before. There is a big toolbox of ideas out there for executives to draw upon. New contexts for using the tools arise every day. It is an exciting time in which to live.

The purpose of this book is to jog the executive's memory—maybe even stretch it a bit—to help him or her bring to mind the universal management truths that get trampled by day-to-day operations and the pressures of management.

Reflect for a moment. Open your mind to the ideas that can enhance your success. Refresh your memory. Learn some new things.

HOW TO USE THIS BOOK

In my formative years of becoming a professional, I was introduced to computer systems. From that point forward, I learned to approach things from a systems standpoint. Regardless of the problem or issue, I learned to gather enough detailed information to begin building the overall context, the big picture. Once the big picture was determined, the next step was to break down the big picture into successively smaller pictures, until all the necessary details were determined or new ones were developed (for instance, a new software application). This analytical approach is reflected in the structure of the book. The basic assumptions are presented first in Part I. Later sections expand upon these basic assumptions.

It is recognized that people are oriented in different ways when it comes to absorbing information or ideas. Although, there are other media for communication, this book uses two: visual and verbal. Diagrams help present visual images of ideas represented by the words in the text. Further, the diagrams provide a summary of the key concepts of a given topic. On a single page, you get a visual representation of the parts that make up the topic, plus see how the parts are interrelated. Thus, you get the logical flow of the parts, how they lead into each other. Not all topics lend themselves to such a diagram; but where a diagram can present a concise visual overview, a diagram has been provided.

There are several ways to use this book. First, the reader can search the table of contents or the index to find a topic of interest (e.g., negotiations) and read that. Second, the reader can just read the book from the first chapter through the last. This is the recommended approach. Then after the book has been read cover to cover, the reader can use the table of contents or the index to find a previously read topic for review purposes. Third, the diagrams can be referenced to get a visual summarization of many concepts presented in the book.

This book is designed to cover three types of readers, who are the following: (1) "I never knew that," (2) "I knew that in the past," and (3) "I know and practice that now." The three types of users represent three targeted levels of learning and experience. It would be very rare for any reader to fit exclusively into only one of the categories. Since the book covers a broad range of topics, it is expected that any executive reading the book will be a cross-section of all three categories. What follows is an elaboration of the three types of readers:

"I know and practice that now." This response might be attributed to the executive who has a full understanding of the topic and practices it regularly. However, this same executive might still derive some benefit from reading the topic. This type of reader is encouraged to think of applying the concepts in combinations not previously considered. Something said in the course of developing a particular topic might trigger the perceptive executive into placing the concept in a different light. This new perspective could pave the way for applying the concept toward a new opportunity, maybe in combination with other concepts presented in the book or ones already known by the executive.

"I knew that in the past." When an executive gives this response to a topic, it is like entering a room in a vast mansion, the contents of which have been forgotten. The contents are useful but have been ignored in the press of everyday events. In this situation, the executive is given a handy reminder of something he or she might find useful in current business activities. Also, the executive

could start to think out of the box, applying the concept in contexts not considered before.

"I never knew that." This might be the reaction of an executive encountering a topic that had never really registered before or was never known in the first place. There are many people out there with great ideas that do not get passed around to everyone. If this is the situation for the reader, the book has been helpful in opening up new horizons of thought. New business possibilities might arise as a result.

In short, the book attempts to present a kaleidoscope of topics, both new and old, that can be applied beneficially in carrying out an executive's responsibilities. If the ideas result in successful action being taken by the executive, the book will have done its job.

I hope you enjoy the book. I learned a lot writing it.

Kenneth McIlroy
kennethmcilroy@pragmaticleader.com
www.pragmaticleader.com
Catoosa, Oklahoma
February 2004

Part I

BASIC ASSUMPTIONS

1

Knowing But Not Doing

The business world is awash with great ideas on successful performance by businesses and their leaders. The ideas come from lectures, seminars, books, consultants, tapes, schools, magazines, newspapers, and other media. The problem is that after business leaders learn the ideas that would lead them to greatness, they do not put them into practice—even after paying big bucks to learn about them. The leaders know what to do but don't do it. Habits, organizational culture, or lack of assertiveness seem to hold them back. Before the ideas can bear fruit, they must be acted upon.

Talking about doing something is not the same as doing it. Company leaders present these good ideas to their subordinates and expect them to be put into practice. Talk is equated to action. Decisions are equated to action. But the proof is in the pudding. If it isn't measured, it doesn't happen. Follow-up by the leaders is necessary. Subordinates should be evaluated on how successful they are at putting the ideas into effect, rather than just giving them good marks for talking the ideas up. Focus on action and results, not talk.

Measure results. Subordinates assume anything managers decide to measure is important. But make sure what you measure is important and not just something that is convenient to measure. Make the measurements simple and few. The more you measure, the more likely some of the important measures are going to get lost in the clutter of unimportant measures. Complex measurements are their own worst enemies. It is hard to focus on many things at the same time. Limit the number of performance items tracked.

Focus on measurements that reflect organizational success rather than individual success. Align measurements with corporate goals and mission. Each employee should identify with the company, not individual departments. Departmental goals and measurements should promote organizational success.

Periodically re-evaluate the measurement systems. Make sure they are effective in translating ideas into results. Consider any measurement system to be a work in process; so, continually refine your measurements. Make sure they are effective.

Remember who your real competitor is. It's not internal people. It's the guy on the outside who is going to steal your customers. Foster cooperative organizational interdependence. Don't let rapid organizational growth result in departmental walls being erected and doors being closed. Encourage people to help one another—even across continents. Balance individual performance measurements with an emphasis on corporate success. Share ideas. Share knowledge. Cooperate. Support the team. Punish those who raise the individual above the team. Punish those who hoard knowledge and refuse to share best practices. Encourage people to be selfless, not selfish.

Simple is good. An idea is not better because it is complex. Some of the greatest ideas are quite simple. But putting a simple idea into effect is not always so easy. Hard work may be required. The more complex the idea or practice, the more likely it will fail. People are more apt to do something if they can easily understand it. Lack of understanding is a natural impediment to getting something done.

It is quite easy to come up with reasons for not doing things, even though you know some other companies have implemented the ideas successfully and benefited from the results. If you know an idea is a good one, reframe the question. First, decide you will do it. Second, make the new question, "How are we going to get around the problems?" Concentrate on solving problems rather than nay saying them.

Don't let common practice or historical precedents throw up roadblocks. Don't be afraid to admit past mistakes. Let go of the past. Look to the future. Be ready to change. Don't continue a practice just because it is an industry standard. Be open to changed conditions. Don't be afraid to experiment. Try something new. And don't wallow in self-pity because of some organizational mistake or an industry downturn. Act on the mistake. Do something to correct it. But don't try the first thing that pops into your head in order to get around the problem. Think through any planned actions; but avoid engaging in paralysis by analysis.

Accept mistakes as a given. They are going to happen. Make failure to act the real failure. If you are going to experiment with new ideas, you are going to make mistakes. If you delegate decision making, you are going get some bad decisions. Learn from the mistakes. Teach others in the organization how to do better. A learning organization is a growing organization. Reward for trying. Punish for not trying.

Leaders set the pattern for an organization. If they know what to do but do not act on their knowledge, how can they expect their people to do any differently? Lead by example.

2

Assumptions about Business

Over the years, some of the hardcore assumptions about business have undergone significant change, particularly in the past few decades. There are so many new facets to modern business and the world's marketplace, that some of the things learned in business school no longer apply. Therefore, executives must open their minds to some new bedrock principles. You as an executive may need to change your previously held beliefs.

Contrary to earlier beliefs, there is no one right organization. But there will always need to be leaders and followers—unless the business consists of just one person or just a few equal partners. Different organizational structures are appropriate in different business situations.

THE VIRTUAL CORPORATION

The virtual corporation, when fully implemented, links discrete businesses into a group of organizations that are tied together by formal and informal agreements. There was a tendency in the past for a business to do as much as possible within its own walls. The enlightened executive of today realizes that a business should concentrate on its core competencies and outsource the rest, including some functions that were rarely outsourced before.

The viewpoint for any virtual corporation is from the company to which an individual leader belongs. In the mind of a participant in a virtual corporation, the top of the pyramid is the core business that defines the company. Assuming you are that person, all other businesses or functions in the pyramid are there to support your core business.

With that viewpoint in mind, look at the rest of the pyramid. Treat the building blocks as separate functions. Examine each and decide which must be housed within your organization and which can be outsourced to some other company. In order to take advantage of your critical resources, meaning skilled people who may be in short supply, you may need to farm out non-core functions—even if it costs more. Why spread your key people too thin? Rapid changes in the marketplace necessitate rapid changes in a company. Minimize what you must change in your company.

KNOWLEDGE OF ORGANIZATION

Regardless of the type of organization you choose to implement, it is essential that all the people in your organization understand the structure of the organization. Everyone needs to know who to contact in order to address a problem or a need. Everyone should have some idea of who is responsible for what.

In a large dysfunctional organization, oftentimes an employee has no idea who to contact on a certain issue. The result is wasted time trying to get the issue resolved. The answer to the problem could be as simple as using a company information website to disseminate the needed information to all employees. With a suitable search engine at their fingertips, employees can search for a function and the person responsible for taking care of it.

There is no excuse these days for a company not keeping its employees informed about the organizational structure, even if it's via a manually prepared directory. Any such directory is well worth the expense of preparing and keeping it up to date.

MANAGING PEOPLE

An inherent aspect of any organizational structure is the way people are managed. The old school of thought said there were supervisors and subordinates—the bosses and the bossed. In essence, there was only one right way to manage employees, from the top down, in an authoritative fashion. And employees were typically in the company for a long time.

The lines are much fuzzier today. There is simply no single right way to manage people. Different philosophies and different approaches apply in different situations. The pendulum has swung from pure management on one extreme, to effective leadership on the other.

The old model was a full-time employee reporting to a full-time supervisor. The current use of consultants and contract employees has blown to shreds the applicability of that model. It no longer applies in most situations the way it used to.

"Body shops" are more prevalent today than in the past. Some of today's professions, such as programmers and accountants, and even CFOs, provide contract employees to fill positions on a regular basis. This is great, since it allows a business to staff up and down to meet changing market conditions; but the impermanence of it can be unsettling.

The pervasiveness of teams brings into question the business of having one person always report to a single person. It is still a valid principle that a person should have one supervisor with ultimate authority over the employee. Such a supervisor provides a safe harbor for the employee in times of trouble, a solid anchor, if you will. The employee is always accountable to this supervisor—even if other supervisors have temporary authority.

However, teams are assembled on a temporary or a more enduring basis, as appropriate, to meet changing needs in ongoing business operations. A team's effectiveness is dependent upon the team member's loyalty to the team and its cause. The team must function as an effective unit, not some loose organization of people. The looser the association, the more likely the team will be ineffective.

Many studies have shown that people draw allegiance to the group they are most heavily associated with. Move a nonunion person into a union and allegiance is likely to change to a union viewpoint. Promote a foot soldier into the officer ranks and that soldier's viewpoint and allegiance are likely to change to that of an officer. Rebellious teenagers become parents over time and drastically change their viewpoints. In short, the allegiance and loyalty of a person can change over time. Where people spend most of their time is typically where their loyalty lies.

The old-time view of loyalty to the organization has undergone a tidal wave change. Companies can no longer expect the same loyalty from employees that was possible in the past. Markets change too fast. Mergers occur too often. In bygone days, lifetime employment at a company was common. Today it is rare.

Respect for authority—e.g., employee to manager—has changed tremendously in recent decades. The newer generations simply do not automatically respect authority. Whereas previous managers used to "manage" people, they must now "lead" their employees. It is no longer acceptable to just order people around because of your position of authority. You must take an entirely different tack these days. You must lead. You must be more considerate of peoples' wants, needs, and feelings.

FOCUSING ON STRENGTHS

There is even the heretical thought by some managers today—which certainly is not politically correct—that a manager's job is to focus on employee strengths rather than weaknesses. They believe you should concentrate on making the best people even better and not worry much about the weak people. Put the weak in some suitable position and not waste a lot of effort on them, because resources and time are better spent on your best people doing what they do best. The payback is greater. Apply the resources where the return is the best A less strident approach is simply to take advantage of the specific strengths and knowledge of an individual and play to those—enhancing them whenever possible—and not worry about the weak points.

Regardless of your views on this, the primary business of business is to make a profit, not concentrate on benevolence or taking care of the unskilled. What would the owners or shareholders want? Although benevolence can be a minor part of business, it should not be the primary goal. That is the function of individuals or benevolent organizations (government, church, etc.). The for-profit organization benefits society in a different way. Its goal should be to provide superior goods and service to satisfied customers—<u>at a profit</u>!

COLLAPSE OF TIME AND DISTANCE

Finally, the scope of management is no longer defined by political or geographic boundaries, or even the internal boundaries of the business itself. Distance as a constraining factor has collapsed. Airplanes and the Internet, for example, have torn down the walls of time and distance. Parochial political governments are under tremendous assault from forces beyond their control. Too many technological changes have inserted themselves into everyday life with profound effect. Culture and mores are constantly changing—and quite rapidly.

IN THE SPOTLIGHT

Today's executive must consider all factors affecting his or her organization, both internal and external. The leader must take into account anything that impacts the company's performance. Too many outside spotlights can be brought to bear on a company's operations. The executive is under a microscope on a well-lighted stage.

3

Corporate Life Cycle

A vigilant executive will pay close attention to the current stage of development reached by his or her company. Knowing the current stage helps the executive know what corrective action, if any, is needed to keep the organization vibrant. Complacency leads inevitably to corporate death or bankruptcy. Different leadership styles characterize or dominate each stage. Some executives can make the transition to the needed leadership style as the business cycle advances, others cannot. First, let's review the life cycle stages:

CORPORATE LIFE CYCLE

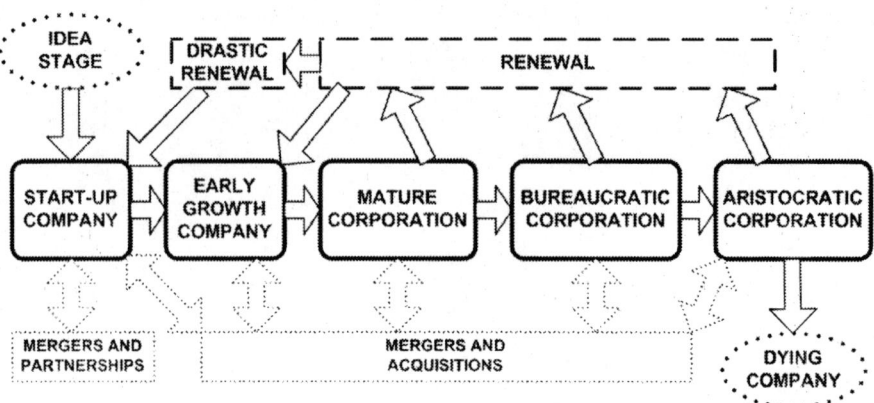

OVERVIEW OF STAGES

Stage 1: In the *idea stage,* a company is just a notion in someone's mind, a dream. A company is said to be at this stage when it starts to form around the idea of the original entrepreneur or founder. A visionary leader provides the impetus to move forward with the idea. He or she is an innovator and has a creative spirit. Ideas are the motivators of this leader, not money or fame. Sacrifice is the norm during this stage. Chaos and constant adjustment rule. Organization and attention to detail are lacking. Excitement prevails, as does risk, since the product or service is unproved. The company, a seed company, is very vulnerable at this stage. Without funding, the seed withers and dies.

Stage 2: The *start-up company* has funding to proceed beyond the seed stage, but is still fighting to survive. The company is still vulnerable. Survival is the driving force. The needed leader is a warrior or barbarian. Action is the name of the game. Damn the torpedoes, full speed ahead! The original entrepreneur may or may not have made the necessary transition to this type of leadership. Money is more of a motivating force for the leader, both for funding and remuneration. The company may or may not be profitable. Consensus building is not emphasized in company culture; nevertheless, the employees need to be behind their leader. All members of the organization should share the leader's vision. There is a unity of purpose. Decisiveness and clearly defined objectives prevail. Focus is needed. Communication is quick. But conditions change. The leader must be adaptive in this stage, especially going into the next stage.

Stage 3: The *early growth company* is in its primary growth stage. The product or service has been accepted in the marketplace and is competitive. Because the company is expanding its market and its operations, a wave of specialization in skills takes over. Sophistication is needed. Leaders and followers are no longer able to do everything. They have to specialize. Staff functions are implemented. Systems and organizational structure start forming. Processes and procedures begin to take shape, but are not yet at the bureaucratic stage. Production and service become separate from sales. Measurement of results in manufacturing and sales becomes pervasive. Customer service is emphasized. Quality control is born. Sales and marketing begin to split into two separate departments. Organizational unity starts to become a problem. Factions begin to develop along departmental lines. Communication takes place, but is less than ideal and sometimes is ineffective. The viewpoint for the company is the near horizon, concentrating on growth. Diversification is explored in order to expand markets. The company is profitable. Cash flow is positive. Expectations are high. All things considered, these are the golden years.

Stage 4: Things start to settle down with the *mature corporation*. Growth continues, but the peak in innovation and growth has been reached. Control starts to gravitate toward the administrator. Order rules over progress. The vision becomes blurred; there are too many competing factors. Performance analyses concentrate on historical facts and figures. Financial reports are emphasized. Predictions about future performance are based on past performance. There is more reaction than action. Processes and procedures reign supreme. Managers spend much time streamlining and improving procedures. Outside consultants and experts are engaged to improve results. Quality control and performance standards are emphasized. Conformance is rewarded. Deviation is punished. Creativity and innovation must overcome immense resistance. R&D groups represent the primary sources of innovation. New products and services are incremental rather than breakthrough. Acquisitions and mergers are actively pursued to expand markets or expertise. Control is stifling. Communication becomes difficult. There is an increased reliance on staff functions rather than line functions. Customers are taken for granted more than before. The sense of urgency is lost. Competitive advantage is assumed. Decay has begun.

Stage 5: The *bureaucratic corporation* tightens the screws. Cost saving and efficiency are pursued with a vengeance. Tighter control is assumed the first answer to any problem. Bureaucratic executives lead the charge. Resentment builds in the ranks. The followers doubt both the company's vision and its leaders. There is a tremendous focus on internal matters at the expense of responding to external challenges. Few people are concerned about developing new products or services. Reorganizations are frequent, since bureaucrats are grasping at solutions. Outside consultants are a fact of life. Mergers and acquisitions are primary sources of new talent and innovation; but the integration of new companies is less than successful. Cultures clash. Fear is in evidence. Loyalty is at low ebb. Communication concentrates on pleasing the executives. Employees and managers feel they can have no impact on company results. Dissent is punished. Negative motivation factors dominate. Selling and producing get little attention. Customers are ignored. Profits decline.

Stage 6: In an *aristocratic corporation*, the leaders feel they have earned the right to luxury and benefits. Position is everything and is more important than the person. Company "royalty" occupy the positions of influence and power.

Self-indulgence is the norm at the executive level. Corporate resources are diverted to satisfy personal projects at the expense of research and development. New products and services are distant memories. Offices are plush. Corporate headquarters are showplaces. Corporate jets are par for the course. Golden parachutes are truly golden. Executives hobnob with the rich, supposedly on company business. The leaders at the top have all the answers and ignore the ideas and needs of employees lower on the corporate ladder. Acquisitions, when attempted, are failures. Debts from acquisitions rise. Reorganizations are constant. Fear is rampant. Safety and security are grasped in a death grip at all levels of the corporation. Cost cutting is epidemic. Executives issue dire warnings in the attempt to raise motivation. Their compensation continues to rise, though. Executives and workers are miles apart. Employees rebel. Talented individuals vote with their feet. Strikes abound. Employees go to work only for their paycheck. Others hang on with the hope of making it to retirement before getting laid off. Customers rebel at shoddy products and service, and at being taken for granted. Competitors win big. The executives fail to notice. The members of the Board of Directors are all good buddies with the executives. Stockholders vote by selling their stock. Stock prices plunge. The company is starting to die.

Stage 7: The grim reaper has arrived. The *dying company* stage has been reached. There is hope, but only if drastic action is taken. Remember that leaders set the pattern for corporate culture. When the culture declines, so does the company. It is up to the executives to turn the situation around before the condition becomes fatal. Regeneration efforts must be instigated as soon as decay is detected. Otherwise, the company is headed inexorably to its death.

Problems can exist at any stage of the business cycle. Renewal efforts are needed more and more in the later stages. The trick is for executives to take the appropriate action when problems arise or decay starts to rear its ugly head. An even better approach is to anticipate the deterioration before it happens and head it off.

    Different leadership styles dominate each stage. The wrong leadership style at a critical juncture will facilitate the passage to a destructive stage. The leadership must adapt or change, or else the leadership must step aside. If an executive fails to recognize the needed change, those around him or her must gently inform the executive. Of course, this is easier said than done if the founder or entrepreneur is the root problem.

    Now let's look at the various stages and the actions that must be taken when an executive takes note of the fact he or she is in a particular stage:

IDEA STAGE

Stage 1: At the *idea stage*, the leader is the nucleus around which everyone else assembles. The idea must be polished and made attractive to investors. Survival means selling the idea and showing potential investors the viability of the business.

Venture capitalists and angel investors are more concerned with investment prospects than they are with the technology or innovativeness of the idea. The danger for the leader is spending too much time on the idea and not enough time on the business plan when courting investors. The foremost investor criteria will be his or her confidence in the management team. Concentrate on selling the team and its business prospects.

Bureaucracy has no place here. Drive and determination must prevail.

START-UP COMPANY

Stage 2: The leader of the *start-up company* must be a hard-charging organizer. The founder may or may not be the person to take the lead here. The leader must be a take-charge individual with a supportive team. People skills are definitely required. The leader must assemble an able team in order to make the product or service happen.

Product and service must both be emphasized. An organizational structure must be put in place rapidly to support getting the product or service to market quickly. Customers must be won. The company's reputation is built in this stage. This is a make or break stage.

Sufficient funding is required to make a go of it. In looking for investment backing, there are a number of sources, none of which is usually a slam-dunk. There are venture capitalists, angel investors, personal funds, family loans, government loans, government grants, and bank loans.

Two start-ups could merge to form one synergistic company having more investor appeal. Investors also look favorably on business partnerships where independent businesses bring supporting functions to the table. Effective partnerships are a sign the entrepreneurs are doing their homework on developing beneficial business arrangements.

Bureaucracy first starts appearing in the start-up company. As organizational complexity grows, so does bureaucracy. This is good so long as it helps the company get organized. It is bad when it becomes oppressive and stifles creativity, like in the mature corporation. Once started in earnest, it is downhill for the remaining stages. Keep bureaucracy lean, mean, and helpful. When it starts to get out of control, you know you have reached the mature corporation level. If bureaucracy gets out of control any sooner, the company can die a premature death.

Complacency has no place in the start-up company.

EARLY GROWTH COMPANY

Stage 3: In order to make a successful transition into an *early growth company*, you, as an executive, must build a fine-tuned racing car—one that will last the whole race. This is the building and expansion stage. Process and procedure are important. How to do things better is a primary goal. You have to get more and more products and service to more and more customers.

Skills have to improve. Specialization must be enhanced and compartmentalized. Delegation is essential. One person cannot do everything. Subordinates must be developed. The number of employees must grow dramatically to support company growth. Never forget the importance of your employees. An effective and unified team is essential to long-run success.

The danger with being an early growth company is that it is too easy to fall into the trap of concentrating solely on day-to-day growth in sales and production. Your innovative product or service may be the only kid on the block for a while, but not for long. There are big, bad wolves out there.

You will be hit from two fronts: (1) improved products and services from competitors and (2) new disruptive or replacement products and services. The former requires doing an ever better job for your customers. The latter necessitates coming up with new products and services. Incremental improvement and growth must be balanced with breakthrough innovation and creativity. Assume some competitor is out there just itching to knock you off the perch.

When you are in a successful growth stage, you could become a prime target for acquisition or merger. Merging with another company or being acquired by another company might make good business sense. All the rules for carrying out an effective merger or acquisition apply. Due diligence is called for when analyzing the possible consolidation of two companies. This is no time for sentimentality or subjectivity. Rational, objective analysis is mandatory.

MATURE CORPORATION

Stage 4: Once you start the transition into becoming a *mature corporation,* you have entered a dangerous minefield. The remaining stages represent various periods of decline—if allowed to go unchecked. A mature corporation often assumes that success has been attained and is rock solid. Progress suffers. Competitors start circling the fort looking for weak points in the defenses. The corporation's leaders feel snug in their quarters, though.

> "We have to face the difficult challenge of changing when things are going well."
> —John L. Chambers

It is time for the executives to concentrate on leadership. There should be a balance between managing and leading. Vision and purpose need to be revisited. The entrepreneurial attitude of earlier stages must be invigorated. Quit concentrating on the organization and start concentrating on the people. Make them feel needed, not neglected. Reward innovation. Break down barriers to creativity. Reinvent the company.

It is time to re-emphasize the forward-looking mindset of the leaders of previous stages. Stop dwelling on past achievements. Your current products or services are likely to be unseated before you even realize they are in danger. Things move too fast in today's world. A disruptive technology may blindside you and make your product irrelevant.

Look both outward and inward. Scan the horizon for opportunities. Look to your own people for ideas. Promote an innovative culture. Take calculated risks. Remember that many breakthrough products were first rejected by the population but went on to become staples of everyday life, things we cannot live without today.

Reawaken the desire to please your customers. Reinforce brand loyalty so you will have a better chance at successfully launching new products or services when they come out. Your customers got you to this point. They are your ticket for the rest of the ride. It is no time to neglect them or take them for granted.

This may be the time to seriously consider acquisitions. They can bring in fresh blood. But remember that the success rate for acquisitions is dismal. Mergers and acquisitions of nonintegrated businesses rarely add value. Proceed with caution if you must. Both sides need to contribute to each other. There must be a synergy of ideas, culture, and talent. There must be a common core of unity. Above all, there must be open communication between the two companies. This is not the time to look at the acquired company as a foster child. Responsible positions must be given to people on both sides. The two sides must become one side. If there is no shared vision and purpose, the acquisition will fail or, at best, be ineffective.

BUREAUCRATIC CORPORATION

Stage 5: The *bureaucratic corporation* is inward looking. Bureaucracy reigns. Kill the bureaucracy. Reduce corporate staff functions. Simplify processes and procedures without sacrificing quality in products and services. Curtail meetings. Delegate authority and responsibility to lower levels. Reward those with entrepreneurial spirit. Give them some running room. Allow mistakes. Encourage risk taking. Define your core competencies. Concentrate on them. Get rid of non-performing units. Don't even think about acquisitions or mergers until you get your own house in order. There is no need to compound the problem.

Reawaken creativity. Open up communications. Search for new ideas. Listen to new ideas. Look inside and outside the corporation. Observe market trends. Review recent technological innovations. Look for opportunities to take advantage of disruptive developments in the marketplace. Give heed to the corporate mavericks. You may not like what they say; but if they have the courage to speak up, they just may be on target in what they are saying. Get out of your ivory tower. Mingle with the troops. Make them feel wanted. Find out their needs. Give them your support.

Renew your partnership with customers. Quit selling products and services. Understand their problems. Sell solutions. Show your customers they are important. Be personal with them. Interface with your customers at all levels—this includes your executives meeting face to face with their executives. Listen to the customer's needs.

Restore a sense of urgency. Take action. Make some hard decisions. Show your people you mean business. Elicit their aid and support. Give them authority to act. Get rid of the non-performers if they fail to shape up after appropriate warnings.

ARISTOCRATIC CORPORATION

Stage 6: The ship of the *aristocratic corporation* is sinking—and fast. Drastic action is needed. We are talking about the necessity for a major organizational culture change. This is not a time for the weak and timid. An experienced turnaround artist may be the only answer. A wholesale replacement of leaders at all levels may be needed. The corrective measures enumerated for the mature corporation and the bureaucratic corporation are all called for—and more. Be aggressive.

It may not be enough to return to the environment of the early growth company. If an analysis of current company products and services finds them non competitive and totally lacking in customer appeal, it may be necessary to catalog the company's strengths and analyze how best to use them as a new start-up. Such a drastic renewal will take courage.

If the outlook is bleak and you have no real authority or influence capable of bringing about a turnaround, it may be time to seek greener pastures. An executive who is simply treading water is no longer an effective leader. Don't retire in place.

DYING COMPANY

Stage 7: The company is dying. Maybe it is headed toward bankruptcy proceedings. Everything said about the aristocratic corporation turnaround applies in triplicate. Drastic action is required on the part of the executives. If action is not taken quickly, a bankruptcy judge may start running the company. By then, it is usually too late.

Unless you as an executive can make a difference in carrying out a turnaround, it is probably best to abandon ship. There is no reason for you to commit professional suicide. Analyze where you can best apply your talents and experience. Decide accordingly. Even if you are the founder, it may be time to admit that your baby is dead.

4

Business Operations Model

All businesses operate as a component of some model or system of interrelated parts. There are many different ways to depict a market-driven system, but the basic model used for this book is depicted on the diagram. It shows the primary players, the significant factors, and the basic elements flowing between the various objects.

BUSINESS OPERATIONS MODEL

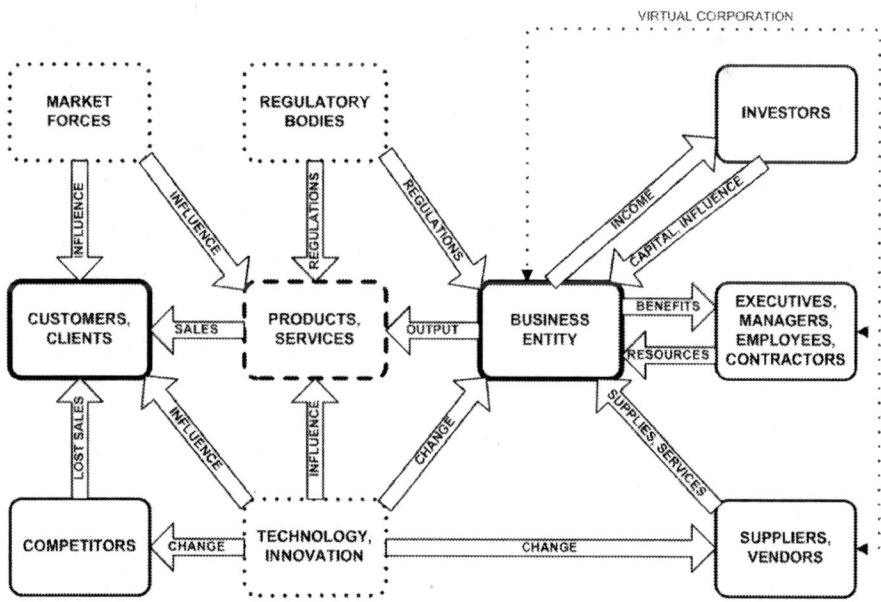

The primary players are customers, investors, company personnel, suppliers, vendors, and competitors. The outputs of a business are the products or services it provides to customers or clients. Having an impact on this whole process are technology, innovation, regulatory bodies, and other market forces.

It is often argued that the customer or client is the most important factor in a business operation. This buyer of goods and services is, of course, essential to ongoing operations. That is a given. However, it is the position of this book that a company's own staff, from clerk to executive, is an absolute requirement for the business to continue to exist in the first place. Without employees, customers could neither be served nor get products delivered.

In short, the customer does not always come first. Instead, a company had better take care of its own personnel and keep them happy. Happy employees are more likely to deliver quality service and products than disgruntled ones. That is why the figure shows "benefits" flowing back to the company's staff. Employees are just as important as customers.

This basic model assumes the relationship between a business and its customers is a mutually beneficial one, a "win-win" relationship for both participants in a monetary exchange for goods and services. It is further taken as fact that it is easier to keep an existing customer than to acquire a new one, at least in the situation where repetitive sales are the expected norm.

The model further embraces the concept that a business entity or company is the focal point of a *virtual corporation,* whose players work together to deliver the output of the business. They are partners in ongoing operations. These partners are the company staff, outside consultants or contractors, and other business entities that provide supplies and services to the business. Each business is the nucleus of its own virtual corporation.

Investors provide the capital that enables the business to get going and to expand into new areas of operation. Although only implied by the figure, customers and clients also help to fund operations—to the extent a profit is received from the sale of goods and services.

Regulatory bodies influence and even control operations of the business and its output. A company must work within the confines of laws, rules, and regulations promulgated and enforced by government or other controlling associations.

Competitors can only be ignored in a purely monopolistic setting—but even monopolies or oligopolies can be unseated. A customer is typically free to choose between a business entity and its competitors. A competitor's success represents lost sales, lost opportunities.

Another assumption of this book is that technology and innovation are factors that cannot be ignored or shortchanged by a business. This is a modern world, and technology is woven into the very fabric of society and the marketplace. Technology and innovation can be supportive or disruptive. In some cases, it is a matter of attitude. In others, it is simply a fact of life and business. The executive who ignores technology has a lot to learn.

New technology and new ideas influence the actions of consumers, competitors, businesses, and suppliers. Technology and innovation are reflected in the products and services provided by businesses. Some seemingly outlandish ideas and concepts can prevail in the long run. An executive should keep an open mind and not reject new ideas out of hand. The notion that the world was round was ridiculed at the time; so was the horseless carriage.

Finally, there are other market forces that influence the behavior of consumers and that influence the goods and services provided to them. Never discount the impact of fads, environmentalists, religion, nationalism, racism, irrational beliefs, terrorism, stock market conditions, fears, natural disasters, political parties, family values, etc. An industry must operate in the context of significant factors and account for all their impact on business operations. Ignorance is not bliss. Vigilance is.

5

Virtual Corporation

With the advent of new technology, such as the Internet, the old operating model of the vertical corporation is giving way to the "virtual corporation." It is easier and less costly to link companies by agreements than to acquire them. Acquisitions require greater capital investment than partnerships. Therefore, part of the answer to increased functionality is outsourcing—where it makes sense. Another part of the answer is instituting partnerships between independent business entities.

In the old-style organization, it was relatively typical to have a whole department or division devoted to a support function, such as payroll, accounting, or manufacturing. Suppliers, for example, would provide the raw materials and sub-parts used in manufacturing; but you did the manufacturing, the final assembly.

VIRTUAL CORPORATION

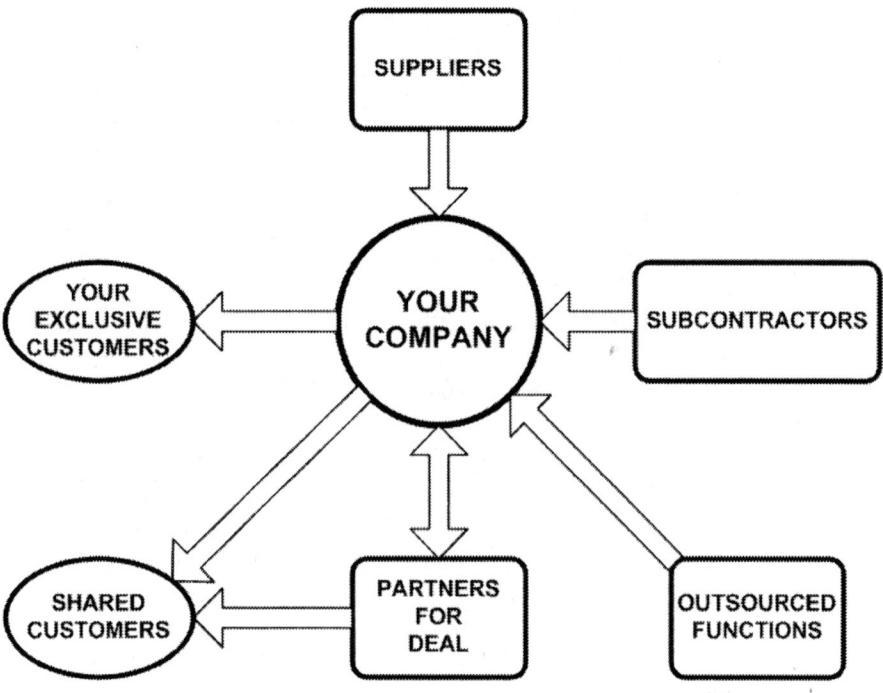

Outsourcing: Today, many global businesses outsource manufacturing entirely. Maybe your company does. These external manufacturers work at your direction and put your label on the finished product. You sell their output under your name, or you arrange for someone else to sell the output on your behalf. The range of possible organizational structures can vary from having your company do everything to your just being the organizer who coordinates all the functions.

Even though manufacturing, for instance, is fully outsourced, you might still have a manufacturing department in your company. In this case, that department provides and coordinates the interface between your company and the actual manufacturer. This internal interface group gives direction to the manufacturer and monitors its adherence to manufacturing requirements. You could have a number of these pseudo departments, which are really just interfacing units.

What are your core competencies? What is it about your company that sets it apart from the rest? Whatever these "things" are, shouldn't they be where you apply the bulk of your resources?

Next, look at those functions in your company that are commonplace outside your company. Can they be outsourced effectively? Why spend limited energy and people on an area that can be outsourced to another company where the outsourced function is its core competency?

Take payroll, for example. Gather the payroll information and ship it outside to a company that specializes in payroll processing. Why devote limited energy to keeping up with changes in payroll programming to handle constantly changing tax or government rules? Apply your programmers to application systems that further your core business. Payroll is a simple example. Think of others.

Remember that the company to which the function was outsourced can spread the cost of its changes across more than one client. You, in turn, would have to absorb the cost entirely within your company. Remember that the cost of updating your own core competency can be spread across your clients.

Alternatives to Outsourcing: There are other choices than outsourcing or keeping something in-house. It may make sense to work as partners in the delivery of products and services. A simple example would be two or more consulting firms working as partners—with equal standing—in a combined deal to reorganize a failing company. Neither consulting firm works for the other; they just work together to solve the shared client's problems. A second example would be a computer manufacturer working with a computer-consulting firm to install a new local area network (LAN) for a client. The possibilities are endless.

If given the choice, apply your people talent to the part of the business that sets you apart, not to an area that just keeps you going. Why waste executive energy on day-to-day management of some function that really just helps you tread water, when you could be applying that same energy to being a champion?

A different type of relationship is the partnership between your company and its suppliers. When there is a free exchange of information and strategy between a company and its suppliers—with the end goal of satisfying your company's customers—you have another facet of a virtual corporation.

The Hub, Your Company: Think of a virtual corporation as your company being the hub with spokes linking it with various business partners in business operations. From this viewpoint, your company is the center of operations—because a company's primary allegiance is to itself. You enlist the aid of business partners and apply their core competencies to help carry out your core competencies. You stick to the idea, or core function, that sets you apart.

At one extreme, you could come up with an idea but just orchestrate its implementation. You could be the point person for a large deal, with very few people on your staff. You are the broker for the deal. An intermediate position is to act as the contractor and outsource the various functions needed to deliver on a deal. (Contractors and subcontractors have been using the virtual corporation model for years.) The opposite end of the continuum is your company doing everything, which is definitely not functioning as a virtual corporation.

One benefit of being at the heart of a virtual corporation is the inherent flexibility provided by the virtual corporation model. You do not have large physical plants or large employee bases that are inherently inflexible. Brick and mortar are just that, immobile brick and mortar. They cannot be reapplied readily to other challenges. Stay flexible. Don't succumb to stationary inertia.

Reevaluation: It is not enough to analyze your business functions one time; you must continue to re-examine your business and see if a function that was once a core competency is no longer unique to your business. If it isn't, then consider outsourcing it to some company for which it is a core competency. Concentrate on your primary business, what you uniquely provide to your customers or clients. Your organization should be tailored to fit the core task at hand. Apply your limited resources in the best possible way.

As a business develops over time, new core functions will come into play. You could get a new core function, for instance, if you enter a new line of business (function) that you uniquely developed on your own. Change your virtual organization to match the new endeavor.

6

Personal Operations Model

The "personal operations model," as shown in the diagram, provides an overview of the way you manage your professional career. The central point, for the present purpose, is your current professional position. That is not to say your work takes precedence over your family or personal life; it is just the focus for this discussion. The title of the diagram is really just a way to make an analogy with the way a business is run.

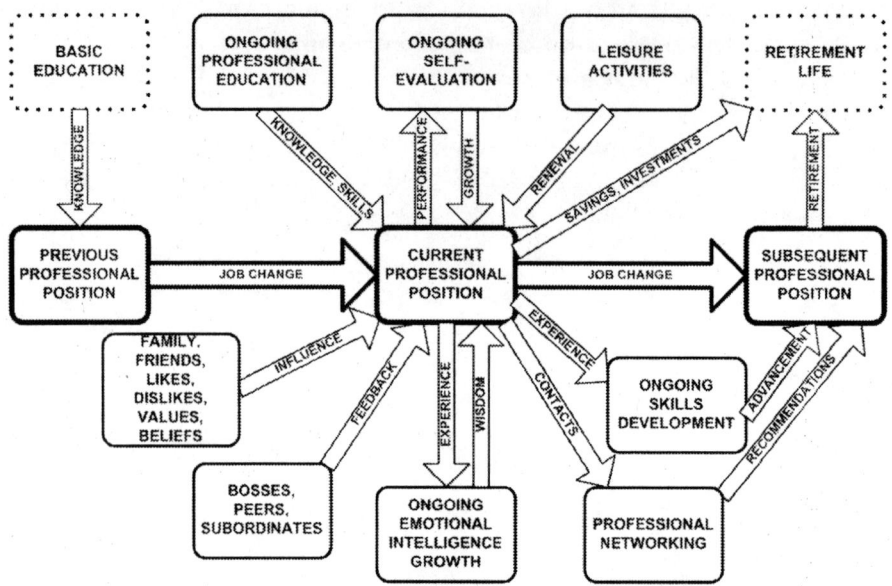

Professionally, you are a self-contained enterprise. You may sell your services to a business or a client, but it is essential you consider yourself an entrepreneur of your own professional life. The old rules have been dashed to the ground. You cannot rely on your employer to take care of your professional career. The ultimate responsibility lies with you. You must take care of your own growth and advancement, choosing your own path through the business world maze. If you can get help along the way, then so much the better; but ultimately you should rely on yourself—always.

Basic Education: You started your professional life with some basic education, maybe even a graduate degree. You may have held jobs while working on a degree. In any event, you received your basic knowledge and training. You got your ticket on the road to becoming an executive. Some people have managed to reach executive status without a bachelor's degree, but that is the exception in today's world.

Having acquired basic education, you advanced through several positions until you arrived at your current position, the focal point of this discussion.

Ongoing Professional Education: Continuing the education line of thought, if you are smart and if you continue to be smart into the future, you will continue to take advantage of professional training. The world changes and so should your professional knowledge.

Professional education might come from formal courses, professional seminars, informal training sessions, or self-study (e.g., reading books). Along the way, you might even have obtained professional certifications. The result of ongoing professional education is new knowledge and new skills. The objective is to keep you updated professionally and advance your professional credentials. If you quit learning, you will shortly become a has-been, totally out of date. So, never stop learning.

"When you're green, you're growing. When you're ripe, you rot."
—Ray Kroc

Bosses, Peers, Subordinates: While on the job you will receive feedback from those who work with you, including your superiors, fellow workers, and subordinates. If you are smart, you will accept 360-degree evaluations from those around you; in fact, you will encourage them. Do not rely on formal performance reviews alone; gather information on your own. Listen to what people say and what they do not say. The information is there; you just need to harvest and process it. This will give you input into the next function.

Ongoing Self-Evaluation: You need to constantly review your performance on the job. What are your strengths? What are your weaknesses? What are your responsibilities? Are you living up to them? Are you contributing? Are you being a drain on the organization? How are your interpersonal relationships? Are you in the right position? Should you seek another position? Should you go to another company? How can you improve? What should you do to improve your value to others and to yourself?

Remember that you are in business for yourself; at least that is the attitude you should take—even if you are a full-time employee. In this case, your employer is your customer. Give full service. Make your customer happy with you. Watch and listen. Analyze what you find out. Take the necessary action to grow. If you are not growing, you are not standing still; you are going backwards.

Ongoing Emotional Intelligence Growth: As you gain experience and learn from your successes and failures, your intelligence will grow—meaning in the area of "emotional intelligence," not the raw IQ you were born with. Emotional intelligence is "learned" intelligence. It produces wisdom that can be applied to your job.

It is an understood fact that most successful people achieve their success through on-the-job experiences. They try hard, persist, and thereby enhance their intelligence along the way. The so-called "brains," people with an innately high IQ, are rarely the truly successful people. They are just too smart for their own good. They expect success without working hard for it. It is owed to them. The typical working stiff knows better. The point is: A brilliant IQ is not necessary for becoming an outstanding executive.

Ongoing Skills Development: As you gain experience on the job, you also develop new skills. With an impressive resume showing a high level of skills and experience, you set the stage for advancement to a better position, a promotion. If you are not advancing, then make sure you are happy where you are. Some people are happy not being a manager or executive. They simply want to be highly skilled in their profession, or they are in management but do not wish to go higher. That is perfectly all right. Just be sure that is what you want.

Professional Networking: One shortcoming of many professional people is that they do not develop professional contacts, meaning friends they can go to when in need. We are talking about networking. If you've done your job on this score, you have people you help and people who can help you. For example, if you lose your job or if you seek a better position, one of the best ways to get in the door for an interview is to know someone who can personally recommend you to another employer.

Networks of professional people are not developed overnight. They are built with tender, loving care over the years. You stay in touch. You continue to give help to others. Remember that you help yourself by helping others. Network! Network! Network!

Leisure Activities: You must avoid working all the time. You must take time off for leisure activities. You need rest and relaxation. Without them, your productivity will fall. Smart businesses know this. Take vacations. Spend time with your family. There is life outside of work. In fact, in the grand scheme of things, family and friends are more important than work. Jobs come and go. Families and friends should not. They are precious and are needed for your own well-being.

Family, Friends, Likes, Dislikes, Values, Beliefs: You are influenced in your job by your family and friends. Your likes and dislikes carry over into your professional life. Your values and beliefs certainly have an impact. There is an old saying, "You can take the boy out of the country, but you can't take the country out of the boy."

Your career may cause changes in your values and beliefs as you learn while working, but your core values and beliefs supersede the influence received from your job. Maintain your honesty and integrity. Engender trust in those who work with you, at all levels. A proper business organization will not attempt to destroy your personal life or your character. Your personal life is important and will enhance your career—when handled properly.

Retirement Life: Finally, if you have saved and invested well over the years—which you should have done working up the executive ladder—then you can retire comfortably. You have earned it.

The above has put a very broad brush to the concepts and factors in your personal life, but they are the basics and must always be kept in mind. If you do not keep the big picture in mind, you can spin your wheels on insignificant details. Keep your "personal operations model" in the background as a reference point. If you forget it, you will wander aimlessly.

Part II
COMPANY DIRECTION

7

Business Success

Before examining business success, some thoughts about the future: The future of business cannot be predicted with any degree of accuracy. People who think they can accurately predict future events are deceiving themselves. In this fast-paced world of technological innovation, all bets are off. The dot.com debacle of 2000 proved the fallacy of trying to predict future business.

"Only a fool would make predictions—especially about the future."
—Samuel Goldwyn

But it is wrong to get mired in the past and its precedents. You must keep your eyes open to what is going on around you. What you never expected could easily blind-side you. So, practice vigilance. Constantly keep your eyes open to new opportunities. When you see an opportunity, act upon it. Indecision is itself a decision. Doing nothing in the face of change is suicide.

BUSINESS SUCCESS

```
                    LOFTY
                    GOALS
    GOOD
    PEOPLE
                    RISK
                    TAKING

    GOOD            GOOD              GOOD
    MANAGEMENT      LEADERSHIP        RESULTS

                    MISTAKES

    NEW IDEAS,
    NEW DEVELOPMENTS,
    NEW INFORMATION,
    OPPORTUNITIES   ADJUSTMENTS
                    AND
                    CORRECTIONS
```

Good Management: The primary key to a business's success is its management. This does not mean executives do all the work and that other people aren't needed. No one person can have all the skills needed for a successful business. Leaders must have followers to do the majority of the work. But everything flows from management. They set the pace and define the rules for business operations. They provide the leadership to take people in the proper direction.

Good Leadership: It is not enough to have good ideas or good products; you must have leaders that can turn the ideas into successful accomplishments. As the marketplace changes, successful leaders must react in the proper way in order to maintain and grow the business. They must be adaptive and decisive.

Good People: Good leaders attract and retain good people. They seek complementary skills in those who surround them. Successful leaders provide a working environment that is supportive of their employees. Work must be enjoyable and challenging, especially to exceptional performers. High turnover is certainly a key indicator that something is amiss in the ranks—and the problem may be at the top.

New Factors and Influences: Watch for new ideas, new developments, new information, and new opportunities. Look for discontinuities. Question why something is changing or not changing. Constantly ask yourself, "What am I not seeing?" Change your viewpoint. Watch for hidden patterns.

Consider successful photographers. They are great because they see things other people fail to see. Perspective is paramount—but seizing the moment is vitally important, too. A great picture not taken is a great picture lost.

Do not forget the proverbial questions: Who, what, where, when, why, and how? Cause and effect must be explored. Sherlock paid attention to clues. Do the same. It's what you don't see that can get you.

Outstanding leaders encourage their people to keep abreast of the latest developments that directly or indirectly could possibly affect the business. They keep the lines of communication open both ways, up and down. Leaders work with their followers to gather information and look for opportunities.

Do not fall into the trap of thinking you, as a leader, are the only one with a vision. Remember that entrepreneurs often have just one good idea in them. Listen to other people. Encourage the imagination of others. Use brainstorming sessions. Brainstorming encouraged "thinking outside the box" long before the latter phrase became fashionable.

Lofty Goals: The best leaders aim high and expect their people to do the same. They raise the bar. They shoot for lofty goals. They grow from their experiences and press their people to grow and expand their skills.

Risks, Mistakes, Adjustments, and Corrections: Successful executives are willing to take risks. Taking multiple risks provides multiple opportunities for success. Good executives are not mistake free; they just know how to recover and learn from their mistakes. Successful executives get up and keep slugging after being knocked down. They adjust to changes in the marketplace and correct misguided decisions. Persistence and good judgment prevail in the long run.

Good Results: So, as the model shows, *good management* combines people and ideas to produce *good results*, a successful business.

8

Choosing a Course

Trying to chart a course for the company is a blend of examining where you are and determining where you would like to be. Look at the opportunities around you. Look at your options. If you were not already in the business you are in today, would you enter it now? Don't close any doors when trying to decide which lines of business to concentrate on.

What about your expectations? What about the expectations of the rest of the company? If you are targeting growth as a positive goal for the company, why not be positive about expectations? Your growth rate will be directly proportional to the expectations of executives and subordinates. Think small and growth will be small. Think big and growth will be big—or, most assuredly, greater than when you think small.

What kind of expectations do your people have? One school of thought says that if you set unreasonable expectations, two things are likely to happen. First, setting unreasonable expectations will force you and your people to think outside the box and consider possibilities you might otherwise have ignored. Second, overreaching expectations will lead to overreaching results. Setting high goals brings greater achievement than setting low, safe, comfortable goals. Be uncomfortable. Be unrealistic. Be surprised at the final tally. An old saying is: "The difficult I do immediately. The impossible takes a little longer." That's certainly a lot better than saying, "I can't do it."

Talk is cheap. Don't expect your people to believe presumably unreasonable goals are achievable without providing some evidence. Give examples of accomplishments from outside the company. Build up a record of successes within your own company. Charge the executives with being business developers. Have them look outside their own division. Don't accept shortcuts, such as deep discounting or price cuts. Concentrate on new ideas, innovation. Let your business model be elastic. Do you want a stay-in-the-rut executive or one who can be flexible and innovative, unconstrained by past practices or history?

The basic income equation says: Revenue less Expenses equals Income. Too often, executives concentrate on expenses. But you can only cut expenses so far. It is going to take expenditures to achieve sustained growth. You cannot continue cutting expenditures and people quarter after quarter and still expect to grow. You get what you pay for, which means you have to spend to grow.

Therefore, you must work on the top line of the income statement, i.e., revenue. Enhancing revenue means coming out with new products, updated products, or whole new lines of business. Innovation is not incrementalism. Innovation requires a different mindset than incrementalism. Innovation takes big leaps on faith. Incrementalism is a more timid approach. America was founded on a revolution. The little colonies took on the big world power and won. The American Revolution was not a time for incrementalism. It was time for drastic action.

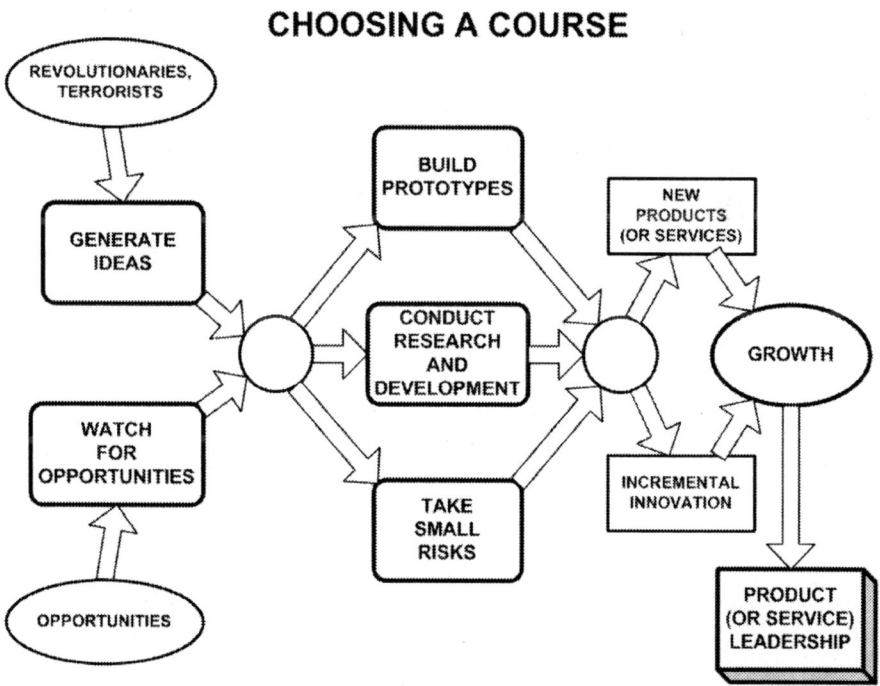

CHOOSING A COURSE

GENERATE IDEAS

Great ideas are the product of fertile imaginations. There is often great wisdom in trite sayings, such as, "Think outside the box." It is easy to dismiss triteness and say it is old hat. If it were totally ridiculous to start with, it would not have lasted so long. So, try it. How can you think outside the box?

Ask WHY? Keep on asking why. Peel away the layers of the "onion" until you get behind the symptoms and get to the root cause. Why think superficially? We supposedly use very little of our brain and our imagination. Stretch yours.

Ask WHY NOT? Ignore conventional wisdom. Conventional wisdom, as espoused by the established church, said the earth was flat. Breakthrough ideas make poor bedfellows with conventional wisdom.

Continually say to yourself that there has to be a better way. Just because nobody has come up with a better way doesn't mean there isn't one. At one time, the horse and buggy reined supreme. We've come a long way, baby—because many people refused to accept the status quo.

Forget exclusivity. Don't assume OR always applies. It might be possible to AND things together. Radio and TV are both in use today. TV did not wipe out radio, nor did either of them wipe out newspapers.

World changing ideas come at the most inopportune and least expected times. Don't close your mind to new ideas. Get your head out of the same sand your competitors have their heads stuck into.

Individuals with new ideas—the *revolutionaries* with revolutionary ideas—can be found in both small companies and large ones. In large companies, these people are often kept in handcuffs by the executive team. Therefore, these revolutionists—who are often depicted as *terrorists* by their management—must leave the company in order to implement a revolutionary idea. What a pity! Compare the cost of using an employee's idea with the cost of acquiring and absorbing another company having the same new idea. What is the old saying, "…Only in his hometown and in his own house is a prophet without honor." (Matt 13:57, NIV)

In an entrepreneurial company, the so-called "terrorist" is more likely to be heard and treated as a "visionary." Large companies so easily forget that a visionary, a person with a radical eye, once led them.

A new idea, a small company, an impassioned visionary, and an environment less averse to risk taking—all these can set the stage for the proverbial act of turning on a dime. A caretaker management team too often concentrates on the status quo, completely ignoring signs of a tsunami racing to sweep them away. They have a steady cash flow, a cash cow—an aging cow. They are comfortable with things the way they are. They are in a destructive rut.

It is wrong to think current competitors are the only competitors. A submarine typically has its sonar adjusted to listen for other submarines. That is little defense against a missile launched from an airplane. The missile impacts and explodes before the submarine's captain ever knew there was a threat. Corporate captains, take time to look all around you. The world is three-dimensional, not two-dimensional. The bullet you never saw nor anticipated is the most deadly. The graveyard is filled with irreplaceable products. The replacement of the typewriter was not a better typewriter. It was a PC, a totally different concept.

Barbarians (new startups) vs. bureaucrats (old brick and mortar); old guard (entrenched management) vs. new guard (new management); youth (Young Turks) vs. age (wisdom); and new ideas (imagination) vs. proven principles (incumbency)—all need to be kept in proper balance. A company is limited only by its imagination, the minds of its employees. You cannot predict the future with great accuracy; but you can make educated guesses about it, seizing upon every opportunity that presents itself—as soon as it presents itself.

Do you think the only answer is to execute better? Perhaps the better answer is to blaze a new path, change the rules of the game. If you have ever been involved in a computer application development project, you know it is more important to first determine WHAT than to determine HOW. Development and implementation (HOW) follow requirements determination (WHAT). Do not fall into the old trap of having a solution that is looking for a problem to solve. First, determine the problem—before your competitor—then seek the solution. Use the tremendous resources of your employees' mental capacity.

Incremental innovation may have worked in your company's past, and it may have its application in the present—but less so, perhaps. While you are making improvements to your existing product line or service, that upstart competitor is creating a brand new product. Aren't you scared? What are you overlooking? What haven't you seen in your peripheral vision? What was that idea your subordinate came up with you thought was so ridiculous? Maybe you should reconsider it. Stop, look, and listen! Put your ear to the ground. A pilot can see the enemy on radar before he or she gets a visual. You, too, cannot rely only on your own vision. Let your troops be an extension of your eyes and ears.

WATCH FOR OPPORTUNITIES

When *opportunity* knocks, you had better be ready to open the door.

> "The reason a lot of people do not recognize opportunity is because it usually goes around wearing overalls looking like hard work."
> —Thomas A. Edison

Time! The clock seems to be racing very fast today. Industries change overnight. Hot products come and go. Dot.coms are here today and gone tomorrow. Something you bought yesterday will be obsolete in a few weeks, if not tomorrow.

Management has long given credence to the concept of opportunity cost, the missed business opportunity because someone was asleep or failed to see the road signs. The problem with today's economy, from a corporate leader's standpoint, is that it moves too fast. It is hard to keep up with what is happening. We are in a state of information overload. Somehow, you must separate the wheat from the chaff, the important from the unimportant. Your success depends upon it.

Timing is key. If you had a good product but were late getting it out the door, you may have lost an opportunity your competitor took advantage of. Market timing is essential to success. If you are too early and there is no demand, the product introduction is a waste. If you are too late, after a competitor has beaten you off the starting line, you are an also-ran.

But timing isn't everything. Flexibility is also very important. You have to roll with the punches. If something doesn't work, try something else. If you have a product, service, or project that is not living up to expectations, scrap it. Why keep throwing good money after bad? If you made a bad decision—in spite of the best intentions and efforts—recognize the mistake and correct it. Don't be so emotionally attached to an idea that you cannot walk away from it. Be objective and logical.

WINDOWS OF OPPORTUNITY

Windows of opportunity come to a business all the time. The sad part is that many golden opportunities are missed because people are asleep at the helm. The wagon train with outriders and scouts deployed on all points of the compass is less likely to be ambushed than one without them. Likewise, executives and their management team must keep their eyes open to windows of opportunity before they close.

WINDOWS OF OPPORTUNITY

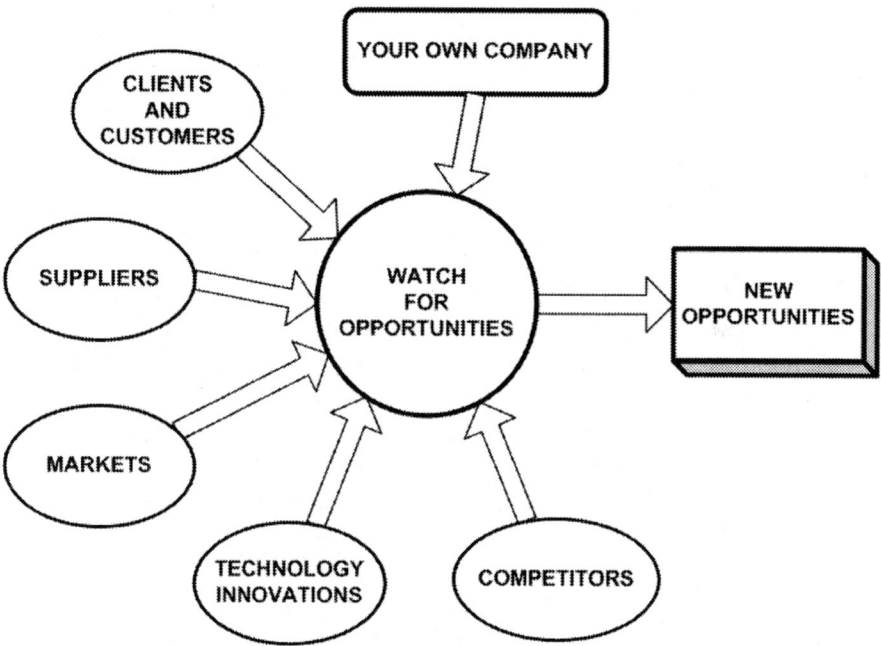

A systematic process should be in place to look for opportunities. There are six major areas where surveillance should be implemented and people assigned to conduct it: (1) clients and customers; (2) suppliers; (3) markets in general; (4) technology innovations; (5) competitors; and (6) the business itself. In the case of the sixth item, your own company, all employees should be instructed and expected to look for windows of opportunity in the company. The other five areas will also provide "targets of opportunity"; but keeping up with them should not be the job of everyone in the company—although it doesn't hurt to have everyone report any opportunities they happen upon by accident. The first five surveillance areas require some specific assignments of personnel, including executives.

Regardless of who keeps watch and where they look, they should keep their eyes open to unexpected successes, unexpected failures, and incongruities in the behavior of customers, markets, competitors, etc. Other things to watch for are changing needs in the marketplace, changes in demographics, changes in viewpoints and attitudes, newly published research results, changes in industry partnerships, new developments in technology, watershed events in society, changes in political winds, and so on.

Let your mind freewheel when you see something that triggers your thought process. Remember that some seemingly insignificant item may be the signal that a cataclysmic event is about to be unleashed. The earlier you figure out its significance, the more likely you can take advantage of it before your competitor does. Also, remember your future competitor could be someone in your own company, someone who saw the opportunity you failed to see, even though that same employee brought it to your attention.

Your nightmares (worries) should come from the possibility of missing good opportunities, things you let slip through your fingers because you weren't paying attention. Sit up and take notice of the world around you. Something is happening—right now—that will impact you. Do not be blindsided.

CONDUCT RESEARCH AND DEVELOPMENT

What is your horizon for R&D? Are you seeking breakthrough results or incremental changes? How much clout does your R&D department have inside the company? How do you feel about R&D having the potential to produce major disruptions in corporate life? Do you have negative feelings about the possible results? You shouldn't.

If your research and development efforts are directed at very long-term innovations, shareholders will have little interest or patience with the expenditures. From a practical standpoint, it makes more business sense to work on a shorter timeframe. In most cases, research should be directed out a few short years at the most. If you plan too far out, some disruptive technology or innovation could make the long-term effort irrelevant—money down the drain.

Direct your R&D resources toward near-term results, meaning a few months to a few years. If some totally unexpected by-product comes out of research, then so much the better. If it has promise, take the ball and run with it. In general, though, executives should direct researchers toward areas that are complementary to the current business—or even a replacement for current products and services.

Unless R&D is the primary business, pure research is quite a gamble for most companies. Someone with a revolutionary idea is more likely to seek fame and fortune outside the company, say, in a start-up, than within a corporation. Start-ups, by their very nature, usually come from entrepreneurs with either an idea or the organizing ability to implement someone else's idea. Small companies have less bureaucracy to fight. Nimbleness and flexibility are their stock in trade.

R&D departments in a large corporation typically have an uphill battle over any revolutionary idea they come up with. The idea is likely to be considered disruptive to current operations. The R&D group rarely has an accomplished salesperson to sell the concept to upper management. There are just too many people to win over before an idea can get approval and funding to proceed. This is true in spite of the fact a large corporation may have gotten its start from a unique idea for a product. How soon we forget our roots.

Because of entrenched roadblocks to radical innovation, incremental improvements are the norm in most corporations. Improvements are good, but this raises an all-important question: Might it not be better to have R&D parceled out to parts of the company that have the most knowledge and expertise about the targeted area? These experts are more likely to come up with relevant innovations, because they work in the area daily. They see the everyday problems and have a vested interest in solving them.

But consider another approach, a change in mindset. Why not maintain an attitude at the executive level that all current products and services are just steppingstones to future products and services? With this mindset, you assume current products and services will be replaced by something more grand and glorious in the not-too-distant future. This mindset could lead to a different attitude about disruptive ideas, including any that come from R&D? Times do change, whether we like it or not. Give R&D a chance to research and develop breakthroughs. Nothing ventured, nothing gained.

BUILD PROTOTYPES

It cannot be said too many times, excessive bureaucracy can stifle innovation. Excruciating analysis and attention to detail in new product development can be self-defeating. An overbearing management that is always pressing for success in every endeavor is actually turning off the stream of new ideas it so desperately needs. Allowing mistakes—even encouraging them—is more likely to produce dramatic breakthroughs and blockbuster products.

Prototyping offers an alternative approach to more tedious regimens. In companies where rapid prototyping is supported from the top, ideas are allowed to flow freely. A rough product is developed, a prototype. It becomes a proof of concept. Although the product or the results it achieves are likely to be imperfect, the result is some new knowledge about what to do or what not to do. This "playing" becomes, in reality, productive learning.

Start with a rough definition of what the prototype should be. Assemble the prototype on the cheap, as much as possible. Enlist the assistance of someone or some entity that can help test the prototype or provide instructive feedback on its viability. Conduct the test. The guiding principles are "quick and dirty." A pilot test can provide valuable insight into product viability.

When developing a rapid prototype, the emphasis should be on the word "rapid." Quickly develop the prototype. Quickly test it. Review the results. Modify the prototype, quickly. Run another quick test. Debrief again. Continue to recycle the prototyping process until it becomes apparent the concept has promise or should be abandoned.

So, test new ideas. Pursue them with vigor, and without imposing bureaucratic perfection. Make mistakes. Don't punish mistakes. Make prototyping a core competency. Open new doors. Achieve those needed breakthroughs.

TAKE SMALL RISKS

Sometimes, in order to expand its horizons, a company needs to follow the lead of venture capitalists (VCs). They have the mindset to take on a bunch of small risks—instead of big ones—in order to score a few homeruns. The likelihood of any particular venture succeeding is not that great. In fact, most will fail. On the other hand, a few will score, and score big. It is a matter of percentages. Even with the best analysis and due diligence, three out of four such ventures will fail, if not more.

The VC might only put $250,000 into a venture to get it started, hoping it will rack up a few wins. If it does, the VC will sweeten the pie with more money. On the flip side, investments that are not producing will not get any additional funds. Feed the strong; starve the weak.

An R&D department will have tried numerous things before hitting on a winner. Drug companies can experience many failures before coming up with a killer drug. You want good people—your best thinkers and innovators—working on possibilities. In the lab, many experiments are tried and most fail, but you still learn from your mistakes. Do not castigate people who are willing to experiment. Don't forget the definition of "experiment."

The point is: you must experiment. The experiments can each be on a rather small scale and with a small number of customers, say. That is what test marketing is all about. When the experiment starts showing promise, it is a no-brainer to throw more resources at it.

It is best to not be too judgmental about which products and services are likely to succeed. Things you might expect to result in big failures, if tried, might turn out to be huge successes.

PRODUCT (OR SERVICE) LEADERSHIP

If you have done everything right, you will achieve *growth* from your *new products (or services)* and from *incremental improvements* to existing products (or services). Seek to be a leader in your defined—or redefined—niche.

The truly successful business is number one or number two in its market. To be more successful—if you are number two—there should be a plan in place to be number one. If you are not or cannot be first or second, stay out of the contest. Follow GE's lead in this matter. Choose another line of business where you can be a leader. If you are an international company, for example, you should shoot for global leadership.

If a company delivers a premium product, it can command a premium price. Commodity products are sold primarily on lowest price—because the products are the same regardless of who provides them. Volume is what counts. But margins are thin and competition is fierce.

When you introduce quality, the equation changes. Either the quality of the product boosts it to premium status; or the quality of delivery (service) moves it up the ladder. In either case, customers will pay more if they perceive the overall value is higher—provided, of course, they can afford it. However, you can always price yourself out of a market.

Therefore, staying power and high profits come from a premium product with quality delivery; but complacency is not a characteristic of the market leader. To keep occupying the leadership position in a business category you must cannibalize your own sales. That means embracing innovation. It is much better for you to steal the market from yourself than to allow a competitor to do so. Don't rest on your laurels. Look for the next product to replace your current product. Being great at marketing is not enough. You must constantly develop the newest and the best.

SELLER VS. BUYER

Let's change our thought process for a moment. The line of demarcation between the two sides of a transaction, seller and buyer, is no longer as clear as it used to be. It is not just a swap of money for goods or service. Technology and changing market forces have muddied this distinction. Both sides can be buyers. Both sides can be sellers.

Sellers offer the customer a cash payment, a gift, or a discount for filling out a survey. Car manufacturers pay car buyers a rebate for purchasing a car. Wireless phone companies give away phones or offer rebates when you sign up for wireless service. Credit card companies give you airline miles for purchases with their cards.

Customers pay annual fees to become a member at a store where they make purchases. The customer can offer the seller more than money, though. Customers provide information and emotional involvement. Sellers enlist the services of customers to join in online user forums. Some products enhance the customer's self-image. Sellers offer tangential goods and services, plus participation in life styles based on common use of a product. The list goes on and on. Customers, by voting with their money give image and prestige to companies.

Technology, because it eliminates time and geographical constraints, can help build an intimacy between buyer and seller that was impossible earlier. More personalized service is available.

The buyer-seller interaction can become quite complex. The resultant multi-faceted exchange gives each party more power than would come from a simple swap of money for goods. An astute executive will take advantage of the many opportunities afforded a business in this modern economy. In one sense, the seller partners with a customer. Both sides of the exchange can offer value. These ongoing relationships must be maintained in an atmosphere of trust and mutual respect.

In short, do your homework, think out of the box, watch for opportunities, act on the opportunities, and become the leader in your market niche.

9

The Mission

What is the mission of the company? What is its vision? What is the rallying cry around which the employees assemble?

> "If you do not know where you are going, every road will get you nowhere."
>
> —Henry Kissinger

THE CAUSE

Without a positive vision, leaders do not know where they are going. Neither do their followers. The vision must not be in opposition to the existing corporate culture. If it is, either the vision or the culture needs to be changed. Changing a company's culture is very difficult because a culture represents ingrained habits; and habits are hard to change. Courageous executives can change culture, though.

For a business to endure and succeed in the long term, the company needs a definition of what its reason for being is. Although most businesses exist to earn a profit, that is not sufficient for achieving success. There has to be more, something people can relate to. There should be some defining concept that expresses the essence of the company.

Once you have a cause, you have something against which to validate any proposed business venture. To take an extreme but illustrative example, consider an airline. For the sake of discussion, let's say the airline's mission in life is to transport passengers from place to place, by air, in the most efficient and satisfying manner.

Now suppose an executive comes up with the bright idea it is time to open up a grocery store chain. The airline definitely does not have the expertise for this line of business. It has nothing to do with transporting passengers from place to place. Clearly, the idea should be rejected. There is no fit with the mission statement.

Next, another executive comes up with a brainstorm to convert 18-wheeler semis into passenger transportation vehicles. It is a novel idea, and it does provide for transporting people. However, it is not transportation by air. Truck suspension systems are designed for cargo, not passengers. The truck does not go by air, so speed of transport is completely sacrificed. Again, there is no fit. It did not pass the mission statement test.

However, one executive puts forth the idea of going into the airline catering business, the provision of in-flight meals to airlines. That does support the company mission and would make sense if it adds to the bottom line without detracting from the core business, air transport. After all, the airline does have other supporting functions, such as baggage handling. Potential profits notwithstanding, the catering business should not divert precious resources that would be better and more profitably applied to the airline's core business.

In any event, the company should have a purpose. Each employee should have a reason for going to work other than getting beans on the table. The yearning to fulfill a company's mission should be instilled in every employee and should color his or her whole attitude about dealing with customers. The mission should be a basic motivation for getting things done, a vision to pursue, a *cause*.

VISION MANAGEMENT

A vision requires at least one visionary. But it is better for the company to have more than one executive who shares the same vision. Ideally, all the executives should share the vision. In any case, the typical scenario is for one person to come up with a vision and then elicit the help and support of others in carrying out the vision. A visionary has creative, imaginative power. The effective visionary also has the ability to convince others to follow him or her and to help make the vision happen. The employees rally around the flag (vision) and march forward.

A vision statement must be developed and put into writing. The earlier the company's position is on the business cycle timeline, the more likely the vision will be the brainchild of one individual—the leader of the start-up, say. Company leaders should back the vision 100 percent, or get off the boat.

An easily remembered slogan is best. It should be easy to articulate. If it is long and complicated it will be hard to repeat and hard to relate to. Simple is good. Embracing what is right and beneficial to others is important. The vision should represent a worthy goal for the company. It should cover both the internal and external affairs of the company. It should be the bedrock of organizational values.

The leaders must sell the vision to the rest of the organization. Before the leaders can sell the vision, they must lead by example. It must be clear to the rank and file that the corporate executives believe in the vision and embrace it all the time, not just on special, public occasions. The vision must be repeated over and over in an all pervasive marketing campaign to every level of the organization. Unless there is a combination of constant reinforcement and repetitive reminders about the vision and its worth, the vision will not become a part of the company's culture. To be effective, the vision must be second nature to everyone.

The effective vision will be a reference point, a standard to which every decision in the organization is compared. It is the lighthouse for direction during a storm, in addition to fair weather times. A decision that conflicts with the company vision is in opposition to company values. Employees should be rewarded for adherence to the vision. Publicly praise employees who act in concert with the company's vision and the values it represents.

A corporate vision is mandatory for success. Write it down and post it everywhere.

CORE IDEOLOGIES

Successful, long-lasting companies generally stick to a certain set of core ideologies. These ideologies set the stage for how a company is run. They may or may not be reflected in the vision statement; but they should be endorsed by the company's leaders and they should serve as guiding principles for all levels of the organization. They represent a company's core values. When company leadership changes over the years, the ideologies remain. They are applied consistently. Company direction may change, but the ideologies continue as before. They are the rules of the road.

If an employee does not believe in the ideologies, working for the company is tough. There is no fit. This is especially true at the executive level. If there is a comfortable fit, stay; if not, get out. Go to a company where you can enthusiastically and passionately embrace their core values.

The success of a company is likely to be a function of the emphasis placed on its core ideologies. Successful companies thoroughly indoctrinate their employees in the core values. Cultures, although differing between companies, should be strong and supportive of the ideologies that define the company. Executives should fit the mold in order to advance. They should be proponents of the ideologies. Star companies are more in alignment with their core ideologies than the also-rans are in alignment with theirs.

It helps, of course, if the ideologies are reflected to a certain extent in the vision statement. If we assume a vision statement is short and to the point, then it might be useful to think of the core ideologies as an elaboration of the vision statement. Whereas the former might make a few points, the latter would consist of a larger number of points, a more extensive definition of the principles that define an organization. However, the number of articulated core values should normally be measured in single digits. Don't have so many you can't keep them straight.

It is wrong to assume every successful company shares the same set of core ideologies as other superior companies. Successful companies have differing sets of core ideologies, and the ones that happen to be shared between any two companies are shared to different degrees. In other words, a particular ideology might be opposed by one or both of the two companies; shared partially by both; or fully endorsed by one or both.

Consider profit as one of the company's core ideologies. Profit is necessary to support all the company's activities. In order for a company to remain viable, profit is required over the long haul. But it is a matter of emphasis. Assuming a basic level of profitability is necessary for ongoing business success, the emphasis might be more on the good the company is doing in society, as opposed to its market leadership. Even market share could be more important than high profitability. On the other hand, profit could be considered the primary measure of business success. It could be used as the measure of competitive advantage.

The view of the customer represents another core ideology. Some successful companies put the customer above all else. Employees are authorized to go to extremes in delivering quality customer service. Some companies seek a balance between customers and employees. Still others say to treat the employees in the proper manner and everything else will fall into line. Customers will be served and profits will roll in.

Honesty and integrity are often core beliefs. It stands to reason, that a company lacking in integrity in its dealings with customers and employees will eventually be found out. Business will suffer. As the old saying goes, honesty pays.

Corporate social responsibility is often mentioned as a core value of successful companies. This can take many forms. It can be directed at improving the quality of life through technology and innovation. It can concentrate on alleviating pain and disease. The emphasis could be on providing high quality products and service at a fair price. It can simply seek to provide happiness. All of these serve the community in different ways, but they still serve.

Product safety and reliability can be two of the company's guiding principles, each taken to different levels. Both support repeat business.

Some successful companies do not compete with other companies as much as they compete with themselves. Rather than trying to outdo the competition, they concentrate on outdoing themselves, constantly raising the bar on performance. They may even try to do the impossible. If they continually outdo themselves, they will beat the competition, or so they believe. Other successful companies frame everything in the context of beating the competition—being there first-est with the most-est.

Individual responsibility and opportunity can be handed out to employees at all levels. Initiative should be applauded in this case. Mistakes might be tolerated and supported, but to different levels. And that is the point: ideologies are applied to different degrees. What is acceptable at one successful company is not necessarily acceptable at another.

It is wrong to think successful companies cannot pursue ideologies seemingly in opposition to each other, such as profitability and excellence. Don't take an either-or approach. It is a matter of balance while continuing to pursue both. Do both—and do them well. The company that prides itself on excellence can seek excellence along more than one path, such as customized products and speedy manufacturing—two more objectives seemingly in opposition to each other. Dell does it.

Regardless of their core ideologies, successful companies do share one trait: they work hard within the context of their core values. They are achievers. They get up and continue in the face of misfortune and setbacks. They press on toward the heights. They do not mimic each other. They have their own rules of behavior, their own core ideologies.

In summary, define a vision, manage it well, and back it up with supporting core ideologies.

10

Deployment of Resources

Whatever direction a company takes, it must deploy its available resources wisely. Resources include intellectual capital, people, physical plant, and fiscal capital. For purposes of this section, emphasis will be placed on the deployment of organizational competencies and capital assets.

Whatever a company does well can be termed its competencies. Those competencies that define it best would be called its core competencies. Other companies could have some of the same core competencies, but the viewpoint taken here is that taken from inside a particular organization.

The company's competencies are said to operate within the context of fixed assets, such as land, buildings, plant, and equipment—capital assets. But capital assets also include intellectual assets like patents and trademarks. When a company combines people, capital assets, processes, procedures, and corporate knowledge; you begin to see what a company is capable of doing—its competencies. So, competencies come from the wise application of all an organization's resources, whatever their nature. The assumption is that resources are limited.

Executives will use available resources in the manner they see fit. This section presents some suggestions for applying those resources to their best advantage. It is an elaboration of the virtual corporation concept.

CORE VS. SUPPORT FUNCTIONS

Diagram: Flow showing "Primary Business" → "Core Function" and "Required Support Activity" → "In-House Support Function" (via Transition). Separately, "New Business Endeavor" → "New Core Function" → (Transition) → "In-House Support Function" → (Transition) → "Outsourced Support Function".

CORE VS. SUPPORT FUNCTIONS

A key concept for the executive to master is the distinction between a company's core competencies and those other functions that are merely supportive in nature. Mastering this distinction is essential for the proper application of expenditures and talent. A simple illustration makes the point.

Assume a company's primary business is developing software to support a fast food operation. The software application covers point-of-sale transactions, plus food and other supplies inventory. The majority of the staff is assigned to software development and software sales.

Since the company has expertise in software development, it would seem logical to have the programmers also work on software to handle the company's payroll, accounting, purchasing, etc. The problem, though, is that assigning programmers to these applications diverts them from the company's primary business activities. In this context, payroll and accounting, for example, are support applications, not core business.

And it is not just a matter of diverting programmers. Take payroll, you must have subject matter experts who are knowledgeable about payroll rules and taxes in all states where the company has people. Sales offices can exist in multiple states, for instance. The subject matter experts must keep up to date on changes in rules and regulations, and maintenance programmers must keep the payroll system updated with the changes.

Further, management staff must be assigned to keep everything running smoothly in payroll. Thus, you have many personnel assigned to payroll. The same applies to accounting and purchasing systems. Why bother? Why utilize resources that could be more profitably applied to the efforts that differentiate the business?

There are plenty of other companies whose core competency is payroll systems, accounting systems, or whatever. They can spread their development and maintenance costs across multiple customers, like the example company does for food operations. So, outsource payroll, maybe even human resources.

Also, keep in mind that your employees will know where the rewards are greatest. It won't be in payroll or accounting, except for high-level executive positions, such as CFO. The employees aren't stupid. In support functions, many staff will consider themselves second-class. They are wrong. They are essential and important; but they are staff, not line. The greatest rewards go to core functions that define the business.

Let the experts concentrate on their core products and services, and you concentrate on yours. Don't dilute precious resources to efforts outside your mainstream. If your competitors focus on the core business and you spread yourself thin doing ancillary functions, who is going to win?

Finally, continue to review what is core vs. support. After a few years, as you move into new areas and markets, what was once a core function might now really be a support function. Also, businesses could have sprung up to do what was once a core function to you. Outsource the functions that are not mainstream to you, wherever you can.

CORE COMPETENCIES

Sometimes companies are sitting on a gold mine. All that is needed is a little spadework to uncover what was there all along.

Look at your core competencies, the underlying skills or processes you apply so well to the situation at hand. Can they, perhaps, be applied to a different problem—in an entirely different context? Do you have hidden treasures you never thought about except as legacy operations? Use your imagination. Think like a kid. Is there a new way to use your core competencies? Would it be profitable? Is it innovative?

CAPITAL OWNERSHIP

Owning capital assets, such as equipment, is not necessarily the best use of a company's funds. With the economy and technology moving at lightning speed today, capital ownership may not make financial sense. Often, as soon as a piece of equipment is purchased, it quickly becomes obsolete. It doesn't even have a chance to wear out. It may still work great, but the work it was doing before may no longer be needed.

The bigger your investment in equipment is, the greater the risk—from a financial standpoint. If you can transfer the risk to someone else, why not do so? There are several options.

Leasing, of course, is one possibility. Depending upon the terms of the lease, risk for obsolescence can rest with the lessor. If you need technologically superior equipment, you may be able to swap the old equipment for newer equipment. If you need more equipment, you expand the lease. If you need less, you reduce the lease—provided the lease allows it.

Another option is to outsource the whole operation associated with the equipment. There are plenty of companies that handle manufacturing for their clients, for example. In other situations, a third party provides the outsourced operation as a package—equipment and service. Web hosting is an example. In this case, the outsourced operation includes equipment (network servers, ISP routers, database servers, etc.) and service (administration of networks, servers, and databases). Service is people, and people require management.

Outsourcing the whole operation has unique advantages for both parties. The outsourcer can take advantage of economies of scale not available to its client. Changes in customer requirements, plus and minus, can be spread across existing capacity. With a broad base of customers, an outsourcer can afford new technology and implement it faster. The company to which the operation was outsourced can spread the costs of technical skills and expertise across many clients. Personnel headaches are reduced at the client company. Thus, economies of scale can accrue to both equipment and personnel.

If you aren't using your equipment up to capacity, you have idle capacity. This is a negative if the equipment is expensive, but is still required for your operation. The outsourcer can use the same equipment for more than one client, thus reducing his or her per-unit cost. You, on the other hand, do not have to tie up costly funds in equipment that sits idle much of the time.

Having much capital invested in obsolete or seldom-used equipment can be like having a millstone around your neck. Your decisions about moving ahead with new technology or continuing with an existing product—instead of starting out with a new product—can be unduly influenced toward maintaining the status quo. When you outsource the function, the problem is not yours; it is the outsourcer's. You have the freedom to move forward unencumbered.

Forget about return on assets. In this fast-paced economy, return on equity is a better measure. Outsource capital expenditures where you can. You will have more flexibility and fewer headaches. Concentrate, instead, on your intellectual capital.

11
Changes in Direction

There is nothing wrong with change, if it is in the right direction.
—Winston Churchill

CHANGES IN DIRECTION

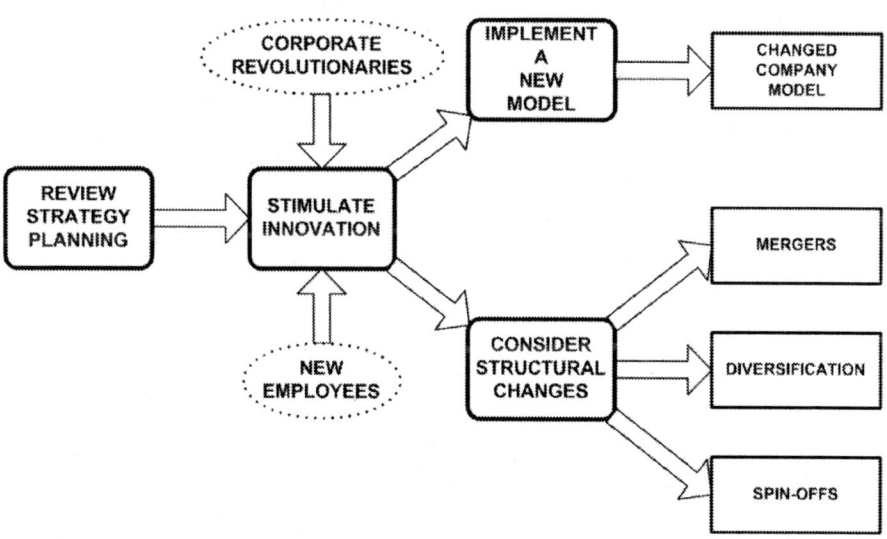

REVIEW STRATEGY PLANNING

Review your whole approach to setting strategy for your company. Why do you have quarterly or yearly strategy meetings? Do you have the luxury of scheduling innovation? Are ideas generated on demand at a recurring meeting?

Believing that regularly scheduled strategy sessions are the answer is like believing you can transform a horse into a bird. The flying horse, Pegasus, was just a figment of someone's imagination. Reality is today's jet plane. But imagination did lead to the reality of jets. It took a number of imaginative steps by innovators, from propeller planes that could barely fly, to jet planes flying miles above the Earth's surface. The steps weren't scheduled, though.

How did you get to the upper floor? You provided answers to your manager. Your upper management didn't have all the answers when you were climbing the corporate ladder. Are you are so different now? Open the pipelines and let ideas flow into the corner offices. The executive view from the top floor can be somewhat different from that of the people interacting directly with the customer?

Major leaps, revolutionary ideas, brought us the ability to travel from coast to coast in mere hours. Think outside the box. Brainstorm with others. Be innovative—now! Don't wait for quarterly or annual strategy sessions. Things are moving too fast.

STIMULATE INNOVATION

Changing Your View: If your business model is a carbon copy of other companies, you are not unique and bring nothing new to the market. Your business model needs to break some of the accepted rules. Success can be self-defeating. It can lock you into a set way of thinking, a mental model that colors your thoughts and prevents you from thinking outside the box.

An example from photography comes to mind. If you place a polarizing filter on your camera's lens, you shut out light rays coming in at certain angles. In other words, the camera is blind to light from the wrong angle. But you, like the photographer, can rotate the polarizing filter so you can see things from a different perspective—in a different light.

Change your point of view. Try to put yourself in a different position. For example, if you want to see the world from the eyes of a child, clear your mind and get on your knees so you are looking from the same height.

Don't let your mental model be set in concrete. It could take a jackhammer to change your thought patterns. Many companies have been flashes-in-the-pan because their management tied themselves to one product and one strategy. The old saying, "If it ain't broke, don't fix it," might be totally wrong in the current situation.

Great execution is the bailiwick of a good administrator; and that administrator may be the visionary of the past, the entrepreneur with no more good ideas. Think about it; does the revolution usually come from the king? Remember, America was founded by little guys, working with far-out thinkers. The upstart New World replaced a British monarchy.

Stimulating Innovation: For an organization to advance and avoid going backward, innovation is essential. To encourage innovation, an environment and corporate culture are needed that support creativity. There are a number of ways to foster innovation. A few possibilities are presented here.

The most obvious is to grant awards, including money, to employees who come up with innovations having great promise. To increase the effectiveness of new ideas, it is essential they be shared across the corporation. Departmental and divisional boundaries need to broken down. The different departments and divisions need to understand that everyone is in this together. An idea could conceivably be developed in one area but have more promise when applied somewhere else. Maybe the idea can even be applied in many areas. One shared idea might lead someone else to come up with a variation to the original idea, or even a totally new idea. This is akin to the process of brainstorming. Company forums and intranets could be used to showcase new ideas and products.

To encourage a sense of entrepreneurial spirit in employees, higher-level awards could be given to employees when their innovations lead to successful new business. Depending upon the situation, the employee with the idea might be given a chance to champion a new product and take it to market—receiving remuneration for doing so. This fosters the development of entrepreneurs. A company could provide funding or grants to researchers for the development of prototypes, pilot tests, or market tests.

Corporate goals could be established that require a fixed percent of annual sales to come from new products within a division. To foster experimentation, certain classes of employees could be instructed to spend a set percentage of their time on projects of their own choosing. This encourages initiative.

It might help to provide career paths for technical and professional people that allow them to advance in rank without having to move into management. They would continue to be "doers" instead of "tellers." Not all people want to be managers nor do they have the talents to do so. Keep the innovators innovating.

Innovative efforts will have failures—many of them. That is a fact of life. The corporate culture should be supportive of mistakes. Lack of trying means lack of success. It usually takes many failures before a breakthrough innovation comes to light.

Risk can be managed by trying out ideas in small steps, meaning small tests with prototypes and pilot projects. Corporate outlays would be minimal. Test the idea for viability before turning the idea into a major corporate effort.

Corporate leaders must encourage individual initiative, tolerate failures, and release tight controls. They must trust and support their people.

Your Competitor's Voice: Listen to your competitors. They are not slow about pointing out your weaknesses to potential clients. They go for your jugular. It can be advantageous for them to put you in a less than favorable light.

Corporate Revolutionaries: The company often owes its existence to the brilliant insight and perseverance of the original entrepreneur. The problem with these entrepreneurial leaders is that they are often one- or maybe two-idea people; there might not be another "vision." The company founder probably assembled people who shared the same vision, and perhaps the same mindset. That was good at the time for effective teamwork; but in later times, that is not necessarily a good thing. Times and market conditions can change.

Let's assume the chief honcho did assemble an executive staff with similar ideas and ideals. That was good for initial growth, but not necessarily for long-term corporate viability. If an executive is surrounded by people who think alike, why are they all needed? You need advisors who think differently in order to come up with decisions based on all the considerations surrounding an issue. The same applies to new products and markets.

When all the executives think alike, or are forced to think alike because of peer or CEO pressure, the company can suffer. Peas in a pod have the same viewpoint, the pod. Therefore, it behooves the chief executive to seek revolutionary ideas outside the executive suite, i.e., from lower rungs on the corporate ladder. Go outside the pod.

The banishment of the corporate rebel—and the death knell of the mature corporation—is the all-pervasive creep of conservatism. Once the entrepreneur and his or her closest executives have achieved success, status, power, and wealth; there is a tendency to look with distaste on anything that threatens the status quo. You've got it and you don't want to lose it. "If it ain't broke, don't fix it," many would say.

The typewriter wasn't broke, but it is now obsolete. The swamp cooler works fine and was a great advance, but the humidified air conditioner was even better. With it, you have, in effect, a swamp cooler inside a modern air conditioner. What about the humidified furnace?

The old suggestion box was a good concept, but not necessarily the best implementation. A better approach is to mingle with the troops. Have your management and their subordinates mingle. Talk to the troops; encourage them to open up. Don't castigate people for their crazy ideas. They could actually have a good or even a great idea, something none of the executives ever dreamed about in their wildest dreams. That crazy idea could also take you in another direction, totally unrelated to the thought at hand. Remember how brainstorming works? Wild thoughts lead to great ideas.

Some of the best sources for corporate rebels, the revolutionaries needed for business advancement, are the lower ranks—even the shop floor. The people lower in the hierarchy are quite likely to be closer to the problems and have better ideas about how to solve them.

Further, do not ignore the benefit of having corporate rebels in the executive ranks. Encourage the executives to challenge accepted beliefs. If you need a yes man, just look in the mirror. But the executive suite needs people that challenge each other onto to bigger and better things, especially new ways of thinking.

Executive meetings are not necessarily the best place for mind-stretching discussions or idea exchange. Some of the best idea exchanges can occur in the hallway or the restroom. Besides, isn't that where most major decisions are made?

In summary, do not treat corporate revolutionaries as anarchists. Rather, treat them as the loyal opposition. Assume they are activists who love the company. If you don't listen to them, maybe your competitor will when they are hired away. Maybe, just maybe, the reason the revolutionary appears to be rocking the boat is that the skipper has turned off his or her intercom.

New Employees: Also, keep in mind that new employees often bring new perspectives to a business. Inbreeding can be counterproductive. Diversity of backgrounds and experience leads to diversity of thoughts. New employees can help inject new blood into an organization. That is often the driving force for bringing in new management, to shake up a company.

IMPLEMENT A NEW MODEL

Times change. Business changes. The company changes. Whether the company is forced into a change or makes it voluntarily, a significant company-wide change cannot be accomplished with a simple "announcement from on high." It is necessary to go beyond mere words. Action is required. The following is a simple, but comprehensive, approach to implementing any company-wide change having extensive impact. The change could be directed at any aspect of the business: line of business, functional realignment, management reorganization, market realignment, ISO certification, culture overhaul, mergers, spin-offs, etc.

Plan the Implementation: Once it has been determined that a major change must be made—a *changed company model* has been decided upon—the executives must meet and plan its implementation. Responsibilities for carrying it out would then be assigned and a formal schedule developed. Making the change happen successfully requires a whole-hearted buy-in from all the executives. They must set the example. They must show by word and deed that they support the change and will do everything necessary to make it happen.

The development of plans for implementation is critical to the project's success. Treat the change as a project. Prepare formal plans covering tasks, responsibilities, resources, and schedules. How and when the plans are developed will depend upon the nature of the company, but guidelines for implementation should be developed at the top. A general plan would be developed first. Progressively lower levels of management would then develop their own detailed plans. Don't forget milestones.

Announce the Change: With this foundation laid, the next step is to start announcing the change in order to prepare the employees. The first step in the announcement is to hold a company-wide meeting, if possible, or a series of meetings to make the announcement to each employee. It would be great if the lead speaker were the head of the company.

The meaning of the change and the company's commitment to the change must be delivered in no uncertain terms during the meeting(s). This shows the employees the company means business. The necessity and benefits of the change must be communicated. Plans for implementing the change should be announced, too. Employees should be told their cooperation is needed and requested.

It is not enough for senior executives to announce plans for change to the whole company. The next step is to proceed down the organizational hierarchy conducting successively lower-level meetings, each chaired by the senior management person for that division, department, or team. The senior management person at each level should explain and communicate in no uncertain terms that the change is going to happen and that support is needed from everyone. The associated roles and responsibilities of the senior manager's subordinates should be delineated.

Implement the Change: Following the development of detailed plans, the change should be implemented and progress reporting put into effect. Unless each level of management shows it means business, the probability of implementation failure will skyrocket. Management should practice what it preaches, plus expect each employee to do his or her assigned part.

Change means transformation. People are resistant to change. Allow people to vent their feelings about the change. Be sympathetic to the fears and misgivings of people affected by the change, but emphasize that the change is going to happen regardless. Incorporate responsibilities for the change into performance objectives, if necessary. Use 360-degree performance reviews at all levels—if you dare.

If appropriate, involve customers and suppliers in helping to implement the change. Ask for their support and cooperation in making it happen.

Provide Training: If implementation requires training, develop the appropriate training classes and train the people. The carrying out of individual responsibilities should immediately follow the training sessions. If what is trained is not put into practice quickly, the training and its associated effort will have been for naught.

Keeping the changes in effect requires ongoing maintenance. If ongoing adherence to the changed model is not reinforced, employees will revert to their old habitual acts. Therefore, regularly reinforce the new model at all management levels. Continually remind the employees, through formal refresher training, if appropriate. Include an explanation of the model in new-employee orientations.

Adjust: Few implementations will be flawless. Encourage feedback from management and employees. Listen to what they say. Where it makes sense, make changes in the change; i.e., adjust to changing conditions by making changes to the model itself.

Do not implement the change and forget it. Never assume it will continue on its own momentum. Monitor results. Reinforce. Adjust. Walk what you talk.

CONSIDER STRUCTURAL CHANGES

The new model could include structural changes in the organizational makeup of the corporation. Consider the pursuit of mergers, business diversification, spin-offs, or some combination thereof.

MERGERS

Remember, mergers are often less than successful. If the merger is designed to convert two lagging behemoths into a more efficient behemoth, is that really a good course of action to take? While the two companies are preoccupied with merging dissimilar cultures, the competition could be applying their resources to an emerging technology or a new concept. Your customer service is likely to suffer during the merger.

Some companies engage in the repetitive acquisition of smaller companies. They see it as an opportunity to improve their stable of products or services. Maybe the target company has the rights to a valuable emerging technology. Perhaps the target company provides a function that is complementary to the acquiring company, one the acquiring company is weak in. These acquisitions are normally less of a problem than the merging of two giants, but the impact on the smaller company can be traumatic. Success is not always assured.

Basic Rules: Regardless of whether a company is actively engaged in frequent or infrequent acquisitions, several basic rules apply. First, perform an effective due diligence effort. Carefully analyze whether the merger is designed to buy market share or to create markets. What are the objectives for life after the merger? Establish a realistic context for the merger. What are the implications? Are there any alternatives to a merger?

Acquisition at all costs should never be the driving force. Be able to walk away from the proposed deal. If there is no long-term strategic potential driving the alliance, the prudence of proceeding is highly questionable. There had better be some strong, rational reason for going ahead. The two companies should share a common vision. Both sides should be supportive of the planned merger or acquisition. Remember that a perceived synergy could be a delusion and a snare in the long run. Today's acquisition could be tomorrow's spin-off. In the cold light of day, a perceived synergy may turn out to be a mirage.

Part of the due diligence effort should center on the people of the company being acquired. An accurate assessment of the key players being brought onboard is essential. Do they have the skills and experience needed? Are they going to devote themselves to making the merger work, or are they going to take flight? How will they mesh with the culture of the acquiring company? Are they compatible? Will they flourish and be happy? Remember that people are the heart and soul of an organization.

Second, mergers should not drag out forever. The longer they take, the more likely that disruption will occur in both the acquiring and the acquired operations. A mother in labor with a baby cannot be distracted with fixing supper. Review the due diligence results, negotiate a win-win deal, and make it happen.

Third, the merging of very dissimilar cultures is a recipe for disaster. There should be a good chemistry between the two companies. If the cultures don't mesh, it would be better to keep the acquired company at arm's length and just treat it as an independent subsidiary. You could simply treat it as an investment.

Fourth, assuming an active acquisition mode of operation is the norm, the integration team from the parent company should be an experienced one. Experience and skills at integration should determine the roles played by various team members. Also, recruit and involve team members from the acquired company. They will have more influence with the acquired employees. The closer the two companies are geographically, the more likely the whole thing will be successful.

Fifth, the employees of an acquired company are automatically going to be scared about the whole thing. Apprehension will run rampant. The acquired employees will expect the worst: layoffs. If they are treated like equal partners to the greatest extent possible, it will be a much easier transition than if they are treated as foster kids. Respect their histories and traditions, but do not dwell on the past. Everyone should move forward and look to the future.

Remember that one of the primary objectives in an acquisition is likely to be the talent in the acquired company. But guess what? Who are the employees most able to get another job? The ones you want most are the most employable. If merging the two companies is not handled properly, trust will go down the tube. At best, it will be shaky at the start. Don't make it worse.

Sixth, assume the acquiring company will have to change because of the merger. Unless the acquired company is treated as an independent subsidiary, the parent company will change, too. Else, why was the merger executed in the first place?

Seventh, produce some short-term wins early in the process. Keep the people engaged and show them things can work out. Do not let them get into a state of mind where they lose interest. Readily admit to an awareness of potential problems, but emphasize the positives. Broadcast the successes.

In short, let the merger be between equals as much as possible. The merged companies are still composed of their people—from both sides. The right merger, conducted properly, should be a shot in the arm for both companies.

DIVERSIFICATION

The Dilemma: Diversification can be accomplished by starting up a new line of business or by acquiring an existing company. Consider a merger. The old management theory of diversification by acquisition does not always pan out. Executives can only handle so much at a time. This is not to say diversification by acquisition never works out. Quite a number have been successful, but the odds can easily be against the player.

A specialized investor is not that interested in a diversified company. The reason is quite simple: the investor could invest in a mutual fund or index fund if diversification were desired. To maximize investment income, the contemporary investor will seek to selectively invest, under the assumption he or she can beat the market average. That means the investor wants a choice in order to maximize his or her shareholder value. Therefore, many investors do not desire corporate diversification. As stated earlier, a diversified company, with many types of business, is just another mutual fund—in one sense.

So, what is the beleaguered executive to do? One group wants diversification for the sake of security. One group wants selective investment for more control over shareholder value. Keep in mind that shareholders vote through buys and sells—and their votes are immediate. However, there are ways a diversified company can attract selective investors.

Consider Reporting More Details: Financial statements often hide the details of diversified operations in order to withhold strategic information from competitors. The company obviously wants to hide problem areas, too. But investors want to know what is happening in each business category. If the investor cannot get enough details to justify a sound investment, he or she can simply seek another company to invest in.

So, one way to satisfy investors is for the company to report operating results by category or market, as appropriate. But after category reporting is started, keep it up. Once the executives start reporting these figures, not reporting them later is automatically perceived as a sign of problems. If things are going great, though, investors will flock to the stock.

The problem with things looking great on the financials is that financial statements do not take into account disruptive changes that are about to erupt in the market. Propeller planes were doing fine until jets and turboprops came along. Mature markets are particularly vulnerable to things looking great, and then encountering an unseen tornado just over the hill.

Therefore, CFOs should make an effort, where it makes business sense, to report forward-looking happenings that will be positive for the company, things that would not normally appear on historical financials. But never report forward-looking events that are unlikely to occur. The stock market can be harsh on false promises.

If a diversified company does not choose to reveal details about its different lines of business, it had better be able to make the case to the investor that there is a synergy between the different types of operations.

Consider Tracking Stocks: Another alternative is for a company to set up "tracking" or "targeted" stocks to concentrate on one aspect of the business. There is much yet to be learned from this practice, however. Tread lightly, if at all.

SPIN-OFFS

Executive management often seeks to expand operations by going into diverse markets. This usually increases revenue, and, presumably, earnings. But as any executive knows—or should know—diversification can fail. A few years after diversification, management may decide diversification—whether by acquisition or by starting a new line of business—was not all it was cracked up to be. Then the reverse course is taken; non-core businesses are divested and management concentrates on the core business.

Reasons for Spin-offs: There can be many reasons for a management about-face: (1) management was spread too thin and lost focus, (2) the parent company's management never understood the newly acquired business and how to run it effectively, (3) the acquired company's future turned out not to be as good as expected, (4) the newly acquired company's culture never meshed with the parent company's culture, (5) key people responsible for the success of the acquired company left before or shortly after the merger, or (6) targeted markets turned sour. In short, things did not work out as expected.

Too often, today's mergers are tomorrow's spin-offs. But consider a more positive scenario for spin-offs. Sometimes a company can establish a strategy for spinning off new businesses when product or service lines achieve a viable mass. Freed from the shackles of corporate bureaucracy, the carved-out portion of the corporation can achieve focus without the distractions inherent in being part of a larger corporate whole.

Even though a company does not have an established strategy for regularly spinning off new businesses, a spin-off may make sense anyway. Perhaps a new product or service has been started that does not really benefit from being under the same roof. Rather than create a tracking stock, the division is carved out and made an independent company.

Benefits of Spin-offs: Regardless of the reason for the spin-off, the new company can streamline its operations and concentrate on one line of business. The leaders can foster an entrepreneurial spirit that helps increase motivation. Talented leaders and employees are thus kept in the fold. Instead of leaving to set up or join start-ups, they can become entrepreneurs with the blessing and support of the parent organization. Additional motivation can come from the shareholder scrutiny given executives of publicly held companies. This can be even more motivating than corporate headquarters oversight.

Part III

LEADERSHIP

12

What Is a Leader?

As for the best leaders, the people do not notice their existence. The next best, the people honor and praise. The next, the people fear, and the next, the people hate. When the best leader's work is done, the people say, "We did it ourselves."

—Lau-Tzu

LEADERSHIP

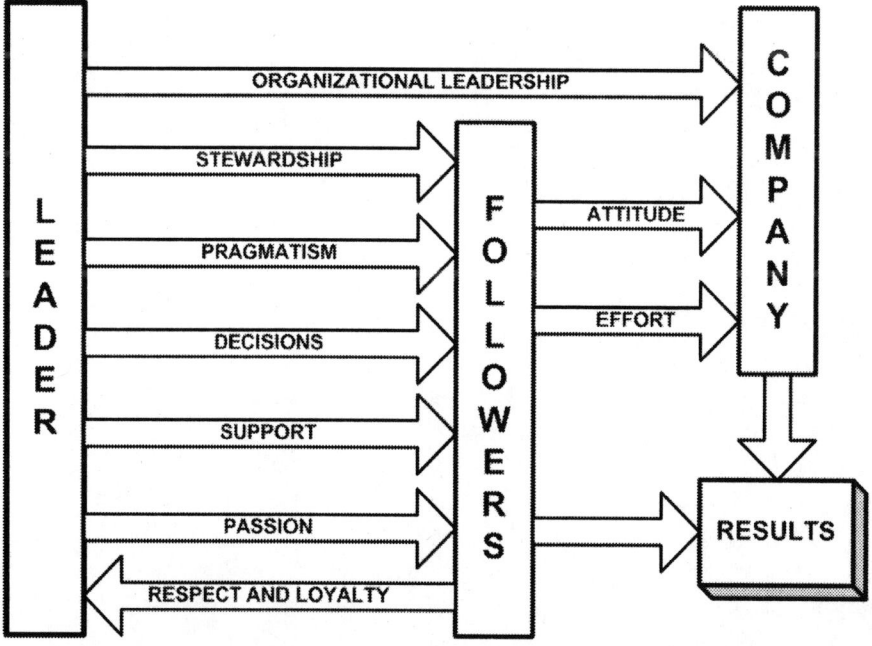

GOOD STEWARD

An organization consists of many assets, such as, people, organizational structure, ideas, experience, vision, inventory, physical plant, customers, suppliers, investments, opportunities, and intellectual property—to name a few.

The Chief Executive Officer (CEO) should not feel he or she is the company. If you picture the company as a pyramid and consider the uppermost point as the CEO, then there is a lot underneath that point. The larger the pyramid is, the smaller the point is, in relative terms. However, that in no way implies insignificance. The larger the company is, the more responsibility the CEO has.

Whatever the CEO does, it will cascade downward. What the CEO does will determine the nature of what flows downward. That puts the CEO in the position of being the chief steward of the company, the chief influencer of how it performs. It is an awesome responsibility!

Therefore, the CEO has the responsibility of being a good steward of the whole company, of the whole pyramid. The proper view is that he or she must lead the people who work in the company. The success of the company and its CEO is dependent upon the rest of the people in the pyramid. The CEO cannot know and do everything. He or she must rely on the knowledge, wisdom, and support of the employees. The people the CEO works with are what make his or her success. The CEO steers, but the others man the oars. Steering in the wrong direction can crash the boat on the rocks.

If you are an executive, but not the CEO, you still have a responsibility. You are an extension of the CEO. If his or her responsibility is the whole pie, yours is a part of the pie. For your piece of the pie, the buck stops with you. You are accountable.

Be an humble but courageous leader. Serve and be served. Never forget that you cannot do it alone. Consider how fortunate you are to be where you are.

PRAGMATIC

Your mother disciplined you for doing something wrong. But she did not throw you out with the bath water every time you made a mistake. Instead, she cared for you, she loved you, and she taught you how to do better. She was a pragmatist, a realist. She accepted imperfection and got on with being a parent. You are the parent of your piece of the pie.

Everybody yells for perfection in all departments. Knowledgeable people demand quality assurance. Employees are called on the carpet for making mistakes. In the manufacture of goods and the delivery of services, the customer or client expects perfection. Accountants also want perfection in their numbers—even though allocations of expenses and revenues are less than exact. So, the pursuit of perfection does have its place and is essential to certain aspects of business; but don't take it too far.

Note that the over zealous search for perfection in decision-making can paralyze a company. From the shop floor to the chief executive, decisions are made all the time. They have to be. The decisions are less than perfect. You rarely have all the needed facts. The decision-maker must make a best guess, an educated guess, and go on. The longer that a decision is put off, the more likely a decision will be made for you—the one to do nothing.

Doing nothing is sometimes the best course to take. The problem may just go away. However, unless you have evidence to the contrary, assume a decision must be made. Gather the facts as best you can. Consult with others who might have better knowledge or a better insight into the matter.

The point is, make the best decision with the best input available. Remember, though, the expense of being 100 percent sure is much costlier than being 90 percent sure. The closer you approach 100 percent assurance, the more costly and time-consuming it will be to achieve any incremental gain in perfection. It may not be worth the effort and expense—and you may not have the time.

"When you see a snake, never mind where he came from."
—William Gurney Benham

DECISIVE

Executives are leaders and have the responsibility to make the decisions necessary to run the business in the most efficient manner; but there must be a balance between short-term and long-term interests. Impatient stockholders look to short-term results, and executives in recent years seem to be giving precedence to short-term decisions because of stock market pressures. However, a business that is built to last must ultimately give due consideration to the long-term—unless the executives are only in the game for a quick buck. In the latter instance, the wrong people are in charge.

Whatever the situation is that calls for a decision, it is the executive's task to balance all competing interests and make the appropriate decision. It is one thing to make decisions when the repercussions are minimal. It is quite another when huge stakes are riding on the outcome. Still, the leader is in his or her exalted position precisely because of an inherent responsibility—and hopefully an ability—to make the big calls. That is why an executive makes the big bucks!

A leader who vacillates or refuses to make a decision when the going gets tough is not worth his or her salt. Such a leader should step aside for others who are willing to lead in good times and bad. No one is perfect, and no executive will make the proper call every time; but he or she must still make the call, after giving due consideration to available facts and alternative solutions. Make the decision!

SUPPORTIVE

The executive who sets a positive emotional tone in his or her relationship with subordinates will get more productivity and loyalty out of them than a leader who sets a negative, demanding tone. The tone set by the executive works like dominoes lined up all in a row. The tone ripples down through the layers of the organization with a high degree of mimicry. You reap what you sow.

An effective leader sets the proper positive and supportive tone. In this atmosphere, there is more likelihood of a free flow of ideas and information to the top. The leader stays informed and can make better decisions. There is mutual support and respect. A cohesive bond and a spirit of cooperation pervade the organization. Performance and morale are enhanced.

A leader who is overbearing and arrogant sets a negative tone. Bonds and cohesiveness, if they ever existed, are destroyed. A domineering and demanding leader forces his subordinates to do the same with their subordinates. Such a leader feels an infraction is an infraction, regardless of degree. The emphasis is on performance without any due consideration to circumstances or care for the people. Team efforts are held together by chains, not by any cooperative unity of purpose. Supportive leadership does not exist in such a scenario.

This does not mean a nice leader should not be tough when the situation demands it. The good, positive leader is assertive and does not back down in tough situations. Saying no or requiring that a responsibility be carried out is a positive factor in an organization's well-being. Being nice, but firm, builds respect and loyalty in subordinates. Petty tyrants do not build respect or loyalty. When times get tough, the goodwill built up by the good leader can pay big dividends. The organization rallies around the flag and tackles the problem. The subordinates of a leader who sets a negative tone just see the orders of the tyrant as unreasonable demands. They do not give their best effort. What goes around comes around.

Be nice. Be supportive. Be fair, but firm. Show respect. You will get better performance out of your people.

PASSION

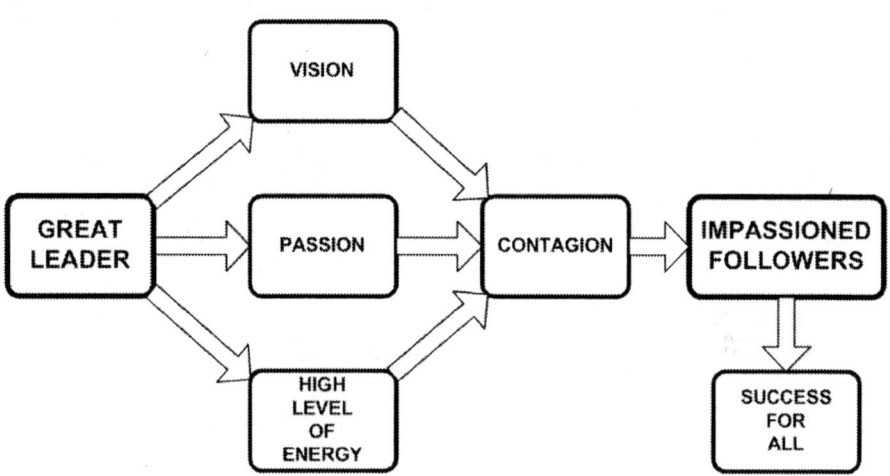

PASSIONATE

A *great leader* has *passion*, is excited about what he or she is doing, and has a *vision*. The vision may need fine-tuning along the way, but the leader sets a course and pushes ahead to the destination with unbounded determination. Money is not the driving force; accomplishment and success are. Leadership is serving, both people and a cause.

There is not only the visionary aspect of passion; there is also the passionate care a leader has for his or her people. The passionate leader loves what he or she does and the people he or she works with.

Passion pervades all action and is communicated to the followers. If the leader cannot instill at least some measure of that same passion in his or her followers, the leader's effectiveness is diminished. Excitement is *contagious*. The vision is the rallying cry, the call to arms.

Passion is drive coupled with enthusiasm. It requires a *high level of energy*. Because pressures that storm the executive can come from all sides, the passionate executive pushes the pedal to the metal. Standing still means being overcome and dragged down. Passion helps the leader break through the waves.

A great leader with *impassioned followers* means *success for all*!

RESPECTED

Giving respect breeds respect. Showing respect enhances people's self-esteem and bestows on them the consideration they are due. Hold people in high regard. Treat everyone with dignity and respect. In short, follow the golden rule, "Do unto others as you would have them do unto you."

When you approach people, do you demand their attention or generate fear in them? A better approach is to invite their participation and ask for their input. Be sure your approach is one of openness and trust.

Watch people's reaction when you interface with them. People's expressions can tell you a lot. Do not be so busy transmitting that you shut down your receiving antenna.

Sometimes discomfort is unavoidable. If you are put into a position where you have to hand out a reprimand or inflict discipline, be sure you do so with respect for the person on the receiving end. Attack the problem, not the individual.

Do not tear down a person's self-esteem. Tell the person you know he or she can do better, then show the way to achieve better performance. Help the subordinate develop an action plan for solving the problem and establish deadlines for deliverables. Assign the employee the responsibility for correcting the problem. Offer your help. These steps will provide a solution without attacking the self-esteem or self-respect of the individual. Be supportive throughout the ordeal.

Be firm if you have to, but still be nice.

RESULTS

Assuming you have laid the proper foundation with your followers, you will get excellent results in your company's endeavors. The followers will have the right attitude and put forth the requisite effort to carry out the work needed in your area of responsibility.

Exercise leadership in the proper manner and watch the company, the employees, and yourself prosper.

13

Leadership in Action

A proactive approach to displaying leadership and inspiring people to follow you requires action on your part. People are going to need some reason to put you on a pedestal. A good starting point is to be a person people can respect, someone they can look up to. Are you trustworthy? Can you be counted on for help and support in time of need? Are you a good role model? Are you consistent? Are you fair? Are you objective? Are you caring? Be a person your subordinates would like to emulate. Be a role model.

Given that you are a person worthy of respect, the next step is to have some goals and objectives. Being a leader means you are the point man or woman who is leading in some direction. There must be a destination. There must be some guiding principles that determine how the journey is to be conducted.

A leader will have a vision, an attractive vision, one that excites people. The vision must be specific and clearly spelled out. It must not be so broad as to be meaningless. The leader will have a commitment to the vision. The vision must be clearly communicated so the followers will understand it. Because the vision excites people, they will want to embrace the vision and make it their own. The vision should be one that can be recited easily by the follower.

A proper vision will represent a challenge, a struggle that requires effort. Being a challenge means that accomplishing the objective of the vision is not an easy task. Carrying out the vision should produce an outcome that is good for those on the receiving end of the effort. The vision should make both the giver and the recipient feel good.

To make the vision happen, the journey must begin. Since the journey is supposed to be difficult and is expected to encounter obstacles, the leader must accept the risks and be the first to start the journey. By definition, leadership means leading.

If the vision is a clear one and the followers believe in it and its worthy goals, the followers will do their part—follow the leader and make it happen. Having accepted the risks; both the leader and the followers must firmly commit to accomplishing the goals, in spite of the obstacles. The buy-in must be from the top down and from the bottom up. Everyone must join the campaign.

Along the journey, the leader needs to act as a cheerleader and encourage cheerleading by other leaders in the team, regardless of position in the organization. Good coaches and good players do not give up before the game is over. They encourage one another to perform at their best and to reach the goal line. They all have commitment.

Never forget to cheer and applaud people's accomplishments along the way. Reward the players for their achievements.

EGO

An executive's ego can be a huge problem in running an organization. Never let your ego get in the way.

> "Pride goes before destruction, a haughty spirit before a fall."
> —Proverbs 16:18 (NIV)

What a company does is a team effort. So long as there is more than one person in the company, it stands to reason that more than one person contributes to the business's success. Do not try to hog the credit from those who truly deserve it. If the executive tries to take all the credit, the other people who contributed to a particular success will get discouraged—and maybe quit after credit has been stolen from them often enough.

Share the credit. Err on the side of giving praise and credit to those who work for you. If your department or division does well, you will ultimately get credit for how your unit performs.

Leave your ego at the door. Remember the little guy. You will go farther and faster.

INITIATIVE

A growing, successful company desires people with initiative. Passive employees are for mature, cash cows. People with initiative act to seize opportunities when they appear, or they solve problems before being forced to by events. When you just react to events, rather than anticipating them, means you lack initiative. Crises and emergencies can become a way of life. Initiative dies.

A true leader is proactive and seeks to anticipate events. He or she plans for the future and acts now to take advantage of any opportunities that are envisioned. A large measure of optimism is inherent in the person with initiative. That person looks for opportunities and is confident they are out there for someone with foresight. Hope springs eternal in these forward-looking people.

The person with drive persists in taking the initiative. Once an opportunity is recognized; that person takes advantage of the situation and then perseveres in taking action. He or she does not give up searching or executing.

But initiative wrongly applied can take a person down the wrong path. When an executive preempts the responsibilities of subordinates—does their job before they have a chance—he or she kills morale and destroys the initiative of subordinates. Initiative must be kept within bounds or it will be self-defeating.

Optimism, the partner of initiative, can help someone bounce back after a setback. The pessimist wallows in self-pity and defeatism. The optimist with initiative gets up, knocks off the dust, and persists in looking for other opportunities. These people have self-confidence. They know their abilities. They keep taking the initiative.

EXPLOITING SUCCESS

One side of the "coin of success" is assembling the necessary resources to correct a problem that has been identified. The problems with the greatest payback for success are corrected first. The remaining problems are tackled in order of priority.

The other side of the "coin of success" is to take advantage of the opportunities afforded by capitalizing upon a company's ongoing successes. In this scenario, the most successful products or services are given even more attention. More resources are thrown at them. It is like the battlefield commander probing enemy lines for weaknesses; when they are found, troops are poured into the enemy's weak points. Reapply this image to breakthrough sales opportunities and you get the picture for business.

Prioritize the successful efforts, then assign your best performers to exploit the opportunities. Keep applying resources, making incremental changes that further enhance the success. After enough incremental advances have been made on the successful ride, there may come a point when a major breakthrough is achieved; that is, given enough changes, you have something that is fundamentally new and different. Hopefully, your competitor will still be playing catch-up.

Therefore, apply your best people and resources to the best opportunities. They will generally give you the best payback for your money.

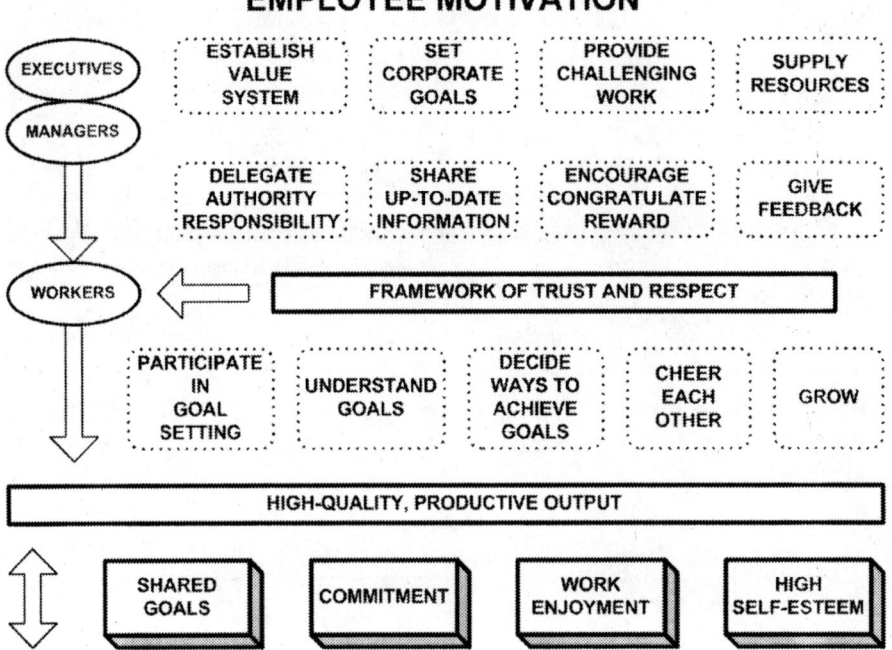

EMPLOYEE MOTIVATION

The chief motivators for on-the-job performance are the sheer joy of doing the job itself and the challenge of doing it well. In short, the worker is most motivated who loves what he or she is doing and who gets extreme pleasure from growing and learning how to do the job better. But executives and managers must establish the proper framework for this to happen.

People work hard when they have a goal and when their work is both worthwhile and important. But the worker must understand both the goal and its importance. This is not about numbers. It is about the value of the work.

The product or service provided by the work needs to benefit someone. Explore what might happen to recipients of the work's output if the work were stopped and they did not receive its benefits. Performing worthwhile work helps build self-esteem in the worker. A boss must communicate the worth and importance of the work in no uncertain terms, in terms the employee can relate to.

Executives Establish Value System: Not only must goals be important, but how you get there is equally important. Neither the goals nor the route to achieving them should violate your value system. This means you need to define another set of goals, the standards that provide context and guidance for everything you do. They are value goals, the framework within which you work and make decisions. These goals must be shared, too.

Management should take the leadership in setting these value goals. They must define a value system that people still adhere to when the going gets tough. You should not compromise on values when they become inconvenient. You stick to them. Your actions tell whether you really believe in your values. Be a role model for your people.

Executives Set Corporate Goals: Executives set the overall goals for a corporation. An organization's goals should be shared, with everyone working to achieve them. It is not enough for some manager or executive to set goals and make some pronouncement from on high. If the workers remain uncommitted to the goals, they never shared the goals in the first place. Awareness does not equate to commitment. The desired results come from a shared commitment to goals. The goals we are talking about here result in productive output. The more employees share in setting the goals, the more likely they will share in a commitment to the goals. Let them participate in goal setting.

Workers Participate in Goal Setting: The more highly motivated person will also set his or her personal performance goals, goals that stretch but that are attainable. Employers need to understand the subordinate's abilities and help the employee to set performance goals accordingly.

There is a lesson here, too, for executives: Seek positions for yourself that are challenging and that offer you pleasure in just doing the job. Even if a current position is not your favorite, it can still be motivating if it gives you a new skill and is a stepping stone to a better position. Learn the new skill, broaden your professional tool bag, and move on.

Workers Understand Goals, Then Decide Ways to Achieve Goals: After the leader has set the primary or critical goals of the organization and has established the value system within which they will be pursued, it is time to let the workers figure out the best ways of getting there. Once the employees understand the goals, let them set their own goals to achieve the organizational goals. Being closer to the action, the worker will often know the better way.

Leaders Supply Resources: Management must provide the resources needed by employees to get the job done. This includes providing a work environment conducive to productivity.

Leaders Provide Challenging Work: If work is boring, motivation takes a holiday. But the more an employee gets immersed in doing a job, the greater will be his or her motivation. Getting a chance to learn new things and to develop new skills is very motivating. An employee needs to be challenged.

So, give employees challenging work to do. They are not challenged by goals that are too easy to achieve. Set goals that make the employees stretch. People can become discouraged, though, if goals are unattainable. Set difficult, but reachable, goals. Make your people feel good when they successfully achieve what they set out to do. Give them a chance to be fulfilled. Everyone needs fulfillment.

Workers Grow: Put your staff in positions in which they feel they can grow. But their motivation will drop if you place them in work in which they have no interest. If the employee feels he or she is wasting time and talent, there is a greater likelihood the employee will leave in search of a more fulfilling job.

The most powerful motivation comes from what is inside a person. External motivators (raises, promotions, bonuses, awards, etc.) are less important. Incentives such as these have their place, but they lack the staying power of a person loving what he or she is doing and wanting to do the job better. Money is rarely the primary driving force. It and other rewards merely serve to keep score on how well a person is doing.

Leaders Delegate Authority and Responsibility: Good bosses establish the framework within which people work, then get out of the way. They let the workers get the job done without micromanaging. This may require adjusting the organization to fit the natural way people want to work, not the way managers think they should work. Let the employees work up to their ability. Let them be in control of achieving their own individual goals. Authority should be delegated along with responsibility.

Leaders (and Workers) Share Up-To-Date Information: Motivation is enhanced by a high level of trust between manager and managed. And trust is improved by allowing the free flow of information between the two sides. That means both parties should provide up-to-date information to the other party.

Leaders Encourage, Congratulate, and Reward: Employees need congratulations to boost their self-esteem and their sense of accomplishment. Cheer your workers on when they do a good job and when they achieve their goals. Also, encourage them to cheer each other. Applaud verbally and enthusiastically. Follow the example of the sports team and the audience who together visibly react to accomplishments on the playing field. Everybody cheers everybody.

Don't be false in your congratulations. Be sincere. Be timely. Do it now. Direct it toward a specific individual or the whole team. Cheer not only the progress, but also the final achievement. Help your subordinates go home at the end of the day with their heads held high.

All of this does not detract from the need to pay a competitive wage, plus provide other rewards for good performance. Although pay is not a primary motivator, it can be a de-motivator. Inadequate pay represents low marks on the professional "scorecard" in an employee's mind. If another company offers the same level of job satisfaction, but at significantly higher pay; what do you think will happen? Feed employees' pocketbooks and their minds.

Leaders Give Feedback: Supervisors should provide feedback. Employees want to know how they are doing, whether good or bad. Criticism, done in the proper way, can be motivating. Support your employees by helping them do better. Doing better can be a positive motivator. Justifiable praise for a job well done spurs the person on to do even better in the future. A kind word of appreciation goes a long way. The praise needs to be timely, when the feat is accomplished—not days later.

Framework of Trust and Respect: A good leader is the boss without being bossy. And good workers get the job done without getting in each other's way. Bosses value their employees; and employees value each other's work. There is mutual trust and respect all around.

High-Quality, Productive Output: Motivated employees are ready, willing, and able to work, to accept challenges, and to work for the common good. In fact, they are eager to do so. They are committed to shared goals. They enjoy going to work. They are an energized workforce. They are high-quality producers. They have high self-esteem. They care. Customers are happy as a result.

Be patient. Be realistic. It takes time—six months, maybe even several years—to turn a non-motivated workforce into a motivated one. It is a culture change. It is culture shock.

Work is fun when you enjoy it. You do not HAVE to go to work. You GET to go to work.

MINGLING WITH EMPLOYEES

Aloofness in the corner office is unbecoming of an executive. If an executive does not mingle with the workers, it is almost universally accepted by them that the leader does not care. Even if the executive does care, and care a lot; if there is no interfacing with the employees, the perception becomes reality in the employees' minds—and perception is reality.

Mingle with the employees not just when the opportunity presents itself, but also as part of a recurrent process. Make it a practice to mingle. Both sides will benefit from the encounters. Each will learn from the other when communication is allowed to flow freely. A listening executive shows respect for the subordinate. The employee is heard. A talking executive imparts knowledge and vision to the employee. The encounters should be two-way streets.

How can the executive conduct these encounters? Start by meeting regularly with employees of the different departments and asking for their feedback. Encourage questions from the meeting participants. This is no time for political doublespeak. Communication must be clear and forthright. If there are situations where competitive realities demand some secrets be kept in the executive suite, then say so and give justifiable reasons for the secrecy. Too many secrets, though, fuel the flames of distrust in two ways: (1) employees wonder what is going on in the back offices and (2) employees get the feeling the executives do not trust them. So, be careful about secrets.

In large organizations with widespread locations, executives often stay close to home, seldom visiting troops out in the boondocks. This is a mistake. It oftentimes leads distant employees to think the "big boss" does not really care about them or their problems and needs. If an important customer asked you to come to their headquarters in a distant city, wouldn't you do it? You have employees out there serving those distant customers, so you should consider them just as important as the customers. These employees provide the primary customer interface and set the stage for productive customer relations. So, visit the distant employees and communicate to them how much you appreciate their efforts and their input. Keep them informed.

Eat in the company lunchroom, if there is one, and sit at the table with employees lower in the organization. Do not always eat with your exclusive club of fellow executives. Eat and communicate with the workers. Have coffees with selected employees and engage in open dialogue. Emphasize their worth to the company without using hollow platitudes. Explain that you need their help in order to prevail over the challenges facing the company. Tell them about the challenges. Elicit their support. After all, without them you could not carry out your assigned responsibilities. It is a team effort.

Bottom line: Use your imagination to come up with ways to mingle. Wander around the company's halls. Go to the assembly line. Talk with the employees on the floor. Make it a regular part of your life. It is impressive for the General to talk to the Private on the front lines. Let them know you know they are in the line of fire, just like you are. Even tell them the pressures you are under. Get them onboard.

14

Company Cultures

Each executive must realize that every company has a culture, and he or she must understand what that company culture is. To fight a company's culture is difficult, at best. To understand and work within the culture is normally the most effective course of action. But sometimes you can't fight city hall; it can be hazardous to your health.

> "When I hear the word culture, I reach for my revolver."
> —Hanns Johst

To change a company's culture is very difficult and normally very time-consuming. Sometimes it is a project worth tackling, but the power and commitment of the leaders to carry through with the conversion is essential. That same commitment must be accepted and acted upon by the employees, too.

A corollary is that any attempt to merge two companies with radically different cultures is a recipe for disaster. Mergers often fail because two cultures did not blend well.

Which type of culture should be used? Which is the most effective? It depends. In some situations, one culture might be superior to another. However, this can be too simplistic a viewpoint. In reality, a company is likely to be a hybrid of several cultures, with one dominant. Different divisions or departments could have different cultures. International companies could certainly have different cultures in their different countries of operation. Regardless, all parts of the company still need to share a common vision.

Because a large company has many different managers with many different management styles, a given department might easily have a culture that is very different from the company-wide culture. It would still need to work within constraints imposed by the culture that is dominant for the company as a whole. This culturally "rogue" department could not adopt an "in your face" approach and expect to survive; at least its department head could not.

The lesson is still the same: The effective manager must recognize the culture(s) and work within the system.

Command and Control: Cultures can take several different forms. One would be the command and control culture that results from a strong leader who wants to run a "tight ship." Decisions come from the top and are passed down through the successively lower chains of command. The company is very hierarchical. Control is centralized. Power and security are emphasized.

A large corporation with a CEO bent on control might fit this mold. However, the size of the company is not the determinant factor, the leadership is. The problem with this tightly controlled culture is that feedback and the free exchange of ideas can be severely suppressed, much to the detriment of company success. On the other hand, the command and control approach is often the best approach during a crisis. It supports decisiveness, but decisions still need the best information available from all parties.

Collaborative: A second culture could be one where the players are very collegial or collaborative. The executives share power and authority. This would typically be representative of a rather flat organization, with few levels of management. Teamwork is emphasized. Consensus is the norm. Executives work as co-equal partners. Pride and ego are subordinated to the well-being of the group.

Leadership is given to the individuals suited for each new situation. The person with the best skills for the job at hand becomes the leader for the situation's duration. As projects change, the leaders change. Teams receive the recognition and the rewards.

Again, the size of a company is not necessarily the controlling factor. Instead, the controlling factor is whether there is a team spirit and the team spirit is communicated—and, thereby infused—throughout the organization. Good communication is essential in this type of company.

Star Player: The third type of culture is the one where individual competence and achievements are emphasized and applauded. Proven skills, expertise, and ability are the factors that dominate the corporate thought-process. Star players are the heroes. If you are not a star, then you are just a camp follower. Objectively measured results populate the scorecards. Recognition and rewards are handed out to star players based on performance metrics.

This type of organization might be more technical in nature, such as engineering. Sales is another example. Piece goods manufacturing is still another. That is not to say this culture cannot be wrongly applied where teamwork is more appropriate. In a situation where teamwork is needed, the star player mentality can be highly disruptive and counterproductive. But in some situations, this approach can be highly productive, call centers for instance.

Charismatic: A fourth type of culture is based on charismatic leadership. Unlike the command and control culture where the leader is the ruler because of the power embodied in his or her position, the charismatic organization has a leader who is driven by a vision. He or she has a mission.

The leader mesmerizes the followers, who, in turn, are drawn to the organization by the magnetism and vision of the leader. The followers share the vision and will do anything to advance it. They are driven by the "cause." Without the charismatic leader, this type of organization dies. Vision and charisma are fine; but if either is lost, the cause is lost.

Individualism: The fifth type of culture heralds the value of each individual as an individual. It is more a loose association of independent people than a cohesive organization. Individual worth is everything. Individual employees are peers to each other. This is different from the collegial or collaborative environment where individuals work together as a team.

Individuals in this type of organization are relatively independent of each other in duties and responsibilities. A consulting organization is a prime example where this type of organization is very appropriate. Research and development groups, where new ideas or products are generated from scratch, are other instances where this type of working relationship is very effective. Bureaucratic processes do not apply.

Different Cultures: Different cultures can work together harmoniously in the same company. The key point is to keep your antennae out for culture clashes. Different departments often have different cultures, simply because companies bring together different professions, and, therefore, different mindsets. It is important that common goals for the company as a whole dominate all mindsets. Everyone must believe in and actively support them. Independent fiefdoms are unacceptable. If you cannot think in terms of the company's bottom line, get off the team.

Choose the right culture. Manage the culture. Blend compatible cultures, if appropriate. Diversity can be both a challenge and a blessing. Thinking outside the box does not come from me-too-ism.

15

The Entrepreneur

THE ENTREPRENEUR

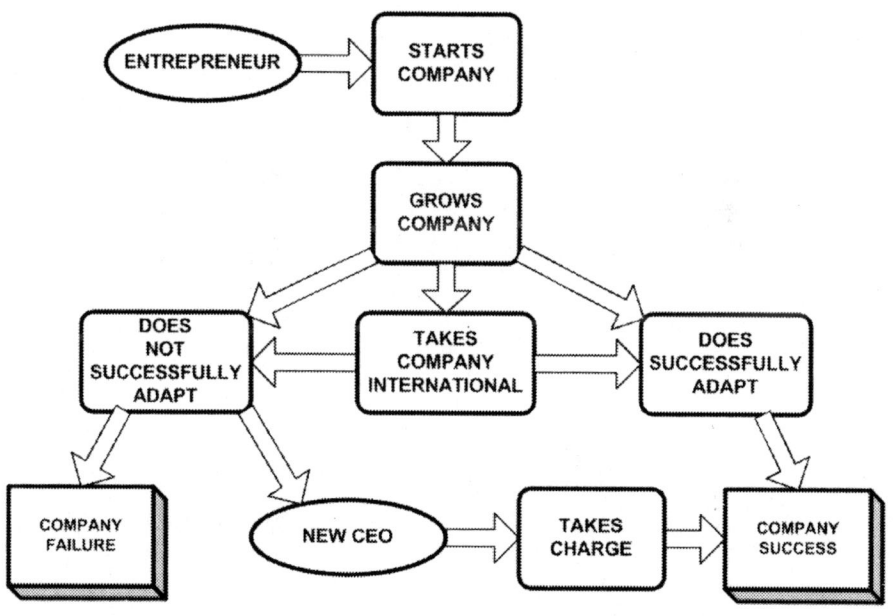

ENTREPRENEURIAL EXECUTIVES

Entrepreneurs typically give a company its start. The entrepreneur is the company's CEO from the beginning and often stays in that position. This can be good or bad, depending upon the individual and the type of company.

Entrepreneurs think in terms of what is best for the whole company. The entrepreneur executive should instill an entrepreneurial spirit in everyone in the company—executives and workers. The employee with an entrepreneurial mindset does not let departmental loyalty override what is best for the common good. He or she will stay vigilant for opportunities and will act to take advantage of things that help the company's bottom line.

Entrepreneurs take risks, preferably rational ones. They make mistakes and are allowed to make mistakes again. No risk, no gain. Employees in an entrepreneurial organization push the envelope, too; they are willing—given the proper leadership and support—to get out of their comfort zone.

Remember, it is often easier to make the transition from an entrepreneurial company to a larger managed company than it is to grow and still maintain an entrepreneurial spirit. Bureaucracy spreads and stifles. People start covering their rears. Having seasoned management does not equate to successful growth. Do you want a static cash cow, or would you prefer a growing, innovative company? Never let the entrepreneurial spirit die.

But some leaders cannot make the transition from being an entrepreneur in a small company to being an adaptive manager of a growing, more mature corporation. When making the transition, you either need people who can make the transition or new people. A wise company founder will recognize this and act accordingly.

TRANSISITON FROM ENTREPRENEUR

The company started with a bang. The entrepreneur had a great idea, buckets of enthusiasm, and an overwhelming passion to succeed. Things went well, the enterprise was funded, and the company grew—and grew some more. That is when the problems began. The company floundered and eventually went under.

The founder was simply unable to make the transition from small start-up to large corporation. He or she was unable to grow and adapt to the changing role of management.

One of the biggest problems facing the entrepreneur of a rapidly growing company is being unwilling to relinquish detailed control. As the organization grows, the point is reached where the entrepreneur has to sit back and trust his or her people to do a good job. The entrepreneur cannot continue to stay involved in every little detail. Instead, he or she must quit doing and start concentrating on guiding. A growing company needs a leader, not a worker.

The key to making this happen is to hire the right people and place them in the proper positions of leadership. Establish the appropriate organization and assign responsibilities. Give the people in leadership positions the authority to carry out their assigned responsibilities.

So, entrepreneur, continually ask yourself, "Is this something I need to get personally involved in, or can I delegate it to someone else?" In most cases, you can delegate. Trust your people.

INTERNATIONAL CEO

It is a matter of faith that if the headquarters of a global corporation is located in the United States, the CEO ought to be an American. If the company was started by an entrepreneur who is still at the helm, it is still true. Or is it? Several thoughts bring this attitude into question.

A corporation that does business around the world, and, perhaps, has offices around the world, needs someone at the top who has a global perspective. If you are going to play in the sandbox, you had better know the whole sandbox. It stands to reason, then, that the person at the top, the CEO, needs to understand the international front.

Given the choice between two otherwise equally qualified candidates for the CEO position, would you give the nod to someone who has lived only in the U.S. or one who has lived and worked in multiple countries? All other things being equal, you should go with the person who has had day-to-day experience in more than one country. Certainly, living and doing business in a country is better experience than just traveling in it.

A touchy situation arises when the founder and CEO only has experience in America but the company has expanded vigorously into foreign markets. When this happens, the CEO needs to become well versed in the implications of foreign operations. At a minimum, the CEO needs to bring in advisors who are experienced in international trade.

If it becomes obvious to the board of directors that the current CEO, even though he or she is the founder of the corporation, is not making the cut on foreign operations, some sort of corrective action is called for. It may mean encouraging the founder to step aside for a more capable individual, or else the board may insist on the founder listening to the advice of people better versed in international trade.

The head of a global corporation occupies a vital position for corporate success. The right person needs to be in the position.

Part IV

ATTITUDES AND EMOTIONS

16

Change

Accepting Change: Change is inevitable. It is a fact of life. In order to deal with change effectively, the executive must be adaptable. That means being comfortable with ambiguities and being able to handle the unexpected. Ambiguity requires dealing with less than perfect information and still being able to make a decision. If the future could be predicted with accuracy and if the predictions were accepted, life would be simple, but boring. If today's executive is bored, he is not paying attention. At a minimum, he or she needs a new outlook or a change in companies.

Self-confidence and self-awareness help the successful executive cope with and master the world of change. Adaptability means being able to respond promptly to a changing situation and decisively act to go forward. A wholesale change in direction may be needed. The adaptable executive must be willing to change the plan and execute an alternate plan when previous assumptions are blown to smithereens. Adaptability in this scenario means being willing to take risks.

> "Companies that learn to manage change are in the best position to continue to take the risks needed to stay out in front."
> —Michael S. Dell

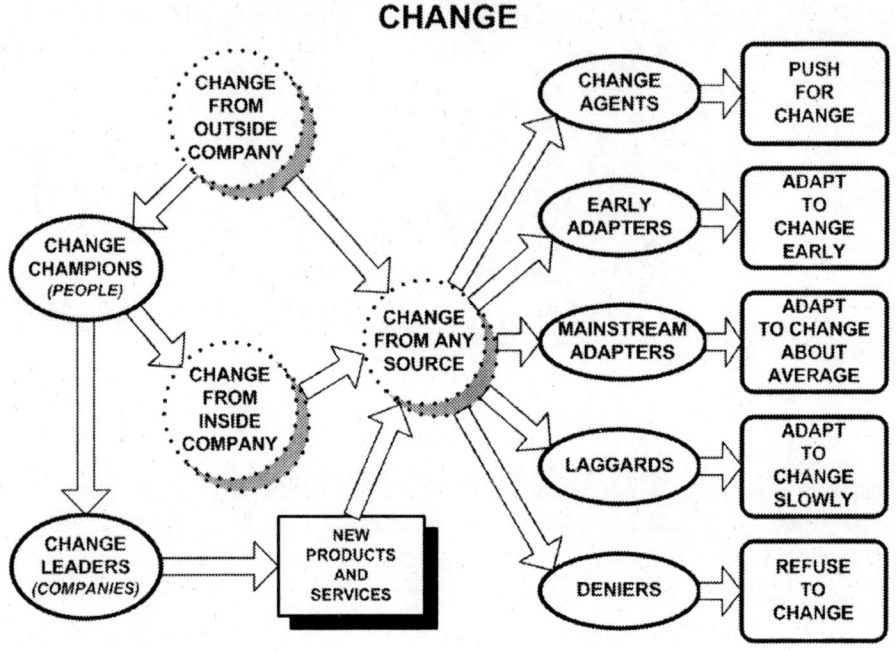

Change Factors: From a business standpoint, change can come from outside the company or from inside the company. Change must be monitored and tracked. There will be those who are champions of change and others who just accept the change. Some will even deny it is happening. If people fail to change over the long haul, they will become obsolete and will be discarded.

Change factors that are external to a company can be many and varied. Advances in technology bring changes to the marketplace. Societal changes, such as the aging of various generations and changes in the distribution of races, bring changes to the business world. Assassinations, wars, terrorist attacks, politics, celebrity deaths, scientific discoveries, fashions, new laws, catastrophes in nature, revolutions, media campaigns, etc., all bring changes. The list of change factors is endless.

Some external change factors cause changes inside a company. Other external change factors cause little or no change within a company. There is always the need to anticipate change and go on the offensive, when appropriate. If a company is faced with a change it did not foresee, it must go into reactionary mode—it must be on the defensive, which is not a good position. Noticing small changes early helps you prepare for bigger changes that come later. You must adapt to change quickly—beat your competitor to the punch.

Reacting to Change: Your reaction to change is important. It is safer to watch for and be prepared for change than to ignore it and hope it goes away. Accept the fact of change. Do not fear it. When you move beyond your fear of change, you will experience a feeling of freedom. Learn to enjoy change. Be ready to change quickly and to enjoy doing it again and again.

> "Today, loving change, tumult, even chaos is a prerequisite for survival, let alone success."
> —Thomas J. Peters

One of the biggest dangers is holding onto the past with a death grip. Old beliefs may have to be discarded because they are no longer true or no longer applicable. The quicker you let go of the old, the sooner you will find the new. Think of change as providing a new beginning. If you never change, you will continue to get the same results and repeat the same mistakes. If you do not move in a new direction, you will certainly never discover anything new. People who stayed at home did not discover America. People who ventured out found it. Those explorers brought a tidal wave of change to the New World.

As paradoxical as it may seem, giving up the security of the present may be the only way to preserve your future security. The more important your current beliefs are, the more likely you will want to hold onto them—in a vise-like grip. While change is enjoyable to some people, it is very scary and traumatic to others. So, whether you embrace change or run from it, you must, in the end, come to grips with it.

> "Change is inevitable, except from a vending machine."
> —Bumper Sticker

Now let's talk more specifically about a business organization.

Change Champions (People): The person who leads change within an organization is not necessarily the innovator who came up with the idea. The change champion sees the opportunity afforded by an innovative idea, then he or she helps remove barriers and helps make the idea come into being. This includes championing the change and enlisting the aid of others in making it happen. The change champion must be an effective leader of change.

A change leader has the confidence to pursue the "dream," i.e., the change to be implemented. Self-assurance and self-confidence provide the foundation, the inner support, to champion change. Maintaining perseverance in the face of organizational obstacles and having the persistence to present the case to corporate leaders are characteristics of a champion of change.

The change leader must articulate the benefits of the change and enlist the emotion of the people who will help implement the change. The followers must be given a compelling vision of the benefits—both to them and the organization. The leader must also bolster the follower's need for achievement and show how the change effort will satisfy that need. The leader will fan the flames of a follower's compulsion to support a worthy cause.

Change Leaders (Companies): For a company to be a leader of change, it must abandon the past. It must be willing to accept innovation, and not just accept it, but also embrace it—take some risks. That means having a willingness to free up resources in order to concentrate on the future. Remember, the future in business is built from a starting point of NOW.

Systematically and regularly, review current products and services. Look for things to abandon and new things to pursue. You must be willing to end commitments to anything that no longer contributes to performance or produces meaningful results.

To take action requires knowing what action to take. This includes conducting an ongoing, repetitive, in-depth review of the following: customer needs, technology developments, supplier innovations, competitor information, market situation, products and services, government rules and regulations, and employee ideas.

Using all the information and insights gathered, the executive team should examine its own business in light of what has been uncovered. This is a time for objectivity, not emotional subjectivity. The change leader must be willing to terminate any product or service that is dying. It is probably dead already.

A telltale sign that a product or service has reached the end of its useful life is hearing people say it still has a few more good years left. Can the resources being consumed by a dying effort be put to better use in another endeavor? Be brutal. Constantly put existing products and services on trial for their lives. Be willing to abandon. Be willing to kill a cherished product or service. This is no time for sentimentality.

When a product or service needs to be abandoned, the next question is, "What do we do now?" Coming hard on its heels is, "How do we do it?"

Determining WHAT means choosing the product or service your best judgment says is most likely to provide the greatest return on the investment of your limited resources. Do not use off-the-wall guesses. Do some serious analysis, and, if practical, some market research. Never assume people in the back office or the executive suite are all seeing and all knowing. Test the assumptions. Consider possible ramifications. Look at the best, worst, and most-likely scenarios. Go with the most-likely possibility, tempered with a due consideration of the best and worst possibilities.

Determining HOW to embark on the new course is not trivial. Explore various alternatives. Evaluate the probable effectiveness of various strategies. Consider alternative implementation processes, marketing approaches, distribution channels, messages to stockholders and investors, competitor responses, customer reaction, employee strengths, and likely government responses (rules and regulations). In general, government will not muddy the water until much later in the cycle.

So, take a systematic approach to constantly re-justifying the expenditure of time and resources on existing products and services. Be honest in analyzing future expectations for existing operations. Look for and embrace change—positive change. Be an innovator. Shake up the competition. Set the stage for wowing future customers. Work on the future now.

Change Agents: Regardless of the source for any change—internal or external, direct or indirect—different people react differently to change. There are, of course, those people who cause the change, the people we will call change agents. They push for change. They produce change. Naturally, they endorse the change, because they are bringing it about. They could come from the ranks of an organization's change champions. They are, in fact, champions of their own ideas. They do not need to be sold on change; they are selling it. They will try to convince executives to experiment with new ideas or products they have developed or conceptualized.

Early Adapters: The next category to be addressed includes those people who do not actually bring about the initial change, but they endorse it and help spread it. They sniff out the change and see it early. They are actively watching for change. Taking technology as an example, and the Internet in particular, early adapters embraced the technology and were the first to use it when it became available.

These people are the avant-garde, the leaders of a movement into new areas. They readily accept change in their areas of interest. They are not afraid of change. They enjoy it. These are the people to reach out to with new products and services.

The early adapter types can help get a new product or service started. They can become evangelists for new things. They like to work in a company that values action. They believe in action. But you have to monitor them to see they do not go off half-cocked. Given the right leadership and direction, they are invaluable in making change happen. If you are trying to institute an organizational change, these are the people to enlist as champions of the change. Optimists abound here. They are open-minded and keep their eyes open to any change that is likely to have an impact on their world.

Mainstream Adapters: Probably the majority of people react to change on a moderate level. These are the mainstream adapters. Ultimately, this group of people helps to ensure the ongoing, sustained viability of any new product or service. They are slower to adapt to change. They want to see if something new is going to survive or if it is just a passing fad. They take some convincing. They fall somewhere in the middle ground between optimism and pessimism. More traditional approaches in advertising, for example, would apply to this group. These are the masses that must be sold on the change before they will endorse it. Peer pressure does apply. The argument to these people is that everyone is doing it or that it is inevitable.

Laggards: This next group is slow to adapt to change. Laggards are either disinterested in the change or else they will only accept the change when forced to by circumstances or their boss. Since they are very reluctant to change, they lack incentive to change, and, therefore, they adapt to change slowly. They are characterized by indecision. They may even get angry about the proposed change. They do not want to give up their security blanket, the blanket they understand and love.

These are the pessimists with negative thoughts about change. They will take some real convincing. Getting their attention is difficult. Sometimes it takes coercion to motivate them. There is no point in spending a lot of time on these people. They will slow things down. However, laggards do eventually realize that a particular change is inevitable and they accept it, but not enthusiastically. They may even enjoy it when they finally get pushed into the change.

Deniers: The worst people to deal with are those who deny the change, who stick their heads in the sand, or who flatly refuse to accept the change. They are happy to do without the change. They feel the change will be bad for them. They deny any need for a change. They do not read the signs, even the flashing ones. Trying to get them to change can take a lot of effort—effort that may be completely wasted.

The world does not stand still. It moves on. If you encounter these people, who are caught up in denial, the only choice may be to part company with them—let them go. They must wake up to the fact they will become obsolete and will self-destruct if they do not change.

So, when change starts making its presence known, act on it after a careful analysis. Anticipate it, if you can. Never ignore change. Adapt to it. Originate it where it makes business sense. Determine which change camp your followers or customers fall into, and act accordingly.

17

Work Attitudes

COMPANY ALLEGIANCE

The good employee's first allegiance should be to the company as a whole instead of to his or her department. Said another way, the guiding principle of an employee, whether executive or hourly, should be to do what is best for the company's bottom line over the long haul, rather than for a department in the company.

In like manner, you must give due consideration to what is good for the employee. A company is the product of its people, the workers at all levels of the hierarchy. If you take care of the employees, they will take care of the company—and its customers.

COMMITMENT

Commitment means making a promise to do something—accepting responsibility for getting things done. It also means having a dedication to something, say, a company. The culture of a company should reinforce personal commitment by a company's personnel—at all levels in the organization.

A person without commitment is someone who makes halfhearted promises or only pretends to mean what he or she says. Sometimes a person does not consciously realize the lack of commitment. Other times that person is fully aware of his or her lack of commitment. Commitment starts with the individual.

The sooner false promises are accepted as a way of life in a corporation, the sooner that corporation starts its downward spiral. If you cannot trust executives or employees to carry through on their promises, people stop caring and they stop trying.

Commitment to a job means aligning one's goals with those of the organization. The company has a vision you can harmonize with your own vision. There is a sharing of values. There is a willingness to make personal sacrifices to support the long-term goals of the company. If the goals are fuzzy, commitment is blunted.

It behooves executives to ensure goals are clearly articulated and that they are in alignment with the organization's mission in life. How can you pledge allegiance to something you can't articulate or don't understand?

Commitment involves an emotional attachment to the cause. It means buy-in. The committed person finds a purpose in the tasks given to him or her. Doing what is right is its own reward and has a greater pulling power than pay. The committed employee feels like he or she is making a difference—is making a contribution. There is a fit between the employee's actions and the company's needs

An executive must display commitment in order to inspire commitment in his or her followers. If the followers fail to see commitment in their leader, then why should they bother? Leaders must be supportive if they expect their people to be committed—that means active, demonstrable support from the leaders, not just talk.

It should be perfectly acceptable to say "No" to fellow workers and management when unreasonable demands are made. An automatic "Yes" is a recipe for lowered expectations. It does not take long to figure out when there is a lack of commitment. Results speak for themselves. Failure and non-performance are the results of false promises.

> "What you do speaks so loudly that I cannot hear what you say."
> —Ralph Waldo Emerson

Commitment is enhanced by effective communication. The fear of communicating "No" or the fear of reporting bad news will result in bad communication or no communication at all. Rampant bad communication—when it is all pervasive in a company—is a sure sign of impending doom. Your people had better tell you about problems before your customer does—or your boss. It is rare for a problem not to be known by someone in the company before your customer tells you about it. Encourage communication, especially bad news. Do not kill the messenger.

It does not stop with commitment inside the organization. You need to honor commitments to your customers and your suppliers. The more you fail in your commitments to them, the more they will avoid doing business with you. Unless you are in that rare monopolistic situation where you are in absolute control, lack of commitment on your company's part ultimately means lost business and lost suppliers. Customers and suppliers must be able to rely on you. They can always vote with their feet—and they will.

COMPLACENCY

In today's modern world, business executives cannot afford to get complacent. Too much is happening too fast. Processes and procedures are very important to successful business operations. However, if you find your company is spending an inordinate amount of its time documenting processes and procedures, it is a good sign the efforts are diverting people from actual operations. Complacency and bureaucracy may be strangling the company.

If too much time is being spent on documentation, the company may have become internally focused. If you are preoccupied with what is going on inside, you are obviously ignoring what is going on outside the company. You will never notice the tornado that is about to slam into your office.

Instead of succumbing to complacency, start questioning the status quo. Don't take anything for granted. Start observing what is going on around you. Become an explorer again. Opportunities are raising their heads all around you. Don't expect them to tap you on the shoulder.

FUN AT WORK

Smiles can be contagious. Humor can grease the wheels. Which company would you rather visit, one where you are surrounded by smiling people, or one where everyone looks terribly serious and even severe? Grumps are not very well liked.

Although some people have a hard time having fun in life, the dream job is one where you are both happy and productive at the same time. It is wonderful to feel you are making a contribution. People will enjoy being around you.

As an executive, you should be a role model; so, loosen up and enjoy your work. Don't be too serious. Make the workplace an environment where employees can enjoy their time on the job. Productivity will increase.

Besides, happy people live longer!

18

Trust

TRUST IN THE ORGANIZATION

An organization built on trust has many advantages over an organization not built on trust. Think about it. Do you want a friend you can trust all the time, some of the time, or never? The answer is obvious, you want a friend you can trust all the time. Consider the four main players in business, excluding competitors: customers, suppliers, fellow workers, and your management. You want to trust all the people you deal with.

> "Man's life would be wretched and confined if it were to miss the candid intimacy developed by mutual trust and esteem."
> —Edwin Dummer

    Customers want to buy from people they trust. Before you can trust a company, you must be able to trust the employees that sell and serve you. It works the other way, too. Employees want to be able to trust the customers they deal with. Trust cannot exist in an atmosphere of suspicion, doubt, or deception
    What about your company's suppliers? Do you want to deal with suppliers you cannot trust? You want them to deliver goods and services you can have confidence in. You want honest dealings with them. But they also want you to be trustworthy.
    Closer to home, what about the people you work with in the company every day, what do they want? Employees want to deal with management they can trust. Executives want employees they can trust and rely upon. It cannot be a

one-sided arrangement. How can you expect people to trust you if you do not trust them?

Trust and loyalty work hand in hand. Which company is more likely to succeed in the long run, the one made up of people who can trust and depend upon each other or the one where everyone distrusts each other? Competitive advantage goes to the company that does not require constant supervision and control over each employee.

The opposite of trust is suspicion and distrust. If an organization has engendered an atmosphere built on fear and distrust, everyone is constantly looking over his or her shoulder and expecting the worst. Efficiency drops. Peak performance is a figment of someone's imagination. Stress abounds. Commitment is nonexistent.

This section asks a lot of questions, but it demands an honest appraisal, starting with yourself. It requires you to apply a single standard to yourself and others. Do not expect from others what you do not deliver yourself. Trust is earned and must be deserved in order to be enduring. Trust is not about self-interest.

TRUSTWORTHINESS

Lack of self-control and low self-restraint are common in the individual who is untrustworthy. The pressures of the moment lead to unethical behavior. The unethical executive will sometimes force subordinates to prepare false reports to avoid making the executive looking bad. The unethical leader is more hype than substance. He or she does not admit mistakes. The executive may take his or her unethical behavior down another path by taking credit for work done by the subordinate.

The paradox is that unethical people generally want others to be open and honest with them. They have a double standard. But when they need the help of a subordinate to carry through on a subterfuge, the executive will then require the subordinate to be unethical and back up what the executive has done or decided. You cannot depend on unethical people. They create problems—unnecessarily.

A trustworthy person is dependable and reliable. Trustworthiness goes hand in glove with being ethical. Ethical people are conscientious. They hold themselves accountable for doing their work and doing it properly. They have self-restraint. They have integrity. They are willing to stand up for what is right, in spite of pressures to the contrary. A trustworthy person is the kind you want on your team. The executive should set the example.

"No virtue is more universally accepted as a test of good character than trustworthiness."

—Harry Emerson Fosdick, D.D.

19

Emotions

EMOTIONAL AWARENESS

An executive, no less than any other person, is driven by emotions. To discount emotions is to delude oneself about their impact. You need to be aware of your emotions and the emotions of other people. Emotions are always present and will shape your thoughts. They can push you around.

Pay attention to your feelings. Learn to recognize your emotions and the impact they are having on whatever it is you are doing. Your emotions have an overwhelming influence on your interpersonal relations. How you interact with others is a primary factor in whether you succeed or fail in your endeavors.

Don't be an emotional illiterate. You can cultivate self-awareness. Start by paying attention to the signals being sent by your body, such as: headaches, pain, anxiety, nervousness, indigestion, etc. Take time to pay attention to yourself—without any outside interruptions. Have regularly scheduled times to reflect on yourself. Even Christ, a god, took time-outs to meditate. So did the great thinkers of our world.

Awareness of your emotions is the first step to controlling and using them profitably. If you don't realize you are angry, you won't know you need to cool it—unless someone points it out to you. Be the first person to know. A divorce or a heart attack might be the first indication you heed, but by then, it could be too late.

Your inner feelings are not irrelevant. You are driven by inner values and credos you may be unable to articulate. Recognizing them is the first step toward understanding them. Until you understand them, you are not going to have much luck shaping and controlling them.

EMOTIONAL INFLUENCE

Our emotions rule more than our logical minds would like. Emotions can have a positive or negative influence. If you pay attention to your own emotions and are receptive to other people's emotions, you will have an easier passage through this life. Sensitivity to emotions is an important factor in executive success.

Emotional empathy helps build strong, productive relationships between you and all the people around you. Recognizing emotions brings understanding of another person's feelings. Understanding another's feelings and needs helps build a foundation of trust. If two people trust each other, each listens to the other in a supportive manner. Communication barriers crumble with the achievement of understanding.

But emotions are contagious. This is true whether an interaction is between two individuals or between members of a larger group. For example, when one person gets angry, it is likely that others will get angry, too. On the other side of the coin, if you are upset and are dealing with someone who is calm and collected, particularly if that person is exerting a soothing influence, you will tend to calm down. So will other members in the group.

If someone in a group has a negative impact on a meeting, say, by constantly contradicting the person in charge; people will tend to get emotionally involved. They will take sides. Emotion spreads like wildfire, whether positive or negative. One inflammatory person can stir up a whole crowd of people. The people become a mob—out of control.

As an executive, the emotions you display when interacting with people can have a tremendous impact on the outcome of the interaction. You are in a position of power and, hopefully, trust. You can build rapport or kill it. You can pump people up or tear them down. You can make them happy or you can make them sad. You can make them mad. It is all in how you convey your feelings and the picture you present with your emotions. Your tone of voice and your body language can easily overpower the words you are saying. Feelings count.

When you make announcements, when you interact with subordinates, you set the tone. You determine in large measure the receptivity and the emotional impact of whatever it is you are trying to tell your people.

Consider some pivotal events and their emotional influence on you and others, such as: changing of the guard in the executive suite, downsizings, mergers, loss of major contracts, reorganizations, new bosses, firings, economic disasters, strikes, wars, terrorist activities, riots, deaths of fellow workers, corporate bankruptcies, plant shutdowns, new blockbuster products from competitors, negative court decisions, unprofitable quarters, hostile takeover attempts, and so on.

How you handle these encounters and the emotions you display while doing so will set the tone for how they are received and managed emotionally by your employees. You can build resentment. You can build anger. You can build distrust. You can build discontent.

On the other hand, you can build consensus. You can build support. You can build sympathy. You can build rapport. You can build enthusiasm. In short, you can build a rocky road or a smooth one. You will travel on the road you build. It is your choice!

20

Personal Stability

SELF-ASSESSMENT

Know thyself. An accurate self-assessment will help you avoid potholes and being blindsided when you least expect it. Sometimes, many times, in fact, a person is his or her own worst enemy.

> "To enter one's own self, it is necessary to go armed to the teeth."
> —Paul Vallery

Make it a point to be aware of your strengths and weaknesses. Some you know intuitively. Some you learn from your experiences. Experience is a great teacher. Reflect on what happens to you and why. Be able to laugh at yourself. Listen to feedback from others. Pay attention to the information you accumulate about yourself. The more you learn, the more you will be able to cope with the ups and downs of life and your professional career.

Try to uncover your blind spots. Are you a perfectionist? Do you spend too much time in detail and neglect the big picture? Are you overly ambitious to the point you set unrealistic goals or misrepresent facts? Do you expect other people to trust you but you don't trust them? Do you always seek the spotlight? Are you afraid to delegate in time of crisis? Do you set a higher standard for other people than yourself? Can you admit failure to others, i.e., can you acknowledge a mistake? Everyone makes mistakes, including you.

As you gain new perspectives, you will learn more about the flaws that need to be chipped away so that the diamond in you can become shining and sparkling. Engage in continuous learning and self-development. Play to your strengths and know your limitations. Polish the diamond.

SELF-CONFIDENCE

To be self-confident you must have a strong sense of self-worth. You must be realistically confident of your abilities. Self-confidence means having the conviction to take on tough challenges in the face of terrible odds—even to the point of risking your job. Self-confidence does not translate into arrogance, which lowers how others feel about you.

With self-confidence, you can fail and make mistakes—and still get up and try again. You are not beaten down with feelings of helplessness, doubt, or ineptness. Your inner strength helps inspire confidence in others around you. You are contagious. Your impact is positive on the company's operations.

You recognize self-confidence in others and you automatically respect it. Build up your own self-confidence. It helps others to respect you. Recognize your strengths, without dwelling on your weaknesses—other than to improve them.

Being self-confident means being able to confront people in authority—your bosses—with unpopular, but true, facts. You are willing to stick your neck out—maybe getting it chopped off in the process. Do not equate this with being suicidal. Self-confidence is knowing you are right and standing up for it in the face of terrible odds.

With an attitude of self-confidence, you have the courage to make high impact decisions—after a sound analysis of the situation. You are not paralyzed with indecision. You weigh the facts, make a decision, and then act upon it.

An effective executive embraces self-confidence and steers the proper course:

> "Fortunate is the person who has developed the self-control to steer a straight course toward his objective in life, without being swayed from his purpose by either commendation or condemnation."
> —Napoleon Hill

STRESS AND DISTRACTIONS

One of the most stressful relationships can be the relationship between you and your boss. Even if you are a CEO, you have a boss, or rather a set of bosses, the Board of Directors. The relationship with your boss is a good place to start controlling your stress. How well you control your emotions and your reaction to stress, determines, in large measure, your physical and mental well-being.

When your mind is calm, your memory and logic functions perform at their best. But your memory and logic functions can be hijacked, if you allow it, when you go into survival mode. Emotions can boil over. Complex, rational thought goes down the tube. It is fight or flight. External sensory perceptions take control.

Distractions cause a loss in productivity, just as anger or anxiety does. We live in a fast-paced world where there are countless distractions. It seems that everything and everybody are demanding our attention. We must take a proactive approach to controlling distractions as best we can. Maintain an open-door policy but do not allow it every minute. Work on cutting down the flow of email to and from your mailbox. Organize and prioritize your work to concentrate on the most important items each day, rather than the trivial.

After a stressful encounter, the most resilient people have a rapid recovery from stress. They maintain their optimism. They think about ways to correct the problem, or just accept it if there is nothing they can do about it. There is an old prayer that has a lot of wisdom in it:

> "God, give us grace to accept with serenity the things that cannot be changed, courage to change the things which should be changed, and the wisdom to distinguish the one from the other."
> —Reinhold Niebuhr

If you practice self-control and do not let yourself get distracted by your emotions, you will perform better, learn better, remember better, and, in general, be more successful throughout your career.

Controlling your emotions does not mean completely submerging them, nor does it mean over-controlling them. You will experience anger, frustration, fear, and so on. We are all human. We react to events. If you externalize your emotions in an exaggerated fashion, like attacking the people around you in a fit of anger, you will *explode*. On the other hand, if you keep you anger inside and harbor the anger for hours or days, you can *implode*. Neither exploding nor imploding is the answer.

The trick is not to let your emotions take over to the point where you take actions you regret later. Instead, let the bad feelings and the bad incidents trigger you to channel your emotions into positive actions, like doing something creative, expending your energy on positive pursuits, etc. If nothing else, just accept the situation as a fact of life and go on.

If you are emotionally competent, you can choose how to express your emotions. Use a measured approach to expressing your emotions. The proper approach varies from culture to culture. Avoid the extremes of explosion or implosion. Stay focused and maintain a clarity of thought when placed in stressful situations. You can maintain your composure, but still let people know how you feel—without tearing them apart limb by limb. You may need to take a timeout or let the other person have a timeout until things calm down and rationality returns.

So, be content and happy, in spite of the crazy things going on around you. Let serenity prevail in your thought patterns. Let stress motivate you to do productive things, rather than destructive things.

INNER PEACE

Constant, unrelenting stress is the enemy of an effective executive. Stress is damaging to both body and spirit. This does not mean the executive lives without any pressures. There are always pressures for an executive—and for most employees, in fact. But how you react to the pressure is key. You need an inner peace.

If you have inner peace, you are in harmony with the world around you. You are aware of the circumstances in which you find yourself. You accept the situation as it is or do what is necessary to make it better—or change it into something altogether different.

Having inner peace includes being at peace with yourself. You know who you are. You are aware of your strengths and weaknesses. You have achieved a happy medium as regards the balance between spiritual, business, and family life. You radiate confidence in handling your responsibilities.

Stated in the vernacular, the executive with inner peace is calm, cool, and collected.

21

Fear

FEAR'S EXISTENCE

Fear is part of the everyday feelings each person in the organization has. Fear can emanate from many different sources. There are so many it would be impossible to list them all. But every executive should realize that fear exists in the organization. Although it can be minimized by the actions of the executives, it can never be eliminated entirely. It is rarely discussed and is rarely acknowledged. But it is there. Even when it does make an appearance, the visible portion is rarely more than a hint. It is like the proverbial iceberg, with only the tip showing.

Survival: The most basic fear is based upon our survival instinct. In the case of employees, including executives, fear of survival relates to the fear of losing your job, income, status, etc. Those fears also expand into apprehension about the potential consequences to those who are dependent upon you, such as family or subordinates. For example, if you lose your job, there will be an obvious impact on your spouse and children, a very negative impact. You do not want your loved ones to get hurt by some action of yours or the company you work for.

Fear can be based on less serious possibilities. You might not lose your job or income, but you could still experience other negative consequences, such as: loss of respect, reduced status, lack of acknowledgement, increased criticism, embarrassment, loss of friendship, isolation, and so on. These can invade the fabric of your life, just like a fungus.

Past Experiences: Fear also comes from past experiences, i.e., what we learned from life or learned from the collective experience of others. These are the learned fears that color everything we do. We may not recognize the fear or even acknowledge its existence, but it is there in our subconscious, nevertheless.

We may have lived through a business decision in the past that had very negative consequences. Even though current conditions, like market factors, are entirely different today; the previous negative result of a similar pursuit may make the executive or subordinate hesitate and miss a "golden opportunity." Fear of failure breeds inaction.

Fear's Contagion: Fear breeds fear. If you do not prick the bubble, it continues to grow. The first antidote to fear is to recognize that fear underlies our emotions. Fear overpowers logic. Accept that fear exists in you and in others.

The next step is to foster good communication within the organization. Oftentimes fear is simply fear of the unknown. Leaders can add to corporate fear by being silent or only telling part of the facts. Lack of information often results in speculation. Speculation can run amok. Speculation leads to false conclusions, often the worst ones.

We all have a vivid and fertile imagination. We can imagine the worst when not allowed to see the whole picture. Obviously, some things have to be kept confidential. But many things are kept from employees for no valid reason. Over concentration on confidentiality can destroy the feeling of trust in an organization. Communicate! Communicate! Clear away the haze, and lower the level of fear.

Risk: Risk is scary if not managed. You must also recognize that risk is inherent to business endeavors. Identify and acknowledge the risk factors in each situation. Analyze and evaluate the risk. Look at the probabilities for success or failure. Decide on a best-case scenario, a worst-case scenario, and the most-likely scenario.

After the risks and their implications have been analyzed and evaluated, choose a "best" path, one based on an educated guess. Never assume you have all the facts. You must make a decision with less than perfect information and go for it. Build support for your decision in the organization. Better yet, get those involved to help make the decision.

Assemble the necessary resources to minimize the risk. Then implement the decision. Make it happen. Periodically review progress toward the goal. Situations can change. Re-evaluate the original decision. Change course, if necessary. If a plane is flying from Dallas to Los Angeles and the weather unexpectedly changes, the new meteorological data must be reviewed and a change in course made.

Changing course does not necessarily imply a change in destination. It may just mean changing the path for getting there. However, never overlook the necessity for changing the destination, i.e., changing the goals. Market conditions may have changed so much that both a new course and a new destination are the answer.

Fear of retribution influences our attitude toward risk. Let your people take sound risks without fear of retribution. Acknowledge the possibility that sound risk taking can result in failure. How many times did Edison fail before he achieved success? If risks are approached as a team—using guidelines developed by and for the organization—there is less individual fear over failed outcomes. Do not punish sound risks, only unsound, reckless risks.

Beliefs: Team beliefs can limit achievements if they have some basis in fear. There are three aspects to a team's beliefs: (1) what a team believes about itself, (2) what a team believes others feel about it, and (3) what the team believes about others, both in an out of the organization. Examine these feelings periodically. Take appropriate corrective action when needed. Stamp out the irrational. Support the rational.

An organization's beliefs about responsibility and trust are important. A long step toward easing fear is to never search for a scapegoat. People in a company must accept responsibility for both their actions and inactions, but they must be assured of an underlying foundation of support through thick and thin. There must be enough trust in an organization—and trust must come from the top—that employees can accept responsibility and run with the ball. If problems do come up, deal with the problems. Quit trying to find scapegoats. Deal with the real issues, not the fabricated failings of individuals.

FEAR AS A MOTIVATOR

Widespread fear and intimidation are the curses of a bad workplace, an environment where people do not want to work and where they seldom work at their best, except maybe in the short-term. In some cases, fear can be a positive motivator for improvement by an employee who is just goofing off on the job. Naturally, this fear is over the possibility of losing one's job. However, fear is generally a very poor motivator in the long run.

Using fear regularly as a motivator is a clear indication of disregard for the worth of the individual being intimidated. An employee working under threat, fear, or intimidation is unlikely to be a happy employee. Unhappy employees do not perform at their best.

Employees in this sense certainly include executives. There are always the Chairman, the Board of Directors, and the stockholders to put fear into the heart of an executive. And an executive's fear may be well justified if the executive is not performing up to valid expectations.

If you are strong willed and have an enormous ego, you need to hold yourself in check. Don't overpower your employees. One of the first consequences of a fear-based relationship with subordinates is a breakdown in communication. An open, trust-based relationship means an open exchange of information, both good and bad.

If subordinates always fear retribution for bringing bad news, communication can suffer. There is the fear that a communicator of bad news will be "shot." ("Kill the messenger.") Negative developments in the marketplace, as far as the company is concerned, might not be communicated out of a sense of fear. Subordinates seek safety in silence.

Employees of a tyrant will sometimes plot or act in a way that is not in the best interest of the tyrant. A breakdown in communication with your subordinates can ultimately get you fired. Is that what you are trying to achieve?

Act in a way that breeds an atmosphere of trust. Both you and your subordinates will be more productive and happy in your work. You will both win. Otherwise, you will both lose.

Part V

SUCCESS

22

Personal Mastery

What are your life dreams? Where do you expect to be ten years from now? What you do in the interim will determine where you are in the future. Have you made any plans or set any goals for the next ten years? In retrospect, how were your last ten years? How well did you do? Did you set any goals for those years? Did you achieve them? Did you have commitment? Will you have commitment for the next ten years? Are you just going to wander aimlessly through the rest of your life?

You must deal with the hand that has been dealt you, but that does not mean accepting the belief that you cannot better yourself. The key to moving yourself off the starter's block is to decide to take action to improve yourself, establish new goals in life, and then act upon your decision—never flagging in your zeal to reach the goals you have set. You must make a commitment in order to be the person you can be. Your decisions in life determine your destiny.

Life will seldom turn out the way you expected or the way you planned. As you go down life's pathways, you must continue to reevaluate how you are doing. If something is not working, make adjustments. Learn from your mistakes. Revise your goals. Revise your strategy. Be flexible in your approach. Continue to make both long- and short-term decisions along the way, but keep your focus on the long term. Commit yourself to long-term results.

Mental associations are powerful. Your attitudes and habits reflect those associations. You avoid sticking your hand into a fire or touching hot things because you associate such action with pain. You do other things, like eat pie, because you associate pie with wonderful tastes in your mouth. The expectation of pain is a powerful motivator. The expectation of pleasure is also powerful.

If the expectation of pain for some action is greater than the expectation of pleasure, the action will be avoided. It is all about mind control, the control of emotions. Therefore, it helps to mentally associate pleasure with the positive goals you set. Likewise, you should immediately associate pain in your mind's eye with anything that will cause you to fail or falter in reaching your goals.

Decide to take action now. Make a list of your immediate goals. Visualize the good and the bad—in the proper context—of achieving or not achieving the goals. Write down the proper negative (painful) and positive (pleasurable) associations to advance your cause, your mission of personal mastery.

Remember, if you do not have a plan for yourself; other people will provide it—and it is unlikely to be what you want. Your body is the ship and your mind is its captain. Take over the rudder with mind control. Don't look for blame, look for solutions. Master yourself. Chart your course and sail to the desired destination.

Now let's examine this in more detail.

PERSONAL MASTERY

```
     STRENGTHS,              LIMITING
     WEAKNESSES              BELIEFS
            \                  /
             ↘                ↙
  CURRENT  →  ANALYZE  ←  CURRENT
   GOALS       YOURSELF     STANDARDS
                 ↓
              DECIDE
   LOFTIER →  COURSE  ←  HIGHER
    GOALS       OF       STANDARDS
              ACTION
                 ↓
              TAKE
 PERSISTENCE → ACTION ←  PERSPECTIVE
            ↙  ↓  ↓  ↓  ↘
                    
  TIME   PHYSICAL  RELATIONSHIPS  EMOTIONS  FINANCES
         HEALTH
```

Analyze Yourself: You must have knowledge of yourself in order to exercise personal mastery. If you do not know what you are, you do not know what you can do. Look at your past to discover who you have become. You have a unique mix of talents and abilities, a unique blend of likes and dislikes. Sometimes people with great potential have their lives slightly out of alignment; they just need a course correction. Do you need a wholesale change or a minor one?

What do other people like about you? What do they think your talents are? Are you your own worst enemy? What motivates you? What de-motivates you? How do you handle compliments? How do you handle criticisms? How comfortable are you with yourself? Do you love yourself? What are you proud of? What are you ashamed of?

Listen to your own language, the way you talk and the words you use. Is there a negative bias or a positive one? Is the glass half empty or half full? Do you always look on the dark side of things? Are you depressed all the time? Are you happy most of the time? Are you bored with life, or excited? Are you secure or insecure? Are you lonely? Are you fulfilled? Do you love others? Are you thankful for your blessings?

What do you want out of life? What are your longings? What do you want professionally? What do you seek in a romantic relationship? What do you want from your family life? What do you seek on a religious plane? What recreational pursuits do you like best? Do you want to be served or to serve? Do you want riches and power? What are you doing you would like to stop doing? What are you not doing you would like to do?

Strengths and Weaknesses: Part of mastering yourself is knowing your own strengths and weaknesses. You need to know what you are working with. Recognize your limitations, but turn them into a positive force. Let them be motivators by picturing them as obstacles to overcome. Use your strengths to further your achievements. Emphasize your strengths. Take pride in yourself and your abilities. Know your greatness and let it empower you to do better.

Catalogue your strengths and your weaknesses. Evaluate them. Be objective in your analysis. Determine how much an impact they have on your success or lack thereof. Which traits need to be emphasized and improved? Which need to be de-emphasized and given little attention? Which ones need to be moderated?

Write a personal resume for yourself, not for some employer. Cover all aspects of your life. Conduct a personal performance review—again, for yourself, not someone else. What are your strong points? What are your weak points? What are your inborn talents? Are you using them all? Where do your skills lie? Which skills need improvement? Are there skills that are totally lacking? What is your expertise? What do you know? What useful experience and wisdom do you have?

What can you offer to others—and to yourself?

Limiting Beliefs: Each time you move from one house to another, you have more and more things to move. If you are smart, you use the occasion to throw away accumulated "junk." Your personal life is like that. You accumulate baggage and let it weigh you down. You must discard your limiting beliefs and move on. Beliefs are powerful influencers. They can make you or break you. To overcome negative beliefs requires powerful resolve and resolute decision-making. Changing your beliefs will change your behavior. Remember, you want positive change.

You can't get rid of all your fears, but don't let them hold you back. Acknowledge your fears and keep them in check. Facing your fears head-on often helps you to realize they were largely unfounded. Visualize conquering your fears.

You cannot realistically expect everyone to like you. Don't hold back for fear of alienating people. You cannot keep everybody happy. In like manner, don't let people set your standards for you. Don't let them saddle you with the belief you will never amount to much. The opinion that someone holds of you will only become a reality if you let it. What matters is how you perceive yourself.

Decide if a relationship is negatively affecting your life. Is it an unhealthy relationship? How does if affect your well-being? Leave a relationship if it is not helping you. Align yourself with people who have a positive influence on you.

You spend a great deal of your week on the job. What happens on the job has a tremendous influence on your attitude toward life. Do you look forward to going to work? Do you enjoy your work? Are you typically in a good mood when you come home? Don't equate being tired from a job well done (hard work) with the negative feelings that come from not enjoying your work? (You can get tired playing.) Decide if your job is affecting your life negatively. If it is, get a new job.

If you believe you can't excel, you will live up to your beliefs. You will be a self-fulfilling prophecy. You must open yourself to your possibilities, your own greatness. Make use of the gifts you have.

Control your inhibiting memories, your burdensome emotions, such as: anger, revenge, sadness, resentment, guilt, and regret. Forgive yourself. Love yourself. Believe you are a worthwhile person. Forgive those who have hurt you. Pray for your enemies.

Quit whining. Start winning. You don't have to be a martyr. You don't have to be a defeatist. Quit trying to change others. Change yourself. Release your brakes. Change your beliefs. Personal breakthroughs come with a change in beliefs.

Look at your beliefs. List the most important ones. Rationally categorize them into the good ones and the bad ones. Look at each belief individually. Is the belief valid or plainly absurd? Ask yourself, "How did I ever come to that belief?" Does the belief help you? Does the belief hold you back? What would it cost to let it go? What will it cost if you do not let it go? Decide to eliminate the most limiting beliefs. Are there other beliefs you should embrace that would help you be more successful? If yes, add them to the list. Decide to incorporate them into your life.

Having dreams is the first step toward making them a reality. You do have the power to change. All you need is the desire and the will power to act upon your dreams. Believe in your vision. Let your vision translate into excitement. Go for it.

You can't change the past, but you can influence the future. To do it, you must believe in the need to change. Then you must believe you can change. Visualize the pleasure that will come from the change. It will help reinforce your efforts to change.

Remember, you cannot get out of life alive; so enjoy it while you can. Don't let negative beliefs put a damper on your potential enjoyment. Each of us has some basic goodness. Be proud of yourself. You are worthy of success.

Current Goals: Look at your current objectives in life? Do you have any? Are you just wandering aimlessly, reacting instead of acting? Do you lack focus? Are you having trouble deciding on a course to follow? Do you know where you are going, or are you just going with the flow? Do you have any immediate goals? What about long-term goals?

If you do have goals, how do they stack up against your capabilities? Do your goals take you where you want to go, or are you just setting goals to please others? Do your goals raise the bar for yourself? Do they just get you by? Are you proud of your goals? Could you have better goals?

Current Standards: Conduct an honest evaluation of yourself. What is the state of your character? What is important to you? Are you bending the rules for the purpose of expediency? Are you applying situational ethics? Would your mother be proud of you if she knew the whole truth? What would your wife and kids feel if they knew? How is your morality? Do you still have honor and integrity? Do you have a code of conduct you are proud of? Are you honest?

Can people count on your word? Are you dependable? Do you practice what you preach? Do you want your subordinates to do what you do or what you say? Are you a role model for others, or just the opposite?

If you were weighed in the balance, would you come out looking shiny or tarnished? Are you living up to your capabilities? What kind of standards have you set for yourself? Have you set the bar too low for yourself? Are you world class, or just an also-ran? Are you just doing what you have to in order to get by, or are you trying to excel in everything you do?

Loftier Goals: Before you started analyzing yourself, you presumably had some goals—even if they just represented maintaining the status quo. You need to harbor a conviction of greatness within your soul. Strive to do better than you did in the past. You have more experience, knowledge, and wisdom than you ever had before. Feel free to dream. Opportunities abound, but you must search them out and grab onto them.

Why aren't you doing what you are passionate about? Be a master of your own destiny. Accept that life is going to be hard, then go forward. Look at your options. Visualize the various alternatives you have. Play them out in your mind. Which ones feel the best to you? Choose the ones you feel most comfortable with—as far as being right is concerned—without regard to how difficult they might be to achieve.

Review your resources, your skills, and your talents. Ask friends, family, and mentors to help you objectively evaluate possible goals. Stay away from negative thinkers. You want positive influencers giving you input.

Set new goals that are important to you. Set goals that are a stretch. Challenge yourself. Pursue your dream. Have a hunger to make something out of yourself. Be better than you were before. Don't be fearful. Dare to think big. Have the courage to set demanding goals. Be willing to go after your goals with sheer determination.

Choose goals on several different fronts. Start with some personal goals, working on you as a person. This falls into the self-help realm. Are there some character traits you would like to change? Are there spiritual concerns you want to address? How is your relationship with God? How about your physical health? Does it need improving? Are you overweight and want to make a change? Are there personal skills you would like to develop, like a foreign language?

What about professional, financial, or business goals? Come up with goals that relate to your income and financial interests? Are there professional skills you need to develop or hone? What level of income do you aspire to? How are your day-to-day finances? What changes would you like to make in them?

What are your investment goals? Do you have some specific career goals you would like to accomplish? Do you want to get another college degree or to complete one you have already started? Are you a principal in a business? If so, what are some worthy goals for your business? How soon can you realistically expect to retire? How will you get there?

Consider fun and games. Do you have any goals that relate to hobbies? Do you even have a hobby? Do you want to learn to dance? Is there some sport you want to learn or improve on? Do you desire some big-time toys, like antique cars, planes, boats, etc.? How would you like to change your entertainment pursuits? Are there any entertainment events you would like to attend? What about travel? Are there places you would like to visit? Would you like to go on an around-the-world cruise? Do you want to master photography? Do you want to learn to sail? Do you want to learn to scuba dive? How about hunting and fishing? Would you like to learn to fly?

Look at personal relationships. How is your family life? Do you need to make changes there? Do you get along well with your parents? How about your kids? Would you like to adopt a child? How is your marriage? How is your relationship with your spouse? What about friends? Are changes needed in that area? Do you need to develop some close friends in the first place? Would you like to get involved with some singles group? Would you like to track down some long-lost friend or school buddy?

Do you wish to make changes in what you are contributing to society? Do you want to help the disadvantaged? What about the handicapped? What about the veterans who have preserved your freedom? Is there some environmental cause you want to support? Do you want to get involved in some volunteer effort? Would you like to help raise funds for some needy group of people? How about making financial contributions to worthy causes? How about going on missionary trips?

Higher Standards: Before you decided to change your life for the better, you had certain standards for your character and for your rules of conduct. If you do set new standards for yourself, you must set standards you believe in. You are establishing a new baseline for what you will accept during the rest of your life. Not setting a standard of performance, for example, makes it easy to succumb to levels of performance that are beneath your capability. Is that what you want?

You cannot always control what life sends your way, but you can control who and what you are. Never believe you are a loser. Believe you are a winner. Constantly raise the bar for yourself.

Protect your character. Uphold your integrity, regardless of the price you have to pay. Maintain your self-respect. Don't betray the respect others have for you. It is all about values, values you have developed over the years through various experiences. If you have let your values corrode, give them a shot in the arm. Restore the values you have let slip. Add new worthy values you were afraid to embrace before. Quit cheating on that expense report. Tell the truth instead of bending it to suit your purposes. In short, clean up your act where needed. Be someone your kids would be proud of. Live what you preach.

Hold yourself to a higher set of standards than other people expect of you. Be proud of yourself. Be the person who has the character you admire.

Decide Course of Action: Set goals and go after them wholeheartedly. Focus on achieving them. You must live by faith and not by sight alone. Life will provide the answers. It is easy to come up with logical reasons why something cannot be achieved. Think positively, not negatively. Enlarge the vision you have of yourself.

You must be willing to take risks in order to grow. Everyone has been given certain talents; use them to advance your dreams. Tap into your goodness in order to make a positive impact on the world around you. Empower yourself. Inspire others.

Once you have decided upon your goals, visualize achieving them. Positive visualization can be used to program your mind. Reinforce your determination by frequently visualizing the pleasurable results of actually achieving your goals.

In order to reach your larger goals, come up with a series of smaller goals that lead toward the bigger goals. Don't try to do everything at once. You eat an elephant one bite at a time. Incremental change is the name of the game. Any big project is a series of smaller tasks done in a logical progression. Like a project manager, go from individual tasks to major milestones to major accomplishments.

Write down your goals. Prioritize them. Spend most of your efforts on the ones most important to you. Discard the unimportant ones you will never have time for. Focus on the major ones. Establish timetables for achieving the goals. Develop a practical plan of action—near-term and long-term. Also, develop backup plans.

Never stop setting new goals. Continue to renew your commitment to personal growth.

Take Action: Having decided upon your goals and a plan for achieving them, work hard at achieving your goals. Take action, and take it now.

Review your goals constantly and your progress toward them. Revise as needed. Set new goals as soon as you achieve your old goals. This will help you to stay in a constant growth mode. As you advance along your path toward success, the accomplishments you make along the way will help build your confidence. You will be able to tackle things you never thought possible. Be open to new possibilities. Think outside the box. Doors will open that were closed before.

Be willing to pay the necessary dues in order to advance yourself. There will be impediments to progress and plenty of setbacks. It will be necessary to energize yourself. You will have to expend a considerable amount of effort to succeed. Achievements will not be handed to you on a silver platter.

Acknowledge your achievements but do not dwell on them excessively. Keep going. Build on your successes with more successes. This will establish a sustaining foundation for future successes. Your successes will help strengthen your self-esteem. They will also help you spring back from failures. Failures will come—that is life—but how you handle setbacks will define your character.

Use positive affirmations throughout your day. Know that it is possible to live your dreams. Change your everyday language to reflect a positive, "I can" attitude. Words shape your beliefs. They determine your actions. Let your newfound, positive beliefs influence your behavior. Actions speak louder than words.

Tap into your talents and move forward. Take responsibility for your actions, for your life. Maintain a sense of urgency about achieving your goals. Have the courage to go after your goals. Believe you can accomplish them. Believe you can live your dreams.

Working toward your goals and experiencing success will encourage you to be positive about yourself. Pursuing your goals helps you have a feeling of fulfillment—but the goals must be ones you find pleasure in achieving, your areas of interest. Be empowered by your dreams.

Rely on yourself and God for your inner motivation. The image you maintain of yourself comes from within. Don't let external images rule your life. Develop positive self-images and internalize them. Make them a part of your everyday life.

Persistence: You will experience failures along the way. Persevere in hard times. Use force of will to overcome life's obstacles. Be unstoppable. Find a powerful motivation to lead you to success. Live for your dreams—all the time. Ignore the critics, the harbingers of doom. Find reasons to go on. Never give up. Commit yourself to your goals.

Don't let circumstances take over your life and prevent you from stepping outside a self-imposed prison. Losers let circumstances overwhelm them. Winners don't. Winners know there are possibilities, ways to grow and improve themselves—in spite of difficulties. Opportunities you never saw will present themselves once you embark upon the road to fulfillment. Strive for new levels of fulfillment.

Perspective: Keep a proper perspective. Maintain a balance in your life. Focus on what you can influence, not what you can't. We worry too much about things that are beyond our control. Don't sweat the small stuff. Ask yourself how important something is in the grand scheme of things? Don't let yourself get sidetracked by unimportant details or events. Concentrate on things of importance.

Use the triage approach. Put your primary energy into high priority items, the things with the greatest potential, or those that are likely to have the most negative impact if left unattended. When the highest priority items have been taken care of, turn your efforts to handling the items that are important but not critical. The third category covers everything else, the unimportant things that would be nice to do but which can be ignored. Never venture into the third category of activities unless you can think of nothing else to do. Even when you think about jumping into this third category, reconsider. Are you just trying to run away from some other more important responsibility?

Remember that the person you become in life is more important than what you accomplish.

Time: It takes time to carry out personal mastery. Use time to your advantage. Time is precious. Don't waste it. Master it. You cannot call back yesterday and do it over. Practice time management. Take control. You only live this life once.

Physical Health: Optimistic, positive, and happy people are healthier and live longer. Someone has said that every time you smile, you lengthen your life. It is an established medical fact that the more you are upset, depressed, and unhappy, the more susceptible you are to disease and infection. A positive attitude makes for a positive body. Your frame of mind is a big factor in your physical health. You control your thoughts. Use them to your advantage.

Assuming you embrace the proper thought patterns to maintain good health, there are actions you can take to further enhance your health. If you have made an objective analysis of your physical health, you know what you need to do. At a minimum, you should get an annual physical; but that is just a beginning. There is no need to go over the specifics of physical health maintenance. TV, movies, magazines, newspapers, etc., barrage you with health improvement activities. There is, also, no need to be a fanatic about it; but you do know what you need to do or where you can go to get help in the matter. Just decide to do it. Don't squander precious years of your life because you neglected your body.

Relationships: We do not live in isolation. We are surrounded by people as we engage in various activities. Human relationships take place in business, family, church, sports, recreation, and other pursuits. Unless you are a total introvert and refuse to deal with people, you know you need to make the best of your relationships. Positive relationships have positive impact on your attitude and well-being. Don't let your emotions destroy relationships. Exercise positive attitudes. Nurture relationships.

Mutual respect is the fundamental mortar of all effective relationships. Set a good example for the people you deal with. Be careful of the people you hang around with. Surround yourself with positive people. Associate with people who share your value system. Interface with people who can help you grow.

The best relationships provide positive results for both parties. There is give and take, of course; but you should orient yourself toward concentrating on what you can give in each relationship. Give and it will be given you. You reap what you sow.

The point is: If you give your time and yourself to others, they will generally repay you in the long run. Even if they don't, you will still have the satisfaction of knowing you gave. As the old saying goes, serve and you will be served. You will feel good about yourself.

Emotions: Negative emotions come to us in many forms, such as: depression, discomfort, hurt, fear, anger, frustration, guilt, inadequacy, defeatism, loneliness, stubbornness, disappointment, etc. Positive emotions include the following: confidence, excitement, determination, hope, happiness, gratitude, love, passion, curiosity, flexibility, etc.

If you wish to succeed, you must master your emotions. You cannot escape them. You cannot always avoid negative emotions. Do not try to deny them. Denial is just a festering sore that will erupt later. But do not indulge negative emotions. Don't let them incapacitate you. Recognize your emotions. Understand them. Search for some positive factors in the things that triggered your negative emotions. Dwell on the positive aspects. Make negative emotions a call to action. Be confident you can overcome the negative influence of bad emotions—both now and in the future.

Finances: As an executive, you at least have a rudimentary understanding of personal finances. They may not be your strong point, but finances are important. You have your day-to-day expenses to look out for. You may have kids whose college education must be funded. You have recreational pursuits to be financed. You have retirement to prepare for. All this requires money.

Finances are not something you can ignore. Overuse of credit is a financial trap. Lack of control over spending leads to disaster. Finances are a major cause of divorce. Bankruptcy is not a pleasant affair. Without proper financial planning and budgeting, you add misery to your life.

So, if your financial house is not in order, take the necessary steps to get it in order. There are plenty of sources for financial help and consultation to help you do it right. It is all a matter of judgment and will power.

In conclusion, you hold the power of personal mastery in your own hands. One person can do a lot. You can do more than you think you can. It is a matter of analyzing yourself, weighing the alternatives for improvement, deciding on a course of action, and taking the steps to make it happen.

> "He who gains a victory over other men is strong; but he who gains a victory over himself is all-powerful."
>
> —Lao-Tzu

23

Controlling Time

TIME THEFT

Time is a most precious commodity. This is no less true for the executive than it is for everyone else. A person has only so much personal time on this planet, not the immeasurable time of the universe. With that in mind, it is illogical not to regret the theft of time—it is loss of life itself. It is easier to defend the theft of time from you by someone else than when you steal time from yourself. You have some control over the former and total control over the latter.

> "Short as life is, we make it still shorter by the careless waste of time."
> —Victor Hugo

Now look at the diagram. Consider all the dotted-line objects as being little explosions that go off when you do not exercise proper stewardship of your time. The time-slot explodes and is lost. The more the explosions occur, the faster that lost time flows to the right. As the losses mount, the greater is the loss of unrecoverable time. But you do have significant control over the faucet of lost time.

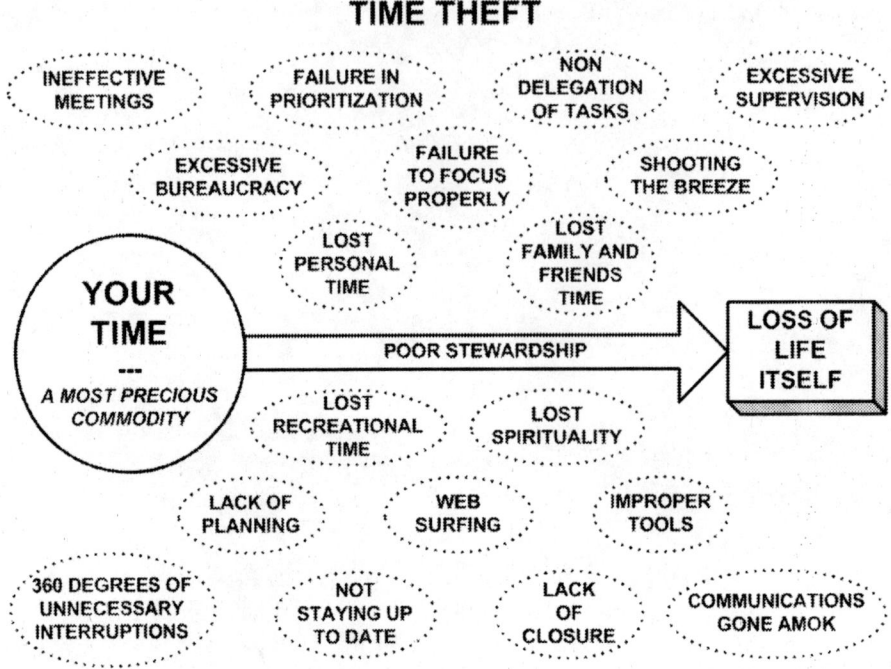

Ineffective Meetings: Let's start by preaching to the choir. Ineffective meetings are a waste of time—usually for a number of people. Meetings are often completely unnecessary; the things on the agenda could have been handled without a formal meeting and with fewer people. Having meetings where nothing is resolved and assigning no responsibility for getting issues resolved is another waste of everybody's time. Therefore, have the right people meet at the right time on the right topics.

Failure in Prioritization: Failure to prioritize is a misuse of time. Unless you prioritize your thoughts and actions, and do so properly, you waste your time. If you focus on low priority tasks at the expense of higher priority tasks, you err in time management. You are, if effect, spinning your wheels. The rule is simple and has been true throughout time: Put your energies into the most important tasks if you wish to succeed and if you wish to get the biggest payback for your efforts.

Non-Delegation of Tasks: A failure in prioritization can result from not delegating responsibilities to your subordinates. If you are a leader, your time is valuable. You are a leader because you have something to offer in the management of those who report to you. By definition, you should delegate those tasks that can be performed by your subordinates. Concentrate on leading and managing. Don't get engrossed in details you have no business worrying about.

Excessive Supervision: Excessive supervision is a problem closely related to delegation. When you allow yourself to get unnecessarily involved in your subordinates' activities, your delegation has been done with an oppressive hand. Coaching is one thing. Constantly looking over the shoulder of your employees is something else. It is a waste of your time and clearly communicates you do not trust the abilities and judgment of your staff. Concentrate on your tasks and let your people do theirs.

Excessive Bureaucracy: Unnecessary bureaucracy is a killer of time that could be more wisely spent elsewhere. Not only does excessive bureaucracy waste money better spent elsewhere, but it also wastes a more precious resource, time. Bureaucracy begets bureaucracy. It is like a communicable disease or a spreading cancer.

> "In a bureaucratic system, useless work drives out useful work."
> —Milton Friedman

Keep processes, procedures, and guidelines lean and mean. Focus on policies and procedures that have an effective payback. Prepare documentation when it is necessary and justified. Don't document when it is unnecessary. In general, bureaucracy must not be allowed to stifle flexibility and innovation.

Failure to Focus Properly: Lack of focus is like being in a ship with no one at the helm. Without rudder control, you are unlikely to reach port. You may sail in circles. You may sail onto a reef. You may crash on the rocks. Focus on high-priority endeavors—a relatively small number of them—and sail toward a profitable port.

Focusing on the wrong things is just as bad as having no focus. There may be a sense of progress derived from focusing on and accomplishing trivial tasks, but the euphoria is misguided. Trivia, by all standards, is unimportant. If some trivial item is a pivotal item, then it is not trivial. Keep things in perspective. Don't let your pet peeves derail you. Concentrate on your major responsibilities, not the trivial ones. Don't spin your wheels.

Shooting the Breeze: Everyone knows what "shooting the breeze" means. Yakking just to yak and kill time is rarely beneficial, unless it facilitates a well-deserved time-out. Sometimes shooting the breeze can be beneficial in building meaningful relationships. The point is: Don't turn shooting the breeze into goof-off time. You have better things to do.

Lost Personal Time: You must balance your responsibilities on all fronts, including: business, professional, family, personal, and religious. There are just some occasions when you need time alone with yourself, time where you can sit and reflect—perhaps while engaged in some activity you dearly love, but which is most enjoyably done alone. Don't sacrifice your personal time.

Lost Family and Friends Time: Family time is important. A well-balanced life means time with family. If you are married to your job, you need to get a divorce. You will be with your family longer than you will be with your job. Your family needs you and you need them. Quit saying to yourself and to your family that you will spend some time with them later when things get less hectic. Time moves fast and children grow up. Nuff said?

Friends are also important. Most people need close friends. They can be enormous Rocks of Gibraltar, or a quiet port of refuge during a storm. Take time for your friends. Friends comfort and refresh you. Like family, they need you and you need them.

Lost Recreational Time: Never forget to take time off and have fun. Recreation is necessary—and it is not evil, you workaholics! Take vacations. Do something fun at night or on weekends. Recreation gives you time to refresh both body and mind—a time to recharge your batteries.

Lost Spirituality: People have spiritual needs. People include executives. Whatever your religious beliefs are, don't sacrifice them on the altar of time. There is a double whammy when you fail to take time off to tend to your spiritual needs: (1) you lose the time you needed to concentrate on spiritual needs and (2) you lose your spirituality. Your spirituality always needs encouragement and reinforcement. When you neglect this part of you, it atrophies. You lose your link with your eternal being. You must live for now AND eternity.

Lack of Planning: It has been said:

"Life is what happens to us while we are making other plans."
—Thomas La Mance

There is a lot of truth in that statement, but planning is essential in the executive world. Lack of personal and professional planning is a recipe for chaos and disaster. If you do not plan where you are going, then the probability of getting there diminishes to almost zero. Making plans and carrying through with them brings success. Planning brings efficiency to the use of time. Lack of planning is like running your car while it is out of tune; gas is wasted—and so is time with no plan. Plan your time wisely.

Web Surfing: It would seem that web surfing has become the proverbial sin. An old saying that might still apply today is, "The Devil made me do it." But you are the one who logged onto the Internet and brought up the browser, not the Devil. The Internet realm reaches the whole world and there is plenty to see. Don't become addicted to the Web and use it to escape your job responsibilities. Time wasted on the Web is time that cannot be regained except by giving up more time in some other area of your life. Invoke the rule of priorities. Let that conscience whispering in your ear prevail.

Improper Tools: When the busy executive uses the wrong tool for a job, inefficiency is the result. Time is lost. If there are tools that can reasonably help you in your job, get them and use them—assuming they are not priced out of this world. Consider, for example, a personal computer, a PC. Any PC in its basic form is just a platform of hardware and operating system software. The PC comes to life for a user when it has a usable application installed. At a minimum, an executive should be proficient in using a word processor, a spreadsheet, and a presentation package—not to mention an Internet browser.

But the rule applies to other forms of technology, too, even common ones. There are many technical helps for communication: teleconferencing, email, specialized software applications, wireless phones, and so on. Proper use of the right tool increases productivity because it saves time for everyone involved. Don't worship technology, but do use it to save time. Take advantage of technology and any non-technical help you can find and master. Conserve time.

360 Degrees of Unnecessary Interruptions: Interruptions are just that, interruptions. They can be good or bad, but the emphasis here is on the bad ones. When your people are busy, don't interrupt them with trivial matters. Their time is valuable, just like yours. But it works both ways. If you have a subordinate who constantly interrupts you, it is time to take action. Gently let the employee know the error of his or her ways. Stress the need to only interrupt with important items.

Peers can interrupt you as well, and you can interrupt them. A collegial atmosphere exists between peers. You are at the same level, with neither person having sway over the other—at least on paper. Respect their time and ask them to respect yours. If you are too busy because of some pressing task, let them know the situation and get back with them later—if the matter truly warrants your attention.

The hardest situation to deal with comes from interruptions by your boss or people even higher up the food chain. It is very hard to say no in this case. The bosses have power and, presumably, the right to interrupt you anytime they feel the need for your attention or they feel you need theirs. But they should respect your productivity needs and you need to respect theirs. Interrupt them when the need justifies, and vice versa. If things get out of hand, VERY CAREFULLY attempt to correct the situation. How to do it will depend upon your superior and your relationship with him or her. Above all, try to avoid getting fired.

If interruptions from all or some points on the compass are getting out of hand, you may need to bend your "open door" policy. As a last ditch defense, you can set aside certain times of the day for closing your door on a regular basis. Communicate the fact to people you deal with. If you have an executive assistant, you can have him or her help you enforce it. Do not abuse this practice, because it can cut down on communication. You desperately need to stay informed in order to survive. Without an air raid warning system, you will never know when bombs are on the way until they hit.

Not Staying Up to Date: This may seem counter intuitive, but not staying up to date professionally can lose you time. Lost time can come in the form of lost opportunities, both from a business perspective and from a personal one. For example, if you do not keep up to date with what is going on in your industry, you will lose out to your business competitors, who, in turn, will get a head start on you. You will lose precious time playing catch-up—and you might never recover the time lost.

From another angle, if you do not stay up with advances in your profession, you lose out to a different set of competitors, other professionals. People lacking an up-to-date skill set do not advance rapidly, if at all. Again, time is lost, but it sneaks up on you without your being aware until it is too late. By that time, the lion has you in its jaws. So, keep up with the latest advances in your career field. Stay current. Pilots have to re-qualify periodically in order to stay current. Take a hint from them. They are forced to do so, but you are going to have to force yourself.

Lack of Closure: Lack of closure steals time. Most people do not take this into consideration. It is never on their radar screen. When you interface with people for some purpose and you go away from the encounter without getting something resolved or without getting responsibility assigned, you have no closure. Time is lost in the encounter. Nothing meaningful is accomplished; so, make the most of any but the most casual encounter. Decide something. Assign responsibility. Do something. Don't waste the time invested in the encounter.

Communications Gone Amok: Readily available communication channels can result in too much communication, communication that is neither meaningful nor useful. Take email, for example. You can get flooded with email that is totally irrelevant to your needs. Going the other direction, you can flood other people with your every thought. Also, either of you can forward every promising thought that comes through your mail server. Spamming can be bi-directional. You know the problem. Do something about it.

Use email-blocking functions. Delete any obviously unimportant messages without reading them—being careful some bit of information wasn't inadvertently buried in the email that could be a time bomb later. Don't email your every thought. Tactfully tell offenders not to send you unimportant emails because your mailbox is flooded and you might miss some important information in the flood.

The same general principles apply to other communications media. Be judicious in using the phone for outgoing communications, and gently terminate incoming calls that have the potential of unnecessarily eating up your time. Conference calls should follow the same rules that apply to having productive meetings. The media is just different.

In short, when you communicate, whatever the media, don't waste other people's time, and don't let them waste yours. Be considerate and courteous.

Repeating the basic principle, your time is precious. When you use it wisely, you make a good investment. When you fail to be a good steward of your time, you lose it. It is very difficult to make up lost time. Often, it is lost forever. Remember that life is a timeline with limited dimensions.

"No minute lost
Comes ever back again.
Take heed and see
Ye nothing do in vain."

—London Clock Tower Motto

TIME VS. MONEY

Which is the most important, time or money? Of course, it depends upon the situation. If the company is about to go under for lack of capital, then money may be the most important. However, the fact that the company is about to go bankrupt might not be the result of a money problem at all. The problem may have been management talent. Money is just a symptom in that case, not the real problem. But time is, in reality, money in the business world.

In this fast-paced economy, when the competitors you need to worry about are running pedal to the metal; it is suggested that time is one of the most valuable resources a company has. It ranks right up there with employees. If you are sitting idly twiddling your thumbs—or, in effect, accomplishing the same thing by what you are doing—then you are squandering something that cannot be easily restored, if at all.

The clock is always ticking. At times, you will think it is racing. In reality, it is just ticking at a steady pace, as your logical mind will readily admit. So, what are the enemies of time?

If you or your people are tied up doing tasks that are not the best use of time, change to other tasks. Many activities are continued simply because of inertia. One of the best things anyone in the company can do is to continually ask if the activity the person is engaged in right now is the best use of his or her time. If not, shut it down and get on with what you should be doing.

Prepare a list of to-do items at the start of each workday. Rank them from most important to least important. Start with the number one item and work down. If you can work on an item in any way, even if it is just setting something in motion so you can work on it later, try your best to make some progress on the item. When you reach a dead-end and meaningful progress is out of your hand, go to the next most important item and start tackling it.

You may only get a few items done during the day. But at the end of the day, what have you accomplished? You have spent your time working on the most important items. That is productivity with a capital P.

The story goes that many years ago a chief executive called in a consultant. The executive was just not accomplishing what he should be. He was not living up to the standards of performance he had set for himself. Valuable opportunities were being lost. So, the chief executive asked the consultant for his advice. What could the executive do better?

The consultant simply told him to start each day making a list of the five most important items the executive should work on that day. Then prioritize them from most important to least important. Start with the first and do as much as possible; then go to the next, and so forth. If the executive could complete an item that day, then so much the better; if not, don't worry about it.

The executive asked the consultant how much he owed for the advice. The consultant told him to try it for thirty days and then send him a check for whatever he thought the advice was worth. At the end of thirty days, the chief executive sent the consultant a check for $25,000. And that was when dollars were worth a lot more than they are today.

So, what do you have planned for the day? Is it what you really should be working on?

24

Being Successful

PURSUIT OF SUCCESS

One Size Does Not Fit All: Executives come in many different sizes and flavors. The leaders of successful companies have different strengths and weaknesses. The companies they work for change over time and face many different challenges in the course of their corporate growth. Leaders change and grow during their professional life, too. Successful corporate leaders are not like peas in a pod. Just look at successful leaders of successful companies. There is no consistent stereotype.

Therefore, it is safe to conclude that successful leaders do not fit one particular mold. It is impossible to say that any one characteristic sets a successful leader apart from the less successful. However, there are some common traits and leadership principles that can be applied, depending upon the situation. Different kinds of leaders with different styles of leadership are appropriate in different circumstances. A bad fit can be ruinous for the executive—and the company.

When going into a new position, an executive must review the situation and ask whether there is a fit. If not, avoid it. In the case of an old position, there may have been a fit earlier, but not currently. If there is no longer a fit, exit the current position. To give a simple example, an introverted engineer is certainly not the person to head a public relations firm.

Just recognize that people differ and that corporate situations vary. Match needs with strengths. But be careful you understand the needs and can objectively identify strengths, yours or someone else's when trying to get a match.

Focus: Failure often results from lack of focus. You need to know where you are going. This principle should be self-evident, but it is too often lost in the shuffle of corporate bureaucracy. It is easy to let distractions get the best of you. So-called emergencies are seldom real emergencies, in the longer perspective of time.

Time spent on distractions is time taken away from primary objectives. Treading water on primary objectives, while dealing with secondary distractions, is great for your competitors. Never forget what your business is all about. Focus on things related to your primary business objectives.

Focusing does not necessarily mean concentrating on only one thing. It is rare when an executive can concentrate on a single item. A more likely scenario is that the executive is trying to focus on a number of things. If too many things are the objects of one's attention, then attention is diluted to the point there is no real focus on anything. Progress does not happen. The leader is spread too thin to be effective.

Assuming you are focusing on too many things—to the point of distraction—you must cut down your areas of concentration. In this case, determine your highest priorities from all the things making demands on you. Choose a subset, say, five, toward which to direct your energies. Then spend most of your time on them. Delegate the rest—if they are really that important.

So, focus on a manageable number of items, the top priorities.

Execution: In order to achieve success you must have a clearly defined goal and a definitive plan for getting there. Everyone involved in carrying out the endeavor must clearly understand the objective and his or her role in making it happen. The proper resources must be in place or allocated. A driving desire to complete the task must be there. But that is not enough.

You must execute the plan. You must resolve to get off the starting line and start the journey, persisting until the objective is achieved. Too many company leaders decide to do something and even make plans to carry it out. They know they need to do it, but they get caught up in the pressures of daily operations and never get around to doing it.

Just do it! Keep at it until the task is completed—not 90 percent, but completely.

Reading the Signs: Keep your eyes and ears open. The same applies to your staff. Different people have different interests; which means they explore and observe different areas. The more your people have their radar screens in operation, the greater your chance for getting wind of some sea change that could have either a positive or a devastating impact on business success.

Keep on the lookout for promising areas of business and professional development. You must be agile. The medium-sized fish concentrating on swallowing the smaller fish can itself get swallowed by an even larger fish.

A major opportunity can be knocking at the door, but it may never knock again. A new idea often has a very short shelf life. If a company misses a critical road sign, all can be lost. Corporations can go merrily down the wrong path wondering why there is little traffic and oblivious to the signs along the way, the ones that were picked up by their astute competitors.

Pay attention to novel things that are happening around you. It might be just a small anomaly; but it could be the tip of the iceberg that will sink your *Titanic* or propel your ship to the moon. The worst dangers are the ones you do not see.

Timing is everything. Whether you are reacting to good or bad events, if you hesitate you may lose it all!

Persistent Drive for Progress: Successful leaders continually shoot for progress. The companies they lead have a persistent drive for progress ingrained in their organizational culture. Their leaders dare to do great things and are confident they can achieve them. They set bold goals for advancements in products and services. They engage in many experiments, keeping what works and rejecting what does not. They may bet the farm. If a company does not have this type of culture, the executive must be a leader in developing it.

The successful company sets specific achievement goals that are clear and unequivocal. Examples might be specific targets for store openings, revenue increases, product development, service delivery, market share, etc.

Setting bold goals means setting goals that are a stretch, but not impossible. If you set mediocre goals, you will get mediocre results. Set courageous goals and you will achieve outstanding results. The magnitude of success is a function of the expectations that went into setting the goals and guiding their achievement.

The persistent drive for progress must be so infused in the company's culture that it reaches cult-like stature. Recurring progress is demanding. Employees either embrace it or they exit. The employees must be willing to make the extra effort, immersing themselves in the drive for progress. They must show concrete results.

To make progress you must try a host of things. You should encourage the development of new ideas—maybe even revolutionary and breakthrough ideas—that you can embody in new products and services. It is not enough that a new idea be "neat." It must be useful and serve the needs of customers.

If a new idea does not quite hit the mark, make adjustments until it does. If it never satisfies the test for being useful and marketable, discard it. You want something the company can run with profitably.

The watchword for product innovation is speed. You must generate new ideas and products at a fast pace. There are many real and potential competitors out there, so you must maintain a sense of urgency about developing new products. Assume your newly released product will be obsolete almost immediately. You need a new product coming down the pipeline. Never rest on your laurels. Move it!

> "This is no time for ease and comfort. It is the time to dare and endure."
>
> —Winston Churchill

Not Good Enough: Never accept a status of "good enough." You must be continually improving yourself. If you are standing still, you are really going backward. A successful leader and a successful company are always trying to do better today than yesterday. Tomorrow can be even better, but only if you believe it and make it happen. The corporate culture must engender in every employee a constant striving to improve.

Complacency is a characteristic of losers, not winners. What is true for athletes striving for new sports records is certainly applicable to outstanding executives. A good leader will constantly promote a discontent with complacency.

Invest in the future today—at the same time you are striving to do well today. Simultaneously work for the short-term and the long-term. If there are problems today, don't rely on short-term fixes. You may need to do a quick fix to keep things rolling, but you still need to work on the long-term solution. In times of trouble, never forget the long-term. Continue to invest in the future even during business downturns. Get the jump on your competitors.

If you are feeling comfortable with today's results, then decay may have set in. Innovate or die. Improve or decline. Continue to raise the bar. Invest in the future early. Invest aggressively. Today is the first day of the rest of your life and your company's.

The Right to Be Wrong: There is an old adage in the military that a mistake can end your career. The same belief often holds true in the corporate world. A mistake can be career killing. There is also an old saying that people continually fall back upon, "Nobody's perfect." Which is right? Which do you follow?

If you are not perfect, why do you expect your people to be perfect? You certainly never have all the facts and you certainly can't make perfect decisions all the time.

The best approach is to throw out emotion and proceed logically. If you do not venture out into the unknown, into the uncertain; you will miss the excitement of future discoveries—future business successes. Where would we be today if Edison had quit after even a hundred failures? He found thousands of wrong things before he discovered the right things.

Bottom line: You have the right to be wrong and you have to give your people the right to make mistakes. World-changing discoveries have come from mistakes!

Gut Feelings: Are there times when you know something just isn't right? You cannot put your finger on it, but your gut is telling you something is wrong. Listen to your intuition. It is coming from your past experiences and learning. It is just working at a subconscious level and has not yet reached the point where you consciously know why your inner voice is saying, "Something's not right with this."

Your gut feelings are often wisdom trying to see the light of day.

Keeping It Simple: The principle of keeping things simple is as applicable in these turbulent times as it ever was. All other things being equal, a simple solution is a better one and is so much easier to implement than a complex one. It is certainly easier to understand. If your people understand it, they are more likely to get it done. Complexity leads to confusion.

This principle should not be extrapolated to mean setting easy goals. That is an entirely different matter. A simple goal can be a very tough and challenging goal. Good goals should stretch the doer into being a better doer.

Keeping things simple requires discipline. It is very easy to make things complicated, more complicated than necessary. Anytime you find yourself making something too complicated, take a break, sit back, and reexamine the situation from a different angle. Maybe you are overlooking the obvious.

Weave simplicity into the fabric of your company's culture and leadership style. Make simplicity itself a goal. Simple can be elegant!

> "There is a master key to success with which no man can fail. Its name is simplicity. Simplicity, I mean, in the sense of reducing to the simplest possible terms every problem that besets us. Whenever I have met a business proposition which, after taking thought, I could not reduce to simplicity, I have left it alone."
>
> —Sir Henri Deterding

NEW EXECUTIVE POSITION

When taking over a new leadership position, there is a great danger in starting with a lot of preconceived notions. Even if you did a proper due diligence before accepting the position, reality is likely to be different than what you expected. Take off your blinders and keep your eyes open. It is best if you have no axes to grind.

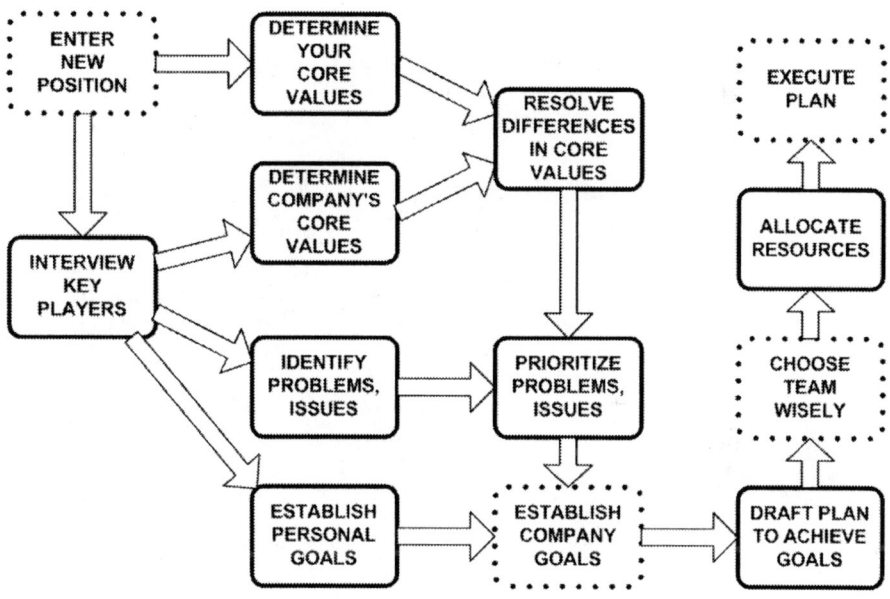

Interviews: Interview the other key players, both in an out of the executive suite. In the interviews, be sure to ask about the major issues facing the company, both now and in the future. Second, ask the interviewees for recommendations on where you should direct your efforts.

Core Values: Determine the core values driving you and the company. Resolve any conflicts or differences. Come to an understanding of what you feel should be the core values going forward. If you plan to change the company's core values, you have quite a job ahead of you. Examine the potential risks and choose the proper course.

Problems, Issues: Identify the problems that must be tackled and prioritize them. Not only should you identify the problems and issues directly related to business operations, but you must also figure out the nature of the company's culture and any problems associated with it. Are you going to accept the culture and work within it, or are you going to attempt the difficult process of trying to change the culture?

Goals: Prepare a draft of the goals you wish to achieve personally and the ones that will drive others in the company. Develop the outline of a general plan to take the company forward. Establish what your guiding principles will be in carrying out the plan.

Team: Now comes a very important task. Flub this and your chances for success are marginal. Think seriously about the kind of people you want on your team. The team should mesh with the goals and values you have established. The team members must have the skills and experience to make the plan happen. A good track record is essential. Your chosen leaders will flesh out the details of the plan and start executing it along with their subordinates. Choose the core members of your team wisely. They are the nucleus around which all the employees will rally. Obtain and deploy the necessary resources. Create and maintain an environment that allows everyone to achieve his or her full potential.

Execution: To implement the plan and its lofty goals, you and your leadership team will need to objectively evaluate yourselves and take the necessary steps to realize your innate abilities. Concentrate on knowing the business and making it grow. Learn about your people, develop them to the extent of their abilities, and support them in carrying out their responsibilities. Encourage communication between all levels. Good communication greases the wheels and helps you steer in the right direction.

TRUSTED ADVICE

The Advisor: Assume you will need advice, whether continuing in your current position or going into a new one. An advisor could be a subordinate, peer, boss, customer, supplier, paid consultant, friend, or family member. There is a saying that you get what you pay for. If that were true, then you should always go to someone you pay for the advice, like an employee or a paid consultant. But the saying is not applicable in this case. Excellent advice can come from many sources, sources that have not been paid directly by you. Whether paid or not, there are certain characteristics of a trusted advisor.

It might seem odd, but good advice does not have to come from someone you like. It will, of course, be harder for you to accept advice from someone you dislike; but sometimes that kind of advice comes as the unvarnished truth. Such an advisor will not be worried about your feelings. They have nothing to lose except their own reputation as an advice giver. Therefore, do not ignore advice from someone you dislike personally. Seek out this type of advisor when it makes sense.

Qualifications: The first qualification of a trusted advisor is normally that he or she be qualified in the subject matter for which advice is being sought. Professional qualifications are a good indicator. Direct experience in the subject matter or a closely related area is good. In short, you want someone who knows what he or she is talking about. For example, you don't want an actor giving you advice about computers; you want a computer expert.

You naturally trust someone more if they speak authoritatively, but that can be a poor indicator. Over the years, you have seen plenty of people who speak with authority but have no subject matter expertise to back up what they say. They can be persuasive and sound logical, but their advice should be taken with a grain of salt. Remember, Mr. Squeaky Voice may really know what he is talking about. If he does, listen to him, in spite of his voice.

Problem Determination: A good advisor is a good listener. The focus is on you; he or she will listen to what you say before issuing an opinion. If a mental patient goes in to see a psychiatrist, the psychiatrist will not recommend treatment before listening to the patient. Listening is a necessity. How can you trust an advisor who does not listen to your problems? You can't. The best advisors seem to listen to you effortlessly. They may use active listening skills to fully define the problem. If something needs clarifying, the advisor will ask for clarification. He or she wants to understand.

Having comprehended the problem, the trusted advisor may start reframing the problem from a different perspective. He or she brings a new viewpoint, which can bring you new insights into the situation. While you are bogged down in details, the advisor can cause you to refocus on the broader picture. In your obsession with the problem, you may have reached the point where you cannot see the forest for the trees. The advisor can help you look up and see the forest.

Objectivity: It is important to have someone come in with an objective viewpoint. You need an advisor who can help you think logically. He or she will help you separate your logic from your emotions. To make a proper decision, you must think with a clear head. Serious decisions should never be panic decisions. You cannot afford to be overemotional.

Common Sense: Common sense will sometimes help you to clear the smoke and see the fire. There are instances where someone totally unfamiliar with a subject can see things more clearly than the expert. A person with good common sense can conclude that something does not compute and be perfectly right. Don't automatically discard the observations of someone devoid of expertise in an area. The priceless advisor will have expertise AND common sense.

> "If a man can have only one kind of sense, let him have common sense. If he has that and uncommon sense, too, he is not far from genius."
>
> —Henry Ward Beecher

Assumptions: Emotion aside, the good advisor will challenge your assumptions. You may be working under false assumptions. The advisor will try to uncover your working set of assumptions, which you may not even be aware of. It is necessary to establish the context of the problem, both assumptions and apparent facts. Whether trying to discover assumptions or facts, you need to peel back the apparent and get to the real. You must dig beneath the surface. Symptoms are seldom the real problems.

Candidness: Good advice will come from someone who is candid and does not pull the punches. You want a person whom you can rely on to tell the truth. Friends and family may or may not be candid with you. Bosses are more likely to be candid because they are talking from a position of power. Peers can be candid, but you need a good relationship to make that happen. Remember, they could be potential competitors.

It is hard to get good advice from subordinates. You are in a position of power and influence over them. Being candid could get them fired, or result in a bad review. It takes a very trusting and respectful relationship between boss and employee for true candidness to come about. Therefore, if an employee is telling you something you do not want to hear and the employee knows you have a differing opinion, you had better pay attention. The employee is taking a risk when knowingly going against your views.

You even have to be careful about the advice given you by a paid outside consultant. That consultant is also in your employ. The consultant wants future revenue. The practice of some consultants is to use a consulting assignment as a basis for determining what you want, then give you advice to support your wants. You have been vindicated in your beliefs and are happy to pay. You just might call that guy back again.

A better consultant, one who is self-confident and does not need your business, is more likely to give you advice you can count on. You want independence, integrity, objectivity, and expertise in an outside consultant.

Criticism, Disagreement: Assuming the proper relationship exists between you and an advisor, he or she will be willing to criticize and correct you gently. A good relationship implies trust, dependability, and consistency in your relationship. You would expect the advisor to be honorable and have integrity. Sincerity should be obvious and not faked.

You want the advisor to be the same person through thick and thin. You want that person to be the real person, without any subterfuge. You do not want a mercurial or vacillating person. A person who seems to put on different hats to suit the occasion is not what you want. The advisor needs to be calm, cool, and collected—with his or her head on straight.

A good advisor will have your interests at heart. That does not mean always agreeing with you. You do not need a "yes" man or woman. You want someone who can disagree and do so because he or she is looking out for you.

Alternatives: Coming in with a different perspective and having a broad—and hopefully relevant—range of experience, the good advisor will be able to present you with alternative solutions after the true problems have been uncovered. A joint review of the risks and probabilities associated with all the options will help you select the proper option to pursue.

Your Decision: A good advisor does not force conclusions down your throat. For a decision to be meaningful and long lasting, the decision must be your own. The good advisor will not substitute his or her judgment for yours. Instead, the advisor will gently lead or coach you into making the right decision, one you can endorse because you reached it on your own.

Good advisors are hard to come by. When you get one, listen.

"To profit from good advice requires more wisdom than to give it."
—John Churton Collins

25

Power and Influence

POWER

Power does not require a lofty title with a big office. Some of the most powerful people in an organization are not high up the organization ladder, nor do they have a high salary. An executive with a corner office may have less power than someone considerably lower in the organization. A few examples will make the point.

First, consider the assistant who reports to an executive. That assistant has power because he or she acts as a gatekeeper to the executive. Assuming other executives report to the assistant's boss, those executives can easily carry less weight than the assistant. The assistant interacts with the boss all the time. If that assistant is wise, full of common sense, and shares a high-level of trust with the boss; the subordinate executives had better not run roughshod over the assistant. They will lose.

Second, consider the salesperson who is a leading sales generator for the company. He or she represents a large revenue stream—ultimately profits. It is not hard to conclude the salesperson could carry more influence with the higher-ups than the salesperson's boss.

Third, a trusted presidential advisor has a good chance of being more influential in world affairs than any cabinet member, including the Secretary of State.

Influence: Power comes from influence. An executive needs to be aware of organizational pockets of power. They are like land mines. The one you don't see can kill you. There are many sources of power, including those that are unearned. An example would be a position of influence coming from a family tie to someone in the organization; power was bestowed, not earned.

Being an executive, you will naturally have a certain amount of influence simply because of your position. Don't misuse your position by becoming a demanding dictator. You have authority, but it is not a license to abuse your position. You occupy a position of trust.

> "The highest proof of virtue is to possess boundless power without abusing it."
> —Thomas B. Macaulay

Proper leadership means influencing people to follow your lead, not commanding it be done. Be loyal to your followers and they will be loyal to you. Remember that lowly people lacking formal authority have toppled world leaders because the lowly people were more effective leaders and had a cause. A vision, one people can believe in, is very powerful.

State of Mind: Be positive in your thinking. Have a positive attitude. Power is often a state of mind. If you feel you have power and influence, you are a long way toward achieving effectiveness. On the other hand, if you feel you have no power or influence, you will likely live up to your expectations.

Networking: One of the premier "power" tools is the effective use of networking. Which are you most likely to listen to, the ad in the Yellow Pages or the recommendation of someone you trust? It is a simple fact that the more people you know and have meaningful relationships with, the more influence you have. Don't burn bridges. Build friendships. Friends will go the extra mile for you. Be a servant to others and they will serve you. When you give, you get much more in return—and it may be when you need it the most.

Therefore, pay attention. Know and use properly the sources of power to which you have access.

POLITICS

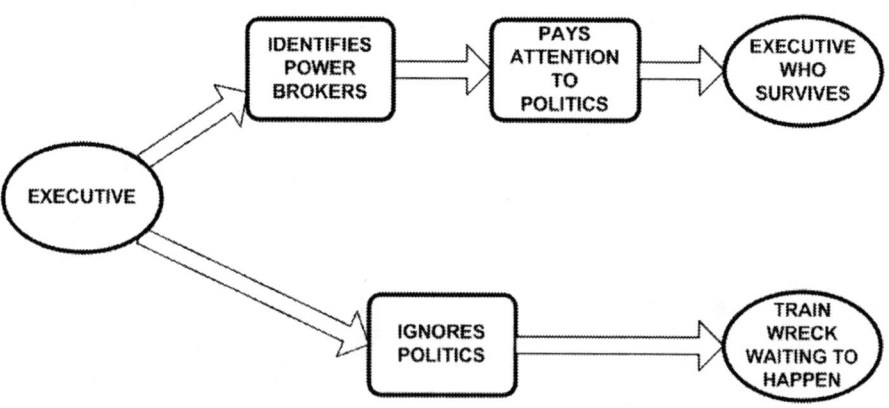

POLITICS

Corporate politics are alive and well—and always will be. You are surrounded by them. To ignore them is to court disaster. Some things you can safely say or do; others you cannot. The situation and the people involved determine what is permissible.

Don't be an unscrupulous schemer, but do not ignore politics. Accept politics as a fact of life—and go on. Perception is reality. Politics create perception. Gossip is like politics, and it is a primary component of office politics. However, you need not encourage nor reinforce it. As with gossip, you do not have to pass it on. Let truth and fairness be your watchwords.

Powerbrokers are not necessarily those people in charge. As stated earlier, the executive assistant often carries more weight than higher-titled executives. Be careful that you do not treat the perceived lowly person as lacking in influence. He or she just might be a nuclear bomb waiting to go off in your life. Treat all people with kindness and respect. You reap what you sow. Don't make enemies if you can help it.

As a matter of efficiency and effectiveness, be painfully aware of where the power lies and who the powerbrokers are. Plan your strategy accordingly. Don't waste your time and effort where power is in a vacuum. Keep your ears to the ground, pay attention to what is going on, and don't ignore the signals that are there for you to grasp. Where it makes sense and is safe, do your best to enlist the support and help of the powerbrokers.

So long as you do not become a brown-noser or suck up to people in authority because they are in authority, you can retain your self-respect. Respect and integrity are everything in your relationship with those above, beside, and below you. Respect does not always win, but it does improve the odds over the long haul.

UNDERSTANDING OTHERS

As an executive, you have a responsibility to provide leadership to others. Being a good leader requires understanding where your followers are coming from. That is necessary in order to lead them where you want them to go.

In order to deal with others, the effective executive must be proactive in trying to understand the feelings and needs of others. Understanding does not imply agreement. You can understand how someone feels and understand what his or her needs are without being in agreement with either the needs or feelings. In fact, you may understand but totally disagree, and even disapprove. For example, as a parent you can fully understand the feelings and wants of your children but still be compelled to say no.

Convincing the other person you understand is the first step toward having a productive relationship. People can strongly disagree on one thing—even many things—and still be the best of friends. Believe it or not, Democrats and Republicans can be friends.

Body Language: You must be attentive to the verbal and physical signals the other person is sending. Pay attention to what is being said and try to figure out what is not being said. Watch the other person's body language, which is usually more informative than the words being said. Keep your radar site in operation and on full alert when interfacing with people.

Active Listening: There is an art to listening effectively. Not only do you listen to the words being said and watch the body language, but you also actively react to what is being said. You either paraphrase what was said to make sure you understand, or you ask for clarification of things you do not fully understand. By actively listening, you clearly communicate you are listening and are trying to understand.

Interrupting: When you constantly interrupt, you send the opposite message. You indicate what you have to say is more important than what the other person is trying to say. You signal you really don't care what he or she is saying. You can also get into trouble finishing sentences for people. Sometimes it can be helpful in avoiding embarrassing pauses. At other times, it causes frustration on the part of the speaker because it reinforces the feeling of being inept at expressing oneself.

Insincerity: When you are not sincere in wanting to understand the other person's feelings and needs, but you say you are; the truth usually comes out in the end. When it does, it takes a lot of fence building to overcome the resultant negative reaction. Trust can be lost forever. Integrity and honesty—again without implying agreement—is always the best policy. You must truly care and show that you care.

It goes without saying, good interpersonal skills and good relationships with people are essential for executive success. The higher up the executive ladder you go, the more need there is for interpersonal skills. Power for power's sake does not win. Insincerity shows a lack of integrity. Integrity does win.

Analyze what your agenda is when interfacing with someone else. You certainly do not radiate empathy when your actions express the desire to overpower the other person, forcing your will upon them. Understand first. Coach and lead next.

RESPONSIVENESS

How do you like it when someone you contact does not return your calls or answer your emails? Set the pattern for the rest of the organization by your own practices. As their leader, you need to set the example.

Your Response: Some would suggest that all communications within a company should be responded to within 24 hours. In certain situations that is impossible. But in any case, let it be known throughout the organization that everyone, including yourself, is expected to respond to queries in a timely fashion. Remember that "No" is a valid response, when warranted.

Note: This level of response does not apply to junk communications, only to serious communications.

In certain instances, it might not be practical to give a full response in the allotted 24 hours. In that case, respond with a brief message saying you will provide an answer by such and such a date. Do not leave the impression with the sender that his or her query has disappeared into a black hole.

Your Assistant: If you have an executive assistant, be sure he or she responds for you in the manner you would yourself, if given the time. The assistant is acting on your behalf and representing you. What kind of representation do you want? Your assistant should shield you from people acting as pests, but maybe the pest needs to be confronted directly by you in order to solve the problem.

On the other hand, if your assistant is blocking access to a greater degree than called for, you will be labeled inaccessible—and that is the kiss of death. You will not get needed communications. People won't try if they perceive you don't care. Communicate the rules of engagement to your assistant and make sure they are followed.

Extend your influence by your responsiveness.

26

Making Things Happen

CLOSURE

The lack of closure in regard to action items contributes to lost productivity. The key items in closure are who, what, and when. Each needs to be addressed in a business interaction.

CLOSURE

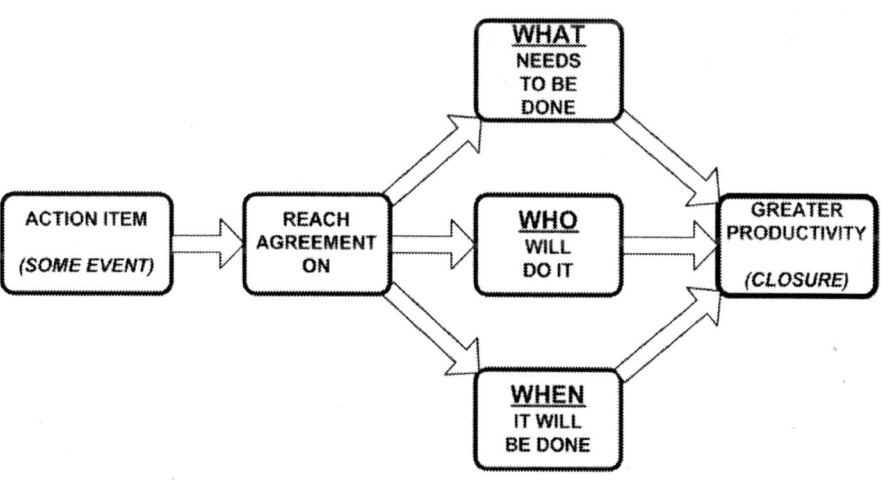

WHAT means coming to some agreement on what needs to be done. You need to fully define the task to be undertaken, meaning the requirements. Defining WHAT includes deciding the expected results, but does not need to include the HOW. In the typical situation, it should be up to the person carrying out the task to determine HOW it is to be accomplished. Therefore, identify the deliverables. And results need to be measurable, to the extent practical.

WHO means determining who is responsible for doing the WHAT. Vagueness in assigning responsibilities is a surefire way not to get anything done. "It wasn't my job," will be the response when failure to act is brought up. Unless you have some eager volunteer straining at the bit, everyone expects someone else to step up to the plate. Since people often have more than enough to do in their normal job responsibilities, volunteerism is not necessarily going to happen. Ensure roles and responsibilities are assigned to take care of the WHAT. Leave each business encounter with an agreement on WHO is responsible for WHAT.

Finally, **WHEN** means setting a completion date for the action item. A target date, especially if it is published, gives added incentive for getting something done. If the person assigned responsibility for an action item does not get it done on time, he or she knows there must be an accounting for failing to do so.

Keep in mind that larger tasks may require setting intermediate dates for phased completions. The larger and more complex the task, the more likely it needs to be broken into pieces. It is not good to have only one completion date, the end one, on a large task and then find out close to the targeted date that the task's completion is in big trouble. Intermediate dates (milestones) for specific parts of the task help provide early warnings that a project is in trouble.

It may be necessary to determine **HOW** before setting intermediate dates. The intermediate dates could come after the original encounter. Let the person responsible for carrying out a task decide HOW, then he or she can set meaningful intermediate dates.

Therefore, know WHO is doing WHAT and WHEN it is going to get done. Instilling closure as a habit in employees and in management cannot but help improve productivity. To give even more incentive, apply the principle that what gets measured gets done. Track and report progress on assignments.

SPEEDY RESOLUTION

A festering wound does not heal itself quickly, if at all. Apply that ugly picture to a problem, an issue, or a task that is not being addressed and you will not be far off track with the analogy. Speedy action, speedy attention to something that is not being handled is the proper approach. Pay attention to inaction. Do not ignore warning signs.

In some situations, a problem will go away or solve itself over time; but the perceptive executive knows better, as applied to most situations. Is some significant problem not being addressed? Are any issues with potentially significant ramifications not getting the attention of management or those assigned to deal with them? If nothing else, unsolved problems detract from current productivity.

Is some seemingly insignificant problem just a symptom of bigger problems? Dig deeper. Keep digging deeper until the source problem is identified, then tackle the root cause. Issues can start out as just differences of opinion, then blossom into full-fledged problems with monumental impact. The sooner you address the issues, the less mess there will be to clean up afterwards.

A dynamite stick is set off by a small fuse having little power in and of itself. If the fuse is allowed to continue burning, it will set off the explosion. Have some fuses been lit in your organization that you are sticking your head in the sand about? Your head may be covered underground, but your backside is fully exposed. Take care of those seemingly minor issues.

How about things that remain undone? Have tasks been assigned that have not been carried out? Are important tasks not being done because no one has been assigned to do them? With limited staff, you will probably have to prioritize outstanding tasks and projects. Prioritize and get the most important tasks done as quickly as you can. Assign people to the tasks.

If you have too many outstanding tasks that are not being taken care of, maybe you need to increase staffing levels. What is the impact on the company's bottom line for not taking care of outstanding tasks? Run the numbers, using best guess estimates, and get the budget changed if you need to add staff.

Untreated sores lead to gangrene. Gangrene leads to amputation—maybe your job. Act and act now.

CONSENSUS

Consensus should not be confused with unanimous agreement. In a unanimous agreement everyone, and that means everyone, agrees with a stand or a decision. The agreement could be about taking some course of action. A unanimous agreement is always the best. But in business, like other things in life, it is hard to get unanimous backing for anything. Everyone has different ideas, values, likes, and prejudices. If you can get unanimous backing on something, great. If not, the next best thing is consensus.

Consensus does not require that everyone totally agree on something. It is not majority rule. Rather, all involved parties simply agree to back something, like a decision. It means everyone supports the stand of the group. Some or all members of the consensus may, in fact, feel they have better ideas, but everyone in the consensus agrees to back the group decision.

A meaningful consensus is never a required decision. To be meaningful, agreement to the consensus must be freely given without coercion. Forced consensus means false commitment. At the slightest bit of trouble, commitment dies. Consensus is an enduring stand, one that survives hard times.

There is nothing wrong with advocates of a consensus using persuasive arguments in an attempt to achieve consensus. However, it is wrong for people in a position of power, like an executive, to demand a consensus. Such an action is the equivalent of telling someone that he or she is being "volunteered" for some action. Volunteering for something, like joining in a consensus, is an act of free will. Otherwise, you have a police state.

So, seek a consensus on critical courses of action, but do not label something as a consensus agreement when it is an executive decision. Be honest about the situation.

GROUP COLLABORATION

There is an old saying that two heads are better than one. No one person is all wise or all knowing. The computer can help us with information and data stored in databases—providing you have the proper information retrieval engine and have stored the information ahead of time; but the computer cannot equal the human mind. The human has more intelligence—usually.

Assuming a team or group works well together, the collective knowledge and wisdom of the group is greater than any one individual. If there is friction among the group members or if individual competitive spirits clash, the group's effectiveness will suffer along with its productivity. The conclusion is that a team can do (1) worse than the average member, (2) about the same as the average member, (3) better than the average member, or (4) better than any individual member. It all depends upon the harmony and cohesiveness of the group. A group can be effective or ineffective.

In very simplistic terms, consider the situation where a group of individuals are taking a test. It stands to reason that the group's combined knowledge is greater than any one individual, assuming no single person already knows all the answers. Pooling their knowledge would help the group score higher on the questions than a single individual. To make this work, though, the group has to know its individuals and their capabilities and defer to the expert in a particular area. In cases of disputed opinion, the collective wisdom of the group will normally gravitate toward the wisest solution. A wise solution means an effective method for carrying out a task.

Consider another situation. Why do you think a President has a cabinet and a staff of advisors? The President cannot know everything or be an expert in everything. When an issue or problem rears its ugly head, the President assembles his or her team and polls the team for alternative interpretations and proposed solutions. The President needs this collective knowledge, wisdom, and insight in order to make the best decision on a course of action. The resultant action will normally be the most effective.

Therefore, collaboration in an organization will help the organization get things done. The company will choose paths more likely to be on the mark if collective intelligence and insight are used.

27

Problem Resolution

Problems arise. They can be the result of conflicts between people, or they can just be problems that appear in the course of business. When the problems involve people, a conflict resolution process applies. For business problems, you can use technology or innovation to help find a solution; or you can fall back on a basic formula for seeking a solution.

CONFLICT RESOLUTION

In business, conflicts are inevitable, even among people who have everything to gain from a friendly, productive relationship. People have different interests and different agendas. They also have different pressures placed upon them, which may or may not be originating from the same source.

The person actively trying to resolve a conflict could be one of the parties directly involved in the conflict, or it could be someone acting as a peacemaker. Of course, it helps if the parties in conflict have the desire to resolve the conflict on their own. When that fails, a third party is needed to help mediate the conflict.

Incomplete Information: Many conflicts are simply due to lack of information. One party may be putting undue pressure on the other party, who, in turn, is in a difficult or stressful situation. Possible causes might include being overworked on the job or having to deal with a family crisis unrelated to work. The possibilities are endless. Don't assume all the contributing factors are out in the open.

Calmness: If the conflict has reached a very heated level, then the first order of business is for the parties to calm down. If you are one of the parties, cool it. Angry outbursts and accusations will not lead to a win-win resolution of the conflict. Exactly the opposite will happen. So, taking a timeout to let things cool down and then reassembling a few minutes later may be the answer. People seldom listen if they are angry or highly agitated. Sometimes a few calming words will help defuse the situation. At a minimum, cool the rhetoric and take the agitation out of your own voice. Speak calmly and listen to the other party with an open mind. Use a neutral language and tone, not an argumentative one.

Understanding: Assuming things have calmed down, you need to get the disagreements out in the open. Encourage an open discussion of the issues. To resolve a heated situation, you must understand where each side is coming from. For example, if you, as an executive, are trying to mediate a potentially explosive conflict, you must first try to understand where each side is coming from. That means listening to both sides and paying attention to what is being said and what is not being said.

But the same applies, in a sense, if you are one of the parties in the disagreement. You presumably already know your side. Maybe the other party does not. If not, you need to explain your problems, needs, and feelings in a tactful, non-threatening manner. The other person should listen with an open mind.

Emotions: Feelings are always involved, which means the conflict is emotionally charged. Try to understand your own feelings and their causes, as well as the feelings of the other party and the reasons for the other person's feelings.

There are at least two sides to any conflict. Try to get in the other person's shoes. Learn to respect the other person's feelings and needs. You do not have to agree with the other party, but you do need to understand.

Cooperation: Avoid placing blame. That puts one of the parties on the defensive. Concentrate on the issues, not the people. If you are a mediator, try not to take sides. Understand the issues. Ferret out the root causes. Both sides should tackle the issues in a cooperative frame of mind.

Compromise: Seek compromise without anyone having to cave into unreasonable demands. Search for the solution that avoids either side losing face or being depicted as a loser. You want a win-win resolution.

Determine the important points for each side and the points that are less important. What is deeply important to one side may be relatively unimportant to the other side. Come up with a creative compromise, one that does not sacrifice principles.

If one party comes out of the situation as a total winner, the thoroughly vanquished loser may harbor a deep-seated resentment that will have negative consequences in future interactions. One side could win the battle now and lose the war later.

So, all parties should calm down, listen to both sides of the conflict, understand the issues, and seek a win-win solution.

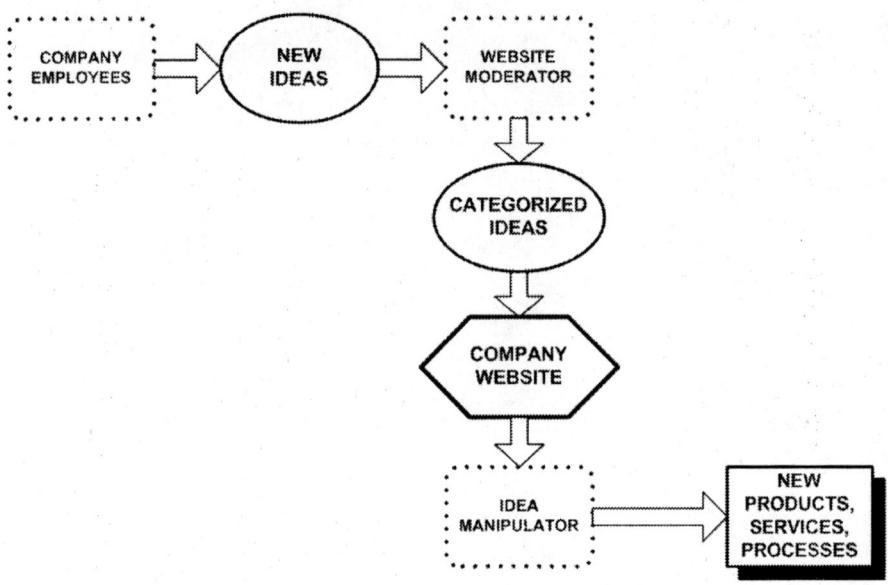

MODERN BRAINSTORMING

The value of brainstorming in problem solving has been proved over and over. Why not apply it in a different context or use a different medium?

The company intranet provides a great medium for facilitating the exchange of ideas. It can be used anytime and anywhere. Set up a company website where ideas can be stored and shared. Encourage people to submit ideas, even seemingly crazy ones. It might be best to conceal the originator of the ideas in order to avoid prejudicing the readers.

Appoint a website moderator or editor to assemble and categorize the ideas that have been submitted. Share the ideas across departmental and divisional boundaries. Manufacturing might come up with an idea that will bear fruit in Operations. Marketing might see an idea from Technology that, with slight tweaking, offers great promise for a new product or a new approach to service.

Any such editor must be an avowed open-minded person. Remember that in brainstorming no idea is a bad idea. Have the editor summarize and forward promising ideas to the appropriate executives or potential implementers. Reward the people who submit winning ideas. They might even be the appropriate entrepreneurs or product managers for the new idea.

But a website may not be needed if the involved parties can easily assemble in one room to practice brainstorming in the traditional manner. Do whatever works for the situation.

SOLVING THE PROBLEM

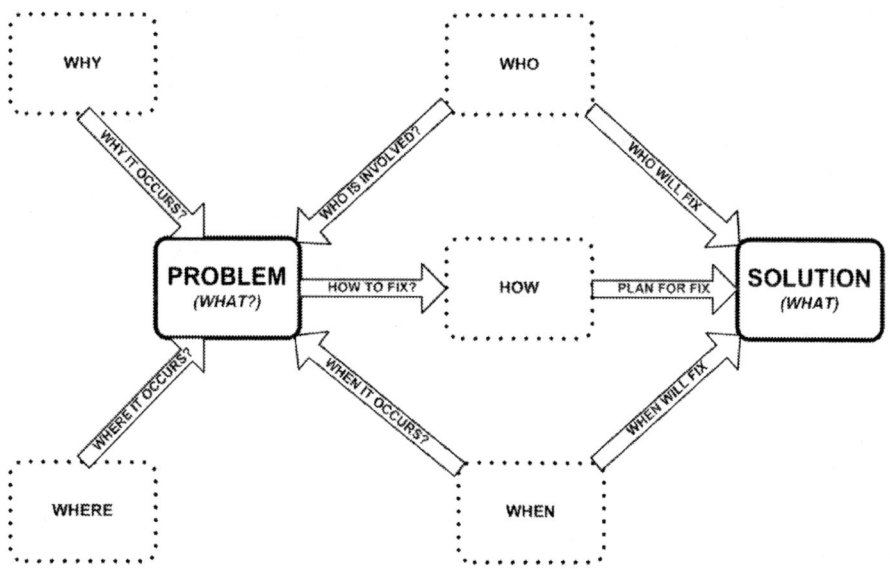

SOLVING THE PROBLEM

Before you can solve a problem, you must know **WHAT** the problem is. A starting point is to formulate a clear, definitive statement of what the "perceived" problem is. The emphasis should be on "perceived," because the perceived problem may just be a symptom of the real problem. In any case, recognize and state what the perceived problem is.

Determine **WHO** the players are in the problem. It is unlikely that some person is not involved in the problem, either as perpetrator or victim. Ignore the bystanders. Are you one of the players? Concentrate on the people directly involved in the problem. Talk to them and determine what each feels the problem is.

Accept the fact that seemingly contradictory statements can be made, but all of which can ultimately be reconciled. Remember the wreck that occurred in an intersection, with witnesses on each corner. Each of the four saw something different. Try to avoid assigning blame here. You are just defining the current manifestation of the problem.

WHERE and **WHEN** is the problem manifesting itself? **WHY** is it occurring? Determine the circumstances under which the problem is revealing itself. Then start searching for the root causes. Peel back the layers of the onion. Try to distinguish between symptoms, or results, and some causative factor. If you find out that B is causing A, next look to see if something is causing B, such as C. Keep uncovering symptoms until you get to the root cause. There may be several. There may be onions within onions. Continue to ask if what was uncovered is just a piece of the problem, not the whole problem. Always explore the possibility that you could be part of the problem.

Ask yourself **HOW** the problem can be fixed? Once you have determined the root cause or causes, formulate a solution to the problem. Explore various alternatives. Do not stop with the first solution that comes to mind. Think about other possible alternatives. Choose the most cost-effective and practical solution, the best **WHAT** to do.

Once you settle on the proper alternative, assemble the necessary resources for solving the problem. That includes assigning responsibility for carrying out the solution, i.e., determining **WHO** will do it. If no one is assigned to fix the problem, the odds of getting it fixed are not very great. Assign specific tasks to specific people.

Figure out **WHEN** the problem can be fixed, given your limited resources? Having seized upon the solution, develop a timetable for getting the solution implemented. Associate specific dates with specific deliverables. If the solution needs to be phased in, set multiple dates that progressively march toward problem solution.

Let people know the problem is being tackled and will be fixed on such and such a date. Track and report milestones along the way. When the problem has been fixed, let everyone know.

Follow the diagram. Reach a satisfactory solution. Celebrate the solution!

Part VI

COMMUNICATION

28

Communication Basics

COMMUNICATION

This book emphasizes open communication throughout. Whether it takes place in business, church, marriage, or other personal relations, communication is extremely important. Like a door, it can be completely closed, partially open, or fully open. The message can be complete, incomplete, or devoid of any meaning. But the analogy stops here.

Communication is much more complex than a simple door and what passes through it. Communication can be done truthfully, candidly, untruthfully, deceitfully, ambiguously, gently, harshly, lovingly, or hatefully. Furthermore, the biggest message may be what was not said, instead of what was said. Body language and tone of voice can override and negate the words said.

> "When the eyes say one thing and the tongue another, a practiced man relies on the language of the first."
>
> —Ralph Waldo Emerson

Because people have different backgrounds and experiences, the same word can have many different meanings and be received in many different ways. The simple word "girl," when said to a woman, is received much differently by the young than the old. "Guys" would never have been applied to women in days gone by, but it is used that way today. Depending upon the individual, some words are like raising a red cape in front of a raging bull. Choose your words carefully. Always try to know whom you are speaking to.

Choosing to tell only part of the facts can result in a totally opposite message than the full message. Mixing some truth with some falsity can produce disinformation, a common ploy of governments and their intelligence organizations.

What is said can be interpreted wrongly because of the way it is said or the setting within which it is voiced. The feelings two parties have for each other can color the message and lead to miscommunication. Negative attitudes toward the person doing the speaking can cause the listener not to give the speaker a fair shake. Parts of the message can be completely missed—or even ignored, on purpose.

Just too many things can go wrong when communicating. There are a lot of potholes out there for communicators to drive into and then experience a blowout. We have lots of wrecks when communicating. Therefore, it behooves each of us to be very careful about what is said and how we say it. Silence can be golden when compared to miscommunication. It may be worse after the communication has been made than before it was attempted.

> "It's still embarrassing. I asked my caddie for a sand wedge, and ten minutes later he came back with a ham on rye."
> —Chi Chi Rodriguez

All this does not mean to give up and keep your mouth shut. We just cannot exist in this world without communication. The same rule applies equally to individuals and to associations of individuals, such as businesses. Everyone must communicate.

In order for communication to occur, there must be a transmitter and a receiver; but preferably, a "transceiver" should be on both ends so communication is bi-directional. This means the two involved parties need to communicate openly and honestly with each other. It does not mean talking negatively behind the other's back.

Look at communication within a team. If only a few people in a team communicate regularly, the full resources and experience of the whole team remain untapped, sometimes with disastrous results. Silence does not mean ignorance. It could be simple bashfulness. It could be fear of saying something wrong or fear of retribution. A person may be afraid of looking foolish in front of others. A supportive atmosphere should prevail between team members. People should feel free to open up with ideas, even crazy ones, without any expectation of being bashed.

The purpose of communication within a team is not to display a know-it-all's purported expertise and vast wisdom. Communication is to inform and set the stage for making something happen. It should be an exchange of information. Every party to the communication should come out better for the knowledge imparted.

The rules about communication between people apply to situations besides when people are in the presence of each other. The media can be phones, emails, telegrams, letters, newsletters, newspapers, magazines, books, etc. There are plenty of media for effecting communication.

In the end, decide what needs to be communicated, understand the audience, deliver the message in the proper way, and communicate in the appropriate setting—at the right time. Remember, people are more receptive at some times than other times. Timing is important.

So, say it, say it right, and say it at the right time!

TRANSMITTING VS. RECEIVING

There is the proverbial question we often raise with our kids, "Why did God give you two ears and only one mouth?" Of course, the point is that we should listen more than we talk. When you are talking, you cannot be listening. When do you learn the most, when you are talking or when you are listening? Would you instruct a spy to talk or to listen?

> "To improve communications, work not on the utterer, but the recipient."
>
> —Peter F. Drucker

Listening doesn't mean just listening to those who surround you. It means listening to many people, such as: experienced, inexperienced, young, old, new hires, old hires, executives, clerks, those in the same location, those in the hinterlands—everyone.

Don't let your ego get in the way. Quit pressing the transmit button. Listen. You stand a good chance of being surprised by what you hear.

WORD OF MOUTH

Information that is spread verbally can be positive or negative, good or bad. That people will talk is inevitable. The tongue, though small in the body, can spread bad news just like a small spark can result in a raging inferno that consumes the whole forest—your company. Therefore, do your part to make sure any talk resulting from the actions of you or your company helps promote your business, not degrade it.

Employees: Counter unsupported bad information with free information flow inside the company. Bad information often comes from inaccurate speculation when there is an absence of accurate information. Encourage and support the free exchange of information and ideas, even if the information is less than positive. That does not mean broadcasting bad news outside the company, but it does mean being candid with employees. Remember that a tiny piece of negative information can be blown up into an unfounded tale of unremitting woe. Communicate within the confidential bounds of the organization. But keep bad news in the family.

Customers: Nurture company relations with customers. Attempt to make each customer's encounter with your products and services a positive one. Happy customers recommend your company to their acquaintances, who, in turn, bring in more business. Unhappy customers tell their family and friends about their terrible experiences, whether perceived or real. The result is lost sales. Keep the customer happy and you will get free, unsolicited advertising.

Suppliers: Be open with your suppliers. Make sure they know the truth, as it relates to them, instead of unfounded rumors. The best antidote for bad information is the truth. Suppliers are your partners. As partners, their word of mouth can help or destroy your business. Suppliers, like customers, talk. Make sure their talk about you is supportive. It is in their best interest to help your business, since more sales on your part mean more purchases from them.

Investors: Investors have many informal lines of communication within the investment community. Attempting to mislead investors about the results of operations can kill needed infusions of funds into your company. It is very unlikely that the results of operations, when bad, will remain hidden. The word will get out. Bite the bullet, get up, keep going. Rumors are like wildfire; you are burned up before you know it.

Competitors: Finally, do not discount the word of mouth of your competitors. Word can get to them via insidious channels. And what do you expect they will do with it? They will tell potential customers how bad you are and give evidence to support it, such as the word of one of your disgruntled customers.

In summary, the best defense against bad word of mouth is good products and wonderful customer service. Serve your customers' needs and bad press will be minimized. Keep your employees informed and they will serve the customers better. They will generate good press. Give them an example to follow. Be the leader you should be.

WRITING IT DOWN

Some people have an aversion to putting things down on paper. It could be they do not want to be held accountable later if they change their mind. They may fear an inability to get something done they committed to do on paper. Some people prefer anonymity. Others might feel the person wanting to get something written down is showing his or her distrust of the second party. Some people might feel it is an affront to their memory.

Fact: People do forget. If they do not forget, they may not remember all the details or may remember them incorrectly. People's memories are short. What was clear at the time may be fuzzy the next day, or even that afternoon. Have you ever played the game of "gossip?" The story is unrecognizable after it goes around the circle.

Putting something down on paper gets the details recorded, for example, the results and agreements of a meeting. Even though the scribe may make mistakes or omissions, what is put down is generally better than nothing at all. If what was put down was wrong, then the people reading the written account can correct any errors. Better communication is the result.

When something is recorded on paper, the written document then becomes an agreement to what happened and what will happen. Assuming names have been associated with "to do" items—and they should—the written document reinforces commitment to get something done. If the person assigned a task knows he or she will have to account for results on a task at some later meeting, that person is more likely to get the task done.

So, write it down. Everyone benefits. Miscommunication is minimized. Tasks get done.

29

Organizational Communications —Special Situations

CONFIDENTIALITY

There is always the question of confidentiality in this connected economy. Where do you draw the line on sharing information outside the company? You have to share information with customers in order to make a sale. The practice of on-time manufacturing and delivery has changed the dynamics of the supplier relationship. Companies are now beginning to share customer order information with suppliers. The result is increased efficiency for both, plus better service from the customer's viewpoint.

There are often barriers to information sharing within an organization, because each department wants to put itself in the best light. This means department heads sometimes become spin doctors. They look out for themselves rather than the company, which is perfectly understandable. But this is a sure sign of culture problems in an organization.

A tougher situation is sharing information with competitors. You certainly do not want to share information about plans, which if known, would alert competitors in time for them to take corrective action—maybe to the complete detriment of your business. Confidentiality agreements with business associates are essential in these situations. Potential partners and suppliers should keep your secrets from your competitors.

At some point, though, you will have to share information with customers in order to prepare the way for future sales. When that happens, assume the cat is out of the bag. Your competitors will find out. When you are far enough along in your plans for product release, you will most likely make a pre-release or pre-introduction press announcement. The timing, of course, is critical. It must give you the start you need in building demand. It must not be so early that competitors will have time to launch an effective counter strike.

But consider another concept. Perhaps there is some justification for sharing ideas among competitors. It will depend upon the type of competition. If it appears that revealing a patentable idea could possibly sink the ship, then don't do it. If competition is less fierce and there is plenty of business to go around for everyone, it might be wise to share ideas, especially if an association of similar companies is facing competition from altogether different types of business.

If twenty people are sharing good ideas, then each of the twenty is receiving nineteen good ideas for each idea given to the others. Perhaps, all can benefit from each other. Good ideas often beget other good ideas. One thought can lead to another. On the other hand, if the group makes a practice of only sharing unimportant information, there is really no point in divulging your great ideas. There is no payback.

Take notice of the situation in which your company finds itself. Do not take the unyielding position that the sharing of information is never allowed. Internally, a company runs best when information is shared freely. Information flow into and out of the company can be beneficial, depending upon who the players are and what the market situation is. Even criminals sometimes share information with the police.

INFORMATION, NOT INVENTORY

A high level of readily accessible information is good. Large inventories are not. The "just-in-time" philosophy has revolutionized many businesses. Sharing customer order information and factory production schedules can enable a business to push the burden of costly inventory back on the suppliers. The suppliers can, in turn, pass the buck to their own suppliers. Everyone benefits. Inventories are reduced for everyone, along with their costly investments.

The key to making "just-in-time" processing work is having the proper information in the hands of the buyers and the suppliers at the proper time. Both buyer and supplier can then intelligently schedule production runs. The customer can benefit, too. If the product being bought allows just a few days lead time, say, for a custom-ordered computer, the customer can still get quick delivery of a product tailored to his or her needs.

The worst case is having to anticipate glitches in supplier deliveries and then stock up on a contingency basis. A threatened strike by a carrier or a manufacturer can be the culprit. However, a costly investment in inventory is seldom required except in very seasonal industries, like toys at Christmas time. The retailers must build up toy inventories to handle the surge of buying at their stores.

Modern information technology can even help track inventory in transit. Transportation companies can tell you where a shipment is so you can properly react to problems in delivery. Radio frequency ID (RFID) tag technology is revolutionizing the tracking of products from manufacturing to distribution to sales. Web services technology is opening doors on the interoperability of computer applications around the world.

The bottom line: Where it makes sense, use timely information to keep inventories down. Technology can help.

TEAM INTERACTIONS

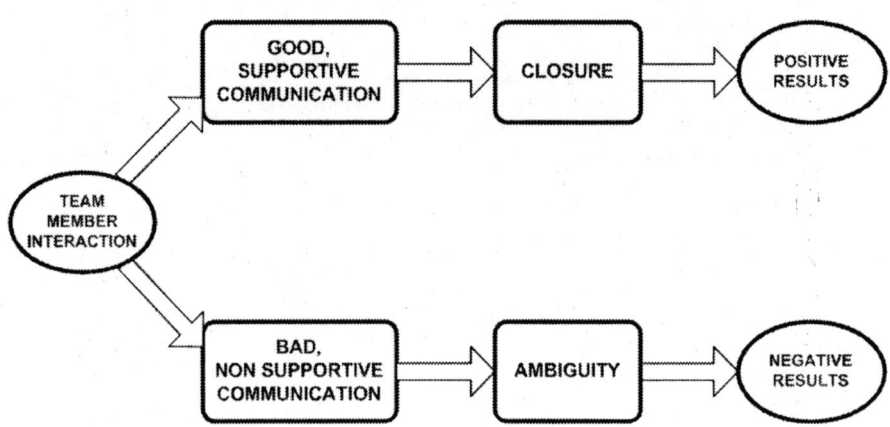

TEAM INTERACTIONS

Any encounter you have with a fellow team member is an interaction with positive, neutral, or negative results. Positive is the best. Negative is the worst. Strive for positive results in every interaction, to the extent it is within your power. Neutral results may be fine in some situations, but they are more likely indications of wasted effort. Remember that time is money.

How do you feel after a team member encounter? An encounter always has some emotional impact. You must do your part to make the encounter as emotionally uplifting as possible. This is true even in a reprimand situation. Do you want the wounded employee feeling beat to the ground, or would you like him or her rising to the challenge of being a better employee? Be supportive, even when reprimanding. Give the person being reprimanded a way out, a chance to improve. Consider the parent disciplining a child. The child should come out of the encounter wanting to do better, not just being browbeat into doing better.

Successful encounters will result in some degree of closure. There should be no confusion on the part of people involved about the outcome of an encounter. An interaction could result in team members being put under a lot of pressure and stress, but they should have no doubt about what is required after the encounter. This points to one of the prime ingredients of a successful encounter, good communication.

A team interaction will always involve some form of communication, even if it is just a supporting touch on the shoulder. Unclear communication is a waste and can be counterproductive. Unclear communication can result in a state of affairs that is worse after the encounter than before it happened. Clear communication is essential. Ambiguity should be treated as an enemy. You always want to know what other people mean. They expect the same of you. Truth always wins in the end, not falsehood.

The other factor in communication is how it is done, how it is handled. Sharp, unbridled comments are like a knife cuts. Blood flows. People's feelings are hurt. Watch how you say things. Whole courses could be devoted to the art of communicating bad or unpopular news. You can be supportively critical of others, provided you are trying to build them up, not tear them down. Examine your motives when being critical. You never win in the long run if you purposefully set out to destroy someone.

A positive team encounter results in some degree of success for those people involved in the interaction. The outcome should be a win for all parties. Teams either work for the common good, or they do not. If teams are working in the context of a company, then, by extension, the team should be working not only for the good of the team but also for the good of the company.

Are you someone the other team members would choose to have on the team if given a choice?

DEBRIEFINGS

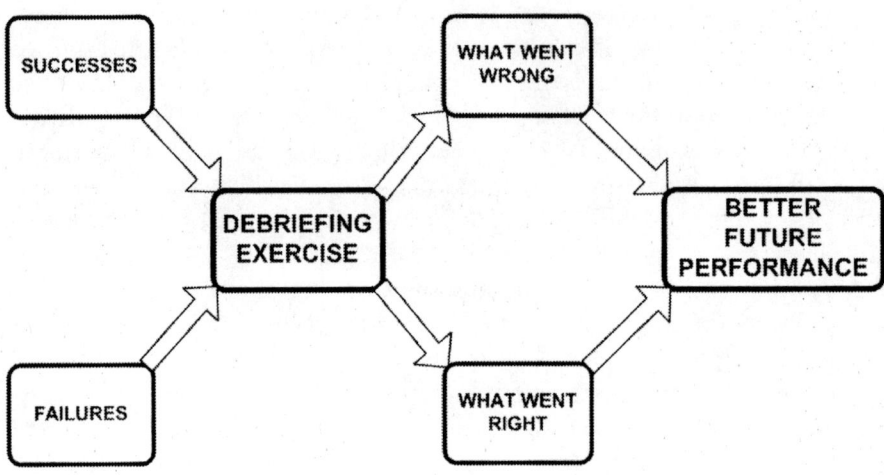

DEBRIEFINGS

It is a rare business, indeed, that does not experience both failures and successes, sometimes on a grand scale. In military circles, failures AND successes result in a debriefing session following the completion, or lack thereof, of a mission. Organizations can learn from the military on this.

The whole objective of a debriefing session is to learn from what just happened, and to do it formally. Business, on the other hand, jumps to the next endeavor or project without duly analyzing what just happened. Managers typically wait anxiously for people to be made available for the next task. As soon as one thing is completed, personnel are reassigned. They move on to the next project. It is rare in the real world of business to conduct an in-depth post-project review. What a waste of available information!

This is not to say that management does not review results; it is just that management works more on a milestone or bottom-line basis, meaning they couch things in generalities. In contrast, the military have lives at stake. The players, say, a group of pilots in an air group, have every incentive to learn how best to deal with the enemy on the next mission. Small details, when overlooked, can result in them getting killed. They learn from each other. To do otherwise is dumb.

Business managers often feel they are under tremendous pressure and do not have time to do all the analyses needed. They are wrong. They should take the time. It is time well spent—when not taken to the point of paralysis by analysis. A debriefing, while things are still fresh on everyone's mind, is just the right time for the most fruitful introspection. Learn from the successes so you can repeat them. Learn from the failures so you will not repeat them.

Figure out what went right. Figure out what went wrong. Then try to figure out why something worked or why it did not work. What can you learn from what happened? What can you do better next time? What might have been a better approach? Separate the chaff (symptoms) from the wheat (causes). Do not conduct superficial analyses that are debriefings in name only.

Debriefings should be a team effort directed at making improvements. Do not look for scapegoats. Instead, look for ways to coach yourself and others into doing better next time, even if this time was a success. Speak openly and honestly with each other—as friends, not as enemies trying for one-upmanship. Egos have to be sacrificed if each team member is going to be open to learning from the other team members.

A successful business is based upon successful teamwork and upon each member of the team believing he or she can do even better the next time. World champion gold medalists got there by incremental improvements over a long period. Effort, practice, and coaching were all necessary ingredients.

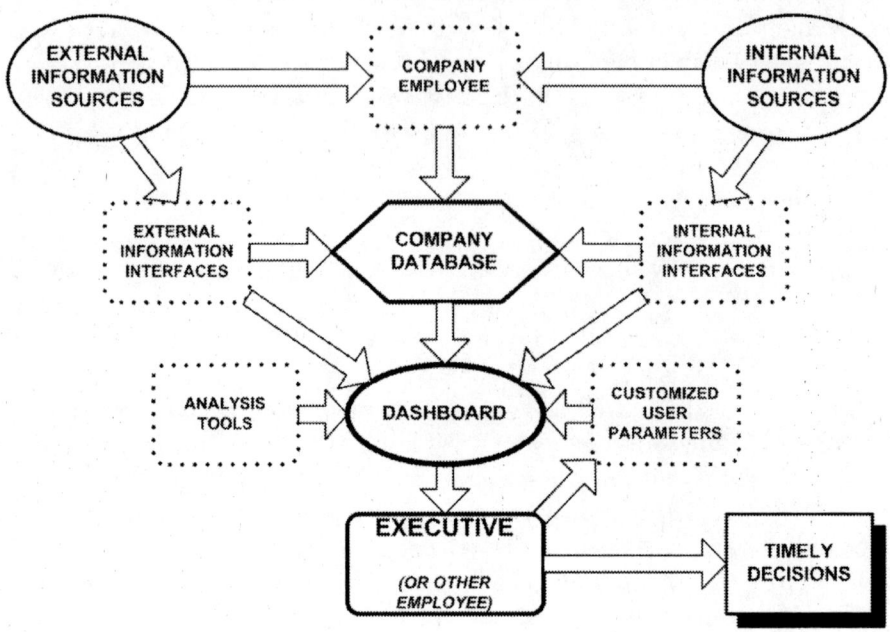

EXECUTIVE DASHBOARD

Information technology in its earlier years concentrated primarily on capturing and reporting data. Computers, databases, communications, and the Internet have all advanced so much in recent years that there is no excuse for executives not having made the transition to proactively capturing and harvesting "information," instead of just data and its summaries. The leaders can now more easily identify trends and spot anomalies. They can view activities as they are happening. They can make intelligent decisions in real-time, not a long time after the fact.

> "Knowledge is a process of piling up facts; wisdom lies in their simplification."
> —Martin H. Fischer

Databases are very sophisticated now. There are numerous data manipulation tools that executives can use to slice and dice the data into all sorts of informational views. This can be done on the fly when the executive wants to do it. Dynamic information software packages are out there that can be bought off the shelf to help analyze data. The good ones will not necessarily be cheap, but the potential payback is huge. These expenditures are very justifiable and make good business sense.

However, to realize the potential benefits, the appropriate data must still be captured and categorized so it can be analyzed. Once the data has been properly coded and categorized—hopefully on many different planes—then it is a simple matter for the executive to dynamically rearrange, summarize, and analyze the information from many different viewpoints. What-if games can be played. But that is not all.

With the advent of the Internet, management can access and play with the information from anywhere, such as from a home, a hotel room, a conference, or the office. Information-gathering people can also input information from anywhere around the globe—in real-time. On the user's side, all that is needed is a web browser and an Internet connection. This means information that does not really fit the normal database model can also be captured and made available to the busy executive wherever he or she is.

Capturing the information, whether raw figures or "news" (textual) information, first requires that management decide what needs to be captured to assist them in their job. Next, people must be assigned to enter the data or write software interfaces to capture information from existing databases. Then it's as if Pandora's box has been opened. The possibilities are endless. Executives can actually know what is going on and make informed decisions! Amazing!

Executives can truly be the captains and officers of their ship. They can gather and analyze information, plus steer the ship, from a "virtual" command and control center—regardless of where they are or what time of day it is. We have the technology to do it, in a near real-time framework, or even real-time in certain situations.

Changes are occurring at breakneck speed in the marketplace, and the changes are coming in from all different directions. The savvy executive needs an "executive dashboard" to give him or her the current "dashboard readings" of what is going on. He or she needs a private news board, a CNN of the organization. The information presented to the executive should be anything that helps him or her carry out assigned responsibilities effectively. Therefore, information in the executive dashboard should be from both internal and external sources.

Further, this executive dashboard should give the executive the ability to configure it to suit his or her fancy. What one executive needs to know is not what another wants to see on his or her dashboard. One person might want access to financial information. Another might want to see the latest industry developments. Still another person might want access to his or her appointment schedule, in addition to all the rest.

Software packages are available that allow the customization of the executive's information portal. The executive can choose the tools (software applications) and information accessible through the private portal. The dashboard automatically configures itself to the desired configuration when the executive brings it up. The executive can even change the configuration as his or her needs change.

The question is, "Why don't companies more effectively share information and ideas with those executives who are in a position of authority and who can act promptly on accurate and timely input?" There is every reason to implement executive dashboards and use them aggressively. There is little justification for not doing so.

30

Negotiations

POWER NEGOTIATING

An executive, just like any individual, hardly goes through a day without some form of negotiation, even if it is on a very small scale. This section concentrates on formal negotiations, but the basic principles apply in other less charged situations.

Although a tough negotiation typically becomes a battle of wits, a regular negotiation should not be treated as an event where there must be a winner and a loser. Nor should it be treated as an occasion for ending the sessions in a draw. The best negotiation is one where each of the two sides goes away with a win; both sides are friends when the negotiation ends.

> "To jaw-jaw is always better than to war-war."
> —Winston Churchill

In the case of a heated dispute, it may not be possible for both sides to win; but being smart in negotiations can even the odds when you are at a disadvantage. If compromise is impossible, then you must go for the exclusive win. Power negotiating will help.

A word of caution: This discussion is oriented toward an American viewpoint. If you find yourself in negotiations with non-Americans, you had better know what you are doing or get someone to help you avoid cultural landmines. A negotiating tactic perfectly acceptable in America could be a disaster on the international stage.

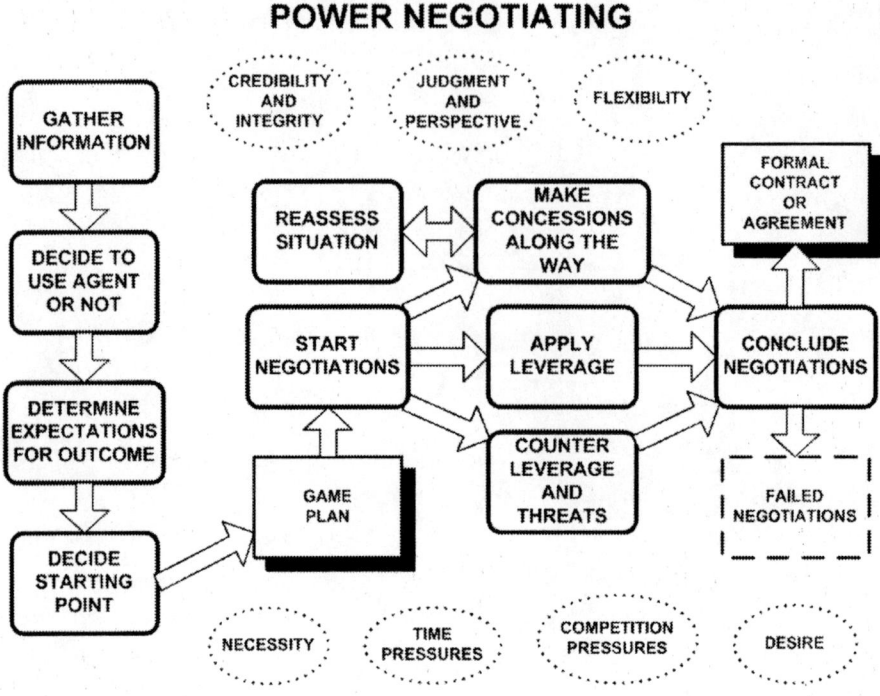

Gather Information: Information is power. The more you learn before negotiations start, the more power you will have during the negotiations. Being informed helps you arrive at reasonable expectations for the negotiated outcome. Information can be used up front to gain leverage, or it can be withheld and interjected at strategic points. Do the necessary research. Learn as much as you can.

Decide Whether to Use an Agent: When approaching a significant negotiation, it might be best to get an agent instead of handling it yourself. Be realistic in evaluating your own negotiating skills. With an agent, you will gain objectivity and minimize the effect of your emotions. Even if you decide not to use an agent, it might be wise to consult a knowledgeable agent in advance of important negotiations.

If you decide to use an agent to handle the negotiations, determine the best way to use him or her. The agent must know what you want to achieve and the role to be played by each of you. Tell the agent everything important, including things that might have marginal significance. An uninformed agent could unexpectedly get caught with his or her pants down at a vulnerable moment in the negotiations.

In a negotiation, an agent and principal should act in concert so that consistent decisions can be made. You must give your agent some authority. It takes movement to generate movement. Don't get into a position where your agent has the authority to make decisions, but the other side's agent does not. You want decision-making authority for both sides in attendance at the sessions.

With the assistance of your agent, work out your strategy in advance of the first meeting. Make sure everyone on your side understands and endorses the strategy. You want a united front. Listen to your agent and any involved lawyers as the negotiations proceed, but always make the final settlement decision yourself.

Determine Expectations for Outcome: Before starting the negotiations, realistically assess your expectations. Where would you like to come out with? Seek a balance between the best and the worst outcomes. Temper aspirations with practical feasibility.

Decide Starting Point: You need to know where to start and when to stop. One of the most basic rules is to start by asking for more than you expect to get. If you don't, you automatically give ground and the advantage goes to the other side. So, give yourself some maneuvering room. Start with a relatively aggressive position; you may have underestimated what the other side is willing to give. Be positive about it; go for the best deal.

Game Plan: Before entering negotiations, you need a game plan that gives you a logical approach for achieving the desired outcome. You may have to change the plan along the way, but construct an initial plan to start you down the path.

Decide from the start what you want. Be realistic in assessing your expectations. Determine your initial position, then devise a constructive concession pattern to get you where you want. Enter the negotiations with an attitude of flexibility. It is highly probable things will change during the negotiations. Be adaptable. Be ready to act quickly in the face of changing conditions.

Start Negotiations: Location and setting are important. Home court advantage most always applies. Try to make the place of the negotiations your own location. It gives you an extra edge. However, if you are coming from an overwhelming position of strength, it might be to your advantage to meet on the other side's turf. They would feel more comfortable and accommodating. If necessary, find a neutral location to conduct the negotiations.

When starting negotiations, one of the initial decisions is whether you will make your starting position known first or let the other side go first. The normal approach is to let them make the first offer. The danger is that they may start with an unrealistic demand, which gets things off to a bad start. If you are well informed and are coming from a position of strength, it might be best for you to make the first offer. Starting first does help you take immediate control of the negotiation. You might even get what you ask for.

When presenting your opening position, present it in the proper tone, not too overblown or too humble. Control your emotions. Throwing gasoline on the fire in the initial salvo is not the proper course of action. It is not a time for being confrontational or argumentative.

Regardless of when you first put your toe in the water, make a plausible case for your opening offer. Be credible. Don't be greedy. Have a good rationale. Back it up with independent research. Set your counterpoint's expectations. In like manner, always ask the other side for the reasoning behind their stance. Use your opening position to provide maneuvering room for the opposite side to gravitate toward your desired outcome. Never make an opening proposal without understanding your realistic expectations. You could easily end up too close or too far away.

Work at getting the other side to make an offer that takes them off their initial position. It is usually a good idea to flinch at their first offer. Not doing so may embolden the other side to harden their position. Never say yes to the first offer; the other side will assume a better result was possible or that something was wrong with the whole deal. Resentment could rise up and blossom into anger. Simply indicate that they will have to do better.

If the representatives on the other side have no authority to make decisions, request that a person in authority attend the session. Do not fall for the trick of the other side appealing to a higher authority not presently at the table. Force them to get the authority in the room. Establish the authority of the negotiating party from the beginning. You want someone with authority at the table.

Be natural. Don't be overly emotional. But you might want to use controlled emotion when the other party steps out of line and misbehaves. It can stop them in their tracks.

Make Concessions Along the Way: Follow a constructive concession plan. Don't give in too quickly. The process is important. Don't make too many concessions or concessions that are too small. Normal concessions are just part of the negotiating dance. Concede in a few meaningful strokes, not in a multitude of small strokes. Don't feel you have to match every counter offer made by the other side. Never go too far. There is always the danger of making a concession that takes you beyond your realistic expectations for an outcome.

> "The minute you settle for less than you deserve, you get even less than you settled for."
> —Maureen Dowd

When making a concession, send several messages, either explicitly or implicitly: First, convey that the concession is meaningful. Second, make it clear there may not be many more, particularly if the concession is not reciprocated. When possible, make any of your concessions accomplish two things: (1) resolve the matter in question and (2) provide bait for a concession on some other issue. Be like the chess player, always looking to your next move.

When receiving a concession, don't let the other side know how pleased you are with the concession. Don't send the wrong signal by how you react. Neither over react nor under react to the concession. Stay in control of yourself, but let them know how you feel. Indicate there is still a long way to go. Don't be afraid of making the first concession, but don't concede if their preceding offer is clearly out of range. When faced with an unreasonable offer by the other side, try to get them to bid against themselves. It is a blunder for either side to engage in overly tough bargaining.

Don't rush to split the difference. Never fall into the trap of offering to do so. It generally will just give the other side a new point of departure. They will want even more. If the other side makes the offer, fine. You then have a new point from which to continue the negotiations.

Don't surrender too much too soon. When someone asks you for a concession, ask for something in return; but do not be specific about it. Let them make the offer. You may get more than you expected.

Credibility and Integrity: Credibility is needed on both sides. Avoid bluffing. Worse, don't let the other side think you are bluffing when you aren't. If your words have been trustworthy throughout the negotiation, you will be more believable.

Do not be caught bluffing. Remember that your bluff could be called, and then you would be forced to back down. You would lose credibility. The other side might then elect to go with someone else for a deal you would have gladly accepted yourself. Only chance a bluff if you feel there will be an opportunity later to graciously pull it off the table if it should fail.

When you are faced with what appears to be a bluff by the other side, ask yourself if you are willing to give in to the bluff. If not, then call the bluff. You will have to make an educated guess. Alternatively, you could nibble around the edges for a slightly better deal, if you are willing to concede most of the bluff. The last resort is giving in to the suspected bluff without establishing its authenticity.

Be consistent. You cannot continually take a "final" position on issue after issue and still give in most of the time. Keep important issues in one camp and unimportant issues in another. Maintain your credibility by giving ground on unimportant items, but standing your ground on important ones. Be consistent and back your stands with a believable rationale. Don't escalate previously insignificant items into deal-breaking status. The results are likely to be negative.

Suspicion and doubt come with the territory. Don't miscalculate and take your own credibility for granted. Continue to reinforce it at every opportunity. Act with consistency. Assume your counterparts are just as suspicious about whether you are bluffing as you are about whether they are bluffing. Assume the other side feels they lack credibility in a bluff.

Be genuine in your dealings. Integrity in business brings success in the long run. Brief lapses in honesty and integrity may bring you short-term benefits, but not long-term success. You are likely to be found out. People have long memories. They also have big mouths. Word will spread. Honesty is always the best policy.

Judgment and Perspective: Exercising good judgment is always appropriate in any negotiation. Analyze the situation. Keep everything in perspective. Strike the right balance in using leverage to reach an acceptable compromise. Have the courage to make concessions when called for; but stick to a position, even an unpopular one, when necessary. Exercise creativity and inventiveness. Use persuasiveness to sell compromises.

The pace of negotiation is important. Never move too fast or too slow. Keep moving toward a positive resolution. Perpetuate a sense of movement. Practice patience and self-control. Act in moderation. Impatience results in bad settlements. Stamina and persistence will come out on top. Balance perseverance with perspective. You won't prevail on all the issues.

> "Patience may be a virtue, but in negotiating it is a weapon of incalculable power. If you can outwait the other side, you can usually outnegotiate them."
>
> —Mark McCormack

Flexibility: Being flexible and adaptable is key to a good negotiated result. Don't let your heart rule your head. You must be willing to compromise without surrendering principles. Don't expect the other side to come up with a compromise. Be creative in finding favorable conditions—a common ground—for compromises. Search for a compromise you can present as a solution. Find the precise formulation that does the trick. Know when and where to introduce the solution—the proper window after an appropriate passage of time.

Most issues in negotiation are ultimately resolvable, if both sides want the deal to happen. Creativity is needed to find the path—not always apparent—to an acceptable compromise. Try to determine the primary concerns of both sides. Add new elements to a compromise in order to induce the other side to drop old elements.

Reassess the Situation: As you gather more information, you can better predict where the negotiations are going and act accordingly. During the proceedings, asking the right questions can force the other side to divulge information that is beneficial to your side. Evaluate what you hear. Determine any leverage potential. Remember that open-ended questions are a good way to fish for unexpected, revealing responses. Pose your questions in low-key terms.

Ask both direct and indirect questions. If the desired information is relevant and there is no potential downside, ask direct questions. Indirect questions can sometimes elicit an inadvertent, but very informative disclosure.

Apply all of this in reverse. Don't give away valuable information to the other side if you can help it. Develop effective blocking techniques. Never lie, but you need not tell everything. Be judicious in what you divulge.

If you reach an impasse or stalemate on some item, the best thing to do is to set it aside for a while. Work on some less important item to get things rolling again. Another possibility is to change the dynamics of the situation by altering some element of the item that is causing a problem. The assumption is that both sides want to work something out. The key is to find a face-saving way to alter the characteristics of the issue in an acceptable way.

It is very rare to reach a true deadlock where no one is willing to budge an inch. In such a situation, it will be necessary to pull in a third party to act as a mediator. If all else fails, both sides may have to walk away from the negotiations.

Apply Leverage: Leverage can be both positive and negative on your part. There are a number of leverage points: necessity, time, competition, and desire. Any of them may or may not be present during a given negotiation.

Apply leverage to bolster your case when it makes sense. The strategic and timely application of information can be used to gain leverage. Use your strongest arguments first.

But you must be careful when communicating strength, even though it is very real. You may not be believed if you lack credibility. Be able to back up what you say. Also, you need to avoid coming across in such a smug and arrogant manner that the other side feels compelled to retaliate, perhaps, in irrational ways. Convey your strength quietly and let your facts speak for themselves. Always behave reasonably. The negotiating table is no place for crusades or power games, but do continue to exploit any advantages gained.

If you find yourself at a disadvantage, aim for limited objectives. Realistically determine what is achievable and what is not. Get your favorable factors out in the open. Minimize your less favorable factors.

Keep your eyes open for the other side trying to apply leverage. Learn to distinguish the real from the unreal. Remember that appearances can be manipulated. Don't let yourself be overwhelmed by your perceived weaknesses, and do not unreasonably inflate the other side's strengths in your own mind. It just might be you are in a stronger position than you realize.

Necessity: If either side is being pressured by a necessity that requires the negotiations to be completed, it can spell big trouble for the person on the wrong side. Results will be less than optimum. For instance, the seller may be strapped for cash and have to make the sale, even at a much-discounted price. In this situation, knowledge is definitely power. If you are on the wrong end of this stick, avoid letting the damaging information get out.

Time Pressures: Time can cut across all other negotiation factors—several ways. People can become more flexible when subjected to a deadline. But people can also become more yielding when there is an indefinite deadline and the negotiations continue to drag out. The other person may grow weary and make more concessions than necessary. After making an offer, it might be best to let some time pass so the other side will learn to accept the offer.

Normally you want to avoid letting the other side know you have a deadline for reaching a settlement, whether self-imposed or imposed by external forces. It is too easy for time to be used against you. It provides a very effective pressure point. Use time in the way that works best for your side.

Pressures of Competition: A potential pressure point is the existence of some competition on the other side. It is great if the other party has to compete with others for your business, for example. Assuming the competition is real, it can be very helpful to let the other side know you have another potential deal cooking if things cannot be worked out. Don't overplay this. If the competition isn't real and the other side finds out, you have weakened your position and have eroded your credibility.

Desire: If either side has an overwhelming desire for a certain outcome and the other side finds out about it, trouble is just around the corner. Since desire is driven by emotions, the heart can rule over the head. If you are the one with an overwhelming desire, don't let it become known. If you find out the other side has such a desire, it can give you leverage in reaching terms more favorable to you. Just be careful not to take it so far that the other side's head suddenly overrules their heart.

Counter Leverage and Threats: One of the most powerful leverage points is maintaining the mindset, from the start, that you are willing to walk away from the negotiations without a deal. This is not always practical; but when it is, it can be very potent. It often takes a great amount of willpower, but keeping yourself reminded of it can help you keep a proper perspective about the negotiations. How many times have you seen a salesperson change his or her tune when you decided to get up and walk out the door? By using this technique, you can often force concessions that were seemingly impossible before. Never use it, though, unless you are willing to carry through with the threat.

Sometimes the other side will attempt to use the Good Guy/Bad Guy gambit on you when there is more than one person on the other side. If that happens, gently confront them about it. Let them know you recognize what they are doing. Embarrassment may cause them to back off. At a minimum, you lessen their leverage in using it.

If the other side keeps hammering relentlessly at you for further concessions, just withdraw your last offer. Be careful, because the whole deal might go down the drain. In any case, it should slow or halt the onslaught.

One approach sometimes used by the other side is to raise some false issue and get you to accept it as a substantial issue. In their mind, it is unimportant; but you are made to think it is substantial. The object is to get you to concede on an altogether different point in exchange for them conceding on the false issue. The result: They give up nothing in the exchange, but you do—and you have been put in a position where you are very relieved at getting rid of an issue that never was. If you suspect this is being tried, probe to see if there are any other problems they will try to bring up later. Get all issues out in the open. Force them to put in writing that no new issues will be raised later. Try to counter with some demands of your own. Don't let them move you into making a concession you are reluctant to make. Force a real trade-off.

Watch for the other side manipulating your objection to an item—to their advantage. They might start by seeming to agree with the validity of your objection—to give you a false sense of security—but they aren't really agreeing. They then gradually change their tune, trying to whittle down your resistance by making small concessions or recasting the facts to suit their own purposes. Listen to all they say, not just the first part.

As negotiations move into the final stage, don't let yourself be intimidated by harsh threats, artificial deadlines, or any other pressure tactics. They are using intimidation to get their way. Anyone trying such a tactic should realize it could backfire to the point of hardening a position or angering the other side. If it is tried on you, consider issuing a warning about the possible negative impact of such a pressure tactic. Also, think about countering the threat with a suggestion that everyone move into a more constructive posture. Don't give in. Tone the threats down.

Play it by ear. You could even try ignoring the threat to show it has no substance. Alternatively, you could make a small point of the threat and downplay it. This could either force the other side to make the threat more explicit or let them ease out of it. But always reply to the threat if it is forced upon you. Never let the other side believe its intimidation has been successful.

For your part, never make a threat you are not prepared to carry out. It might only cause the other side to stiffen their position.

Conclude Negotiations: Try to arrange the ultimate deal for yourself, but know when to stop the music and grab a chair. You may not have another chance. Keep your emotions in check. Reanalyze any offer that will force you to stretch beyond your expectations. Can you handle the consequences rationally? It might still be best to walk away from the negotiations. Make an unemotional decision.

Consider taking all night, if necessary and appropriate, to conclude the negotiations. If the other side is allowed to sleep on it, you may come out a loser. They may decide the deal is not worth it or there is a need to renegotiate on some points.

If the other side is particularly proud of their negotiating ability, it is possible they will try to take things too far and make it hard to come to a final agreement. If this is the case and you feel a deal is close, make a small concession that will make the other person feel good. Timing is everything. It must be done at a logical stopping point in the negotiations.

There are times when the other side will presumably reach an agreement with you, but then start asking for more concessions—nibbling for further advantage. It this technique is tried, counter with a warning that it will cost them for you to concede. You will want something in return. They may even try it after both sides have left the table. Getting the final agreement in writing will help head them off at the pass.

So, come to terms if favorable ones are at hand. Keep everyone at the table until agreement is reached. If a deal isn't possible on favorable terms, walk away from it.

Formal Contract or Agreement: Always get a contract or formal agreement drawn up as soon as possible before people have time to forget what they agreed to. Do not rely on oral agreements. If it is not put into writing quickly, conditions may change. It will be much harder to negotiate the second time. Everyone thought it was over and will resent reopening the discussions. Always read the contract before signing it. Pull in a lawyer, if appropriate.

It makes a big difference who draws up the agreement. If possible, shoot for your side preparing a draft of what was agreed to. There may be misunderstandings or even some blatant changes if they do it. You are in a stronger position if you do the draft. You then have control over timing and wording.

There is a real danger if you and your attorney are not working as one in any dealings with the other side while arriving at the final wording of the agreement. You are more likely than the attorney to remember pertinent business issues. If the attorney was not there throughout the negotiations, he or she will not be aware of all the fine points. Therefore, work together and respond as one voice.

Failed Negotiations: Negotiations can fail because it was just not possible to strike a deal or because an impasse was reached. In the latter case, consider mediation or arbitration. Use court action only as a last resort.

Taking a different slant, consider a dispute. In a normal deal, the parties start fresh. In a dispute, however, somebody is upset from the beginning. Emotions are rampant. If things do not work out, there is no neutral exit position. One side may be demanding an unconditional surrender. A lawsuit will likely result if no compromise is reached and if arbitration is not acceptable.

Negotiation is a process. Follow all the steps. Experience helps you be the most successful. Remember that the goal is mutual satisfaction. Don't think in terms of just getting your way. Keep alert to what is happening during the negotiations. Stay focused on achieving the desired outcome. Don't let the pressures get you down. Maintain your perspective.

> "Allowing your opponent in a transaction to walk way with his dignity, his humor, and his hearing intact, and a pretty good deal in his pocket, is the right way to do business."
> —John Rutledge

MEDIATION

When negotiations bog down and two parties can't get something resolved, it is helpful to bring in a mediator. Unlike an arbitrator, a mediator cannot make a judgment or ruling. The purpose of bringing in a mediator is to facilitate the process of two sides finding some compromise to one or more issues. Since the mediator has no power but persuasion, he or she may or may not be able to broker a resolution. However, the influence of the mediator can be enhanced if there is a threat of court action if no compromise is reached.

Both sides should perceive the mediator as impartial and trustworthy. A good mediator will be someone with a professional understanding of the issues. Further, the standing of the mediator is greatly improved if he or she has been a successful mediator through tough situations in the past. The mediator should not be someone having extensive dealings with either side. That would destroy the feeling of impartiality.

Mediation is much less expensive than litigation. It is also faster. Legal proceedings can be quite lengthy in comparison. Court decisions are likely to be appealed, and thereby take even longer to get resolution. A mediated settlement usually has the full backing of the two parties and is likely to be complied with. It is reached on much less contentious grounds.

The mediator will initially ask each side to present to him or her the issues and a playback of the events that led up to the impasse. The two sides will need to communicate to the mediator the impact the issues have had and the proposed resolution. All this is to brief the mediator and get him or her up to speed. The mediator can ask for clarification in private. Presumably, the two sides will open up to the mediator more than to each other. With a thorough understanding in hand, the mediator can then help each side thoroughly understand the other side's position.

The objective is to bring about unemotional communication. By the time a mediator is called in, there is a good chance that effective communication between the two parties has broken down. Neither side may be listening.

Assuming the mediator has the respect of both sides, they will open up to him or her and fully communicate their respective positions.

Of course, the primary task is for the mediator to explore possibilities for compromise with both parties and help them reach a suitable resolution. By mitigating the rhetoric and emotion in the proceedings, the mediator can help the two sides concentrate on the facts and real issues. For true compromise to be reached, it is essential that both sides understand where the other is coming from.

There will be both joint and private meetings. The mediator will sometimes meet with a given side in private. At other times, he or she will bring the two parties into a joint meeting, where he or she will act as the moderator of the meeting and control the agenda. The first joint meeting should be used by the mediator to explain the process and to emphasize that each side must concentrate on facts rather than emotion. There must be a three-way understanding of the issues, meaning between the mediator and each of the two sides.

In the private meetings, the mediator can help each of the parties see the weaknesses in their respective positions, ones they might not have thought about. Each side might be more forthcoming in discussing alternative solutions in a confidential setting. The mediator can act as a sounding board.

At some point, the mediator will ask each side to propose terms for settlement. The mediator can then present the proposal to the other side. Acting as a go-between, the mediator can lead the parties through a series of compromises until a final settlement is reached.

Once an agreement has been reached, it should be reduced to writing and signed by both parties.

PART VII

MANAGEMENT

31

Management Fundamentals

The responsibilities of an executive fall roughly into two general areas: (1) being a leader within the organization and (2) being a manager who sees that the assigned responsibilities get done. The first area includes deciding the direction an organization is going to take, then inspiring and motivating others to join in the effort with enthusiasm. The second area covers the management of people and other resources to see that organizational directives are carried out effectively and efficiently. Whereas the former area is a blend of inspiration and strategy, the latter is a mixture of tactics and control. *Leadership* addresses the big picture, the forest. *Management* is concerned with individual pieces of the picture, the trees.

Look at successful companies. Look at their leaders. The leaders of successful companies are not clones of each other. What does that tell you? There are many different management styles. They are applied in many different scenarios. What works great in one situation could have disastrous results in another.

However, certain management practices, depending upon the situation, are more likely to succeed than others. This book covers many different management styles and practices. Earlier sections of the book addressed leadership and organizational direction. This section is where the rubber meets the road. The grand vision comes to nothing without detailed execution.

"The devil is in the details."

—Anonymous

> "A little neglect may breed great mischief…for the want of a nail the shoe was lost; for the want of a shoe the horse was lost; and for the want of a horse the rider was lost."
>
> —Benjamin Franklin

That rider could be you; so, manage and control the execution of your directives. This and later parts of the book present management concepts for you to consider in carrying out your company's vision and your management responsibilities.

MEASUREMENT OF RESULTS

One bedrock principle in management is: "What gets measured gets done." Put the spotlight on an activity, and the commitment to its completion goes up. Nervousness aside, if people know they are being watched for results, performance will be better. Where the boss concentrates his or her attention is important to an employee. After all, the boss is the one doing performance reviews. If the boss doesn't seem to care about something, why waste a lot of energy on it? It apparently is unimportant.

But the next question is, "Which results are being measured?" Picking unimportant measurements defeats the whole purpose of doing measurements in the first place. If the selected results are not a real factor in a particular business's success, the choice is misplaced. For example, the number of potential customers a salesperson talks to is less important than how many sales are closed during the day. Unless the talks result in completed sales, now or later, they are probably not very effective.

Therefore, after deciding what is to be measured, the next question is, "How is it to be measured?" For instance, assume you are running a call center that handles technical support calls from customers. Next, assume you want to measure the success of those calls, which is a measure of customer satisfaction. How to measure the success of phone agents is not a trivial exercise. Are you going to survey customers after calls, or are you going to use quality assurance representatives to monitor calls, or both? How to carry out the measurement determines the effectiveness of the whole measurement process.

Meaningful results, meaning those that truly reflect successful activities, are the ones to be measured. What they are will depend upon the nature of the business activity. Choose the objects of measurement wisely. Don't stop here, though.

Make it a regular practice to review the measurement process. Conditions change. As a result, goals and objectives are likely to need revision. Not only might the objects of measurement need to be changed, but also the way things are measured. Don't establish a measurement process and assume it should remain in effect indefinitely. Periodically reanalyze the whole process and make appropriate adjustments.

Decide to measure. Decide what to measure. Decide how to measure. Perform periodic reviews of the whole measurement process. Adjust the process, if needed.

SLIPPAGE

Slippage is going to occur. Schedules are going to slip. Assigned tasks are not going to get done on time. Unexpected events may be the cause. Commitment on the part of one or more players may be lacking. Bad estimates may be the culprit. There may be unexpected resource shortages. Perhaps insufficient time was allowed. Management may have been inattentive. There could be any number of reasons for missing a targeted completion date.

Awareness: What do you do about slippage? First, you must know it is occurring. The good leader will have earlier established and will continue to nurture good lines of communication. People must feel comfortable with reporting either good or bad news. Slippage is bad news. It is critical that bad news be reported. Take corrective action when slippage occurs. Be proactive.

Assigning Responsibility: Assign the responsibility for completing specific tasks to specific people, as early as possible. If more than one person is going to work on a task, one of them should be assigned overall responsibility. The person having overall responsibility is then responsible for reporting progress on the task. The recipient of status reporting could be the immediate supervisor—and maybe someone higher up, also.

Control Mechanisms: The most concrete mechanism for making sure slippage is reported is to have formal project plans showing expected completion dates for each task. Adherence to schedule or the lack thereof must be reported. When schedules are first developed, they should allow some slack, a buffer for contingencies. The unexpected WILL happen. Things seldom go as planned.

It takes meeting a number of deadlines to overcome the bad press of not meeting just ONE deadline. Therefore, it behooves the person developing deadlines to include buffers in the estimates. It is great when you are able to report an early completion. You get applause. Even if things do not go according to expectations and an unexpected delay does occur, you can still report on-time completion if you managed to stay within your buffer. There is still applause. Not meeting a scheduled completion date means boos and hisses.

A less definitive control mechanism is simply assigning someone a task with an agreed upon completion date, but without a formal project plan being in effect. In this situation, the person assigned the task should also be assigned the responsibility for periodic status reporting that covers progress toward task completion.

The essential point is that a task that is not monitored is less likely to get done than one that is monitored. Not conducting any follow-up is a very good way for your subordinate to conclude you do not place a high importance on the task's completion.

An undesirable control mechanism is assigning responsibility but not coming up with a completion date. Then the person assigned the responsibility has little incentive to get the job done. The perception is that the supervisor does not care that much.

The absolute worst control mechanism is to identify a task that needs to get done but not assign anyone to get it done. It will not get done.

So, assign responsibility, monitor progress, and make sure the assignment is carried out—on schedule.

Causes and Solutions for Slippage: Now, what about the case where slippage has occurred, despite everyone's best intentions? The first step is to figure out what happened to cause the slippage. The diligent employee will report both the slippage and the cause. If the reason is not reported, the supervisor or other lead person must ferret out the cause.

When investigating the cause, it is not a good time for heavy-handed Gestapo tactics. Start with the simple, non-accusatory question, "What happened?" Set the stage for a respectful problem-solving approach to determining the cause and coming up with a solution. Be a supportive partner in problem resolution. You could be partially to blame for the slippage, anyway.

> "You do not lead by hitting people over the head—that's assault, not leadership."
> —Dwight D. Eisenhower

Once you have determined the cause, there are several possible options. First, you could decide the task was unimportant or unnecessary after all, especially in light of the factors causing its slippage. The landscape may have changed. Before taking this tack, make sure no insurmountable repercussions will result.

Second, the person assigned to the task might not have been the proper person to get it done in the first place. This usually reflects a mistake in management or a shortage of resources. Therefore, management is the primary culprit. The solution is either to assign someone else to help with the task or to reassign the task to some other person. Either is a touchy situation and requires good interpersonal skills on the part of the supervisor. Do the reassignment in a way that does not destroy the self-esteem of the person being replaced. Remember, the original problem was with management.

Third, the slippage may have been the result of a bad estimate; it just takes longer than expected. The solution is to adjust the schedule or add more bodies to the effort. At a minimum, the person making the original estimate should file the bad estimate away for future reference. Experience is a good teacher, especially with estimates. (Establish the estimating tendencies of the estimators and adjust accordingly, before the estimates are finalized.)

Fourth, the hardest situation is where the schedule cannot be slipped and there are no other resources to apply to the task. The reasons for slippage may or may not be under the control of the person assigned the task. This will need to be handled with tact and firmness. Be supportive. The solution can take several forms. If the person has other concurrent assignments and this is the most important, slide the other assignments and concentrate on the one in trouble. If this is the only assigned task, then relief can only come from two sources: work harder in the allotted time or work more hours each day and on weekends (overtime).

Fifth, the slippage could be ignored in the hope it will solve itself. Taking no corrective action is a decision itself. Hoping the problem will go away is often wishful thinking. Disaster could be just around the corner. Therefore, do not ignore slippage. People will think you do not care and act accordingly.

Commitment to task and schedule is essential. Elicit buy-in from the start. Get the help of the person doing the task in estimating the time required. Avoid imposing a deadline, if possible. If the person assigned the task had no say in determining the deadline, then the deadline is not his or hers. That person has no ownership of the outcome.

MANAGING EXPECTATIONS

A proverbial problem in the two-sided equation, manager vs. managed, is when the manager makes huge demands on his or her employees. Sometimes the demands can be met; sometimes they cannot. An executive can be on the other side of the equation, too. Even a CEO must report to the Board of Directors.

There is no fail-safe answer to the problem of managing expectations, but there are some possible scenarios to take into consideration. First, if the manager continually demands more than the employees can deliver; morale will suffer—and probably so will productivity. If the manager sets standards of performance that cannot be met, the employee is put into the position of always under-performing and never succeeding. A constant feeling of failure is the result. An astute employee might recognize the problem, and then harbor resentment toward the supervisor. Any employee in this predicament could decide to hit the exit saying, "I don't have to put up with this."

But the manager can get into other problem situations. If the unreasonable schedules and performance levels were also reported to someone above the manager, then the manager is put in the position of not delivering on promises. There is not much to recommend the promising of unreasonable results. At best, it is over optimism. At worst, it is outright lying.

Second, if the manager sets goals that are attainable, but which force the employee to stretch, the results can be positive. As a rule, a supervisor should always encourage his or her employees to raise the bar. Successful athletes continue to raise the bar for themselves in order to force improvement. It contributes to their being winners.

This is all a careful balancing act, though. If the pressure is unrelenting and most projects are put into "crash" mode, people will burn out. They will either slack off or leave the company. Crash projects are a fact of life in business. If they are frequent, it is likely the problem is with the leadership; they are being too demanding or else they are not doing a good job of managing—which is also true in the demanding boss scenario discussed earlier. If schedules or performance levels are being missed frequently, then something needs to be changed. It cannot be continued. A flameout is just over the horizon. (The assumption is that the employees are a capable lot.)

Third, setting goals that are too easy is not the answer. The employees will not be stretched and will not develop as much as they should. Company productivity will not match reasonable expectations. Profits will not be what they should be. Competitors will have a field day. Opportunities will be missed.

Never overlook the problem of politics or perception when setting goals and establishing deadlines. If you, as a manager, frequently fail to meet published schedules or productivity levels, then you are likely to be portrayed as undependable. Your estimates will be taken with a grain of salt—you will have no credibility.

The answer is to always build in a cushion when developing a project or performance plan—when allowed. If you meet or exceed published dates and performance levels most of the time, you will be perceived as being dependable, someone who can be counted on to deliver as promised.

It just makes sense to include a buffer in estimates. One failure can eliminate the positive effects of quite a number of successes. If you include a reasonable cushion in estimates—in order to account for the unexpected and for the danger of being overly optimistic—you have a better chance of bringing in projects ahead of time. There is much praise for that, but being on time and on budget is great, too.

A reasonable executive should abide by a code of reasonable expectations.

MANAGEMENT COMPETENCE

Many executives lack basic management skills, such as being able to effectively supervise, develop, motivate, evaluate, and coach subordinates. Oftentimes, the primary job of middle managers is simply to make their bosses look good. That, of course, is not in the best interest of the company or its employees. Leaders should focus their attention downward toward helping subordinates carry out the corporate direction.

One of the primary reasons managers lack the ability to carry out their assigned function is that they rarely receive the proper training, whether by self-study, formal classes, or on-the-job coaching by a superior. Most managers need some preparation before they are moved into a management slot. Even when training has been provided and is ongoing—as it should be—it is still best to develop the manager by moving him or her into positions of progressively more responsibility. Experience is a good teacher—sometimes a brutal one.

If a manager has the talent—meaning raw ability—to become a successful executive, it will become apparent as the person moves up the corporate ladder. (This assumes objective evaluation of the manager's performance, which does not always happen.) Managers should earn the right to move up to higher levels of responsibility by their demonstrated performance on the job. "Time in grade" is not the same thing as talent and skills.

Too often, a manager gets promoted into a position beyond his or her capability, but the person responsible for the promotion is never held accountable. The promoting boss may simply refuse to admit the mistake because of ego, and, therefore, does nothing to correct the problem. The result is that both the business and the subordinates suffer. Until some sort of reorganization or downsizing occurs, nothing happens to correct the problem.

Potential managers should be asked if they want to move into management before they are pushed into a slot they neither want nor have the skills for. Much of the time a person is made to feel a promotion into management is the only option for advancement. The problem is compounded by the fact many organizations do not provide a path for advancement outside of management. There should be an advancement path for the professional who does not want to become a manager.

A simple determinant of a manager's competence is just to ask his or her subordinates. Most subordinates will know—assuming they aren't on one side of a good-ole-boy relationship with their boss. Being friends with your subordinates is not wrong. Letting friendship lead you to overlook a subordinate's incompetence or sub-par performance is wrong.

Remember, some obstacles to basing promotions on competence are the following: politics, nepotism, patronage, ego, favoritism, and simple friendship.

Develop the individual. Evaluate for performance. Assess for managerial competence. Promote based on competence and performance. Protect the company and its employees.

32

The Best People

The best executive is the one who has the sense enough to pick good men to do what he wants done, and self-restraint enough to keep from meddling with them while they do it.

—Theodore Roosevelt

BEST BOSSES AND BEST EMPLOYEES

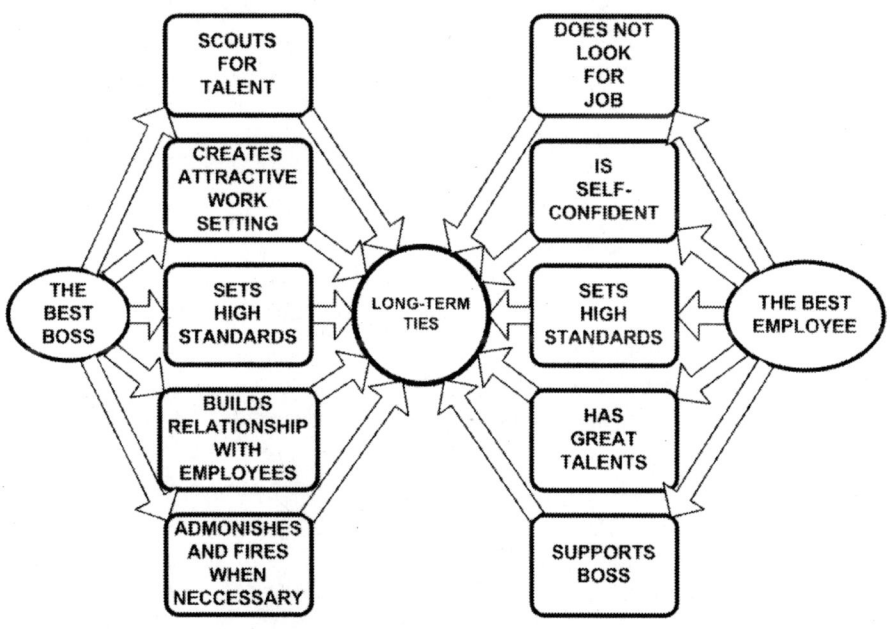

BEST BOSSES AND BEST EMPLOYEES

The Best Boss: The best boss wants high-quality people surrounding him or her. In order to make that happen, the executive must become a talent scout and actively search for high-quality people. Hunting grounds can be places where experts appear, like conventions or other professional gatherings. The executive might also ask customers whom they would like to work with—maybe the employees of competitors. Another approach is just to ask a knowledgeable individual who the best person is in a particular field of expertise.

When potential candidates are identified, they are added to the executive's candidate list—Rolodex or otherwise. If possible, contact is made and relationships started—and nurtured. If the executive's own employee decides to move on to another position, the executive could already have a potential replacement candidate waiting in the wings. The executive may even have been a supporter of the move in order to better an employee's professional career

This does not mean the boss wants to lose his or her good help. The best boss just wants what is best for the employee. (We are talking real strength of character on the part of the boss.)

Credentials or not, any potential employee should undergo an effective pre-employment interview to properly qualify the candidate for a position.

The best boss is intelligent enough to know high-quality employees are in great demand. To keep them, the executive must create and maintain an attractive work setting, an enjoyable place to work. The best boss communicates and constantly reinforces the message that the workplace is no ordinary one. Slogans, signs, pep talks, etc., can be used to constantly reinforce the message. But the message must be backed up by reality. It must be a great place to work.

For example, the good executive will insulate employees from bureaucracy. He or she will fight it tooth and nail. When bureaucracy gets in the way of progress, the executive will try to work around the bureaucracy, if nothing else. This applies, also, to the boss's supervision of subordinates. He or she will stay out of their way and let them get on with their job, trusting them to take the initiative in carrying out their assigned tasks.

Like a good teacher, the best boss asks leading questions, such as asking an employee if there is a better way to do something—even if the boss already knows a better way. The employees are given a chance to figure out the answers. The answers are not provided to them on a silver platter. The boss might also ask if something is the best the employee can do, thus encouraging the subordinate to do even better.

If the executive has done a good job on the work environment, there will be happiness and laughter in the workplace. A visitor should sense an aura of well-being when in the area.

The best executive sets few rules but does set high standards for achievement and performance. Authority is delegated along with responsibility. High standards establish the setting for doing greater things. In fact, the good boss will help his or her employees grow by putting them in uncomfortable positions that force growth. Excellence compounds itself.

The work environment, the encounters with subordinates, and the constant encouragement are all designed to build a rock solid, mutually beneficial relationship with the employee. The executive should go beyond just nurturing a team spirit; call the result a friendship, an alliance, a kinship, or whatever, the best boss and the best employees enjoy being around each other. Each is free to admit mistakes and get on with it. Trust abounds.

The best boss dwells on strengths, not weaknesses. Employees are praised, not criticized, in the normal course of events. The executive should remember that it takes many positive statements to counteract one harsh, negative statement.

That does not mean the executive abdicates his or her responsibility to admonish non performers—even to the extreme of firing someone when necessary. In the context of good performers and bad performers, the slacker's hand must be called. A boss loses the respect of other employees, the performing ones, when non-work is ignored. And there are the occasions when an otherwise excellent employee drifts into nonperformance. Like a good coach and mentor, the best boss will give the employee a tactful nudge—even a hard push—in the right direction. This will help the boss maintain the employee's respect.

The good executive will recognize when people need to be fired, even employees who previously were excellent workers. When this happens, the boss should engineer a graceful departure, one that does not destroy the dignity of the fired employee. Done in the proper manner, the employee knows it was the right thing for the employer to do.

Sometimes, when the firing finally happens, it is anticipated so much that it is almost a non-event. By laying the proper groundwork—warnings, feedback, etc.—-the fired employee, along with everyone else, realizes there was no other option. The executive, either alone or in concert with others, then helps the terminated employee explore options for other employment. The best boss will show that he or she cares—and is sincere about it.

The executive should not overlook the possibility of rehiring a good employee who went off the deep end but came back. For example, divorce, a spouse's death, drug use, or something else may have put the employee in such a sustained, long-term tailspin that the employer had no other choice. But the best boss will—under the proper circumstances—hire back a fired employee who has crawled back from the brink and recovered from the fall. Wouldn't you want that to be done for you in similar circumstances?

The Best Employee: Once his or her professional reputation has been established, the best employee does not have to look for a job. The best bosses seek out this type of employee and provide exceptional environments to entice them in.

But it can work in the other direction, too. An astute employee will recognize a good boss and an exceptional work environment and try to work for that boss. The best employee will know a good thing when he or she sees it.

The best employee is self-confident and wants to be challenged. The employee wants new assignments that test his or her abilities. The employee is good and wants to prove it. He or she wants more than just responsibility and authority; there is the desire for a certain amount of ownership of a task, the chance to put his or her personal brand on an assignment.

Inherent in the best employee is a self-imposed set of high standards for performance and achievement. Second-rate work is not allowed. The employee is his or her own worst critic. He or she sets the curve in a department and thereby raises the bar for other employees.

The high-quality employee has great talents, or else would not be a best employee. But it goes even further; if there is a proper match between boss and employee, the employee will provide complementary skills and talents to the boss. The executive will seek to hire those people having supporting skills and talents.

And the best employee supports the boss's endeavors. The employee will jump in and help without being asked. He or she will share the boss's vision and support the boss's agenda. If there is a crisis, the best employee is right there, Johnny-on-the-spot. Possibilities for solutions will be presented to the boss for getting around a problem or issue.

In like manner, if the best employee interfaces with customers, he or she will have an affinity, or close relationship, with customers. He or she is there to help. The employee is a partner of the customer.

Long-Term Ties: If all of the above are practiced by the best boss and the best employee, a bond and a kinship will be established that can last a lifetime, through different companies and different careers. The best boss doesn't forget a great employee, and maintains contact over the years. The best employee will nurture the long-term relationship, too.

Having the right boss is more important than being in the right company, and, perhaps, even more important than being in the right job. Such a relationship should be treasured.

EMPLOYEE CHARACTERISTICS

For a company to be successful, the executives must instill in the employees a common vision, common goals, and common values. The employees need to be headed in the same (company) direction and have a positive attitude about getting there. Making this happen is the responsibility of the executives. They must bind everyone into a cohesive team. Having said that, what are the characteristics of the good employee?

Positive Attitude: The foremost characteristic of a good employee is a positive attitude, one that is unmistakably communicated to all those around him or her. Greeting the world with a smile is much better than being a grouch and letting everyone know it. Both a positive attitude and a negative attitude can be contagious. You want an epidemic of positivism.

Attitude includes more than being positive. It means having the desire and the passion to succeed. An employee with the proper attitude will get up and persevere after falling down or being knocked over. Attitude brings success in the face of many failures.

Good Interpersonal Skills: Some executives think brains are everything. Brains are important, but are certainly not everything. If the person who is a genius cannot get others to work with him or her, ineffectiveness prevails. You certainly want smart people for your workforce; but you need them to be team-oriented, working for the good of the whole. They need to be team-builders. They need to be able to work with others and show an interest in the people they deal with.

Thus, interpersonal skills are important. An excellent employee will be able to interface with and work with other people in harmony. Good relationships between employees help grease the wheels and clear the sand from gears when problems arise. Not being able to get along with people ruins the effectiveness of an otherwise excellent employee.

Good Communicator: The good employee is a good communicator. That includes being able to listen as well as communicate effectively. As a supportive team member, the employee should be willing and able to share his or her knowledge with others. Understanding another's position does not mean agreeing with it. Effective communication means making the other person understand that you understand.

Ambition: It is all right for someone to be ambitious; in fact, it is essential for people to have ambition and want to excel at anything they do. However, they should not let their ego get out of hand. They need to keep it in check. A self-centered, overly ambitious person is very unlikely to be an asset to the corporation.

Adaptability: Good employees adapt to and accept change. We live in a world of change. You must be nimble to survive. Your employee should have an open mind and be able to objectively consider new ideas and concepts. New problems or obstacles should not cause panic.

In fact, if you are going to push the business envelope, you must have people who can think outside the box. You must set the stage to promote innovation and new ideas. This requires an executive who will listen to some far out ideas and not castigate the wild thinker. The wild ideas of the past are things we cannot live without today.

Courage: The employee must be courageous. It does not mean sacrificing principles, the values he or she holds dear. Courage does include being able to reach a decision or to concur with one and march forward with its implementation. Being courageous does not mean being stubborn and unwilling to change your mind. It does mean being open to both the revision of goals and the means of achieving them when situations change. Courage means being willing to champion a new, revolutionary idea whose time has come, in spite of the many forces that would kill the new idea on the spot.

Self-Worth: Finally, a good employee should have a well-developed sense of self worth. With that assurance in hand, the employee should have the good insight to objectively know what he or she is good at and where he or she is going. That includes having the confidence and persistence to make it happen.

Choosing the right employees is key to management success.

EMPLOYEE TALENT

The most important factor in organizational success is the talent of its employees, from clerk to executive. Stellar corporate performance comes from stellar employee talent. The best leaders, both executives and managers, succeed because they have above average talent and surround themselves with the same.

Best: Your goal as an executive should be to assemble a team of outstanding performers. Pro sports teams excel because they acquire the best talent, as found in their potential player pool. The starting lineup consists of the best player for each position. You, too, should strive to put the best person in each position. By "best" person, we are talking about someone in the top 10 percent of available talent.

Better: The "better" talent might be the next tier down, those who are more than just above average. Where you draw the line percentile-wise is a matter of judgment. Let's assume you want the best of the above average people, say, people in the 71 to 89 percentile range. That means your "best" and "better" people are the top 30 percent of available talent—for the price you are willing to pay.

Mediocre: Everyone else can be roughly categorized as average to poor performers. They are the bottom 70 percent. Let's call them "mediocre."

Talent Pools: But here is the kicker: You can move the whole scale up or down according to the amount you are willing to pay and according to the professional opportunities you offer the candidates. Your available talent pool will change to meet the perceived opportunity afforded by a position as regards pay, benefits, and opportunities for advancement or growth. Said another way, you can sometimes get better talent than would normally be available for a certain level of pay if the position is viewed as offering above average opportunities.

A start-up company could offer incentives—such as stock options or business ownership—to offset a lower starting salary. Sacrifices in pay might be totally acceptable for the potential employee in such a case. Executives who come to work under those incentives are gambling, but they feel the potential rewards are well worth the risk.

In short, to get the best talent, you are going to have to pay for it with actual salary and other incentives. Don't just throw out a bunch of money in the hope of getting the right talent. Be careful you don't get the top talent from a low-talent pool. The result will still be some low-talent employees. Search in a high-talent pool. Crack military units start their search with the best of the best, not the above average.

Fitting Talent to Position: What about the people who do not fit into the "best" ranking for a given position? The theory is that everyone can be a "best" player in some position. There is a right person, for example, for a clerical position. That person would perform in an outstanding manner and would enjoy the work and the satisfaction it brings. An excellent clerk is not a candidate for a CEO position; nor is an excellent CEO a candidate for a clerical position.

Therefore, the goal is to get the best and the better people in every position, with an eye toward moving better people into a best level of performance, either by finding the appropriate position where he or she can be a best performer or by converting the better player into a best player through coaching and training.

Unless you can find a suitable position for the lower 70 percent of employees—where they can be the top 30 percent performers—you should consider getting rid of them. The hard-nosed approach is to convert them or terminate them. When filling new positions, you can more nearly match the proper people with the proper position through effective employee interviews and screening. Properly structured in-depth interviews can greatly boost the success rate for new-hires.

Inheriting Talent: When you inherit an existing group of employees because you are newly hired, transferred, or promoted; you have a much rougher situation to deal with. If, after conducting in-depth interviews or observing performance on the job, you discover you have some under-performers, it is decision time. If you are a believer in the concept, you must upgrade the people, transfer them to another position they are suited for, or else part company with them. The appropriate decision will depend upon the situation and what the corporate culture and politics allow.

Before you get all bent out of shape and consider this to be a cold, hardhearted, uncaring approach to managing people, remember the theory: Everyone can perform in top form, i.e., be a "best" player, in some position. It is just a matter of achieving the proper match.

INVESTORS AND EMPLOYEES

Executives should take a lesson from investors. Investors know that the key ingredient to having a successful company is for the company to attract and keep the best employees. A company must build the kind of work environment that focuses on attracting and keeping talented employees. Investors expect the companies they invest in to value employee loyalty and the productivity that dependable employees bring to the operation.

Investors in start-up companies place an extreme premium on the chief executives and the teams they surround themselves with. Even if you have the greatest product in the world, if you do not have the proper team to execute the plan, success doesn't have a chance. Astute investors are vitally interested in the executive team of going companies, too. When leadership deteriorates, employee productivity deteriorates, and the company fails.

So, if investors care about employees, you had better care, also. The investors can certainly ruin your stock's value by taking their money to another company with a better team of executives and employees.

33

Hiring Process

One of the functions most critical to an executive's success is effective hiring of the right people. A company's success depends upon its people. A few hours of hiring determines the productivity of an open position for months and years into the future. The hours spent hiring should not be wasted. There is too much at stake.

> "First-rate people hire first-rate people; second-rate people hire third-rate people."
>
> —Leo Rosten

EMPLOYEE MIS-HIRES

First, let's define a *mis-hire* as putting the wrong person into a particular position, a situation where the employee only performs in a mediocre (average to poor) manner. This could result from an external hire or an internal hire (promotion, transfer, or upgrade without promotion).

Now, assume that 50 percent of hires are mis-hires—not an unreasonable assumption—meaning you fail half of the time to get outstanding performers, the ones needed to make your company an outstanding company. Mis-hires are a management problem. In general, the hiring manager has the last say and is, therefore, the one responsible for a mis-hire.

An exception can occur when someone higher up in the organization forces the hiring manager to take on a new person. Many times, this hire is a result of political considerations, which is never a good reason. Hire on merit and talent, not because someone is a friend, family member, or the object of someone's benevolence. A company is in business to make a profit, not provide welfare.

Money Costs: What are the costs of mis-hires? First, there are the direct costs associated with hiring someone, e.g., interviews, travel, relocation, and testing. Second, you have the start-up costs while the new employee gets up to speed and becomes at least minimally productive in the new position. Third, there are the direct ongoing costs of salary and benefits while the mis-hire remains on the job, reduced by any marginal effectiveness provided to the company. Fourth, there are the costs of mistakes—above normal—caused by bad decisions on the part of the below par employee. Fifth, add in the cost of opportunities missed because you did not get the performance you could have gotten with a good hire—which could be horrendous. Sixth, consider the support (overhead) costs associated with maintaining the position in day-to-day operations. Seventh, include any costs for severance, which could embody bad press and stock price erosion caused by the exit of a high-level executive. If the person had an employee contract with a severance payment clause, this cost can take an even greater jump. Finally, remember that it is going to cost you to bring in a new person to fill the position—and if you make another mistake in hiring, it will cost you dearly, *again*.

The cost of mis-hires is a function of the level of the position. It costs the company less if a mistake is made hiring a clerk than it does if a mistake is made hiring an executive. The higher the position is in the corporate hierarchy, the greater is the cost for a mis-hire. Common sense will tell you that a mis-hire at the executive level can be quite expensive, many times the cost of that person's annual salary. The cost could easily reach into the millions, depending on the position and the responsibilities associated with the position.

Time Costs: Never forget the cost of time. When the wrong executive is hired, the minimum time before the executive can be removed is likely to be at least six months. More typically, it takes a year or more for the mis-hire to exit. That is a long time in the life of a business, a time for many lost opportunities.

It takes a while to figure out the wrong person was hired. There is a honeymoon period when the new executive is given time to prove his or her merit. Then there is the time it takes to carry out the termination. Ego often enters into the picture. The hiring manager may initially refuse to admit he or she has made a mis-hire. When it can no longer be denied, the hiring manager must build up the courage to carry out the termination. For some positions, this may require building a consensus in the executive ranks or on the Board of Directors.

Review Previous Hires: Evaluate your previous hires. How successful have you been? Shoot straight with yourself. This is no time to look at the past with rose-colored glasses. Be brutally honest about your hiring success, because hiring success is a key factor in your overall professional success.

The bottom line: Mis-hires are likely at least half the time, in the average scenario. Mis-hires are costly, especially the higher up you go in the organization. Mis-hires waste precious time and money. Take the right approach; hire the right people the first time. Shoot for a 90 percent success rate. It is achievable—done properly.

HIRING EMPLOYEES

Question: Who hires the best employees, you or your fiercest competitor?

It's not very hard to hire mediocre employees. But you need to populate your company with people who excel. This requires finding not only people who excel but also those who fit in your company. The best-qualified person in the world for a particular job may be the worst person as far as your company is concerned. Hire someone who is a good fit, both professionally and culturally.

One of the most important functions a company has is hiring new and replacement employees. Company success depends upon the results. Executives should make sure it is done right and oversee the process, being active participants when needed. A company is defined by its people.

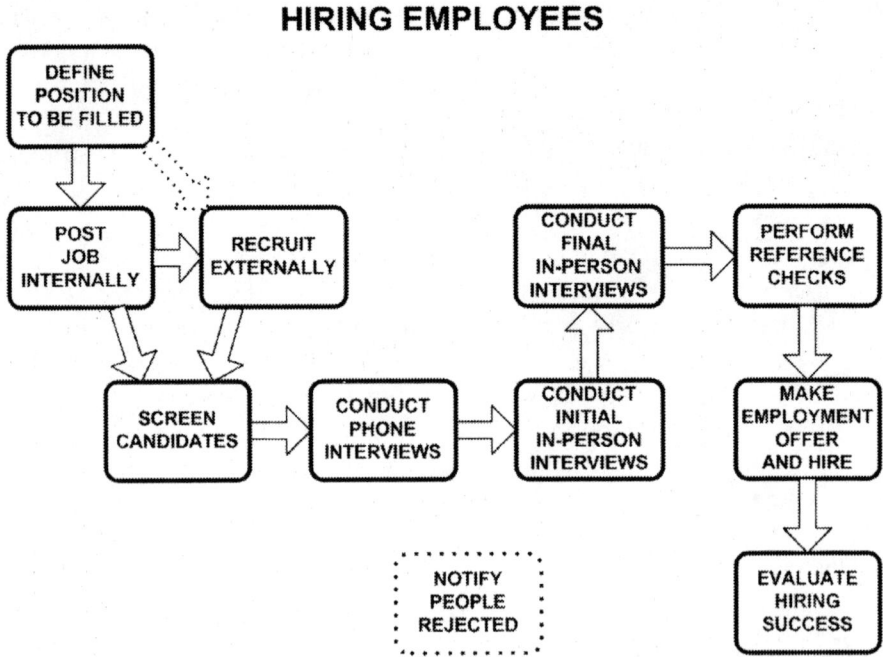

HIRING EMPLOYEES

Define Position To Be Filled: Job descriptions tend to get too long and too detailed. When they do, they can become too restrictive, too much of a straightjacket. Leave some running room for you and the candidate. It is unlikely you will find someone who perfectly matches a lengthy list of details. Stick to the required generalities: experience, achievements, skills, education, professional training, and general attitudes. Interviews can be used to determine other characteristics of a potential candidate. Distinguish between "must have" and "nice to have" attributes. Make sure everyone directly involved in the process understands the type of people being sought.

Don't forget to put down any skills that will be needed in the future for the position. If your company is planning to venture into a new area, you may need someone already experienced in that skill set, international operations, for example. Hire for the future as well as the present. Remember that the future is as early as tomorrow.

Post Job Internally: Never overlook capable in-house talent when trying to fill open positions. Someone in one position may be qualified to fill another position. Advertise the opening through internal job postings. Support an environment that allows employees to move from one position to another. An internal transfer is certainly better than losing a good employee to a competitor.

Another variation on acquiring in-house talent is to train a person in one position for movement into another position. Considering the expense of outside hires, in-house training can be quite cost effective. You have already seen the employee in action. You know his or her talents and productivity. There is less guessing to do. The likelihood of making a wrong move is much less than bringing in someone new from the outside.

Recruit Externally: If you are unable to find someone within your company to fill the position, you must look outside the company. It is possible the position you are trying to fill requires going outside the company in order to get a special type of talent never before needed in the company, or just to get a fresh viewpoint. In any case, there are a number of possible sources of new employees.

Current employees are often a good recruiting source for outside talent. A person in a profession, say, programming, is likely to know other good programmers at other companies. Offer your existing employees a finder's fee for any new hire. Also, use your own network of family, friends, and professional contacts.

Employment ads can often work, but this can be a shotgun approach. In this scenario, the hiring company must do all the resume screening. If you do not have the resources for an effective, high-volume screening process, forget employment ads.

Internet ads can sometimes bring in good employees. The web approach works two different ways. First, a company can advertise available positions through one or more Internet job posting services. Second, an employee can post his or her resume on the Web to advertise he or she is available for hire. Many sites allow this type of posting. In general, although not always the case, initial screening of candidates rests with the hiring company. Again, consider the resources you have available for screening candidates.

If you are a company just starting out or otherwise have ties to venture capitalists, use the venture capitalists' networks to find good candidates. This is especially effective if the venture capitalists have invested directly in your company. If so, they have a vested interest in helping you succeed, and good employees help a company. They want you to hire the best.

Consulting firms, those who provide contract-for-hire employees (consultants), many times will give an employer the option of hiring their consultants after a waiting period. A premium payment may be required, though. In any case, bringing in a consultant, with the option to hire after a certain period, provides a good way to evaluate on-the-job performance of a potential employee. You get to see him or her in action, for a number of months, before making any offer of employment. With the cost of hiring the wrong employee so high, the expense of starting the employee as a contractor can be, in reality, very cost effective.

If you can build a good, working relationship with high-quality employment firms, do so. A professional firm—either on a fee-for-hire arrangement or on a retainer—can do some effective screening and be well worth the expense. The more an employee search firm understands your company and your needs, the better job it can do in presenting qualified candidates.

But search firms are often prohibited by professional ethics from recruiting candidates from their client companies. This reduces, sometimes significantly, the reach of their search, especially if the search firm has many corporate clients. Make sure you know the restrictions under which your search firm is working. Ask for a list of companies on their prohibited list. Client companies will sometimes even engage a search firm infrequently just to keep them from fishing inside their company. The smaller search firms are likely to be working under less restrictive constraints, if for no other reason than they have fewer clients. Search firms are in the business to make money. Make sure they are not feeding you inferior candidates just to increase their revenue—volume over quality.

Before you even consider using search firms, decide if their fees—which can be quite hefty—are worth the expenditure. At the executive level, search firms may be the primary source for high-level candidates. On the other hand, if a company is actively engaged at all levels in an ongoing, personal recruitment of outside talent, search firms may be unnecessary for a particular position—even at the CEO level. Networking does work. Objective, personal knowledge of candidates can be powerful.

Screen Candidates: When screening candidates, decide who will do the screening, and for what. The screeners could be the hiring manager, an HR recruiter, a member of the organization particularly well versed in the professional field of the desired candidates, or an outside recruiter. When deciding who will do the initial screening, it is essential all screening personnel understand the job requirements.

It may fall to the hiring manager to do the initial screening if no one in HR has the knowledge to do an effective job of screening candidates. The best solution is for HR to screen out the obvious bad fits and pass the good or the questionable fits on to the hiring manager. The hiring manager would be well advised to help the HR recruiter learn what to look for if the recruiter does not already know.

If an outside search or consulting firm has been engaged to provide candidates, they will automatically perform a first cut screening of candidates they want to present. If they are making mistakes in their screening, let them know so they can correct their ways. If necessary, sever the relationship if they are causing you too much extra work.

A good working relationship between a search firm representative, an HR recruiter, and a hiring manager can be especially effective and efficient; if they all know each other, trust one another, and are well versed in the hiring manager's requirements and preferences. Exceptional candidates can come out of this relationship.

The primary source of information for this screening step is the resume provided by a candidate or whoever is representing him or her, such as a search firm. In the case of someone representing the candidate, the representative can be quizzed to help decide whether the candidate being presented even meets the basic requirements of the position to be filled.

All candidates making it through this screening step at least pass minimal requirements. Little time should be spent on obvious rejects. This is the killer step for most candidates.

Conduct Phone Interviews: Phone interviews are a good next step after the preceding resume review step. All candidates at this point at least meet basic position requirements. This step does not typically apply to internal candidates, unless they are remote to your office. HR can be employed in this step to talk to the candidates and get a better feel for their qualifications.

This is also a good place for the hiring manager to do some screening. For more technical positions, those where HR does not have the expertise to make a proper judgment, the hiring manager should definitely be brought on the scene. For high-level executive positions, a hiring manager or some screening executive should be engaged to start personal contact with the candidate.

A phone interview should be relatively brief, a half-hour, or so. It should verify basic requirements, what the candidate is looking for, and, most importantly, start building a picture of who the candidate really is, the person behind the resume. This interview will start to determine if there is a professional and cultural fit.

If the candidate lives in another city or state, the length of the phone interview should be increased and more information elicited about the candidate. The hiring manager is the one to handle the longer phone interviews. A long phone interview can be very cost-effective compared to interview trip expenses.

Any person passing this screening step is a promising candidate and has qualified for an initial in-person interview.

Conduct Initial In-Person Interviews: Either HR or the hiring manager should schedule the first in-person interview. HR is the obvious choice to make arrangements and coordinate the visit in complicated situations, e.g., an out-of-town candidate who will meet with more than one interviewer. But only one interview need be promised or even hinted at to the candidate when setting it up. A minimum of two hours should be reserved for this face-to-face interview. It might last even longer than that.

Normally, the hiring manager would start the in-person interview. He or she could begin somewhat informally to build rapport; but if time is limited, you might as well jump into the formal, structured interview (described later). It will start the process of really determining if there is any sort of meaningful fit for the candidate. Properly conducted, a formal interview will determine within 30 minutes if there is obviously no match.

Assuming there is the potential of a match with what the company needs and what the candidate wants, continue the formal interview as long as time permits. If several people get involved in this interview—which is more likely for a high-level position—each can possibly take a different portion of the structured interview form.

An interviewer should not let ego get in the way. Even doctors cannot always remember to ask a patient all the needed questions during an examination session. Stick to the structured interview form and take notes on the answers given and the observations made. Since the structured interview form seeks to ferret out inconsistencies, it might be better for one person to take the candidate through the whole form, or at least the portion tackled in the first in-person interview. Other interviewers could conduct less structured interviews, but ones that still probe the viability of the candidate. Unless one interviewer has the more pertinent experience in one part of the structured interview, it is still suggested the hiring manager be the one to take the candidate through the whole form, whether covered in one or several visits.

If the candidate makes it through this part of the interview process, this might be a good place to give the candidate a tour of the company premises. Either the HR recruiter or the hiring manager could conduct the tour; but for the place where the candidate will be working, the hiring manager is the obvious choice as a tour guide.

If appropriate and if the candidate is still a potential choice, general employee benefits could be described here.

Unless unavoidable, compensation should not be brought up in this step, except maybe to ask the candidate what he or she expects. Until all candidates have been evaluated, no compensation offers should be put forth.

Since it is harder to schedule high-level executive candidates for interviews and since their position is so important, the more company people who can be brought in for this first face-to-face interview, the better. An executive interview should be neither unstructured nor superficial. Find out as much as you can about the candidate and his or her capabilities while you have the candidate's undivided attention. Milk the interview for all it is worth.

Candidates that make it through this step are in the playoffs.

Conduct Final In-Person Interviews: After reviewing the qualifications of all candidates who made it through the first in-person interview visit, the final set of candidates should be selected and invited back to a follow-on visit of in-person interviewing.

If the formal, structured interview form was not completed earlier, it should be completed here. Again, the hiring manager should be the one taking the candidate through the structured form, preferably. And again, if we are talking about an executive position, the more people involved in the interviewing, the better. It would be good for the other executives to get involved, especially those the candidate will be working with closely. Hiring executives is serious business. Better safe than sorry.

[If executive mis-hires exceed 10 percent, the hiring process is flawed.]

The second in-person interview could be used to explore technical and professional qualifications in depth. This need not be the hiring manager. Somebody else on the staff could be a better choice for this interview. For a lower-level position, this interview could be done on the same day as the first. In fact, a second visit may not be required; this is at the discretion of the hiring manager.

Perform Reference Checks: Preliminary reference checks, meaning simple requests to verify information provided by the candidate or the candidate's representative—education, dates of employment, etc.—can be performed by the HR recruiter. For in-depth reference checks, the job should fall to the hiring manager who conducted the in-depth structured interview. Only he or she will be privy to all the pertinent information, and the hiring manager would have the most in-depth understanding of the candidate. He or she will have spent the most time with the candidate.

In-depth reference checks may or may not be allowed by previous employers. Many companies refuse to allow them because of potential legal ramifications. Usually, if the candidate is still employed by a previous employer, the candidate will not want you to talk to them—for obvious reasons.

Assuming the candidate provides some references you can check or you can come up with some on your own, you are essentially looking for an evaluation of the candidate by someone who has worked with the candidate or knows him or her in some other capacity. Remember, though, any references provided by the candidate are likely to be good ones—not necessarily ones to give you a balanced evaluation. Bias may be involved or there might be some other agenda in play.

Ask probing questions. Verify qualifications, experience, and achievements. Ask for opinions. Ask for reasons for the opinions held. Try to uncover any snow jobs. Find out the true relationship between the candidate and the reference. Explain what you expect of the candidate and see if the person being talked to feels the candidate is right for the job.

This is your last formal step for uncovering information about the candidate.

Make Employment Offer and Hire: You have determined your final candidates at this point in the process. All interviewers should pool their information, evaluations, and opinions. Choose your top candidate.

Once the decision has been made, the next step is to decide on compensation, benefits, and terms of employment. If salary negotiations are in order, the hiring manager will need to be on the front line in order to make final decisions. In some cases of limited authority, the hiring manager may need to get higher approval for a salary exceeding what has been authorized.

In any event, the hiring manager will probably make the first offer over the phone. As soon as a final salary has been agreed to, a formal written offer should be made that satisfies all HR and legal requirements.

If the top candidate refuses all offers and counteroffers, move down to the second best candidate and repeat the process. If, for whatever reason, no desired candidate can be hired; the search will have to be reopened and started from the beginning. Do not settle for a less-than-capable candidate. Remember, you want a company staffed by the best people so you can achieve the best results for owners, partners, stockholders, and current staff.

Notify People Rejected: Follow normal HR and legally approved procedures, as necessary, and formally notify all non-selected candidates. Don't keep them in a state of suspense any longer than you have to. Let them get on with their lives and other options.

If you have any obvious non-matches, let them know ASAP. As long as a candidate is still a "possible," don't issue a formal rejection. Keep your options open.

Note: In times of economic downturns, there may be so many candidates that it is impractical to notify all rejects. You should at least notify those you have been in touch with on a personal basis—meaning something beyond automatic email confirmations of resume receipt. Canned responses to application submissions can simply state that further contact will only happen for those candidates you are interested in.

Evaluate Hiring Success: Continually gather information about the company's success in hiring, yours in particular. That means doing periodic follow-up on the success of new-hires on the job. Track employee exits and the reasons for them. Periodically review results and determine where improvements in the process can be made. Also, address the sticky situation of hiring managers being less than successful in their hiring performance.

You want good gatekeepers to keep out non-performers.

STRUCTURED INTERVIEW

The primary tool for an effective structured interview is a formal interview form that guides the interviewer through all the areas that need to be covered. Each executive should have an interview form tailored or adaptable to the types of positions for which he or she normally interviews. As an example, a Chief Information Officer could have an interview form that covers anyone from executive to programmer, manager to worker. When interviewing some prospective employee, the hiring manager would simply skip those sections that do not apply. A versatile form will handle anyone up to the CEO level. Remember, it is not uncommon for a lower-level executive to interview candidates for higher-level positions.

Whether an executive uses a single, comprehensive interview form or has different ones tailored to specialized positions, the idea is to provide a structured framework for conducting interviews. Further, the form should be comprehensive enough and the interview spaced over a long enough period that the true nature of the candidate can be determined and any inconsistencies ferreted out. The implication is that enough time be spent with the interviewee, perhaps, over several sessions, to get a good reading on the candidate's nature and capabilities. Unless the position is relatively unimportant—and the question is whether any position is unimportant—a significant amount of time should be spent with the potential employee.

In the final stages of selection, a minimum of two hours should be spent by the hiring manager in interviewing the candidate. For more important positions, four to six hours ought to be spent in formal interview sessions, at a minimum. This gives time for the interviewer to build rapport with the candidate and to let the real person behind the candidate make his or her appearance. Time erodes facades. Assuming you are hiring someone you expect to occupy a position for months or even years, a few extra hours getting to know the person is not a bad investment. You need to be as certain as you can that there is a match between person, position, company, and company culture.

The same principles apply to external hires and internal transfers or promotions. The primary difference might be a shortening of the interview time if the candidate is already well known by the interviewer. A word of warning, though: A thorough interview just might uncover some falsely held assumptions about an internal candidate. You may not know the person as well as you thought you did. A structured interview can force you to go into areas you never explored before. You might uncover either a better or worse fit than you imagined.

Another application of a structured interview is the situation where a manager is newly placed in charge of a department or division within his or her company. The formal interview—maybe conducted over a number of days at times convenient to both participants—can be used to learn more about your new subordinates. Since you already employ the subordinate, you can freely give information and beliefs as well as fish for them. It is a great way to bond with your new subordinates. Rapport can be enhanced. They get to know you and you get to know them. The subordinates can reveal things about themselves you would never uncover in day-to-day conversations. The time is time well spent—a great investment in your organization's well being.

Considering that the cost of hiring the wrong person is out of sight, time used to develop structured interview forms is an excellent investment. Questions should be a blend of specific and open-ended questions, with a preference given to the latter. You want to give the candidate a chance to talk. Explore some issues from several different angles. Give the potential employee a chance to prove the validity of answers to previous questions, from different viewpoints. The point is not to trick the interviewee, but to probe the substance of key subjects. Strip away the superficial and get to the bedrock. The candidate may even experience some self-discovery.

For the most part, specific questions will not be presented in this section of the book, but general topics will. A good starting point is to ask what kind of position the candidate seeks and what kind work he or she likes best. To make the candidate more at ease, delve into formal education, starting with high school, if you like, and continuing through all college degrees. Find out schools attended, major courses of study, grades, honors, and degrees pursued and earned. Ask which courses were liked best. Ask the same for activities. Question the candidate about his or her high and low points while attending each school. Find out the person's goals coming out of each school. Ask about jobs worked while in school, both full- and part-time.

Finding out a person's attitude about education can give you insight into the real person. Continue the investigation by probing the candidate's pursuit of professional training. Find out the type of training (subjects) received and the candidate's opinion on various ways of learning (formal classes, seminars, tapes, self-study, and hands-on). Ask the person's preferred way to learn. Check into the person's reading habits.

Next, explore the candidate's work history, from most recent through pertinent past. For a previous position, determine the following: starting expectations (vs. reality encountered), working conditions after coming onboard, responsibilities, hours worked, major challenges, successes, failures, what was enjoyable (vs. not enjoyable), major areas of growth, reasons for leaving, supervisors' strengths and weaknesses, and what the supervisors felt about the candidate. What would the candidate's assistants say his or her weaknesses were?

See what the candidate's future plans and goals are for this next job. Ask what the ideal position would be like and why. Ask how the offered position squares with the ideal position. Find out what the candidate's expectations are of the people around him or her, from a 360-degree viewpoint, including internal and external clients.

Explore the interviewee's accomplishments: greatest successes and failures, what was learned from them, and how they were handled. Have the candidate elaborate on major projects and the normal role performed.

Look into the management roles and positions of leadership held at previous companies. Include task force assignments. Ask for the number and types of employees supervised. Find out how problem employees were handled, as well as terminations. Explore the candidate's leadership in action: vision and its development in the previous job, vision for the sought after position, how change has been orchestrated, nature of followship (by subordinates and peers), building of teams, maintaining team effectiveness, and handling team problems.

Next, see what the candidate's management philosophy is. Does he or she micro-manage, or is authority delegated along with responsibility? What are the perceived roles of supervisor, assistant, and subordinate? How are decisions arrived at? What are the views on company vs. departmental loyalty? How often should meetings be conducted, and in what manner? How should information be disseminated at all levels in the organization, and in which direction? What is the candidate's experience on management reporting: methods, subject matter, and audience?

What about change? How should it work and who should be involved? What experience does the candidate have in implementing change?

How are goals established by the candidate, how are they communicated, and how is achievement monitored? How should performance measurement be implemented and who is accountable for what? What about 360-degree evaluations? Which criticisms are hardest for the interviewee to accept? What would the typical subordinate consider the candidate's strengths and weaknesses to be?

Then delve into the interviewee's intellectual competencies by asking for a description of learning ability, analytical skills, judgment, and decision-making. Ask in-depth questions about decision-making: best decisions, worst decisions, hardest decisions, and general approach to reaching a decision. What about ability to conceptualize? Is the candidate most comfortable with long-term or short-term issues; concrete or abstract concepts; or the big picture or details?

What about creativity? Ask for examples. See if the candidate is more of a visionary or more of an implementer. What about strategic planning? Does he or she stay up on developments in the industry or profession? What has been the candidate's experience in strategic planning, including successes and failures? Where is the industry headed?

Get the candidate to describe and evaluate other professional competencies: oral communication, written communication, interpersonal skills, corporate political savvy, teaching experience, purchasing of goods and services, and negotiating skills.

Look into the interviewee's skills at customer relations: client partnerships, diagnosing customer needs, customer acquisition, and contract negotiations. Ask what the clients and the candidate's own management would consider his or her strengths and weaknesses in customer relations.

Delve into the candidate's viewpoint on diversity in the workplace, including giving examples of confronting discrimination and prejudice. Have any employment charges (EEOC, sexual harassment, etc.) been brought successfully against the candidate?

Next, get the candidate to elaborate on his or her personal characteristics: perfection vs. speed, team vs. star player, visionary vs. pragmatist, progressive vs. conservative, and risk vs. cautious orientation. Which risks have worked out and which have not? Is the interviewee willing to stand up to the boss? What is the candidate's attitude toward technology? How literate or illiterate is he or she with computers and other technology? What about personal integrity, what is the candidate's experience on taking courageous but unpopular stands?

Ask about experience with personal initiative. What initiatives would the candidate pursue in the first weeks on the job? What obstacles have been faced in the past and how have they been overcome? Does the candidate work best initiating multiple tasks or just working with a few? How much supervision is needed or wanted? Does he or she ask for permission first or ask for forgiveness afterward? What are the candidate's skills at persuasion, organizing, and planning? Are deadlines normally hit or missed?

What about assertiveness, including successes and failures? Ask the candidate to describe how he or she has raised the bar for self and others? Explore motivation level and causes of motivation and de-motivation? What are the person's self-ratings in the area of enthusiasm and charisma? Which people or things have had the most influence on the candidate's career, and why? How does the person react to stress? What causes stress and what brings out anger?

What are the candidate's most favorite and least favorite: tasks, attitudes of self and others, and behaviors of self and others?

Some other attitudes to explore are feelings about the following: change, chaos, travel, overtime, working from home, relocation, documentation, quality assurance, standards adherence, status reporting, employee training, and self-training.

Now the rubber really hits the road. Explore the candidate's self-appraisal some more: How does he or she feel about his or her own self? What are the areas of strength and the areas for improvement? How has he or she changed in recent years? What organizational changes are easiest to accept? Hardest? Is the candidate considered by others to be stubborn or inflexible? What kind of first impression does the candidate typically expect to make on others? Does he or she have a sense of humor? What kind of business vs. personal balance exists in the candidate's life?

Then ask the candidate to look back on his or her whole career and to comment on the most successful jobs, the least successful jobs, the biggest challenges faced and overcome, and what he or she is most proud of professionally.

Next, develop a set of questions to probe the technical or professional expertise needed to handle the position being offered. This will vary between professions.

Finally, close with questions about these: expected length of stay with the company, availability for being hired, salary expectations, relocation expectations, and any other expectations. Ask for any additional points the candidate would like to make or any questions that need to be answered. You might even ask how the candidate feels about the interview just conducted. Then close with an agreement on what the next step is.

Never give candidates or their representatives any copies of the interview questions! You do not want a candidate to rehearse or be coached on the answers. You want spontaneous responses.

It is strongly suggested you have your interview form thoroughly reviewed by an HR specialist to determine if there are any questions that could cause legal problems. Federal, state, and local regulations that you are not aware of could get you into trouble.

Remember that an interview is some of the most important time you can spend with someone. Hiring people or transferring them into new positions can be a success or a failure. Make sure there is a fit and that the candidate is qualified. A company runs on its people. Your own success depends upon them.

NEW HIRE PRODUCTIVITY

When a new employee is brought onboard, that person should not be placed in a "sink or swim" setting. It is counterproductive for a company to ask new employees to fend for themselves without any support. The logical approach is to bring them up to speed as soon as possible. This means being supportive, both morally and materially.

NEW HIRE PRODUCTIVITY

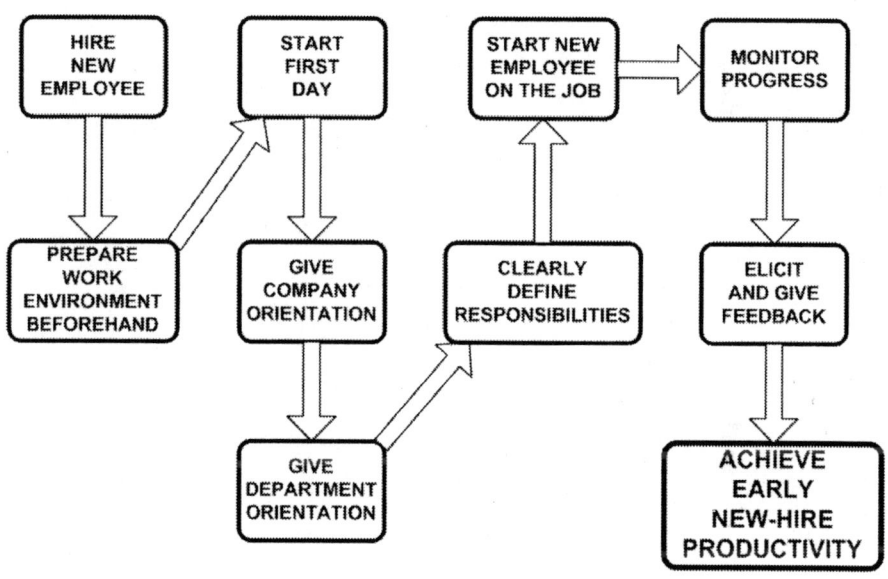

Before the new employee's first day, the hiring manager and HR need to work together to prepare for the employee's first day. Assign a desk. Procure the necessary personal computer and software, if applicable. Have the computer configured and ready to run as soon as the employee arrives on the scene, including setting up appropriate network access. Get the phone(s) configured for immediate use. Obtain any other necessary supplies and materials.

Briefing the new hire is essential. A formal new-hire orientation is a good thing. This includes going down a checklist to make sure the new employee is thoroughly briefed about the company, its policies, its vision, its role in the business world, and specifics about the hiring department and its place in the company.

One of the first things that must be communicated clearly to the new hire is his or her job description. What are the duties and responsibilities that have been assigned? What is the initial project he or she is to work on? What is the project all about? Who are the other team members on the project? What other groups are involved? What are his or her specific responsibilities for the project? The new employee should have a clear understanding of what he or she is to do.

Put the new employee to work, but do not leave that person to cope alone. Provide ongoing attention and support, especially in the early days on the job. Monitor the new hire's progress and give constructive feedback. Elicit feedback from the employee to see how things are going. Make him or her feel like a valuable member of the team.

It is going to take awhile for a new employee to become fully productive. It just makes good business sense to make productivity happen as soon as possible. Lost time in this case is lost money!

34

Keeping Employees

After you get your employees, you want to keep them. If you went through the proper hiring process, you got good employees. But it takes some time before they become truly valuable to your company. After a year or two, your investment in an employee is quite huge. Don't throw it away. Keep your employees. They will be expensive to replace if they leave.

EMPLOYEES—KEEPING THEM

Question: Are your competitors or some other business concerns likely to steal your best performers?

It is a common belief that customers are the most important factor in business; but how can you serve without a server, the employee. Assuming you have a good product or service, the key to the organization's success is a good cadre of employees. Without them, you cannot carry out the business functions necessary to deliver a product or service to the customer. Even a one-person consultant company requires at least one employee, the consultant. He or she had better be good at getting along with customers.

Salaries: The management team often lives in a fantasy world where it is taken as a religious commandment, an irrefutable fact of life, that salaries must be kept at a minimum, where no one employee is paid significantly more than another in the same type of job. That is wrong!

Does it not make sense to pay a highly skilled professional double the salary of a less productive, inexperienced person? If the highly skilled professional turns out three or four times the work of the less capable person, do you not come out ahead paying the better employee twice the salary? Do the math! Yet, the accounting types are some of the biggest opponents of disparities in pay. They seem to forget simple profit and loss principles, their area of expertise. Go with the model that produces the greatest return.

Other Monetary Incentives: In addition to pay, other monetary incentives are possible motivators: profit sharing, stock options, employee stock purchase plans, bonuses, raises, medical benefits, etc. There are many tried and true ways to reward employees with financial incentives. But money is not enough.

Motivations: People are different. They have many different likes and dislikes. What motivates one person is a de-motivator to the next. You must allow for different personalities and work styles. Diversity training may be called for, at all levels in the corporation—that includes the executive suite. Diversity training helps build awareness and tolerance.

You must offer employees stimulating and challenging assignments. Since people are different and have different motivators, place people in situations that fit the individual. An assignment could be challenging to one person and totally boring to another. Use assignments to help people grow. Encourage them to develop themselves. Coach them into greatness.

Supportive Environment: Employees want to work in a supportive business atmosphere. A company's culture is very important. The employee must feel comfortably "at home" when at work. Remember, culture is largely driven by the company's leaders. They must infuse a supportive environment throughout the corporation.

Employer Loyalty: For many years, companies demanded worker loyalty; but in the fast pace of today's workplace and with so much emphasis on the bottom line, companies have destroyed that bond. There have been too many layoffs by companies and bosses who supposedly were advocates of employment without layoffs. The trust relationship has been destroyed. Instead of a buyers' market (employers), it can be a sellers' market (employees). Steadfast loyalty has gone down the tube. Employees have been taught to have a "me first" attitude. The company can't be counted on.

It is now up to the company to make employees want to stay. That means commitment on both sides. It must be a win-win relationship. Most employees will bend over backwards to help and support their employer. They just need to feel appreciated and be given meaningful work.

Meaningful Work: Meaningful work translates into giving the worker the message that he or she is making a real contribution to the business. *Employee* loyalty and satisfaction are the first steps in *customer* loyalty and satisfaction. Customer relations are based upon good employees. Keeping employees happy helps keep customers happy. The server must get enjoyment from serving the served.

Upbeat Work Environment: Never discount the appearance of the workplace itself. A drab looking work environment cannot but help lower morale. A good atmosphere supports a good attitude. A cheerful atmosphere leads to cheerful employees.

Keep in mind that when employees start to leave a company, the first to leave are the best and the brightest. They are the most marketable. They know enough to seek better surroundings. They realize they do not have to put up with a drab environment.

DELEGATE DOWNWARD

Part of keeping an employee is showing him or her you have trust enough to delegate authority along with responsibility. Issues should be handled at the lowest possible level in the organization. Let the subordinate run with the ball. This places problem solving at the level where the problem is best understood. The person with his or her ear closest to the ground has the best understanding of the situation and normally is the person best equipped to handle it.

Executives should never assume they know it all and are the best equipped to handle all issues. It is likely that some subordinate will be more knowledgeable, particularly if the issue is in the area in which the subordinate works and has his or her expertise.

Many companies talk about pushing down authority to lower levels. Most employees assume it is just talk, that all they get is responsibility and accountability—but no authority. So, give them authority commensurate with their responsibility. Walk the talk.

Build an employee-driven company. Push decision-making down as far as it makes sense. This makes the people accountable and responsible for their actions. Reward them when they do well and act in the company's best interests. They will have an attitude of ownership in the bottom line. They and the company will perform better.

EMPLOYEE PAY

There are many ways to value an employee: customer satisfaction, interpersonal skills, ability to follow orders, contribution to the bottom line, optimism, cheerfulness, effectiveness, etc. Too often, though, pay rates are set according to rigid guidelines. The guidelines do not reflect the worth of an employee. To put this in perspective, forget the human side of the equation and think of the employee as a machine. This may seem heartless, but listen for a moment.

What if you were buying a machine? One of the first things a company considers is the payback that piece of machinery provides over its lifespan. For example, assume a machine life of two years with proper maintenance. Next, assume machine X has a purchase price of $1000. Now consider that machine Y has the same productive life but will cost $2000, which is double the cost of X. In this example, both X and Y are assumed to have comparable maintenance costs. However, machine Y can produce at three times the rate of machine X. Machine Y costs 200 percent but produces 300 percent. Given that both machines will manufacture products providing revenue many times their original cost over their productive life, which machine would you buy? You would choose machine Y, of course.

Now change the setting. Employees X, Y, and Z are each paid the same, $50,000 a year, not counting benefits. All three are medium performers. Employee S (for Superior) can outperform X, Y, and Z put together, plus turn out a higher quality product. Rather than being paid three times what either of the others is paid, the more likely scenario is a pay premium of maybe 50 percent over just one of the others—and even that percentage might be optimistic.

If you want a quality product in a shorter length of time, which employee would you prefer working on your project? The answer is obvious, unless the whole objective is to train the less capable employee. But let's assume all four employees are experienced.

Look at this from a return on investment (ROI) perspective. It makes perfect sense to pay the superior performer twice that of one of the lesser performers. Assuming three times the productivity with a higher quality result, ROI certainly justifies twice the pay for the superior performer. If a competitor decides to go after this superior performer, the long-run cost of losing that employee could be astronomical. It costs a bundle to get a new employee up to speed, particularly to the level of being highly skilled and very knowledgeable about the company and its product (or service).

The lesson: Pay superior employees more than the market rate. If you get the right employee and can hold onto him or her, the payback more than justifies the cost. Use your calculator instead of your emotions. High pay for superior performers can be relatively inexpensive. Average pay for mediocre people can be expensive in comparison.

EMPLOYEE STOCK OWNERSHIP

Employee stock ownership can take several different forms:

Executive Investment: Incoming executives might purchase stock in a new company simply because they feel it is a good investment. They are about to invest their professional life, which means they believe in the company and what they can make it into. Depending upon the size of their investment, they may be betting the farm. This can happen, for example, when forming a new company.

Stock Options: Stock option plans are another way to enhance employee interest in the results of operations. Stock option plans, when they start reaching a meaningful size for a given employee, become golden handcuffs for employee retention purposes. When additional stock options are given to good employees as rewards for outstanding performance, the result is the golden handcuffs becoming even more binding.

But stock options can have a negative effect in several different ways. If market conditions, like the recent dot.com meltdown, make stock options meaningless, the employee might look upon the options in a negative light. All the efforts put into making the company more profitable are suddenly lost because of stock market ups and downs. The employee suffers huge losses financially. Belief in stock options takes a beating. In retrospect, hard cash rewards would have been better.

In the worst case, the employee starts living beyond his or her means, building up huge debts in expectation of huge rewards when the stock is sold or the stock options are exercised. Exercising stock options but keeping the stock can result in huge tax obligations that cannot be met when the stock price plunges later. Bankruptcy may be just around the corner for the employee.

Vesting schedules for stock options, when spread over many years, become less than meaningful. Things move very fast in today's economy. The ability to exercise options several years down the road is a bird in the bush. If a good job offer comes along while the company's stock price is low, the employee is out the door. The golden handcuffs have become clay, easily cracked open.

Perceived fairness in the awarding of stock options plays a big part in the effectiveness of the stock options program. When stock options are awarded to all team members as a reward for successful team efforts, team building is enhanced and there is a perception of fairness—at least within the team. Outside the team is another matter.

When stock options are awarded to star players, particularly those perceived to be "pets" of the executives, resentment can take place. If the other players feel the award was not fully justified, the other players can get bent all out of shape. The star player has positive feelings about the company. The other players—who are more numerous—have negative feelings. Their productivity can fall. The negative impact of the award can be greater than the positive impact.

An emphasis on star players rather than team players can destroy the mortar holding teams together. You, of course, want to reward the best players more, but it is a careful balancing act. Give the best players recognition, but be generous in the treatment of other players. Remember that people often play up to the expectations of those in control. Who is most likely to succeed, the one being praised or the one being torn down? It is a mind game. Perception is reality.

Fairness is key. Generally, fellow employees know the best performers, perhaps even better than their managers. There will be more acceptance of rewards fairly given than those based on favoritism. Be objective in making rewards. Reward the best performers but still encourage the less productive people to perform at their best. Be fair AND supportive.

Many companies try to keep the fact of stock option grants and the names of the grantees secret. The assumption is that there will be no resentment from those not receiving the awards because they are not even aware of it. Wrong! People talk. If employees are being granted stock options, the word will get out, maybe not completely or even accurately, but it will get out. Resentment will rear its ugly head.

If a company is going to make stock option awards, everyone should be made aware they are being made. The objective would be to place a carrot before all the employees to encourage good performance. Team awards can help deflect resentment against particular employees. The amount of the awards for each individual need not be disclosed, but hiding the very fact people are getting awards can be counterproductive. Promotions are published. It may be best to announce special stock option awards as an incentive measure. Why is this so different from other awards, such as employee of the month or best performer on a shift? The other employees have less trouble over awards fairly given.

Following the dot.com meltdown, stock options are much less appealing than before. The vagaries of the stock market can have a chilling effect on stock awards. Expensing of options when they are granted is being pushed in some sectors. So, weigh all the factors. Be very careful how stock plans are designed and administered. Concentrate on the positive aspects and mitigate potential negative effects. It is suggested that some granting of stock options be made in addition to more immediate awards, such as bonuses and pay raises.

Stock Purchase Plans: Employee stock purchase plans are another item in the cafeteria of employee benefits. Unlike stock option plans, there is a much lower possibility of resentment coming from employees who purchase stock with their own money. Whereas stock option awards are done at the whim of management, stock purchases are the choice of the employee. All decisions rest with the employee, which makes it much harder to shift blame.

Stock purchase plans should offer stock to the employee at a favorable discount, e.g., applied to the lower of the starting and ending prices of the stock over the applicable stock purchase period. That period might be six months. A longer (six months) rather than a shorter (three months) period helps alleviate problems in stock price fluctuation leading to dips in stock prices. Whether a stock's low price occurs at the beginning or the end of the period, the employee gets the lower reference point. If the stock price generally rises over time, the employee cannot help but win.

There should be limits on the amount of pay that can be deducted for stock per paycheck and limits on how often the deductions can be changed—but do not make the restrictions too severe. Give the employees some freedom in the matter. After all, they are betting their own money on the company's performance.

From an investment point of view, too much concentration by an employee on his or her company's stock violates the principle of diversification in investments. It is very dangerous to have all your eggs in one basket. If the basket gets knocked out of your hands, the eggs will get broken. Broken eggs aren't worth much.

All other things being equal, an employee's interest or ownership in a company's stock is a positive influence. It helps encourage good performance. Self-interest is involved. But the interest can go south if conditions change to the point that resentment raises its head. A balance between immediate reward and potential future reward is essential. The positives and negatives must be clearly analyzed in light of the current situation and expected conditions down the road. The company should clearly communicate potential problems in order to put the monkey on the employee's back as much as possible.

35

Developing Subordinates

DEVELOPMENT

An executive has a responsibility to see that people below him or her in the organization carry out their responsibilities satisfactorily. The subordinates represent a resource over which the executive has stewardship. Good stewardship of a business resource means getting the best performance possible from the asset.

Employees are people, and people can improve. Maintaining status quo in regard to employee performance is a misuse of one of the most valuable, if not the most valuable, resources a company has—its employees.

Determining Needs: Developing subordinates starts with determining their developmental needs. The executive, or applicable manager, must make it a point to understand a subordinate's strengths and weaknesses. Observation is a prerequisite to this determination. Performance reviews are a formal requirement, but the messages delivered in reviews should not carry any surprises for the employee. If they do, the supervisor has failed to give timely feedback between reviews. Feedback, to be useful, should be given promptly at the time of the referenced action, not weeks or months later.

Working on Weaknesses or Strengths: One school of thought says to work on people's weaknesses, i.e., eliminate weaknesses, rather than enhance strengths. It certainly makes sense to correct weaknesses. However, unless the weakness is critical to job performance, perhaps it is best to give very little attention to the weakness. Instead, the best payback could come from strengthening the strong points. If the player has the skills to be a good quarterback, helping him become a great quarterback would benefit the team the most. You should not spend time helping the quarterback become a good kicker.

Right Position: But the question remains, do you have the employee in the right position to start with? If the person is good at finance but not sales, then why spend time developing his or her sales skills. The answer seems obvious, put the person in finance and enhance his or her financial skills. You want the individual in a position where he or she can do the most good. If the person has no natural ability with numbers or math, why waste time on financial training?

Necessary Understanding: An aside for the moment: It does make sense to provide introductory training to develop awareness, understanding, and appreciation for topics for which the person, say, an executive, has just a smattering of knowledge but no natural ability. Continuing with executives, they need to understand computers, software, communications, and networks in general terms in order to get along responsibly in business. But detailed knowledge and skills belong to the IT division in this case. The CFO need not know network server administration. Even the CTO doesn't need that skill. The CTO should hire a skilled network administrator to handle that function. The CTO's job is leading and managing, not administering servers.

It also makes sense to give rising executives and managers experience in different divisions of the company. But it does not make sense to put them in positions for which they have no aptitude and where they will perform badly—just so they can get some experience. We have different professions for a reason. Everyone cannot do everything.

Unnecessary Skill Building: Returning to the main premise, you should not waste time and expense on building skills for which the person has no inclination or talent. Consider the network administrator again. If the administrator has a tough time getting along with people, use someone else in the network department to interface with users. Some people are technically oriented and some are people oriented. The fortunate people are both.

Forget those standard performance metrics—usually subjective, anyway—that you attempt to apply across the board to a whole department. Tailor performance objectives to specific job responsibilities. Assign responsibilities and positions to people who can best handle them, then enhance the requisite skills. Payback will be greater.

Concentrating on Best Employees: Now to a more controversial subject, concentrating your development efforts (money and time) on your best employees. This, of course, results in neglecting your under-performers. It violates the rule of spending most of your time on your problem people. Maybe you should just get rid of the problem people. But the question of fairness comes up. Why shouldn't you treat all employees the same? Why not, for example, spend an equal number of dollars training each person in the department, adding to his or her skill sets?

Maybe, just maybe, it makes more business sense to concentrate on enhancing the performance of the best employees. Enhance their strong points, but spend little time on their weak points—unless the weak points are seriously detrimental to the individual's overall job performance. Spending $2000 on training the expert to be an even better expert may bring a higher return than spending $2000 on the under-performer.

This is a complicated and emotional issue. There are many scenarios. What happens to team spirit and cohesiveness? Will not resentment build up from the underprivileged? Morale could suffer.

Each situation is going to have to be examined in its own context and framed properly, maybe as an acknowledged reward for exceptional behavior. Even a quarterback needs a team surrounding him. Without team cooperation, there is no scoring. Just be careful how the whole thing is handled.

Manager Time and Budget: Regardless of the approach taken, coaching and training are needed. Coaching means manager time. Training means a training budget, and training is usually money spent wisely, unless taken to the extreme.

One of the most important aids to employee development and well-being is personal time spent by the boss with the subordinate, one on one. This kind of time builds solid, productive relationships. It builds followship. Person-to-person time is invaluable. It should be used to praise and encourage. It should also be used to provide constructive feedback. It should result in improved performance.

Develop your people.

COACHING

The majority of executives are very poor coaches. Perhaps, it is because they get so caught up in their everyday pressures they forget the need to coach their subordinates to greatness. The executives may feel development is the responsibility of the subordinates themselves. On the other hand, executives may avoid coaching activities because they feel inadequate to the job. It takes a combination of being supportively critical and being sensitive to the feelings, needs, and deficiencies of the employee. Good coaches are not found on every street corner.

Good coaching starts with good interpersonal skills; so, if you are a good executive, you probably already have this set of skills. Now apply it to coaching. For coaching to work, the coach must be viewed by the trainee as being trustworthy and caring, including being sensitive to the employee's shortcomings. To understand the employee's needs requires awareness of an employee's performance, and that requires perceptive observation. You have to know the person being coached. You have to be patient while guiding the employee through improvement exercises.

The coach and the trainee must have a partnership arrangement. Each must be properly accepting of the responsibilities of the other. The coach is the authoritative source for knowledge and techniques. The person being coached must bury pride and allow the coach to provide constructive criticism. This means being willing to accept the fact of having shortcomings that need to be addressed. But it is not a one-way street. The coach must actively listen to the employee during training, plus be willing to correct any misconceptions about the person being coached. Feedback is needed in both directions. The partnership includes the trainee's willingness to follow up on the instruction, to be proactive in making improvements in performance.

Both coach and trainee must have a positive attitude about the whole process. Each must believe in the process—emotionally and actively. Each must be committed to the effort.

Now, let's shift gears a moment. In the preceding discussion, the coach was a superior and the trainee was a subordinate. Reverse the situation. A good executive is open to coaching by a subordinate who has greater expertise in some area. All things considered, a superior is typically more of a generalist, while the subordinate is more of a specialist. The superior should put his or her ego aside and admit shortcomings and blind spots. There is nothing wrong in being coached by an expert lower in the organizational tree. You can even coach your boss. You and your peers can coach each other. Learn from anybody who can teach you.

Therefore, coach and be coached.

MENTORING

Some leading executives feel mentoring is a waste of time and can simply result in a person becoming someone he or she is not, just an imitator of the mentor. But that stance reflects a lack of true understanding of what mentoring is all about. Gifted bosses are gifted mentors.

A mentor is someone who acts as a wise and loyal advisor. To mentor means to be a teacher and a coach. If a leader does not coach followers, then the wrong person is leading. A mentor cares about the person being coached and takes a personal interest in the protégé, the person being guided in the furtherance of his or her career.

To be a guide, the mentor must have an influence on the one being led. There must be trust and mutual respect. Both must listen and respond. Both must take due consideration of the other's feelings. The mentor, because of the inherent responsibility of being the influencer, must lead by example. The mentor is a role model and must accept the responsibility that goes with it.

A mentor is in there during wins and losses. It is not a one-time affair of short duration. Mentoring means investing time over the long haul. The ultimate mentoring relationship does not require both parties to be employees of the same organization. Although mentoring between professionals is likely to begin while both are in the same company, it need not end when one of the two leaves the company. Even though the number of encounters may drop, they can continue at critical junctures in the life of the one being mentored. The relationship can last for years.

The good mentor, one who really cares, is not concerned about any personal benefits accruing from the mentoring effort—other than the satisfaction of guiding the protégé into the professional growth of which he or she is capable. The analogy is the teacher who watches a student grow and develop, one of the greatest joys of teaching.

The ultimate payback to mentoring comes when the mentored person reaches the point where he or she becomes a mentor to someone else.

PROMOTING FROM WITHIN

It is not a foregone conclusion that the best new leadership must come from outside the company. Many of the most successful companies have developed their leaders from within their own ranks. Good leaders can come from inside the organization. People can be developed and then enticed to stay in the company.

If the company has the right atmosphere and treats its people right, they will grow, develop, and stay with the company. You know more about your current employees than someone coming in off the street. Look for the gems in your own backyard. There could be some real diamonds.

Consider yourself. If you have continued to develop over the years and have not retired in place, you should be at your professional prime. You were not always the skilled professional you are now. You learned and trained. You grew. Why can't that be true for your own employees?

Always having to go outside the company to get the best people may, in fact, be an indication there is a management problem within the company. If a company grows, new people will be needed, of course. But ignoring the possibility of developing and promoting internal staff is a big mistake. Current employees know the ropes. They know the company and its products. They can be productive immediately. That is not the case with new employees. It takes time to bring them up to speed.

In short, keep your internal staff in mind for new positions. Realize they can grow. Help them grow. Don't let your familiarity breed contempt. A prophet CAN have honor in his or her own house. Take off the blinders and be objective.

DIAGONAL PROMOTIONS

By definition, a promotion means moving up in pay AND responsibility. A vertical promotion typically involves moving directly up the organizational ladder in your own division. You take your boss's position. However, you could be promoted to a similar position in another division. Either way can be limiting in several ways. First, it may be awhile before your boss or another superior vacates his or her position. Second, moving up the corporate ladder in this fashion sometimes merely reinforces your existing skills and knowledge—unless the new position has a myriad of functions and breadth to them. There is another possibility.

Think in terms of diagonal promotions. If an organization wants to develop well-rounded leaders, it needs to promote with the idea of broadening their experience and increasing their toolbox of skills. Therefore, it is often better to promote a person into a position requiring different skills and having different areas of responsibility, such as: new functions, new product lines, new locations (e.g., overseas), new divisions, new markets, new cultures, etc. Of course, the person must have the requisite talents—not necessarily skills—to successfully fill the position. Skills can be learned.

One result of such a move is increased breadth in the executive. Both the individual and the company benefit from this. Another result is that there is more opportunity for advancement if there are more paths for moving up. There is more hope for the ambitious leader. Finally, barriers in the company are torn down. Diversity and its acceptance are the results. There is cross-fertilization. People get to know each other. Networking increases. There is a common community.

EMPLOYEE INTERDEPARTMENTAL MOVES

As new opportunities arise within the company, employees should be allowed to move to the new opportunity, within bounds, of course. Too often, an employee, particularly a good employee, gets stuck in a specific job or function for a long time, much longer than justified.

The manager of a good performer does not want to lose that exceptional employee. But the bigger danger is that the company loses the employee. If the employee sees a better job or opportunity in the company and is qualified to fill the role, he or she should be allowed to pursue the opportunity. Formal job postings support this concept. You recruit outside employees, why not internal?

Of course, movement should be allowed only within reason. When an employee has been assigned to a critical position on a critical project, there should be a commitment from the employee to complete the assigned task. He or she owes it to the employer. But a time constraint does exist. If the assigned position lasts for many months, say, six months or more, the limit is being stretched. In a society that has been conditioned by TV and movies to expect anything to be solved in one hour, or two hours max, the thought of being on one continuous effort for upwards of a year is not always going to be acceptable.

Therefore, it behooves supervisors to provide employees with work that is challenging and enriching. For good employees, it is a seller's market. Remember, an employee can always vote with his or her feet if denied the opportunity to work in meaningful and satisfying positions. Opportunities abound outside the company. The first mistake is maintaining an environment that encourages an employee to look elsewhere. If the employee enjoys the work and finds it challenging, there is less likelihood he or she will jump ship.

Attract, don't repel.

36

Training

> What I know, that you ought to know but do not know, makes me powerful.
>
> —Anonymous

LEARNING PATHS

Everyone does not learn the same way. Public schools often use the same basic approach to teaching, regardless of student; but students do not all learn the same way. If the executive expects to have his people trained in a first-rate manner, he or she must make sure the trainers allow for differences in students.

Best Path: Some people are visually oriented. They need to see pictures to get the point. Others are aurally oriented; they are listeners. They need to hear something to understand it. Still other people learn best by doing something, i.e., on-the-job training. For some, reading is the best teacher. For others, writing something down themselves helps.

Some of the greatest writers of all time did poorly in school, thinking of it as sheer torture. They learned best by writing. But there are other people, not authors, who also feel the best way to think something out is also to put it down on paper. They might make notes to crystallize their thoughts, and then never look at the notes again. In a simple case, writing down a new acquaintance's name helps some visually oriented people get the name to sink into their memory.

Discipline: People lacking self-discipline may need formal classrooms to enforce study. They cannot learn without an instructor leading them through a study. A combination of things may be at work. They need to hear the lesson because of their aural learning path, but they also may lack the discipline to study on their own.

Disciplined people excel at self-study and often prefer to learn that way. It is possible they are poor listeners while in class, with the result their best learning comes from going home and reading the study materials in quiet concentration.

Multiple Paths: Abstract thought comes easy to some people. For others, concrete, real-life examples are necessary to get the point across. A combination of the two may work best in some instances: (1) tell them the concepts and (2) show them real-life examples.

The aural person may need to hear something then talk it over after a visual presentation. They think things through on their feet, in real-time mode, in order to grasp the meaning. Hearing someone else present an idea and then verbalizing it themselves provides the best avenue for learning. Class participation exercises help these people.

Multi-Pronged Approach: In short, effective training materials must usually hit the students from several different angles. If a student can only be reached through one approach, then that avenue must be one of the approaches used in a class if each student is going to learn. If a student can be accessed through several different angles, then the multi-channel approach is doubly effective. Training is reinforced by more than one path in this case.

Executive's Path: On a more personal level, the executive should make the effort to figure out how he or she learns best and act accordingly when seeking and receiving training.

TRAINING NEEDS

If we work under the assumption that part of the organization's responsibility is to use training to improve the skills and performance of its employees, then the first thing that must happen is to determine the areas for needed improvement. In some cases, it requires teaching new subjects. In others, recurrent training is needed to improve and upgrade existing skills.

TRAINING NEEDS

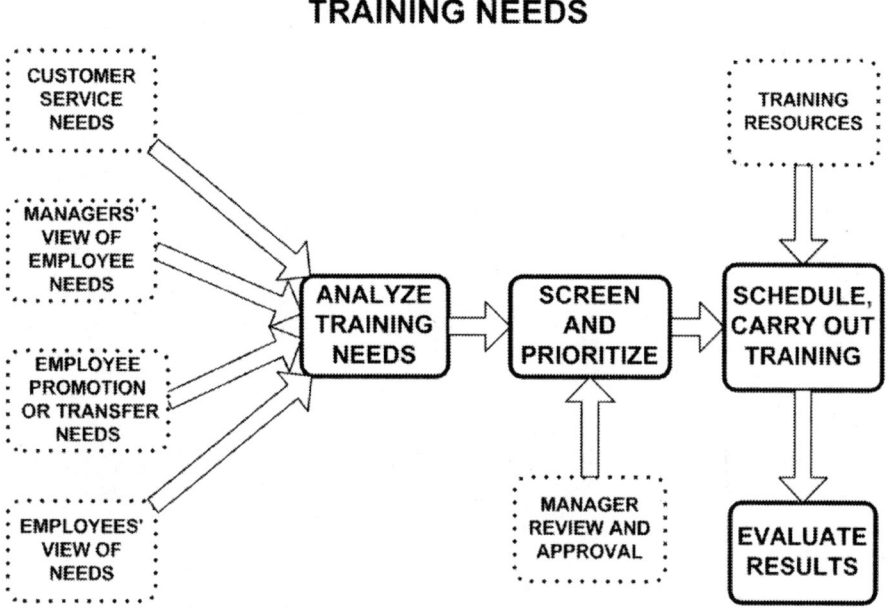

Analyze Training Needs: So how do you determine training needs? First, if your company has entered into a contract to deliver a service to a customer that requires specific training, the choice of training material is a given. It is covered by the customer contract.

Second, to determine training needs within the company, go to managers of the organization and ask what training their subordinates need. The managers are responsible for performance in their group, so they should know their subordinate's training needs. This includes asking bosses of executives about the training needs of the executives that report to them.

The highest-level executive has no boss but the board of directors, so he or she can ask them for areas of weakness where training might help. Also, the highest-level executive can ask subordinates for suggestions on training. This will take courage on both sides.

Third, anytime an employee is being promoted or moved into a new position, that employee may have specific training needs. These needs are easily determined on a case-by-case basis.

But why not add a fourth, more radical, approach to determining training needs? Just go to the employees and ask what additional training they need to better carry out their assigned responsibilities. The employees will have a vested interest in improving both their professional skills and their job output. Money spent on improving job performance almost always has a multiplier effect on performance.

Screen and Prioritize: There can always be the problem of an employee trying to improve his or her skills with the objective of getting a better job outside the company. The applicable managers must give guidance in this case. They will know the employee best. In any case, you should restrict the training to areas that improve performance on current responsibilities or future jobs the employee might realistically be expected to move into—in the company.

Even assuming some safeguards are in place, you may still lose an employee to another company after a skills upgrade. You never know when this is going to happen. There is not a lot you can do to prevent it. But don't assume the employee had planned to leave soon after receiving the training. There may have been other reasons that actually drove the employee away. Maybe the company or its management is to blame.

Once training needs have been determined, priorities for training must be set by the training department, after consultation with the applicable managers and potential students. Concentrate on areas with the greatest potential impact on productivity.

Schedule, Carry Out Training: After priorities have been established, course schedules can be established to carry out the training, with due consideration to available resources.

Evaluate Results: A word of warning: Corporations seldom evaluate the effectiveness of their training dollars. Measurements of job performance before and after training would be helpful. The evaluation should concentrate on areas being addressed by the training curriculum. Further, the post-training assessment should occur at specified intervals after the training, say, one month then six months after training. The idea is first to see if the training produced any immediate change and second to see if the training had any long-term impact.

Habits are hard to break. Training may have short-term impact but no long-term effectiveness. The training material might be at fault, or the corporate culture may blunt any positive effects of training. In the latter instance, a culture change may be necessary.

Training is important to the organization, so make it happen. Reap the potential rewards.

PROFESSIONAL TRAINING

One of the sad facts of corporate life is that people lower on the corporate ladder are more likely than their managers to take advantage of the professional training offered by their company. There are two major reasons for this: (1) the subordinates have been ordered by management to attend company-sponsored training classes or (2) the employees simply have a burning desire to improve themselves—they are willing to get training.

Executives seldom attend company-sponsored training sessions unless forced to do so. Sometimes it is because of pride. They don't want to admit they need training. At other times, the executive feels he or she cannot learn much, if anything, from those lower in the corporate hierarchy. This is an ego problem, too. The reality is that we can learn something from almost anyone, if we take the time to let it happen.

> "The man who has ceased to learn ought not to be allowed to wander around loose in these dangerous days."
> —M. M. Coady

An older executive certainly needs to keep abreast of developments in the world. It is very easy to let yourself fall behind professionally. For an avid reader of professional books and materials, this is much less the case.

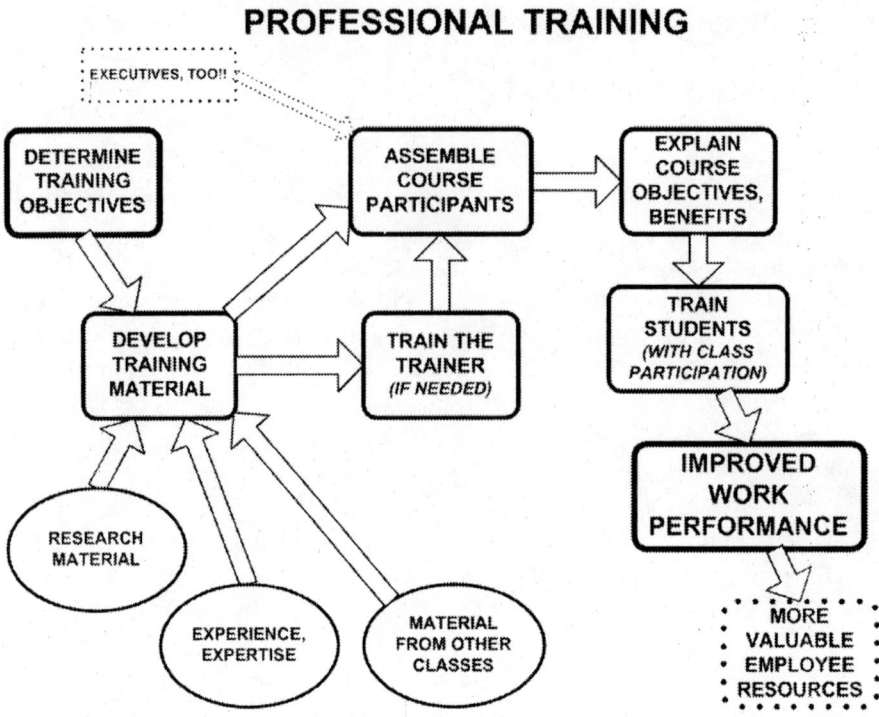

Determine Training Objectives: In preparing the course material, there should be clear objectives driving the training in the first place. The objectives need to be specific, not broad generalities. Furthermore, the objectives should be communicated to the students so they know the purpose behind the training and what it is supposed to achieve.

Develop Training Material: Formal training materials can come from research, past experiences, existing classroom material, expertise, and newly determined material that needs to be taught. There is more out there to learn than we can possibly absorb, but there is plenty we can learn and put to use.

Train the Trainer: If the instructor needs training, then a train-the-trainer effort needs to be mounted. Preferably, this training would be done by an expert, a subject matter expert (SME). The SME could come from the client, for example, when the company has a contract to provide service on an outsourced basis for the client and the client has the SME. If an expert is not available, the instructor will have to embark upon the necessary self-study. In any case, the instructor should be involved in the development of course materials.

Assemble Course Participants: Training needs, student availability, and instructor availability will determine who can attend and when.

Explain Course Objectives, Benefits: At the start of the class, a good instructor will explain to the students how the training can add value to the individual. A student will be more interested in how the training benefits him or her personally than any benefits accruing to the company. The course material needs to be relevant to the student's needs. Assume the student is silently asking, "What's in this for me?" Tell him or her. The student needs to care enough so that he or she will have an incentive to get with the training program.

Train Students: Getting the student involved in the training will go a long way towards making the training effective. The instructor can use role-playing, real-time exercises, student-teacher interaction, and so on—anything to get the students actively participating in the class. If the instructor just lectures, the student will just listen. Straight lecturing can easily go in one ear and out the other. The instructor can gauge whether the students are getting the point by using techniques that trigger feedback. If nothing else, the students will pay attention to avoid being embarrassed.

Improved Work Performance: If the training has been successful, the results should show up in the individual's work performance—provided the training is directly connected with on-the-job activity. If the student cannot apply the training shortly after the course is completed, most of what was taught will be forgotten. Do not give classes weeks before the training will be used.

Some training material, by necessity, will be more general in nature. In this case, it will be hard to observe measurable results of increased effectiveness on the job. For example, the effects of courses on sexual harassment will be unlikely to show up in a person's work if there were no problems there to start with. Many courses are simply designed to raise awareness of potential problems and head them off before they occur. So, benefits to training are not always observable. Absence of problems could be the indication of success.

More Valuable Employee Resources: If an organization has a good training department and if corporate management funds the training properly, there will be a good line-up—at all times—of courses that help the individual and further the cause of business. Training can raise the value of one's personal self, which, in turn, raises the value of the employee to the company. Keep the employee trained and feeling good about his or her own self and you will be less likely to lose the employee. If the employee is happy, walking out the door is less likely to occur.

When an organization tries to avoid spending much money on training its employees, out of the fear of making them so valuable they will leave, that fear is just a symptom for other problems in the workplace. Continually helping the employee grow is a good way to keep him or her happy with the company. The employee has incentive to stay.

If a person is not learning as fast as the world is changing, he or she will get left behind and will eat other people's dust. The executive who stops learning is destined to be a has-been, someone who has lost his or her usefulness.

TRAINING BY MANAGERS

There are very few executives who do not believe in the power and effectiveness of training. Whole departments are set up to provide organizational training. However, it is very seldom that managers do the training themselves. They leave it to others, supposedly those better able to teach.

Professional Approach: There is no doubt that professional instructors know how to teach better than the average manager. The professional instructor studies and becomes well versed in the subject matter and how best to deliver it; he or she becomes an expert in what is taught.

For job-specific courses, unless the instructor has firsthand experience with a specific skill set or a group of job responsibilities, the good instructor will seek out the appropriate reference material or someone who is an expert in the subject matter. If you want to learn the best way of doing something, go to the best, the subject matter experts, and learn how they do it.

There is the story of a person who would go to an organization and make the claim he could improve performance of the organization's people. He always delivered on his promise. His technique was simple. He just asked who was the best in the organization on the skill that needed to be taught. He then went to that person and learned how the expert did it. Then the instructor would teach the expert's techniques to the rest of the staff. Organizational performance got a boost. The instructor delivered on his promise.

Use the Manager: But a manager has skills. A manager has been moved into a position of leadership because he or she was good at something—at least that is the assumption. That means the leader—in theory—has something to teach his or her subordinates. Further, since the leader is held accountable for the performance of his or her group, it stands to reason that the leader has every incentive to do his or her part in upgrading the performance of the group.

So, why not have the manager teach his or her subordinates? Keep in mind that since the leader is charged with carrying out performance reviews, he or she is supposed to be knowledgeable about the strengths and weaknesses of each subordinate. The leader will know the areas of improvement needed for each individual.

Payback: Therefore, the manager should teach his or her subordinates how to do things better—where it makes sense. This can be a very highly leveraged activity with huge payback. One hour spent teaching is automatically multiplied by the number of students. Then, assuming the productivity of each student is improved multiple times, you have a manager improving the bottom line: manager training hour *times* number of subordinates *times* improved performance factor *equals* a large increase in productivity.

So, managers, teach what you know to the people you depend on. You and the employees have much to gain. So does the organization you are all a part of.

DIVERSITY TRAINING

Differences: People are different, even in the same family. Work brings together an even broader cross-section of people, including: different age groups, different incomes, different races, different parts of the country, different countries, city background vs. country background, big city vs. small town, different education levels, male vs. female, environmentalist vs. non environmentalist, gun control advocate vs. gun advocate, Christian vs. Jew vs. Muslim, atheists vs. agnostics vs. God-fearing, extrovert vs. introvert, heterosexual vs. homosexual, single vs. divorced vs. widowed vs. married, sports vs. non sports, soldier vs. pacifist, Army vs. Navy vs. Air Force, Texas vs. Oklahoma, business vs. non profit, big government vs. limited government, slender vs. overweight, intelligent vs. unintelligent, normal vs. retarded, computer literate vs. computer illiterate, conservative vs. liberal vs. moderate, conservative vs. progressive, meek vs. assertive, passive vs. proactive, strict vs. permissive, North vs. South, labor vs. management, union vs. non union, domestic vs. foreign, free market vs. price controls, regulation vs. deregulation, English speaking vs. non English speaking, delegation vs. tight supervision, nationalist vs. internationalist, leader vs. follower, and so on.

Hopefully, the point has been made: There are many different types of diversity in individuals. Do you know anyone with whom you agree on everything mentioned above? It is doubtful. Even husbands and wives in a wonderful marriage have different likes and dislikes, but they manage to get along—and quite well. Marriage does not require fights. Neither does the workplace.

A Changed Society: With the exponential change in technology in recent decades, time and distance have been compressed. There has been a profound change in society and in business. A simple example: TV, radio, movies, and a mobile labor force have all conspired to blend the speech patterns of people. There are fewer differences in accents than in times past. But the blending of regional accents is not representative of other aspects of life. Other differences still remain.

People are being brought together in close proximity, to the point that differences are becoming a source of frequent abrasion. As our country was being formed and melded together, we were called the melting pot of the world. We welcomed people from all parts of the globe. They came in search of freedom and democracy. We were Americans first. For the most part, we shared a common vision. We were proud to be Americans.

Now differences are being highlighted. Special interest groups abound and wield an influence all out of proportion to their numbers. If you visualize tolerance from two aspects: (1) tolerance for sin and corruption and (2) tolerance for differences; we seem to have more tolerance for the first than the second. We have our values reversed from what they should be.

Responsibility of Executives: Business executives cannot hide their heads in the sand and ignore the problem. They are surrounded by employees having very different needs and wants. Global operations compound the problem. Cultural differences abound in the workplace. Tolerance and forbearance are essential to a smooth-running organization. That does not mean letting employees slack off from job responsibilities. It does, however, mean recognizing and allowing for diversity in the workplace. Executives must take the lead and set the example.

Training: One thing that can be done to raise awareness and acceptance of differences is to have company-sponsored diversity training. The training can emphasize how different people are. The training can show, for example, that one word can be inflammatory when said to the wrong person, someone from a different background than the speaker. Also, a person within a race or a family can say something to another member of the same group and no offense is taken; but when an outsider says the same thing word-for-word, the response can be anger and resentment.

Diversity training cannot be accomplished in a one- or two-hour session. Effective diversity training requires more than one session. It is best to have sessions spread over a number of weeks to give the teachings time to sink in and be accepted. It helps if people of totally different backgrounds are required to interface with each other in class exercises that build understanding and acceptance. When you put people one-on-one with each other, you start to tear down the barriers that reinforce bias and prejudice between races, for example. You find out there actually are some good people out there who do not share your beliefs.

Tolerance: Diversity training is not about changing basic values. It is about tolerance. It is about fact vs. opinion. It is about the right to disagree without being disagreeable. People need to cast away their selfish viewpoints. They need to see and understand the other side.

> "Tolerance is the positive and cordial effort to understand another's beliefs, practices and habits without necessarily sharing or accepting them."
>
> —Joshua L. Liebman

Diversity training cannot but help the bottom line. Cooperative, understanding employees will produce better profits than contentious, quarrelsome employees. We cannot all walk in the other person's moccasins; we cannot all go through the experiences of other people's lives. But we can try to understand. It starts at the top.

Promote diversity training. Attend yourself. Show them you care. Show them you believe.

37

Employee Exits

FIRING PEOPLE

If the executive has never fired anyone, the executive is probably not doing his or her job. It is rare for a manager to avoid making at least a few mistakes in the hiring process. By extension, there is a high probability that a manager taking over an existing department or division will find some deadwood. The previous manager will have made some mistakes. So, count your blessings if you have no one to fire. But in case the situation arises, do what you have to.

> "Firing people is unpleasant, but it really has to be done occasionally.... Purging the bad performers is as good a tonic for the organization as giving sizable rewards to the star performers."
> —Robert Townsend

FIRING PEOPLE

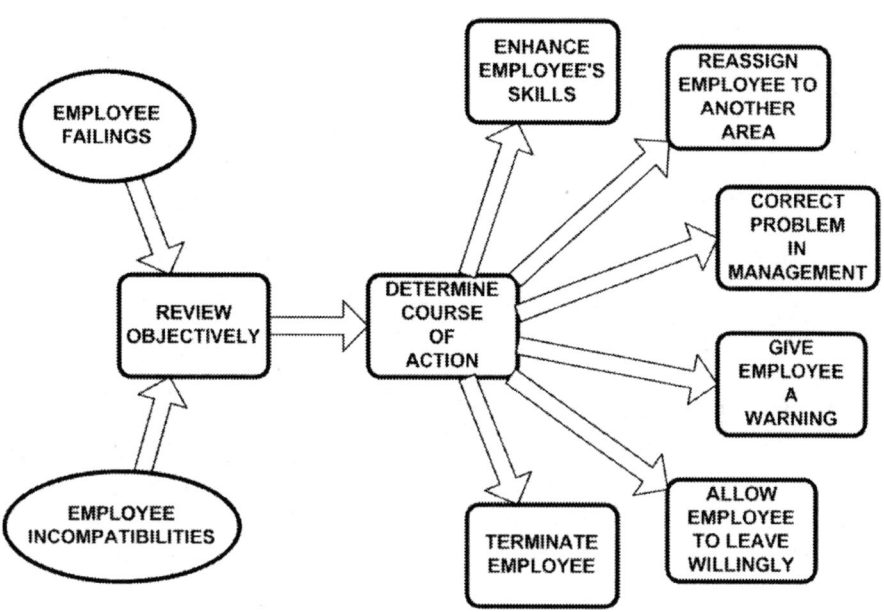

Review Objectively: When reviewing performance on the job, make sure you look at the whole picture. Also, make sure the problem is not, in fact, a problem in management. Be objective in coming up with the causes for underperformance. Thoroughly investigate the reasons for lack of performance. Leave no stone unturned.

There are a number of justifications for firing someone. The reasons can generally be categorized as employee failings or incompatibilities. But you must examine the situation without bias before deciding what to do.

Employee Failings: Breaking a trust is serious, especially if it is a matter of honesty and integrity. Falsifying records, paying bribes, accepting bribes, lying about achievements, lying to customers, covering up serious incidents, lying to management, etc., are examples of things that could be justification for letting people go. It is not enough to talk about and encourage integrity; you must enforce it. If you wink at it, your people will, too.

Company rules, assuming they are reasonable and in the best interests of all, should be documented. They should be communicated and re-communicated to the employees. They lay the foundation for carrying out job responsibilities. They are the rules of the game. Repeated violations of company rules should be dealt with forcefully, which includes invoking termination procedures.

Repeated violations of safety rules in hazardous working conditions are not only bad for the bottom line; they also show a disregard for fellow workers. Safety infractions, unless isolated and unintentional, cannot be ignored. Repeated offenders should be fired.

Lack of performance on the job is certainly a starting point for determining if an employee should be separated from the company. But not so fast, please! It is not enough to determine an employee has not performed up to expectations. The involved manager must also investigate and come to a solid understanding of the true cause for not performing up to requirements.

Were the performance standards clearly communicated to the employee? Were the performance standards reasonable? Does the employee have the right skills for the job? Could the employee have done better with the proper training? Was the employee provided with the necessary resources to get the job done? Were there circumstances beyond his or her control? Was the original analysis correct about the situation into which the employee was placed? Did some factor change after the task was started? Is this a one-time blip on the scope or a repeated occurrence? Was there a breakdown in management coaching?

Employee Incompatibilities: Now let's look at a more difficult situation, but one that must certainly be addressed by the effective executive. Every successful company has a culture, a set of core values and beliefs shared by all in the company. Executives and all managers should be role models for an organization's value system.

Sometimes a person just does not fit into a company's culture. It is not his or her fault; it just happens. Different people have different needs. The different company cultures are neither right nor wrong. Events can happen that change company cultures. Market conditions can change or mergers can occur that result in an alteration of a company's culture. The employee was a fit before but no longer is.

It is easier to deal with culture compatibility problems when core values are simply not shared by the employee. But the more nebulous situation occurs when there are differences in opinion about the way the business should be run. This situation is harder to deal with. If serious differences of opinion persist over the long haul, they must be addressed. If resolution is not possible, a parting of the ways may be called for. This is certainly true if the company's vision is not shared. People need to get onboard or find another ship.

Determine Course of Action: There are alternatives to firing. Maybe the employee just needs to have his or her skills enhanced. Maybe the employee is not the problem; management may be the problem. If the latter is true, correct the management problem rather than forcing the blame on the employee.

If someone is not cut out for a particular position, look for an alternative position, one where the employee can perform up to standards. This alternative should always be explored. Work under the assumption there is a right position for any person, a position where that person can do an excellent job. If the company and the employee cannot agree on a compatible position, then the employee must leave.

Regardless of the best efforts, the point may be reached where there is no choice but to let someone go. If it can be handled by the employee making the decision to leave, that is the best course. It will save face. If not, and if all other possibilities have gone down in flames, then do what you have to. Be careful that government regulations are followed and that legal ramifications are considered before action is taken.

Always start with a warning, unless the problem is an infraction so serious that an immediate termination is the only answer. After a warning, get the employee to commit to improvement. Provide the necessary support. Monitor progress. Follow the appropriate procedures. If acceptable improvement occurs, great! If not, proceed with termination.

Be sympathetic. Be humane in how you go about it. It is rare for any person not to have been laid off or fired at least once in his or her career. Remember how you felt when it happened to you. Expect it to happen to you sometime in the future, if it hasn't already. It could even happen again. Just be considerate of other people's feelings.

Executive Firings: Firing executives is harder than firing non-executives. You are talking about a company leader. The ramifications are greater. If the executive has no interest in the job or does not harmonize with the rest of the executive team, the out of sync executive needs to leave. If the executive does not have the respect of his or her subordinates, the executive cannot be an effective leader. Failure in communication with subordinates or other executives is a key shortcoming. Of course, general lack of performance is certainly grounds for dismissal. Review the situation objectively and do what needs to be done—and do it without delay. Go to the executive, present the facts in a straightforward manner, and show compassion. Then get a replacement for the leader.

LEARNING FROM THE PAST

A person, at his or her own peril, ignores the lessons of the past. The most impressive lessons are the ones learned in the first person. The mistake is failing take into consideration the experience of those people who surround you—which was learned in their own first person.

One of the biggest mistakes in a corporation is laying off or forcing into retirement older employees who have some of the best judgment and the most to contribute to a corporation's success. Grey hair is often the badge of wisdom. Of course, this principle does not apply to those older people who have ceased to learn or who have retired in place.

GOOD EMPLOYEE LOSSES

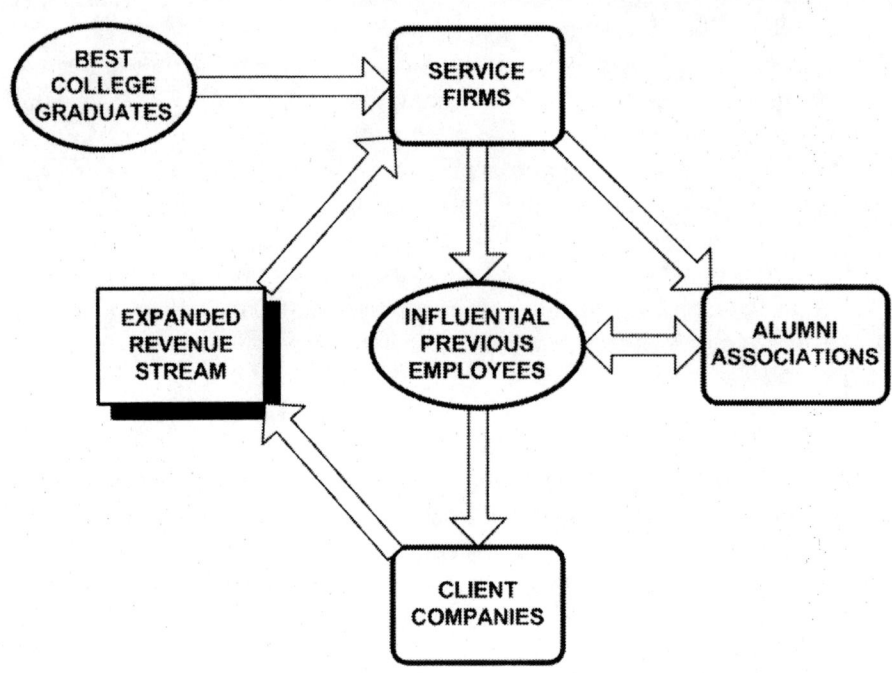

GOOD EMPLOYEE LOSSES

Some companies lose good employees and still come out ahead. An accounting graduate knows that a job with one of the big accounting firms is potentially a ticket to success. As a result, accounting firms are able to recruit the best graduates. The firms take the graduates and mold them into executive material, e.g., CFOs. When they become "graduates" of the accounting firms, they are even more valuable. Corporations eagerly bring them on board.

Why do the accounting firms spend so much effort and money on developing these "green" college students? First, the students perform needed services for client firms and thereby bring in revenue for the accounting firms. Second, when these students move on to another company, they are often placed in positions that allow them to purchase services of the accounting firms they graduated from. Assuming the previous accounting firm of the new CFO treated him or her right, preference is likely to lean toward the old firm for an audit engagement. A bonding took place. The revenue stream of the accounting firm spreads out as a result.

Consulting firms follow the same practice. One difference is that consulting firms are likely to cover a broader range of executive skill sets, which means they can fan out into more varied executive positions. A company engaging the services of a consulting firm may go after a consultant if they are greatly impressed with his or her demonstrated ability while on assignment at their company. After the client company hires the consultant, there is a strong tendency for the new executive to recommend the services of his or her old employer. The client organization will already have a positive feeling about the consultant group. The wheels are greased.

Accounting and consulting firms support active alumni organizations. This is a win-win situation for the firms and for their "graduates." The influence of the firms continues and the former auditors and consultants are able to network with people they know and have confidence in. It is a beneficial "good ole boys" networking opportunity.

By acting like professional schools and placement organizations, the firms are making an excellent investment in future revenue streams. In the meantime, they have gained the benefit of talented people with new ideas who were not afraid to get their hands dirty working up through the ranks. It is a win-win situation.

Can your company take advantage of this concept?

38

Meetings

Meetings are indispensable when you don't want to do anything.
—John Kenneth Galbraith

Meetings are the bane of productivity, but they can be better. There are keys to making meetings more productive.

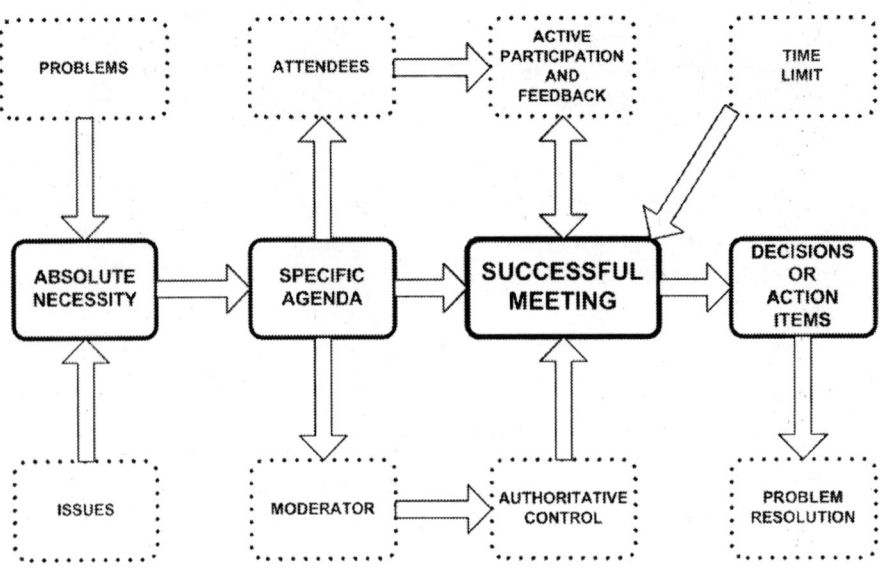

Rule 1: Never call a meeting unless it is absolutely necessary. There should be some pressing problem or issue that can only be addressed in a meeting. While you are in your meeting tying up a lot of people's time, what is your competitor doing? Is your competitor in a meeting? Multiply the meeting hours *times* the number of attendees *times* their equivalent hourly salary (plus benefits). Is the meeting worth all those bucks? Time is money! Too many meetings are a clear indication of entrenched bureaucracy.

Rule 2: Always have an agenda. Know why the meeting was called in the first place. Just having a weekly status meeting because you have always had one in the past is not a sufficient reason. Status updates can be handled using status reports, whether published by paper, email, or website. The agenda should cover substantive subjects, things that cannot be handled except by a face-to-face meeting or by video or voice teleconferencing. Publish the agenda to all attendees before the meeting.

Rule 3: Stick to the agenda until the closing period in the meeting when "other business" can be taken care of. It is too easy to get sidetracked on miscellaneous topics and not cover the primary subject(s). Remember, there was supposedly an overriding reason for having the meeting in the first place.

Rule 4: Chair the meeting with an iron-fisted moderator. It is suggested the person having the most at stake chair the meeting. However, the personalities involved may dictate another choice. The person in charge of the meeting should see that the agenda is followed and that an appropriate pace is maintained to ensure adequate time is given to each agenda item. Do not wait until the last minute to cover the remaining topics on the agenda. The chairperson should step in when discussions or people get out of hand. The person leading the meeting should have some recognized authority over the meeting, either because of position or influence (power).

Rule 5: All attendees should participate in the meeting. The chairperson should make sure this happens. People who are silent in the meeting do not need to be there. Why were they invited if not to make a contribution?

Rule 6: Set a time limit for conducting the meeting and start it on time. This forces the meeting to proceed with dispatch and not drag on forever. People have tight schedules already—without the meeting. Be considerate.

Rule 7: Come out of the meeting with decisions made or action items to do. An action item should not be to have another meeting to continue the discussion. In some cases, though, an action item could be for a smaller group to meet and resolve a problem or issue. In short, at the close of the meeting the attendees should feel that something was accomplished. A business meeting is not a social gathering—or at least it should not be. The moderator should summarize the action items and decisions coming out of the meeting. Publish the results.

So, follow the rules. Have a successful meeting.

39

Board of Directors

It may seem overly trite to bring this up, but corporations sometimes forget what makes for a successful Board of Directors. Every board member should bring something to the table. Directorships should not be just plums handed out as rewards for some past action or because of favoritism. Boards should provide oversight and guidance—without messing in day-to-day affairs.

Any board member should bring a positive contribution to the corporation. There are any number of contributions a board member can make. Most of the board should come from *outside* the company. That means they should bring experience, presumably experience the corporate officers do not already have. Experienced people, provided the experience is relevant to the business, can provide wise counsel in setting corporate strategies.

One benefit often sought in board members is the large number of business and government contacts they have built up in their professional lives. A good board member can open doors to people not otherwise accessible by the corporation. There is tremendous power in personal networking. The recommendation of someone you trust can be invaluable. It carries a lot more weight than anything said by a stranger.

If a board does its job properly, it will monitor and stay abreast of the results of business operations and the performance of people on the highest rungs of the corporate ladder. Business strategies developed by the executives should pass muster with the board. If the company's leadership is taking the company in the wrong direction or if the executives are not performing up to par, it is the Board of Directors' responsibility to take corrective action. They should keep their ear to the ground, learning of problems before they come to the attention of shareholders. Vigilance is necessary; otherwise, shareholder suits are possible—and against the board members, too.

But a good board has another responsibility, being an effective cheerleader when things are going right. If the company is going through a major transition or if the company has just brought on a new CEO, the board members should be supportive of the transition effort or the change in leadership. Such events can bring on some troublesome times. The board should be a source of encouragement. They can and should be a major factor in maintaining morale in the executive suite. If the directors are always acting the part of policemen, they have missed the boat on effective participation.

If a board member does not perform, he or she should find the exit door.

40

Miscellaneous Management Notes

EMAIL

Company email can be both a blessing and a curse. With everyone's company email address available via a company email directory, you have a quick and easy way to reach someone when a phone or in-person contact isn't the best solution.

Group Lists: Group email lists allow an email sender to select one email address that automatically sends the email to everyone on the list. Separate multi-address lists can be set up to handle different situations. A group list for all team members assists in keeping team members updated on team activities. Status reports, for example, can be routed via email to everyone on the team.

Although group mail lists are an effective means of notifying team members, especially if they are widely dispersed, they can be a problem when you start moving up the organizational levels. Generally, setting up a group list for a department is good. All people in the department can be notified at once. The caveat is that the department list should only be used for important information, information that is needed by all people in the department. Don't flood everyone in the department with emails.

When you move up to the division or overall organization level, there is a real danger in using group email addresses. First, they are hard to keep up to date. Second, if you do not have an excellent traffic cop controlling email addressed to the whole company or division, the junk email ogre will start raising its ugly head and people will ignore the company- or division-level emails. Email should be important to most, if not all recipients, before it is allowed to go out.

An Alternative: When whole division or whole company emails start becoming too numerous, consider using an internal company website to make the information known. If structured properly, the website will allow people to choose only the information that is pertinent to them. Emails give you very little choice. You look at the subject line and hope it is descriptive of the content before you decide to delete a seemingly unimportant email—you just hope it is unimportant.

Other Dangers: Group email lists offer a means for a recipient to hit the "Reply All" button, thereby sending everyone on the list a reply. It is rare that everyone wanted to see the reply, even though the one sending the reply thought they should. Also, a person will sometimes accidentally hit the "Reply All" button when he or she just wanted to send a reply to some specific person on the list. When the accident happens, everyone else on the list suffers; and if the reply was confidential or very personal, so much the worse.

Emails are a great way for hackers to spread viruses. The hackers can use group email lists to spread the virus, starting with a snowball that turns into an avalanche—one group list to successively more group lists. Mail servers need to have virus protection installed to prevent this from happening; otherwise, the replicating virus can bring a mail server to its knees.

Spam blocking mechanisms are needed. Be sure proper safeguards are in place to restrict spamming. Getting rid of spam on company time is a waste of employee expense. Use automatic spam blockers and controls.

In short, emails are great communication tools when used judiciously. When they are used inappropriately, they can seriously degrade people's performance on the job. Most of you have heard of people who receive hundreds of emails a day and automatically delete them. They do not have time to critically review them. Executives should make sure emails are used properly from the top of the organization to the bottom.

EMPLOYEE INTERNET ACCESS

As computer software systems evolve, there will be fewer applications that do not provide a web browser interface. Web-based systems offer many benefits to workers. Your PC's web browser allows access to internal intranets, extranets, and the Internet—the world!

Unless you totally shut down access to external Internet websites, your people are going to surf the Web while at work. If executives surf the Web but prohibit their employees from doing so, they will be found out. All it takes is an unexpected walk-in at your office while you are surfing. The word will get out. So, if you are going to use the Web for personal reasons, it is hypocritical not to let your employees do the same.

That employees will goof off is nothing new. It is an age-old supervisory problem. That employees have a new tool, the web browser, is relatively new to the workplace. Somehow, employers must deal with the resultant problems.

Unless a manager sits at his or her desk all day and never walks around the department, the manager will know which employees are shirking work on a regular basis. Setting up a policy which completely bans employee use of the Internet, except in the regular course of business, is a mistake.

What should your reaction be when a good employee spends a few minutes web surfing during a well-deserved break? Maybe the employee needed a change of pace to relieve job stress. With a policy embracing a complete ban, consistency of enforcement means punishing the good employee. If you apply the rule to the shirker but not the productive worker, you stand the chance of big-time trouble, especially if a fired employee's attorney finds out the rule was applied on a discriminatory basis.

So, institute a rule that says web surfing unrelated to work is only allowed during a valid rest break, during lunch, outside normal working hours, or during justifiable lulls in workload. If an employee is stressed out from too much job pressure, web surfing just might be good, inexpensive therapy.

Excessive web surfing is normally just a symptom of other problems the supervising manager should be addressing. Performance standards, properly applied and made the subject of performance reviews, will normally take care of the problem. Don't let web surfing be a scapegoat for the real problem, supervisory management.

TEAM SKILLS

Teams are often assembled just to apply more bodies to a large task. There is nothing wrong with this. Another reason for assembling a team might be to exercise a form of representative democracy. In this scenario, each team member is selected as a representative of his or her department. This lets each department have a say in the output of the team.

But sometimes managers forget that one of the reasons for assembling a team is to combine into one group a diversity of skills and viewpoints. Not all people are clones of each other. Each person has certain talents and skills. In other words, each person brings a different set of strengths to the group. For example, a football team is an assembly of people with diverse football skills. Each has a specialty, and the effective coach places the right person in the right position, into the role the player is best qualified to handle.

Another benefit of a properly assembled team is that the various members bring varying viewpoints to the group. The different insights and perceptions allow the group to think on different planes and from different vantage points. The result is a more comprehensive foundation for determining the group's course of action.

HOARDING

Hoarding can manifest itself in many different ways. It occurs when people in the organization feel there is some perceived scarcity of an item, typically some resource. Hoarding can be both destructive and expensive.

People: Let's start with the most valuable resource a company has, its people. Many managers tend to put the good of their department and its assigned responsibilities above that of the company as a whole and above that of the individual employee within the department. This can be very counterproductive.

If someone on your staff could be used more profitably in some other area of the company, let the person transfer to the other area. Consider the needs of the company. What is best for the bottom line? Also, consider the needs and desires of the employee. Does he or she wish to make the transfer? Would the move help the employee grow and be even more valuable to the company in the long run? If yes, do not become a roadblock to the move. You may be able to keep the employee from going to the other department, but you cannot close the door on that same employee going to another company. In the latter case, who wins? The other company does. Your company suffers the loss of a good employee.

On the other hand, interdepartmental transfers should not be permitted on mere whims or without a proper wind-down in the first department. The employee does have a responsibility to both his current management and the company to carry out an orderly shutdown and make the transfer in the least disruptive manner possible.

Supplies and Equipment: A second type of hoarding is the hoarding of supplies and equipment. This is generally either the result of (1) close control—usually repressive—of expenses or (2) a true shortage of resources. If people have a perceived feeling of scarcity, it is in their own best interests to hoard supplies and equipment whenever they can. The same attitude prevails when a true scarcity exists. Possession is nine points of the law. If you have it, keep it until you need it. Forget sharing.

The problem with this line of thinking, particularly if forced by unnecessary bureaucratic control, is that the opposite result can occur. Expenses can go up because people hoard supplies and equipment whether they have an immediate need or not. In the case of supplies, it is quite easy to be penny-wise and pound-foolish. If you expect people to get their job done, you are obligated to supply the employees with their justifiable needs. In the case of equipment, hoarding can be very expensive and the consequent utilization of the hoarded equipment very low. People will work around any restrictions. They can be very creative and completely defeat your attempt at minimizing expenses.

Information: Another type of hoarding involves the hoarding of ideas or information. This defeats the whole aim of effective communication. Good communication within a company is a requirement for business success. Don't hoard information.

OMBUDSMAN POSITION

Some companies have had positive results from installing an ombudsman-like position in the company. This person acts as an intermediary between management and subordinates. The ombudsman handles things employees feel they cannot take through normal channels for fear of retribution. The ombudsman-like position is normally only applicable to larger organizations. The term, ombudsman, is most likely to come up in regard to governments and other institutions; but the concept is equally applicable to large corporations.

Installing an ombudsman who is directly accessible by all employees has the immediate effect of putting a damper on criminal or unethical activity. It gives everyone in the company a confidential way to report illegal or suspicious activity. Any would-be perpetrator would always wonder who was watching over his or her shoulder.

The person filling the ombudsman role would need to be an understanding, wise, well-balanced, and well-adjusted person. He or she should not be judgmental. The position requires verifying the authenticity of submitted material. The ombudsman should be a good investigator. If any suspected wrongdoing is uncovered, policies and proper procedures should be followed to resolve the issue.

The ombudsman needs to have the full support and backing of the executive suite. That includes occupying the position with no fear of retribution from any accused management. The ombudsman should have access to anyone, from Chairman on down.

Just remember, the cost of the ombudsman position could be a drop in the bucket compared to the cost of defending a lawsuit that might otherwise have been prevented. Whistle-blowing is a last resort for well-meaning employees who have no other safe way to bring wrongdoing to the attention of those in charge, the leaders who can take corrective action before the situation blows up.

If it makes sense for your organization, install someone in the role of an ombudsman. Provide an 800 number for discreet long distance communications from outlying parts of the company.

GOING WITH THE FLOW

Sometimes, choosing the best is not the best answer. "Best" can be interpreted several different ways. To illustrate the point, consider written communications. In the past, typewriter-prepared documents prevailed. Anyone could accept and read the output of typewriters. There were no compatibility problems.

Nowadays the story is different. Documents are frequently exchanged in "soft" form, such as in attachments to emails. For this to work efficiently, the recipient must have software capable of deciphering the document. To be more specific, if the originator of the document used Microsoft Word, the recipient had better be able to read the Word document—using the version the document was created with. If the originator uses WordPerfect and the recipient uses Word, never the twain shall meet; unless someone goes to the trouble of using a version compatible with both products.

Let's suppose, at a given time, WordPerfect is the far superior product; so, the purchase agent chooses WordPerfect. However, Microsoft dominates the market, but its latest version does not support WordPerfect's latest version. Without reverting to a previous version that is compatible, users of the two packages cannot communicate with each other without a lot of trouble. The problem compounds itself when you are trying to send documents to many recipients and you do not know which version of which software each person has.

The lesson is: go with the market leader so long as it has the basic functions you need and is affordable. Apply the standard throughout your company. If you stick with the market leader and there is the need to interface with other packages, the likelihood of problems is reduced if you go with the flow. This is particularly true in technology-dominated situations.

If you choose to use a non standard approach that requires interfacing with other software packages, you are buying a lot of grief; unless a new emerging standard is about to displace the existing standard. (The transition period could get bumpy.) You need to speak the same language, even if it is not necessarily the best. Why put yourself at an unnecessary disadvantage?

ROMANCE AT WORK

As an executive, you should never encourage romance on the job, whether it is between you and someone else, or between others. That is not to say it will not happen or even that it should not happen. The workplace consists of men and women. People interact at work. Hormones run strong. Accept it and deal with it. But you must not stick your head in the sand.

First, the greatest danger is for two people to get romantically involved when both work in close proximity to each other, say, in the same department or group. Romances have their ups and downs. The downs lead to discord, and discord invariably leads to lost productivity. Lost productivity leads to lost corporate income. Couples expect the best of each other. When it does not happen—and it will not always happen—a fight can ensue. The fight spills over into their work, and maybe even into the work of others. Not only can the lovebirds fight with each other, they may fight with other people at the same time.

There is another factor to be considered in a workplace romance. The two lovers are obviously close to each other and tied to one another. That means they are supportive and protective of each other. Do something perceived as bad to one and the other feels injured, too. If you give one a bad performance review, do not expect the other to sit idly by. In simple terms, make one mad and you may be making two employees mad. It makes little difference if the action was justified. Loved ones want to defend each other, regardless.

"It is love, not reason, that is stronger than death."
—Thomas Mann

If a romance results and lasts for more than just a short period, then the two individuals should be moved into different departments or one should leave the company. If the romance fails and the two part with feelings of enmity, they certainly should be separated. Feelings matter. Feelings impact productivity.

SAFETY CONCERNS

Accidents are more likely to happen in some companies than others because of the nature of the business. For example, a financial consultant is less likely to be involved in an accident on the job than a production worker in a steel factory. The executive's awareness of and attention to safety factors should be a function of the potential risk for worker accidents.

If you truly care about people—and you should—profits must take a backseat to worker safety. The goal should be zero accidents. When the number of accidents increases, you will have higher insurance premiums, and, therefore, higher costs. But more importantly, people get hurt. Business may involve the act of going to war with competitors, but do not accept the viewpoint of the General on the battlefield that casualties are inevitable. Employees aren't cannon fodder.

Attempt to have the lowest accident rate in your industry. Shoot for zero accidents. Preach the word. Have your people preach the word. Reward managers whose people achieve a minimal accident rate in the workplace.

The person who gets hurt in an accident could be someone's spouse. Would you want your spouse hurt?

Part VIII

COMPANY OPERATIONS

41

Business Focus

One rule of thumb for concentrating your focus on anything is to limit yourself to five (5) items, the five items with the highest priority in your sphere of influence. If you apply the same principle to business in general, you could summarize business as needing to concentrate on five areas: customer satisfaction, product (or service), cost, people, and quality. Master them properly and you can roar down the road to success.

FIVE AREAS OF BUSINESS FOCUS

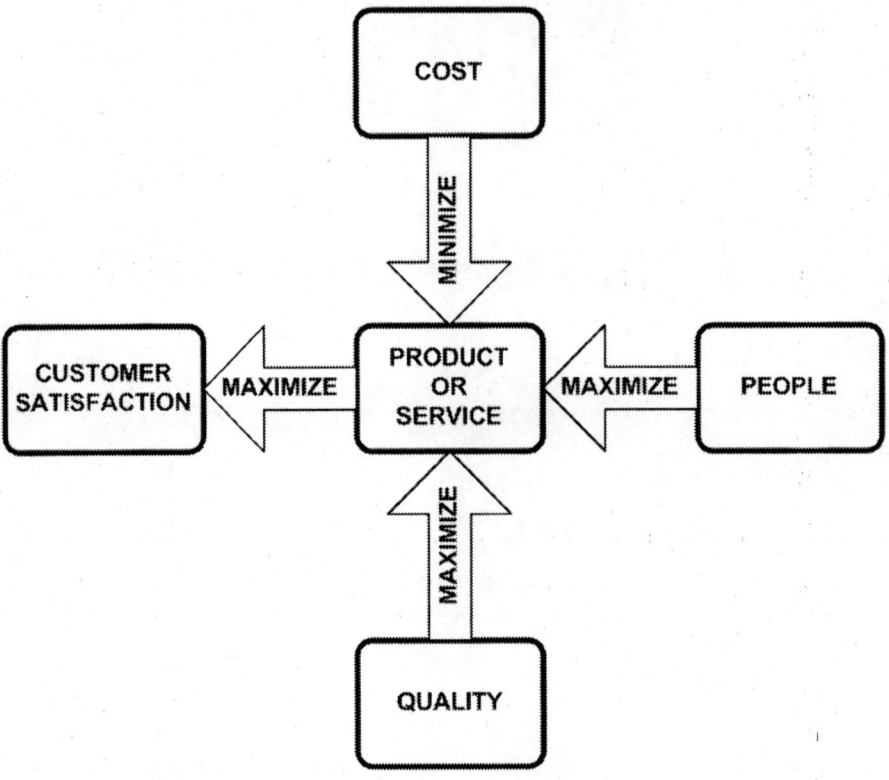

Product or Service: First, the output of a business is its product (or service), what it delivers to the customer. It must be the right product delivered at the right price at the right time to the right customer. As the diagram suggests, the product or service is central to business and is its reason for being. It brings in revenue.

Sell current products. Work on new products.

Customer Satisfaction: The goal is to *maximize customer satisfaction* and, thereby, foster repeat business. A loyal, happy customer comes back to the business again and again. The satisfied customer spreads the word to other potential buyers, which helps to expand revenue. Without revenue, you can have no profits.

Cost: It is not enough to maximize revenue; you must *minimize cost* in order to maximize profit. That means you wisely control expenditures in the areas of cost of goods and delivery of product or service. Cost covers all expenditures related to business operation.

Customer satisfaction ultimately determines profit. First, the customers must want or need the product or service. Second, they must be able to afford it. That requires minimizing cost in order to price the product or service reasonably.

Quality: Quality of product or service has a direct impact on customer satisfaction. Shoddy products or services result in shoddy sales. Low quality destroys repeat business—and revenue. So, *maximize quality* of product or service.

People: People make things happen in business. They are essential to business operation. They are the mortar that holds everything together. *Maximize your people's performance* as it relates to the development and delivery of the product or service. Everything they do should lead to customer satisfaction and maximum profit.

This may seem like an overly simplistic view of business, but the whole point is that executives sometimes lose their focus and get dragged off into trivial pursuits. They forget the areas that should be their primary focus. They forget the five focal points for business, upon which everything else hangs—including their careers.

42

Product/Service Delivery

Speed and connectivity are blurring the distinction between product and service. There are many ways to communicate with a customer or client. If you work under the assumption that a business's function is to solve a problem for a customer, the distinction between product and service becomes a little hazy. Besides, a company wants as many hooks into the customer as possible.

PRODUCT/SERVICE DELIVERY

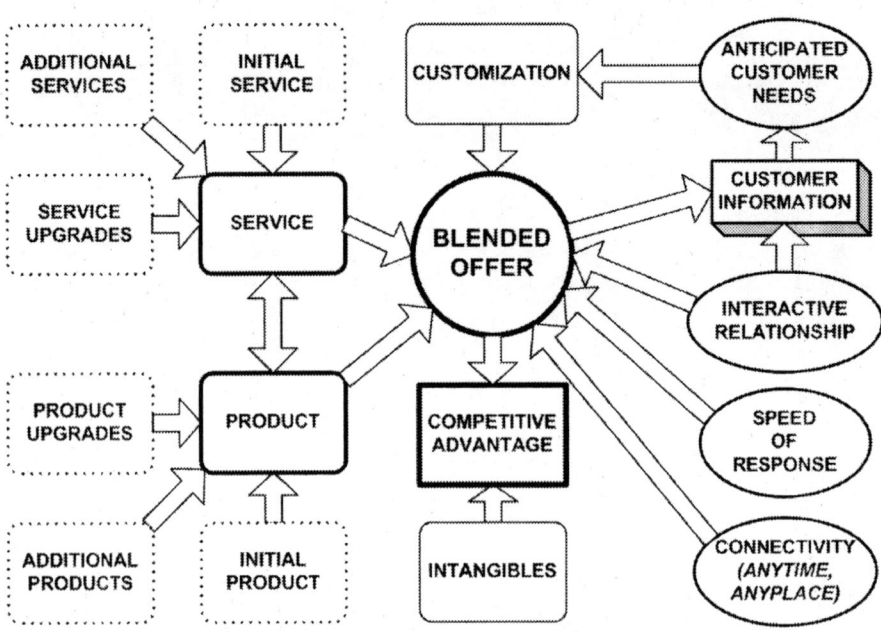

Blended Offer: Products and service can be offered in an appealing package. For instance, when you buy a computer device, like a printer, the seller will offer you an extended service contract. Many companies bundle consulting with product installation. An example would be a software company selling you an accounting package, plus ongoing support for it. Car dealers sell you a car and provide an extended warranty contract—for a price. Consulting firms bundle products with consulting contracts.

With the speed of communication and commerce growing every day, and with the paths of connectivity between businesses, customers, and other businesses on the rise, executives must take advantage of every pathway to the customer that makes sense. The economy and the market place are moving at light speed. Executives had better keep up.

A blended offer is possible for a company delivering both products and service. But products can be sold without service, and vice versa. Ideally, both should be sold together. Using the technology available today, including the Internet, all sorts of possibilities exist for making sales.

Product: Starting with products, a company gets its foot in the door by selling an *initial product* to the customer. If the product proves satisfactory, the customer starts developing trust in the brand and buys *additional products*. The revenue stream can grow even more if the company can make a profit from selling *upgrades* to one or more of the products owned by the customer. Computer software and hardware products are prime examples of upgrade possibilities. A more drastic upgrade is getting the customer to trade in an automobile for a newer model. Thus, upgrades can be typified by complete replacement instead of just changing a portion of the product.

Service: Initial service offerings can take several forms. First, service can be a one-time affair, such as the initial service provided at the time a product is sold. This can be as simple as professional, supportive sales assistance. It could also be a limited level of service and support for a short period after the sale, say, 90 days.

Second, service can be an ongoing affair. This type of service normally involves an ongoing maintenance and support fee, which can be packaged with the initial sale. The period covered could be one year, at the end of which the customer is offered a chance to renew or extend the maintenance agreement for another year.

Service upgrades can provide additional revenue. A company could offer several levels of service, based on hours per day covered or the comprehensiveness of service provided. Basic customer support might be given during normal working hours. 24-hour support would be at a higher cost. On-site support, with a vendor's support person resident at the customer's premises, would come at an even higher price. A service upgrade would come from convincing the customer to move up to a more expensive level of service.

Once a company has proved itself with one type of service, the company has a better chance of selling *additional services* to the customer. For example, a well-rounded computer consulting company could sell network consulting services in addition to business software package installation and support. They could even offer an overall technical analysis of a customer's installations around the globe. Having a consulting arm in the company that sells products offers many possibilities for additional revenue streams.

Customer Information: Customer information should be captured at the time of sale or from information discovered by the people interfacing with the customer. Past sales are a great source for determining customer buying habits. The emphasis here is on capturing information that is used by the original selling company. Privacy rules should be in place to cover the sharing of information with other business entities. Building a trust-based relationship with the customer means respecting the customer's desires in regard to the privacy of personal information.

Anticipated Customer Needs: A customer's needs can be anticipated. A simple case would be renewing a subscription or a prescription. Blending knowledge about (1) a customer's past purchases, (2) purchases made by classes of customers, (3) new products, and (4) trends taking place in the market place, a business can be in an excellent position to make informed recommendations for additional products and services. This supports customized offers.

Customization: As a company learns more about the customer, customized offers can be presented that tailor the product and/or service combination to the specific needs of the customer. Any information gathered by computer systems can help establish buying patterns. Customer likes and dislikes can be determined and recorded for future use.

Another type of customization is allowing the customer to customize a product at the time of purchase. With the Internet, for example, a customer can order a computer from home. It could be configured to suit the buyer. The desired product would then be custom manufactured and shipped directly to the customer within a few days. There is no more need to take one of the standard configured models off a showroom floor. The customer is happier and inventories are kept at a minimum.

Interactive Relationship: With the coming of age of the Internet and web-based customer activity, a business can offer a more advanced level of interaction between company and customer. The customer can seek information on the company's website and enter requests for service or information. Further, the technology of today allows a customer to get real-time assistance from a real, live person while the customer is logged onto the website.

A company representative can even see what the customer is seeing on his or her browser and coach the customer interactively. There are many different possibilities for meaningful and fulfilling interactions between business and customer. The whole way of conducting business has been turned on its heels.

Speed of Response: Technology, like the Internet, has greatly increased the speed with which a company can respond to its customers. Computer applications can respond around the clock. 24x7 call centers can also respond around the clock, if provided by the company. Account executives can still respond face-to-face.

Connectivity (Anytime, Anyplace): Connectivity has been greatly enhanced. Customers can connect to businesses with less effort. Businesses can connect to suppliers effectively. Businesses can share customer order information with suppliers. The Internet allows connectivity anytime and anyplace. All that is needed to make a connection is a browser and an Internet hook-up. We have plenty of computer-to-computer options for connectivity that allow automatic sharing of information between companies. Responsiveness improves for everyone directly or indirectly involved in a customer transaction.

Competitive Advantage: There are a myriad of ways for a company to conduct its business. Competitive advantage is achieved by: (1) a mastery of the alternative ways to conduct business; (2) superior products and services consistently delivered in a timely manner; (3) intelligent use of customer information; and (4) effective, responsive interfaces with the customer. Taken together, they can do wonders for enhancing competitive advantage. Technology has done a lot to level the playing field, but it still boils down to choosing the best alternative and performing at a higher level than the competition.

Intangibles: A high-quality tangible product you can see and put your hands on is not enough. Intangibles are the deciding factor in business success. Level of service is key. Wise use of available information is imperative. Emotions of the customer can have a decisive influence on customer loyalty and the trust he or she feels for a company and its brand. Nurture the customer relationship. Provide value over and above what is expected.

We live in a fast-moving and dynamic economy. Speed and connectivity provide opportunities never before available. They also bring danger to a business if not embraced wisely. Take advantage of them. Be a success.

43

Internal Functions

It is not enough to perform well in your interactions related to products and service delivered to the customer. The internal functions of a company are exceedingly important to an organization's success. They must be performed well. They must support or enhance regular operations.

BUREAUCRACY

How bureaucratic is your company? How bureaucratic is your management process? How hard is it to get things done, especially the things with obviously good paybacks? Are there too many decision-making layers?

> "Bureaucracy is the death of any achievement."
> —Albert Einstein

What is the size of the corporate staff? Small is beautiful. Big means lack of trust in the rest of the corporation. Corporate leaders should set corporate goals, but they should not decide the tasks and responsibilities of every level. Limit corporate staffing to those functions that can only be handled at the corporate level.

The more people there are at the corporate level, the more people there will be throughout the rest of the organization just to respond to headquarters' requests and interference. While people are reacting to corporate staff, they are not concentrating on their primary responsibilities. Things slow down. Don't let the sand of bureaucracy get into the company's gears.

The approach taken for communications within a company can be indicative of a flourishing bureaucracy. When communications are always forced to go through strict channels, communication can get smothered. The extreme is when leaders themselves enforce tight control over communications inside a company. Freedom of speech is stifled. You must communicate information to the people who need it. Encourage communication between people who can best address the problems and issues.

In general, if profit planning is always controlled by headquarters, it indicates a lack of authority at lower levels to go along with their assigned responsibility. Authority is often given to a lesser degree than responsibility, even though they should go hand in hand. Both should be given at the same time. If they are not, bureaucracy is at work.

Delegate planning and control of revenue and expenditures to the people most likely to have the greatest impact, the ones in the know. Delegate authority and responsibility downward—without giving up accountability.

DEPARTMENTAL SERVICE

Let's say you are an executive heading up a major department. (The concept also applies to a manager in charge of a small department.) Further, let's assume your department does not normally have a direct interface with customers. Presumably, your department was set up to serve some useful function. You serve someone or some other group in the organization. You have clients—they are internal clients.

> "The vocation of every man and woman is to serve other people."
> —Leo Tolstoy

Whatever kind of professional you are, you are still in the client service business. Your clients are just people inside the company. Your reputation in the company and your influence with other executives depends upon the kind of service your department delivers. Think client.

Mount a client relations campaign directed toward the people you serve. Remember the old adage, the client is always right. Don't become a bureaucratic foot dragger. Treat your clients as you would like to be treated. Provide service, high-quality service, and you will get cooperation and service in return. Give respect and you will get it in return. Nurture client relations.

Think of ways to improve your service. Spend time on research and development related to your service product. Ask your clients how you are doing?

Take corrective action as needed, and do it promptly. Encourage all your people to nurture client relations. Tie performance evaluations to client relations.
Be a positive addition to corporate well-being, not a drag on profits.

BEST PRACTICES

There is much to be said for finding and using the best practices, however determined. Say, for example, that a corporation surveys its far-flung operations in search of a great idea that can be implemented at other sites. It would be foolish not to replace a good operational practice with a much better one. That is just common sense. The sad case is when company communications are so bad that good ideas are not shared, even though applicable to common situations or even entirely different ones.

Determining best practices within a company should be initiated by a dedicated team, a group of people focusing on finding out the things each part of the company does best. Once the survey has been completed and the results have been categorized and summarized, the information should be shared with leaders throughout the company. Then, company leaders can review and implement the practices that are appropriate in their area.

Why re-invent a wheel that has already been developed and proved in some other part of the business? Leaders might also find that some practice or concept can be successfully applied in a novel way to an internal operation. Be imaginative. Think outside the box for a new way to apply the best practice.

After the initial project to uncover best practices has been completed, the next step is to set up a mechanism for sharing best practices that are developed following the initial project. An internal website could be used to communicate newly developed best practices. Reward individuals and groups that come up with new best practices. Reward them handsomely.

EFFCIENCY

There is always a limit to how much additional profit a well-run, efficient company can achieve. Chasing that last percentage of improvement in efficiency is not necessarily the best use of resources. Going from 95 percent efficiency to 98 percent could be cost-prohibitive. The same effort might be better spent on a more innovative function in an entirely different area.

Perfection in efficiency is not perfection in corporate profits. Instead, seek the exponential leap along a different path. Be suspicious of rising profits but not revenue, especially over an extended period. Your support might be for a primary product or service that is reaching the end of its life.

"There is nothing so useless as doing efficiently that which should not be done at all."
—Peter F. Drucker

44

Consultants, Friends and Foes

> Consultant: any ordinary guy more than fifty miles from home.
> —Eric Sevareid

> Don't follow any advice, no matter how good, until you feel as deeply in your spirit as you think in your mind that the counsel is wise.
> —David Seabury

> To accept good advice is but to increase one's own ability.
> —Johann Wolfgang von Goethe

CONSULTANTS

The executive who engages a consultant puts his or her own career on the line; because the findings of a consultant, if followed, can impact the company's executives, employees, directors, owners, and stockholders—not to mention its customers and suppliers. Since the primary motivation of a consultant is often the engagement fee, the consultant's findings can sometimes be brought into question. Therefore, the parameters surrounding an engagement and the people involved, on both sides, are terribly important. Overt and covert agendas must be uncovered. Why are you bringing in a consultant in the first place?

Avoiding Responsibility: Consultants are sometimes brought in because executives are afraid to take a stand. They want to cover themselves. Their excuse is that the consultant said it, not them. In this scenario, the executives are just doing what the consultants say to do. That is a complete abdication of executive responsibility. Shareholders won't make that fine distinction; neither will customers.

Executives of a company simply cannot escape their responsibilities by bringing in a consultant. They should not be puppets of the consultants. The hiring company must set the objectives of the engagement. Once the engagement has been completed, the final decision on what to do must be made by the hiring company. Consultants sell advice; they should not sell decisions. Their advice can be heeded or ignored—in part or in whole. It's up to the executives—who have the final responsibility.

Objectivity: The advice you pay for should be objective, but sometimes it is not. It all boils down to the integrity of those doing the hiring and those being hired. There are many good consultants who are truly knowledgeable and who are very objective. But consultants, by their very nature, are politically sensitive and will play their cards VERY CAREFULLY. They have to. They want return engagements, plus referrals to other potential clients. They may even be jockeying for a full-time position as an employee with the client company.

Deference to Outsiders: Organizations typically give more weight to pronouncements coming from outside the organization than from inside. Familiarity breeds contempt. An outside consultant can reach the same conclusion already reached by someone on the inside, but it will carry more weight coming from the outside. Customers, creditors, regulatory bodies, special interest groups, and stockholders can also influence you. But some insiders' opinions do carry weight, such as the head of the company (the boss) or someone he or she relies on for advice (a trusted assistant).

This all points to an obvious conclusion—if you are willing to be objective and open-minded—listen to your own people before you start paying big bucks to some outside concern. Your insiders will usually have a better understanding of the business than the outsider. The outsider may bring perspective and objectivity, but his or her reference point is still from outside the company. Also, the outsider will have to charge you for the time spent becoming familiar with your company. Inside people do not have that start-up problem.

Going Overboard: Large corporations can go consultant crazy. They bring in consultants for everything. Management approves consultant engagements without really analyzing the need for each individual engagement. The right hand does not know what the left is doing. Millions are spent without knowing the effectiveness of the expenditures. The consultants are happy, of course, because they are generating huge revenues.

When consulting fees spiral out of control, everyone loses except the consulting companies. If, when walking down the hall, you see a lot of consultants; assume things are out of control. It would be cheaper to hire employees with the desired skills and experience instead of constantly engaging consultants for the long term.

Not So Unique: Consultants learn by experience, meaning they learn from their consulting assignments. In short, they get paid by the client to learn. Once they have learned something, they use what they have learned in future engagements. Thus, every subsequent client benefits from previous clients. So long as an engagement is not led by a novice, everyone can profit from the process.

Although consultants, in theory, provide results customized to the client; in reality, many business problems are just repeats of problems found at other clients. Consulting firms usually have a generalized formula or several standard formulae they apply to different assignments. The output is much the same as they have provided elsewhere, but slightly customized to fit the occasion. Your unique solution is probably just a variation of some common solution. That is not necessarily good or bad, but it should be kept in mind. Judge a recommendation by the fruit it delivers. Ignore promises of uniqueness. That is a marketing tactic. It is often harder to sell a commonplace solution; so, they sell uniqueness.

On the other side, though, there is a situation where the consulting firm will sell a common solution and emphasize the fact it is a proven product. This is the case when a consulting firm, like some of the big consulting firms, has a methodology it sells. This proven methodology is generally a formal process with predefined steps, forms, formulas, etc. It may be computer-based. These methodologies are usually quite expensive, but they can be very effective when implemented properly. However, it may be more advantageous and a whole lot less expensive to develop your own, with the emphasis on simplicity, not complexity. Going either route will consume a lot of time.

Over-Extending Themselves: A consulting firm is very unlikely to have expertise in every area, so you are wise to check their credentials before engaging them for a particular assignment. There is a huge temptation for a consulting group to be all things to all people. Businesses sometimes try the same approach. It is a mistake for both. In any case, ask for examples and references from similar projects. Make sure they can walk the talk, that they are experts in the required area.

Too Much Jargon: Avoid consultants who constantly talk in jargon you do not understand. Don't let your ego get in the way. No executive should expect to be an expert in every discipline. If you don't understand what a consultant is saying, make him or her talk in terms you can understand. A good consultant knows how to communicate effectively.

Junior People: One recurring problem from consulting engagements is that the consulting group will often woo you with their best consultants, and then assign junior people to handle the day-to-day tasks of the engagement. You want the best people you can get because what they recommend could have a profound influence on the direction your business takes. You have to pay more for the better people, but you get what you pay for. For mundane work, the junior people are fine; but for critical work, you want consultants with high mileage on their odometers. You most definitely want a senior person in charge of the engagement. Monitor results and ask for more qualified people if the assigned personnel are not performing up to par.

Competitors: One thing to consider when engaging a consulting firm is finding out if they have a client who is your direct competitor. If they do, there could be a conflict of interest. It is strongly suggested you steer away from engaging a consultant who is cozy with your competitor.

Hiring-Company Responsibilities: There are two partners in a consulting engagement, the hiring company and the hired consultant group. Don't ignore problems on the hiring side, meaning your company. Integrity can be lacking. Critical bits of information can be withheld. The responsible executive on the hiring side could be totally inept and lacking in common sense and judgment. This is not a good working environment for the consultant.

The hiring company could be using the consultants as hit men, to do their dirty work. Consultants can sometimes be coerced into giving an opinion the hiring company has preordained. Remember, a consultant wants to please the client.

> "All too many consultants, when asked, 'What is two and two?' respond, 'What did you have in mind?'"
> —Norman R. Augustine

Remember, the consultants could give the right advice but be totally ignored. In short, there is a potential for many problems on both sides. Lawyers have made plenty of money trying to sort out problems from consulting engagements gone astray.

Information Sharing: Consulting firms want to build long-term relationships with clients. This can be beneficial to both sides, because the consultants are able to develop an in-depth knowledge of the company, which makes any recommendations come from a stronger knowledge base. If the consulting firm is a good one, there is a strong argument for letting them get in bed with you. If they aren't, why are you engaging them in the first place?

But be careful how much you reveal. It might be best to take a "need to know" approach when doling out information, especially closely guarded strategic information. If you are too restrictive, though, you will place handcuffs on the consultants and may prevent them from doing their best. Play it by ear. Use non-disclosure agreements, where appropriate.

Pseudo Employees: Sometimes a client organization will place a consultant in a position that would normally be filled by an employee. That means putting the consultant in a decision-making role with the same authority as an employee. In the right circumstances, this could be a good choice. The consultant's firm probably would not have a problem with this, but it is better to have your own people in positions of authority.

In this scenario, the consultant will not be around long enough to suffer any of the long-term consequences of his or her decisions. It might be better, if you are having trouble filling a position, to let one of the other executives run the position, with advice from the consultant, until the position can be filled. Don't let consultants take over your company.

Politics: Beware of the situation where a consultant gets so entrenched in a client's affairs, because of a long-term relationship, that he or she becomes a major player in corporate politics. If you see this happening in your company, you can probably make the safe assumption that objectivity on the part of the consultant has taken a hit. Too cozy a relationship means his or her recommendations may not be free of bias.

Put-Downs: Also, keep in mind that some consultants will see it as advantageous to downplay the quality of a company's people in order to raise themselves in the eyes of the client's executives. Some of your employees will figure this out eventually, if it happens.

For any endeavor, you need a team composed of cooperative members from both sides of the aisle. Make sure your people are cooperating with the consultants and that they understand the benefits consultants bring to the equation. Get rid of any consultant who continually tears down your employees. The engagement will not work without the full cooperation of all parties. Trust and respect are required on both sides.

Simple Is Good: A consultant is expected to come up with some high-powered advice—the more complex, demanding, and painful, the better. Complexity is its own justification. But simple is best. It is certainly the easiest to implement, and it will require less follow-on work (expense) by the consultants. The most elegant solution is often the simplest. It just may take a while to figure it out. The more complex a solution is, the greater are its potential risks and difficulties.

Incentives: When you start giving the consultants monetary incentives, such as bonuses, to accomplish specific results, like finding a certain number of positions to be eliminated through layoffs; the more likely it is that objectivity will fly out the window. The consultants want to maximize revenue. Impartiality may not be achievable. Besides, layoffs are a management problem, not some outsider's responsibility. The appearance of consultants can often mean leaders are not managing. The captain's chair is empty—and an iceberg is coming up fast.

Worth It When Needed: Don't let all the warnings in this section deter you from engaging consultants when you need them. If you need help, you need help! ***The right consultant with the right expertise at the right time can be worth his or her weight in gold.*** Consultants do have their place in the scheme of things. Don't necessarily reject a consulting firm because of some bad project in the past. Consulting organizations are just like other organizations. They can and do make mistakes. They can learn and grow. How they handle their failures is important.

In summary, use consultants when you need them, but be wary of how you use them. Never give them a blank check or a free rein to do whatever they see fit. Give them specific assignments. Monitor the results. But remember that a good consultant is no substitute for a good leader.

CONSULTING ENGAGEMENT PARAMETERS

In order to have an effective and meaningful consulting engagement, certain parameters should be put in place before the engagement begins. First, if you really want an objective, unbiased consultation, you must communicate to the consultant that you do not want him or her just to tell you what you want to hear. If you are investing time and expense to bring someone in, you need to hear the unvarnished truth. You want objectivity, not subjectivity. You want the consultant to be candid.

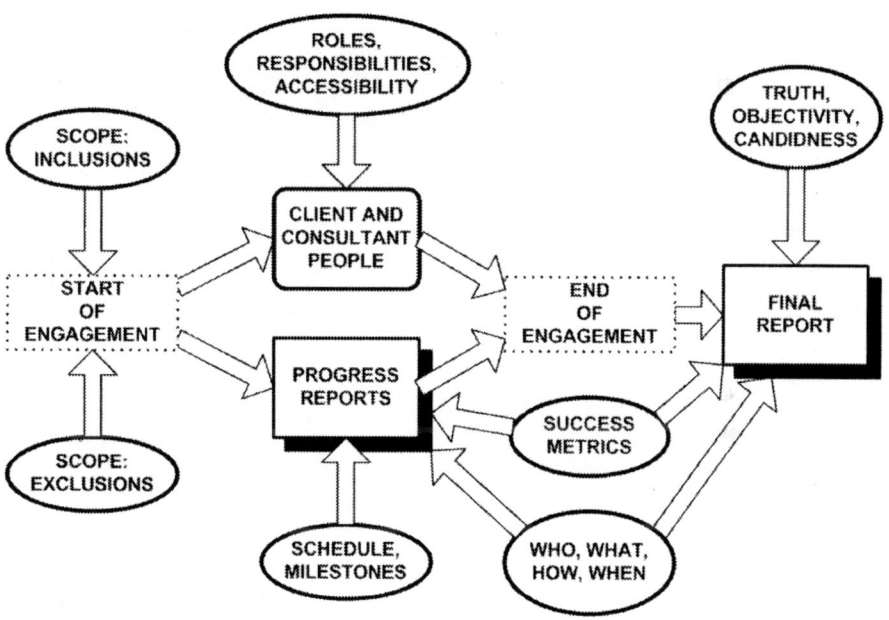

The scope of the engagement needs to be clearly defined from the start. Establish, preferably on paper, the areas that will be addressed by the consultant. If needed, indicate areas or topics that are not covered in the assignment. If there are things you do not want the consultant involved in, let the consultant know. The same rules apply if you do not want the consultant talking to someone in the company.

Laying down the parameters of an engagement includes indicating the responsibilities to be carried out by both the consultant and by your company. The roles should be listed along with who will fill each role. Accessibility to people in each role should be defined. There should be a primary spokesman (contact point) for each side. Problem resolution should be covered in order to handle any issues that happen to come up during the engagement.

There should be a published schedule with milestones in order to measure progress on the assignment. The methods and frequency of communicating should be agreed to. This would include the topics to be covered in progress reports and which people are to receive the reports. The agreement should indicate who is responsible for contributing to the reports, who will prepare them, and who will actually deliver them. Part of the reporting should include face-to-face meetings, both regularly scheduled and impromptu ones.

Part of the agreement should describe how success is to be measured during the course of the engagement and upon its completion. Measuring success could be as simple as the preparation and delivery of a final report. The agreement could go further and lay out some complicated metrics to be used and reported as part of the assignment.

In general, you need to come to a definitive agreement on the working arrangements and the deliverables expected from the consulting assignment.

Part IX

SALES AND MARKETING

45

The Sales Cycle

The standard sales cycle is fairly simple and straightforward. It is just presented here to give context for later chapters in the book.

SALES CYCLE

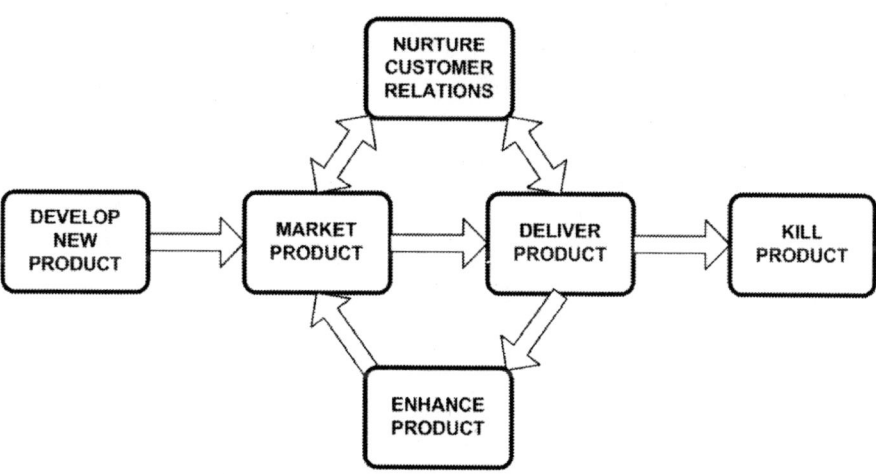

The sales cycle can be summarized as a process that starts with the development of a product (or service). (Whether it is developed directly by the company or is outsourced to another business entity is not pertinent to this discussion.) The company then markets the product to potential customers.

Upon its purchase, the company must deliver the product to the customer. When marketing and selling the company's output, the company must develop and nurture a good relationship with the customer. A satisfied customer returns for repeat business.

As time passes, the product is enhanced—maybe even a new product is developed—and sold to the customer.

At some point, the product becomes unprofitable or is superseded by another product. The company must then call it quits and kill the product. The sales cycle has ended for that product.

46

Marketing Factors

MARKETING BASICS

You can carve out a highly profitable market niche by being very selective in choosing your targeted customers. Do not go after customers that do not match your expertise or fit your business model.

New Products: There are a number of potential sources for new products, including: research and development, market research, and internal entrepreneurship. To promote internal entrepreneurship, you reward the product author with returns from the new product. If appropriate, make the product author the product manager.

Being first in the market is the goal and is the best way to preempt your competition. If you are late getting off the starting line, you might never catch up. Whoever achieves the number 1 and 2 positions in the market are those who acted the fastest. It is hard to dislodge the leaders. Speed to market is everything. "The early bird gets the worm" certainly applies here.

Being first to market does not always mean having the best product. Superior marketing can overcome a better product. In the long run, you still need to turn your product into the best in order to maintain market leadership.

> "It's the first company to build the mental position that has the upper hand, not the first company to make the product. IBM didn't invent the computer; Sperry Rand did. But IBM was the first to build the computer position in the prospect's mind."
>
> —Al Ries

Being the market leader has a domino effect and helps you draw in even more customers. The more customers you have, the more you will get—call it peer pressure, crowd influence, or whatever.

As fast as today's clock is ticking, the market race is not for the faint of heart. You must move quickly. Although you must do your homework about potential market conditions, there is never time for the "perfect" market survey. You must make an educated guess. New markets are "unknown" markets, by definition. Taking a risk is essential.

Do you want to be a perpetual follower?

New Product Rejection: Blockbuster products are typically rejected by customers, sometimes for years, before gaining wide acceptance. Then they become necessities; you cannot live without them. If you ask customers what they want, their reference point is usually the stable of current products. They want the same products, but jazzed up with new colors or new features. People are uncomfortable with new products. They are set in their ways and reluctant to change. But they can and do.

Even the greatest new technology can have a slow start. Until other people start embracing the new technology, the average person will have no partnership with the new technology. If you are the first to use a revolutionary communications technology, it will take some time for everyone else to acquire the technology so you can use it to communicate with the other people.

Personal computers took a while to get going. Even the Internet was slow in gaining acceptance before it took off like a rocket. Other examples of products that were slow in gaining marketplace approval, but which are necessities now, are Post-its®, VCRs, cellular phones, and minivans.

It is tough to introduce a new product. It takes time, pain, and expense on the part of business leaders to make a new product a success. Perseverance does pay off, though.

Solutions: Emphasize and sell solutions to problems. Promote the business value proposition that is provided by the product.

> "Last year our customers bought over one million quarter-inch drill bits and none of them wanted to buy the product. They all wanted quarter-inch holes."
>
> —Anonymous

But another, sometimes more effective, tactic is to sell the financial benefits of the product, such as savings in purchase price or savings in maintenance costs over the life of the product.

Spreading the Word: Spread an awareness of the product. Use conferences, public appearances, media contacts, and interviews to promote products and services. Try to get favorable product reviews by approaching the right influencers. Use company evangelists, meaning product specialists, to help promote the product. Use CEOs as media celebrities, if they present a positive image over the media.

Build online web communities. Set up focus groups to draw attention to the product and to provide feedback to your marketers. Publish success stories. Promote partnerships with other firms, where it makes sense and the partnerships create market synergy.

Build public awareness of the brand in addition to the product. New product introductions are easier when associated with a well-respected brand. Sell the reputation of the company. Perhaps sell the company brand more than selling the individual products, assuming the company has multiple products.

In regard to brand loyalty, you need 360-degree branding. A company sends out many messages about itself through many different media: press releases, sales brochures, websites, TV ads, radio ads, order forms, showrooms, customer contact people, etc.

The company's messages must send a consistent message, a message that reinforces itself every time a potential customer receives a message. Make sure the message is always the same and is the one you want to be delivered, quality and trust, for example. Embed a core idea that is unique and instantly comprehended. Then live up to your brand.

Brand Loyalty: Brand loyalty means that when you are given a choice between two brands of the same product—not knowing the respective merits of the individual products—you choose one because it carries a brand you trust.

Over the years, you learn to trust a particular brand because it has produced quality products you can count on. You look upon the brand as providing a good value. You know what you are getting and you feel the provider of the product knows what it is doing. The brand is dependable. Your first-hand experiences have proved it.

But remember, your company can lose brand loyalty by turning out shoddy products and service. Once you lose a customer, it is extremely difficult to get that customer back. It can take years, if ever. You must keep earning the trust of your customers. Be vigilant in product creation and delivery.

In the early years of the Internet, brand loyalty had minimal impact. The initial users of the Internet had an overriding desire to get on the Web and take advantage of whatever it was beginning to offer. With the Internet moving into the mainstream, brand loyalty is becoming more important. Mainstream consumers lean more to familiarity and affordability than the early users did. The pendulum is swinging back to business basics.

COMPETITIVE ADVANTAGE

Who is your closest competitor? How close are they? Are you in the lead or are they? If you are in the lead, can you sustain it? How long can you sustain it? If they are in the lead, can you close the gap? How long will it take?

> "In business, the competition will bite you if you keep running; if you stand still, they will swallow you."
> —Semon Knudsen

Normal Revenue: Normal business revenue is derived from the sale of core products and services. This represents market share. It is the primary target of the marketing department, the reason for the business. Revenue *less* associated expense *equals* income from operations. Company resources should be concentrated in this area.

Other Revenue: Then there is revenue that has nothing to do with market share. This is revenue or income that comes from activity outside the normal revenue stream. It could be income derived from selling company property that is no longer needed for operations. It could be interest income or income derived from one-time changes in accounting practice. This category of income is nice to have, since it does increase owner's equity, but it has nothing to do with market share. The sophisticated investor is not interested in this type of earnings. It does not add to shareholder value in the long term.

Bad Revenue: Finally, there is revenue that is bad revenue. It is bad because it comes at the expense of market share. This is true if valuable company resources are diverted to products or services in an area that is not strategic to a company's core business, especially if the diversion delays time-to-market for core business products.

For example, if manufacturing and sales are diverted to some product that produces half the gross profit as the same effort could produce if applied to core products, you have bad revenue. This is even worse if the same effort could have been applied toward building long-term market share, like for a new product.

Bad revenue could come from some pet project of the CEO that is done at shareholder expense. Unless the CEO owns most or all of the company, it is not justified. The astute shareholder would conclude it is bad management.

Bad revenue might also result from an effort to produce good figures in an otherwise lackluster quarter, but the short-term gain is done at the expense of a later quarter. The chickens will come home to roost, eventually.

Choosing Markets: Always consider the type of market share you are seeking. You want to be a leader. If the market is overcrowded and the effort to obtain or maintain market share is overly expensive, you may be in the wrong market. If a market has been relatively untapped and the company has the resources to capture an extremely profitable niche, go for it.

Choosing markets is a choice between opportunities—given the proper resources that cannot be applied better elsewhere. It is all a question of numbers and is based on an analysis of market size, potential market dominance, ability of the company to dominate the market, and availability of company resources.

Inattention: But these are all basics, so why bring them up? The problem is the devil within us; the maintenance of status quo is too easy. You do not have to think, or at least you fail to do so, until the competitor—who did think—suddenly races by because he or she saw the opportunity while you were dozing. Once you lose market position, it is harder to regain that position than it would have been to maintain it. Playing catch-up is hard when your competitor is accelerating. You should have been the one out in front with the pedal to the metal.

The successful leader needs to constantly keep his or her antennae up and turned on. In today's speedy economy, there is no time for standby mode. The shareholder is looking to the future. Are you?

BUZZ MARKETING

Traditional marketing campaigns have lost their punch. Marketers are seeking other avenues to spread the word. One approach that is being explored in recent years is buzz marketing. The idea is to seek out influential trendsetters in selected niche markets, then use these messengers to spread the word—

buzz. It is a soft sell as opposed to a hard sell. This grassroots approach has the potential of sparking an epidemic of national proportions.

Rather than using traditional marketing media (TV, radio, newspapers, magazines, billboards, etc.), the companies try to use more impactive, word-of-mouth selling. In this scenario, the messenger tells a friend, peer, admirer, fan, or acquaintance how good the product is. The recipient of the message then tells other people. These first converts become evangelists for the product. They serve as trendsetters—consciously or unconsciously.

Targets of Buzz: Buzz marketing works for people in their twenties, who are skeptical of traditional advertising. It comes across as spontaneous, but it isn't. It is meticulously planned. Markets and trendsetters are carefully selected. The idea is peer communication, spreading the word through a peer group. The voice of a friend is, of course, more believable and credible than mass communication. Potential consumers are reached person-to-person, where the people live, work, and play.

It is unlikely that buzz marketing will ever work for commodity products. It is probably more applicable in niche markets rather than broad-based ones. The effectiveness of buzz increases for products the consumer is likely to be passionate about. This category of products helps give the consumer an image of being cool, on the cutting-edge.

Messengers: The choice of messengers is critical. The marketer should seek out people who are perceived as being trendsetters in the community. They can be celebrities, peer group leaders, or people who are paid and dressed up to look like trendsetters. You want these people to influence other people, who then talk up the product to their friends and admirers. So, the messengers might be paid or unpaid.

A company will give a product to the messengers, or will loan a more expensive product, like a car, to them for a short period, say, six months. Then people who want to emulate the trendsetters see one of them with the product. The messenger could also hand out mementos, trinkets, or souvenirs related to the product. The trendsetter might try to give an impression of revealing guarded secrets. Fake shoppers can be employed to pass the message to other shoppers. Messengers could even give impromptu performances. They could also use Internet forums and chat-room sessions to pass the word.

Underground Avenues: Alternatively, an underground approach could be used that embeds messages in other things, such as games, websites, performances, etc. The marketing connection may not be apparent at first. The sponsor may or may not be revealed.

Low Cost: The beauty of all these methods is that the cost is relatively small compared to regular marketing channels. Buzz marketing lets the consumer—an unpaid salesperson—carry the message for you.

Risks: Buzz marketing is a stealth strategy and is full of risks. Its results are hard to measure. When uncovered for what it is, there is a risk of severe backlash from consumers who feel they have been hoodwinked. As buzz marketing becomes more pervasive, consumers will become more wary and more skeptical. Buzz will be perceived as a negative message of contrived manipulation. It can come across as being totally deceptive in nature. The result might be a public-relations nightmare; and this has already happened to some marketers.

If you do decide to use buzz marketing, be wary. Enter at your own peril.

PRODUCT TRAINING SCHOOLS

Leading technology companies provide schools for technician wannabes. There are several benefits to this practice. The most obvious benefit is that it strengthens the brand name. When the student graduates he or she has bonded with the brand because that is where his or her newly acquired skills lie. He or she has invested time and money into the brand. As "branded" students spread throughout the industry, they are likely to be positively disposed to buying products of the company that sponsored the schools. The students are evangelists for the cause.

PRODUCT TRAINING SCHOOLS

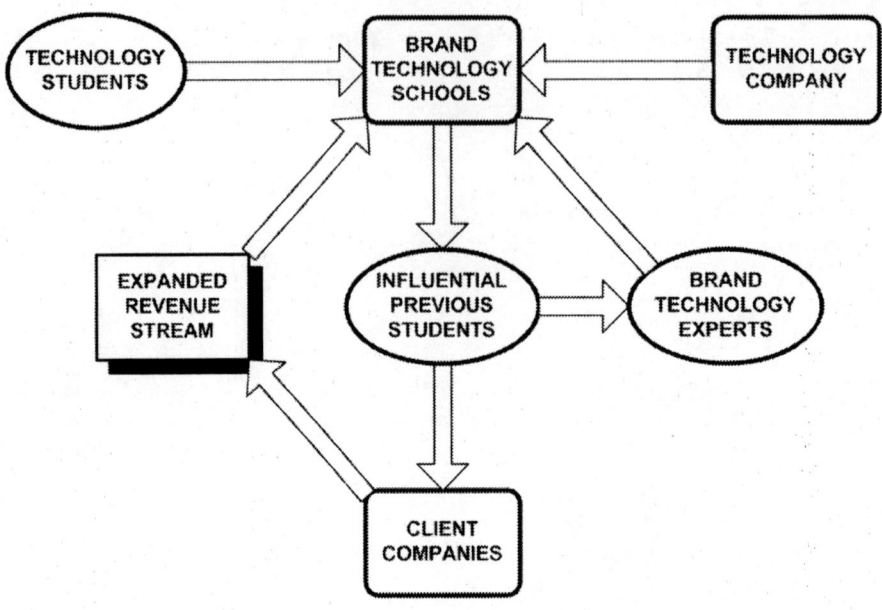

Influence occurs in three possible ways when the trained technician goes to work for a company. First, if the company already uses the technology, the new employee just adds one more voice in favor of keeping the brand. Second, if the technician has moved up to a position of influence and there is a choice between brands, the technician will normally lean toward the technology brand he or she is comfortable with. Finally, if the technician is hired by a company that is trying to decide on a technology in the first place, the previous bonding can lead the technician to recommend going with the known technology brand.

The technology schools may or may not be owned by the technology company. As a brand becomes popular, that popularity leads independent technical schools to include the branded technology in their curriculum. Training opportunities expand. This reinforces brand awareness.

Schools bring in the experts of a technology to teach new students. This not only reinforces the evangelism of the brand, but the experts bring in valuable experience from the real world. If the technology company runs the schools, the instructors, as employees of the technology company, bring valuable insights into problems and opportunities for existing and new products.

Overall, technology schools can exert a powerful influence for the successful spread of a brand's awareness. Revenue grows as a consequence.

Are you in a company that could apply this principle?

47

Selling

SELLING A SOLUTION

One of the best ways to sell products and services is not to sell them as individual items having standalone merit. Instead, operate under the assumption your customer or client is making a purchase to solve one or more problems. Therefore, you should be selling a solution.

SELLING A SOLUTION

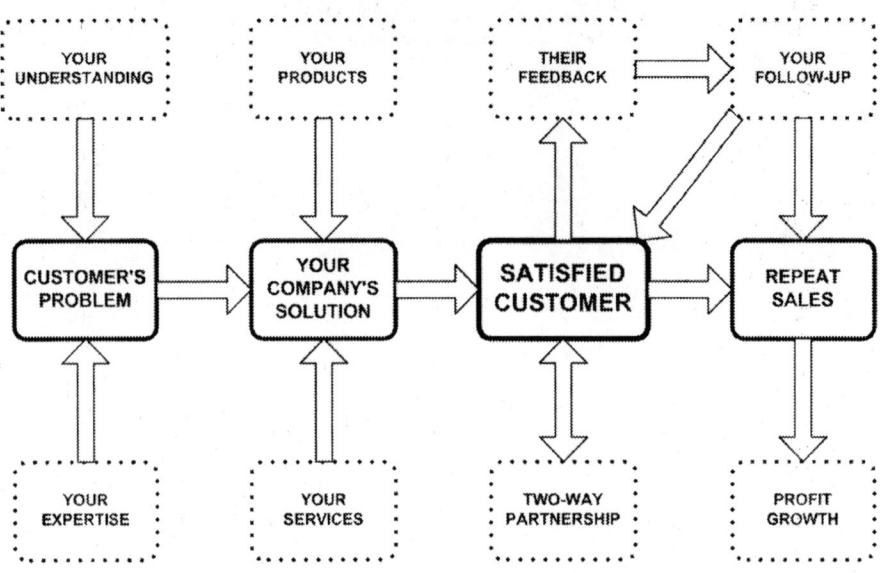

Customer's Problem: In order to come up with a solution, you must understand the customer's problem. That means applying your expertise to the situation so you understand what the problem is. Problem solving is a two-way street, with both sides talking. You must listen to the customer's problems and concerns. By listening—instead of the more typical sales approach of talking so much—you gain an understanding of the problem.

Your Company's Solution: Using your knowledge and skills to perform an analysis of the information gathered, you start to work toward a solution. Since you are coming in with an outside viewpoint—hopefully with a certain level of objectivity—you may determine the problem is not what the customer thought it was. In any case, the problem is identified.

Next, you look at your company's stable of products and services to see if you can help the customer. If so, you assemble a solution to the problem. If you cannot provide a solution for a particular problem, you let the customer know. Remember, you are desirous of maintaining a long-term relationship. In this scenario, you must avoid the temptation of trying to make a sale at any cost, whether it is right for the customer or not.

If you do not have the solution, there other alternatives that can help build and maintain your relationship with the customer. One possibility is to partner with some other company to provide a solution. In this situation, you might even be able to get a piece of the action. Another possibility is for you to refer the customer to an altogether different company. This will also reinforce the customer's trust of you as a consultant. You have given advice at no charge.

Satisfied Customer: This model of selling assumes you want to engender an ongoing two-way partnership between your company and the customer. Information flows both ways. Both sides work together. It is a win-win relationship. It includes actively requesting feedback from the customer after the sale, then acting upon what you hear. If there are problems, you follow up with some corrective action. If there are no problems, you have at least shown the customer you care.

Repeat Sales: The immediate result of all this problem solving is that you acquire and maintain customer satisfaction. As you continue to follow up with the satisfied customer, you lay a firm foundation for repeat sales. Repeat sales lead to increased revenue and long-term profit growth. The business grows.

> "A salesman is one who sells goods that won't come back to customers who will."
>
> —Anonymous

Therefore, take the IBM approach and sell a solution. Establish a relationship of trust where the customer is loyal to your company, not particular products.

SELLING DOLLARS

Some people buy because of the real or perceived benefits offered by a product. Others buy the solution to a problem that is besetting them. But the best sales technique is often to show a customer the dollar benefit represented by the product. The benefit could be an increase in revenue coming from your customer's use of the product. Alternatively, the benefit could be a savings in your customer expenses.

Regardless of whether the dollar benefit is increased revenue or reduced expenses, a good salesperson will sell the dollars. This requires doing some homework. Determine who your competition is. Dig up supporting figures. Analyze potential return on investment. Spread the cost of your product over its lifetime. Show the cost of going without the product.

Talk in terms of total cost, not original purchase price, particularly if your purchase price is higher than the competition. Show the dollar benefit of using your product as compared to using that of the competition. A simple reduction in your product's cost might be the reduced maintenance resulting from use of your product.

$$\text{Total Price} - \text{Reduced Maintenance Cost} = \text{Net Total Price}$$

Showing per unit figures can often help clarify benefits. Restate the dollars in terms of benefits per customer unit versus that provided by your competition. This lets you reach your true per unit net price. For example, spread your product's total price over the number of customer units, say, a customer's own manufacturing output units—if your product can be related to things produced by your customer. Then spread the savings in product maintenance, for example—versus the maintenance costs with your competitor's product—over the applicable number of customer units. Finally, reduce your product's applicable purchase price per customer unit by the comparative savings per unit; which gets you to true cost per customer unit.

$$\text{Total Price} / \text{Customer Units} = \text{Price per Unit}$$

$$\text{Total Savings} / \text{Customer Units} = \text{Savings per Unit}$$

Price per Unit - Saving per Unit = Net Price per Unit

The goal of all these calculations is to arrive at true cost or true savings, both in total and per unit figures. There could be many variations in the figures used, but the overall concept is the same: Take attention away from original cost and focus on net cost. Be sure to restate your figures in terms the customer can relate to.

DYNAMIC PRICING

Today's all-pervasive connectivity and numerous communication channels—all functioning at the speed of the Internet—have changed the dynamics of pricing for goods and services. Financial markets and commodity exchanges used to be the leaders in real-time pricing. The Web gives everyone access to real-time pricing, both buyer and seller.

The common person can enter bids for items offered on the Web. Auctions no longer are restricted to specific locations. Auctioneers are no longer needed. A computer program controls the bidding process. Auctions can last over extended periods and over extended distances.

With the Internet as the communications medium, a person at home can bid on airline tickets. Energy and bandwidth can be auctioned and sold online. Using an online brokerage account, a regular stockholder can enter buys and sells for stocks, just like the big boys—all the time getting real-time quotes and real-time trade confirmations.

If a company decides the price for a product offered online is too high or too low, the price can be changed instantly. The volume of sales before and after the price change can be tracked. Adjustments in offerings can be made quickly. Business leaders no longer have to wait for monthly, weekly, or even daily sales reports. They know the results instantly.

The new playing field is strengthening the customer's position. If a customer does not like the posted price, a price search for competing products or dealers can be started instantly. Information gives new power to both sides. Some companies even post competitors' prices. And some websites' main purpose is to provide a listing of lowest prices from various distributors—with a link to a place to purchase the product at a certain price.

Use dynamic pricing capabilities to your company's advantage. Regular markets are beginning to follow the lead of financial markets. Real-time pricing is coming in like a tsunami. Think outside the box. How can you take advantage of the system? How can you achieve a competitive advantage and still make a good profit?

CROSS-SELLING

The concept of cross-selling is important to an executive's thought process. He or she should always consider expanding sales to an existing customer or client. Cross-selling occurs when a selling company takes advantage of a new opportunity to sell a product or service to an existing customer. We will ignore the simple case of just increasing sales of the same product or service to an existing customer contact. With that out of the way, there are three categories of cross-selling opportunities:

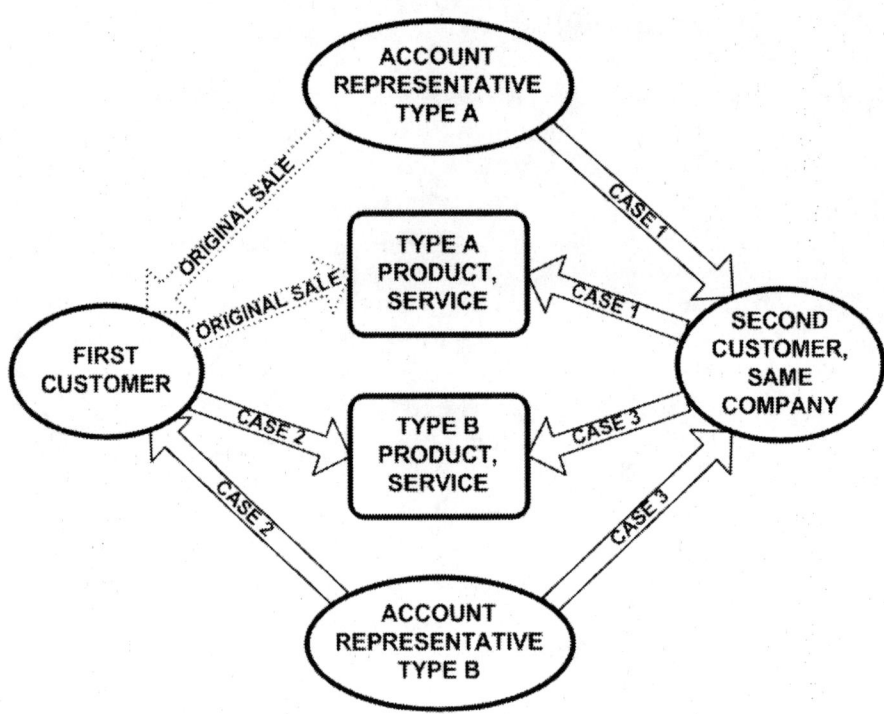

Case 1: The first account representative (type A) gets an opportunity to sell his or her specialty (type A product, service) to a second customer contact in the same company where the first sale was made. The contact with the second customer may or may not involve a recommendation or introduction from the first customer contact, the one that first opened the door to business with your company.

Case 2: A second account representative (type B) has the opportunity to sell his or her specialty (type B product, service) to the first customer contact in the client company. Either the first customer contact or the first account representative (type A), or both, could have been instrumental in opening this door.

Case 3: A second account representative (type B) gets an opportunity to sell his or her specialty (type B product, service) to a second customer contact in the client company. Three possible avenues to the new sale could be the original account executive, the original customer contact, or the second customer contact—or some combination thereof. The second customer may just need another type of product.

The bottom line: Make sure to explore all avenues for selling products and services to an existing client company. Once the door to the client company has been opened to one sale, other opportunities may arise. Just because your company has made a (first) sale, don't forget about trying to open other doors at the client company. A large company will have many departments and many divisions, thus, many potential customer contacts.

INTERNET CHANNEL CONFLICT

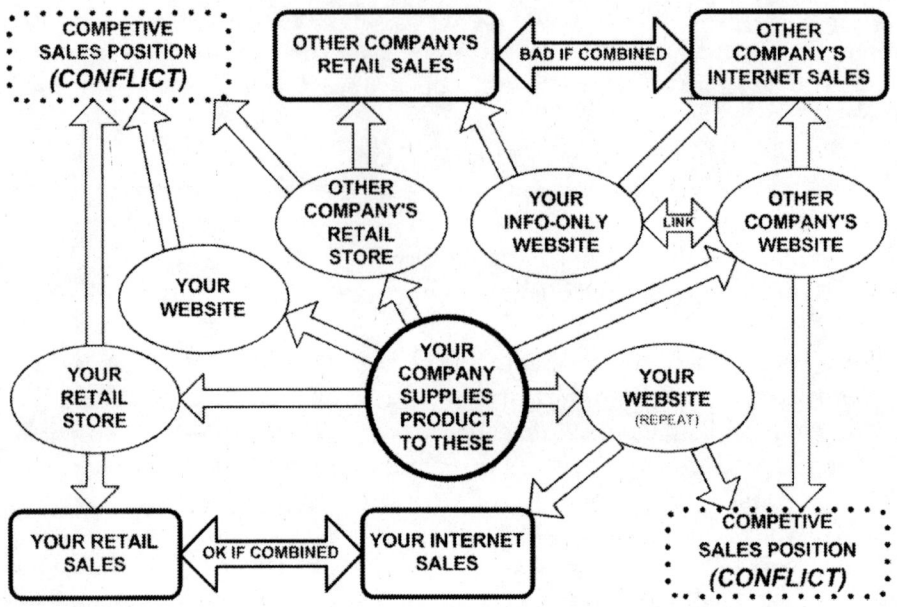

INTERNET CHANNEL CONFLICT

Channel Conflict: Channel conflict can come into play when a manufacturer has a choice of several different sales distribution paths, or channels. Suppose a manufacturer has always sold its product through independent retailers, but suddenly starts selling directly to the customer. The retailers will likely get bent all out of shape. This is a change in the business model, and it shatters the previous understanding about the way products are sold. Now the manufacturer is in direct competition with the retailer. The retailer is losing sales it had before.

Next, look at a manufacturer who starts out selling product directly to the customer. No middleman is involved. Company stores are set up on the East Coast. The company starts spreading west. Assume there is a huge demand for the product, but the manufacturer cannot set up new stores fast enough. So, it starts selling the product through retailers on the West Coast. Retailers are getting a piece of the action they did not have before. They are happy in spite of the manufacturer also engaging in retail sales.

Retailer Alienation: The different reactions are due to the positive or negative impact the change is having on the retailers. The Internet opens up possibilities to manufacturers who never before sold directly to consumers. From the manufacturer's point of view, a whole new vista of opportunities has rolled into view. Why not take advantage of the new possibilities? The profits could be huge.

The potential problem is alienation of retailers who were in the driver's seat before and whose position is now threatened. A trust has been broken with the retailers. But what does the manufacturer do about the Internet? The manufacturer cannot ignore it.

Retailer Websites (maybe linked with company information-only website): Retailers could demand that any Internet sales be made only through their own retail websites. This could be a problem since all retail websites are not created equal. There is a danger of the retailer damaging the manufacturer's image because of customers having a less than enjoyable time on the retailer's poorly designed website. Maybe not all of the retailers want to set up websites. So, you have a mixture of good sites, bad sites, and no sites.

This is not good, especially if the manufacturer has set up a website to give information about the company's products and where they can be bought, including links to retailer websites. The potential customer survives the website's marketing blitz only to find out (1) the selected retailer's website is a terror to deal with, (2) the online consumer must drive to a retail outlet since the retailer has no website, or (3) there is no nearby retail store even if the customer were reluctantly willing to make the drive.

The customer goes away with a bad taste in his or her mouth. If other brands are available and if they provide a positive experience, you can guess what will happen.

The manufacturer might try to set up and enforce website standards when it comes to dealing with the manufacturer's products. But that would be hard to enforce on the retailers. There are too many players, from web developers to retailer marketing types.

Company Information-Only Website (no links): One approach is for the manufacturer to set up an information only site, with no links to retailers. The problem with this is that the Internet user may have gone on the Web with the distinct goal of buying the product online. When not allowed to do so, the frustrated customer can simply search for a new brand, one that can be found somewhere else on the Internet. In one sense, you have driven the customer to the competition.

Company Internet-Only Sales: The manufacturer could decide to abandon its retailers and go with the "direct Internet sales only" model. This is a drastic step. The retailers are definitely alienated. The customers who are accustomed to dealing with the retailers and who are repeat customers are alienated, too. Then, of course, there are the customers who prefer dealing with a brick-and-mortar store. They are alienated, too. That adds up to a lot of alienated people.

A slight modification to this approach is for the manufacturer to partner with independent Internet-only retailers. The positive aspect to this is that the manufacturer doesn't have to set up any website; but the negative aspects of the approach in the previous paragraph are still in effect.

Unless there is a very strong case for the Internet only model opening up huge markets, markets that weren't there before and that would totally offset lost brick-and-mortar sales; this choice would appear foolhardy.

Company Integrated Sales: Then there is the possibility of replacing the independent retailers with a combination of manufacturer brick-and-mortar sites and websites. This has all the disadvantages of alienating pre-existing customers, plus the ramp-up time and expense for opening brick-and-mortar stores.

If the manufacturer starts out selling through its own website, there would be no conflict because no other independent retailer ever had a shot at selling the product. No trust was ever broken. If the manufacturer started with its own brick-and-mortar stores, it could add a retail website—with a cooperative blending of sales between the two. Such an integrated sales operation is a very effective operations model. It is one that old-time brick-and-mortar companies have returned to after trying to keep Internet sales completely separate from retail outlet sales. A shared warehousing and distribution system makes very good sense.

When trying to go the Internet route where the manufacturer has to convert from wholesale distribution to customer-direct distribution; the leap is equivalent to trying to jump across a huge chasm. Remember that distribution problems brought down many dot.coms when they tried to distribute directly to consumers.

Distribution and delivery to individual customers is no piece of cake—even if you use the likes of UPS or FedEx. The number of manufacturer-to-customer pathways—and relationships—would skyrocket. They have to be managed. Inventory problems are different and more complex.

Analyze First: No one with any sense said moving to the Internet would be easy for an existing manufacturer. Before making the plunge, the manufacturer should (1) consider all the alternatives, (2) look at the positives and negatives of each alternative, (3) weigh the probabilities of each alternative, and (4) play what-if games with the consequent financials.

One possibility might be to dabble in the Internet on a test basis without abandoning the loyal retailers. The experiment could uncover possibilities not hitherto expected. A synergistic solution might come from testing the pilot operation and closely monitoring its results.

In the end, the manufacturer must weigh the relative strengths of all the players before choosing a course of action. Who has the greatest bargaining power? Who is most likely to be successful? What are competitors likely to do? A compromise may have to be reached. Retailers may have to give in.

The manufacturer's leaders must take a stand. That means they must choose a course of action and carry it through—making appropriate adjustments while proceeding with the implementation. Vacillation or delay in making a decision could result in corporate death.

Part X

CUSTOMERS

48

Enthusiastic Customers

It takes considerable effort and dedication to develop enthusiastic customers, but that should be your goal. However, you must lay some groundwork first.

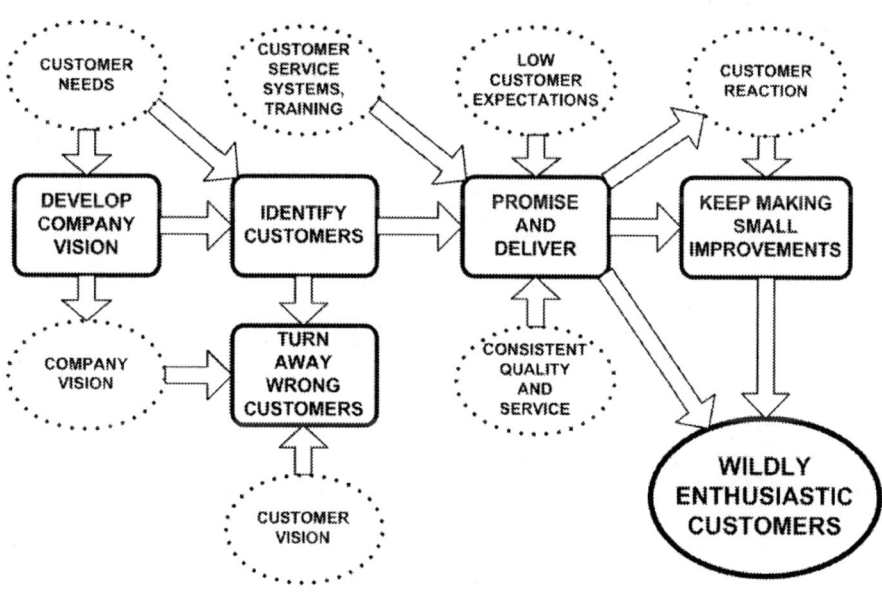

ENTHUSIASTIC CUSTOMERS

Develop Company Vision: You need to decide who you are as a company and the vision to use to guide you into the future. This is something you must develop—not outsiders, or your customers. Be sure to differentiate yourself from your competition. Let the vision be your goal.

Visualize what you want for your business. Identify customer needs that can be satisfied by your vision. Create a vision of perfection that is centered on the products and services you deliver to your customers. You can never achieve perfection, but you can keep it as a vision in your head—a guiding force—a target to shoot for.

Once you have come up with your vision, superimpose it on your business. Compare the realities of your business with your vision, i.e., actual vs. goals. Identify any discrepancies, the places where your business fails to live up to your vision. Work on eliminating or reducing the discrepancies.

> "Before you build a better mousetrap, it helps to know if there are any mice out there."
> —Mortimer B. Zukerman

Devote your time and attention to making the vision happen.

Identify Customers: When you have formulated your vision, it is time to concentrate more on determining who your target customers are. Identify the perceived customer needs you are trying to satisfy. When you determine what any particular customer really wants, it will probably turn out to be just a few things. But you need to satisfy needs customers aren't aware of. Keep in mind that customers will use your products in ways you never envisioned. Be open to possibilities you never thought about before.

When trying to determine who all your customers are, remember they are not necessarily the ones you will sell to directly. Consider everyone who touches the product, from original buyer (e.g., purchasing agent) through the end customer (e.g., end user). You must satisfy all your customers along the way. Breaks in the links mean breaks in sales.

Customers have their own visions, but they are typically very incompletely formulated. They tend to concentrate on one or two immediate needs; i.e., they focus on just a few, not many needs. Research existing and potential customers for any information you can find out. Work customers' visions into your own vision, but it may be necessary to reject their visions. In the end, hold fast to whatever vision you come up with for your business.

Turn Away Wrong Customers: Always operate within the confines of your own vision. Determine your customer's vision, what is needed by the customer. Compare the customer's vision with yours. Any customer's vision only has some meaning through its relevance to your company's vision. Remember, you can't really relate to a customer's vision without having one of your own as a reference point.

After learning a customer's vision and seeing how it fits with yours, you may need to tell the customer you cannot satisfy his or her needs. It may go against your basic feelings about selling, but the customer will need to be turned away. Always stay within the bounds of your own vision. Be true to yourself. It is a well-known fact that leaders in the marketplace operate within a well-defined window of service. They know who they are and the business they want to be in.

Promise and Deliver: Customers will initially come to you with very low expectations. They are conditioned to accept low quality products and service. Surprise them with high quality. You don't own the customers. They will leave if you don't deliver what they need.

So, pay attention to customers' needs. When you interface with them, ask what they want in the way of goods and services. Listen to what they say and, particularly, to what they don't say. You cannot assume they will list all their needs. In fact, they may say something that hides their true wants. They may focus on immediate problems, their "hot buttons," without looking at their broader needs, what they truly need the most.

Customer silence is a big problem. Most customers believe complaining will do little good, so why bother? When they receive bad service, they just never return—unless there is no competition and they have no other choice. They fail to complain. Their silence can itself be a message. Therefore, when someone does voice a complaint, listen to it. Pay close attention. More than likely, they really mean it. But pay particular attention if you do not hear complaints. Use customer reactions to your failing to serve their needs as a call to arms. Use customer feedback to identify any changes needed in products or services.

> "Those who enter to buy, support me. Those who come to flatter, please me. Those who complain, teach me how I may please others so that more will come. Only those hurt me who are displeased but do not complain. They refuse me permission to correct my errors and thus improve my service."
>
> —Marshall Field

Your company must provide consistent quality in products and service; therefore, set high standards for delivery. Whatever you promise in advertisements or whatever your people say to customers, deliver on your promises.

Customers expect you to do what you say you will do. If you don't, after awhile you will have no credibility with your customers. Consistency in high-quality products and service is a powerful message. It has "stickiness." When you act in a manner that is inconsistent with what you advertise, it takes a lot to overcome the negative message spoken by your actions.

Consistency on your part helps overcome resistance on the part of a customer. It is more important for your company and its people to meet expectations consistently than to exceed expectations.

To help achieve consistency, you must have some established customer service processes, systems, if you will. Predefined systems that are actually used on a day-to-day basis help reinforce consistency. Further, employees who deal with customers must be trained in the systems designed to handle customer interfaces. We are talking customer service rules, processes, and standards.

Treat your customers as people with their own individual needs. Personalize your service to them. Fulfill their needs. Give them respect. Show them you care. Let them know what they say matters.

Don't overlook your employees in this matter. Managers should recognize when an employee does a good job with customers. Reward employees when their actions create enthusiastic customers. Tie raises and promotions to success in customer service. As the old saying goes, "Look after your people and they will look after your customers."

Keep Making Small Improvements: Using customer input and their reactions to your products and service, always strive to improve customer service delivery. Be flexible and change systems when necessary. Visions must be flexible. Alter course when needed.

Introduce incremental improvements. Continually raise the bar, but do it in small increments—increments that can be consistently delivered on a high-quality level. Deliver what you promise, all the time, without fail. Incremental increases do add up. It is a mistake to make big promises and not deliver. So, start with achievable levels of service and continually add to them. Don't raise expectations you cannot satisfy.

Wildly Enthusiastic Customers: If you just satisfy customers, you have not done enough. You must go beyond just satisfying them. You must strive to make them wildly enthusiastic about your goods and services. Make it a joy for people to do business with you. Help them reach a level of satisfaction where they genuinely support you. Give them reason to spread the word about your good deeds. Add customers to your sales force.

49

Managing Customers

Customer expectations are rising. They want new products, and often they want them customized to their specific needs. Customer relationships are increasingly complex. Customers have more power and aren't averse to using it. There are new products and new channels for distribution. Intermediaries are proliferating. Competition is fierce.

> "There is only one boss: the customer. And he can fire everybody in the company, from the chairman on down, simply by spending his money somewhere else."
>
> —Sam Walton

CUSTOMER RELATIONSHIP MANAGEMENT (CRM)

Customer relationship management (CRM) includes acquiring and retaining the best customers, plus increasing their expenditures with a company. You want a long-term, profitable relationship. That relationship must be managed—effectively. Customers are valuable assets. A customer-centric business strategy is essential.

The Internet has greatly increased the avenues for marketing and selling products. Around the clock access is the norm. Self-service is on the rise. Competition can spring up overnight. Advances in technology can change the marketplace in an instant. More customer data is available because of advances in technology and systems. More CRM applications are being developed and sold to corporations. Innovation is essential on all fronts, including: development, production, marketing, sales, delivery, service, and customer relationship management.

Customer Loyalty: Companies must keep customers loyal while continuing to make a profit from them. Loyal customers are more profitable than casual consumers. It is less expensive to retain current customers—and you must make the effort to do so—than to win over new customers. CRM requires a coordinated application of all available resources, meaning technology, information, experience, skills, technique, and people.

Customer loyalty is not a given. True loyalty is an emotional bond reinforced by the quality of products and service. Remember, customers have access to an increasing body of information, which is available from an increasing number of sources. Competition abounds. Exit barriers are breaking down.

Employee Loyalty: Getting and keeping customer loyalty is very difficult without having the loyalty of all employees involved in the customer relationship. Your employees must be loyal and committed to a customer-centric company. The employees must believe the company is also an employee-centric organization. You need customers AND employees to be successful. Once customers are lost, it is difficult and often quite impossible to get them back. Employees are an important factor in keeping them.

Coordination of Players: Contact management is not enough. Sales and service must be coordinated and information shared. Quick delivery of products is expected for direct customer purchases, such as through the Internet. Self-service websites that provide product information, sales, and service are common. Self-diagnostic tools can be made available to customers for applicable products. Providing a user-friendly function can solve common problems.

Even though the Internet has revolutionized the sales and distribution network, it has not eliminated the need for normal distribution channels. Distributors, brokers, resellers, and brick-and-mortar retail outlets are still needed. Channel partners continue to be important. There are just more options for market outreach.

Suppliers are more tightly integrated into the sales cycle, with companies sharing customer order information with their suppliers to handle just-in-time manufacturing and delivery requirements. Partner relationship management (PRM) systems are coming into existence. E-commerce is alive and well from supplier through seller to customer. The goal is to actively integrate and manage all the relationships with appropriate systems and procedures.

Customer Experience: There will be bumps in the road. Things will not go as planned. That is when you need customer loyalty to get you through the tough times. Poor rapport can mean a quick customer departure. Good rapport means the customer is more likely to stick out the bad times.

Keep in mind that a customer has the choice of more channels in which to conduct his or her business. If the customer has a bad experience in one of the channels, say, the Internet; the effects of that bad experience can spill over into the company's brick-and-mortar outlets, for instance. A company is the sum of its parts. Each part represents the whole company. More vigilance and coordination are required than ever before. A customer may use any or all of the channels in his or her relationship with the company.

Never discount the need for human contact. Technology has not eliminated it. There are times when the customer wants to talk person-to-person with a real person; and that could either be using a phone call or a face-to-face encounter. Be prepared to blend all channels of contact. People will frequent both websites and brick-and-mortar sites. Technology cannot completely replace personal contact.

With more avenues open for contact, there could be a significant growth in the number of contacts and the resources needed to handle them. You do want the higher number of contacts, though. They represent an increased stickiness with your customer. But the contacts must be responsive and timely. We live in a fast-paced world and consumers expect fast service. Requests for service must be handled quickly. Complaints must be dealt with promptly.

In this modern world, competitive advantage is more tenuous. You must stay alert. You must innovate, collaborate, and manage.

CUSTOMER LOCK-IN

If you have made a preemptive strike in the market, i.e., cornered the market by having a controlling patent or some other intellectual property; then you have achieved an enviable position.

Example: Microsoft has controlled the PC operating system market for years with its Windows technology. This has allowed Microsoft to take over associated areas, such as word processing and spreadsheets. Microsoft products ultimately edged out WordPerfect and VisiCalc. In the end, it made little difference who had the best product.

However, Microsoft had better beware. Linux is coming on strong in the operating system arena. Apache is doing a number on Microsoft's Internet

Information Server. Software that is downloadable from the Web, meaning software tailored to the needs of the user rather than being the full-blown version—such as Microsoft Word—may ultimately redefine the landscape. Downloadable software applications offer users the hope of always working with the latest version.

Open-source software is even available for database management systems. Free versions can be downloaded. Microsoft and Oracle are both under assault. And these are the big guys.

Remember that IBM was the preeminent computer manufacturer at one time. They set the rules. Then along came Intel and Microsoft. There is no reason to assume Microsoft or any other company is immortal.

CUSTOMER ISSUES

Instant and all-pervasive communication has changed the rules of the game. The effective communicator no longer has to be someone with power and influence, or someone able to get the attention of our biased reporters. The Internet has leveled the playing field. The key word is TRUTH. The corollary is EXPOSURE.

Small Voices: Large corporations and powerful individuals used to hold tremendous sway—and they still do—but the Internet has been a great equalizer. Exposure of news that is detrimental to a company is much easier to accomplish today. The previously insignificant person can now move mountains. Matt Drudge, in his Internet newsletter, the *Drudge Report*, opened up the Clinton-intern affair that led to impeachment proceedings. The more powerful news media were unable to hide it. The Internet is a mighty communications force.

A company with something to hide had better beware. If a company is unwilling to talk about something, the customer can—and he or she will be heard. Ignoring the issue just makes it worse. Executives must be paranoid and expect that when they try to hide something, it will be on national news before the week is out. It is easier to defend yourself if you say it first than if you have a TV reporter asking you on live TV.

The Internet has chat rooms, instant messaging, bulletin boards, forums, news sites, email, etc. Wireless phones can take and transmit pictures and videos in real time. There are numerous ways to get the message out. Anyone can be a reporter.

The CEO does not stand a chance against a persistent, crusading customer who has been given a raw deal. And it does not have to be a customer. It could be someone who finds out an unflattering bit of information and takes on the issue as a cause.

A website need not be a very credible site to have influence. People will post information that consists mainly of rumors and innuendos. It costs little to set up a new site targeted at a specific company. Opinions often prevail over fact.

The sources of damaging information aren't just dissatisfied customers or other unhappy people in the marketplace. A disgruntled current or previous employee can wreak havoc with a company's reputation. An employee is an insider and is automatically believed by many on the outside.

Defense: Executives must be ever vigilant to potential problems and try to head them off before they become full disasters. Use websites to give your customers a chance to vent their problems. Listen to what they say. Take corrective action—and take it quickly. This means responding to customer complaints now, not later.

One of the biggest problems is dealing with the situation where a dissatisfied customer does not let you know but does let the rest of the world know. As soon as the first whiff of smoke is detected, call in the fire department to do damage control. Denial is no answer. The clamor of many voices can easily overwhelm denial. The Internet is a community of many voices with powerful sway over public opinion.

As the negotiator or debater would tell you, the easiest way to deflate a negative factor is to admit it right up front. You have announced it yourself. You have admitted the problem. But you must promise to correct the problem and take the appropriate corrective action ASAP. Truth, although damaging, can be mitigated with positive action on your part.

CUSTOMER QUESTIONNAIRES

Difficulties: Questionnaires can be used to gather information, both positive and negative, about your customer relationships. The problem is that most people hate surveys. How often do you throw a survey in the trash, even if someone will pay you to complete it? The fact that organizations will pay you to complete a survey ought to be an indication of how hard it is to get a response. Even if people do complete a questionnaire, they will only reluctantly be totally candid. Usually the more helpful information is what was not said.

Personal Contact: It stands to reason that a piece of paper cannot reveal the customer's body language that is visible to someone doing an in-person interview. Eyeball-to-eyeball contact helps you read the signs and pursue alternative lines of questioning when you sense the customer is not telling you everything. Many people are a lot quicker to hand out praise than hurtful criticism. Out of your presence, they bring up the negatives.

If there are thousands of customers who make relatively small purchases, it is not practical to make personal contact with each of them. The cost would be prohibitive. In that situation, sampling could be used.

For companies with fewer customers, but customers who bring in large amounts of revenue, personal contact is essential. It shows you care. It shows you are willing to take the time to understand a customer's problems and needs. Unless you have a terribly demanding customer, there is a good chance problems will get swept under the rug. Resentment builds, perhaps, to the breaking point. Building a strong, partnering relationship means building a bond of sincere care and trust. If communication is allowed to implode, the customer will leave without your ever knowing why.

Communicate one-on-one with your customers, if possible. Search for the slightest hint of dissatisfaction. If any is uncovered, take corrective action quickly and forcefully. Avoid impersonal questionnaires.

One-on-one conversations may even turn up ideas for blockbuster new products. Listen to the customer and learn.

Part XI

INFORMATION TECHNOLOGY

50

Information Technology and Business

TECHNOLOGY'S INFLUENCE

Technology affects us in almost every aspect of life, whether business or personal. A good business leader should have a basic understanding of the capabilities of information and communications technology, plus any technology directly related to the business. To deny or ignore the influence of technology in the marketplace is to be like the ostrich that sticks its head in the sand. Technology is here to stay, and it does have a profound influence on business. Therefore, ignoring technology is not really a valid option, unless you consider business suicide a valid option.

> "Technology is a queer thing. It brings you great gifts with one hand, and it stabs you in the back with the other."
> —C. P. Snow

A business can take several approaches to dealing with technology, not all of which are positive. Technology should be considered a resource, something to help in conducting business. In most cases, it should not be an end in and of itself. Treat technology as a tool, like money or equipment. It should provide a service or some useful function. It is not an enemy, unless you refuse to let it be your friend.

Deciding How to Use It: Therefore, assuming you recognize the importance of technology, the next step is to decide how to deal with it. In any event, you must keep your eyes and ears open to old technology, new technology, and future technology. That means trying to stay abreast of developments in technology. It does not mean the executive has to have an intimate knowledge of all technology impacting his or her business. It does mean that someone on the company's staff does need to keep up with advances in technology and impart the general concepts to company leaders.

Giving due consideration to the business model desired, the CEO must define the role technology is to play in business operations, or rather the relationship the business will have with technology. If the company's business is technology, that is one thing. If technology just occupies a supporting role in business operations, that is another. It is hard to conceive of a company that does not use technology. Using a PC word processor is using technology. A phone is technology. Who doesn't use a phone?

A company's definition of itself determines the role technology plays in the business. (Note: It is imperative for a company to have a working definition of itself.)

Follower: First, let's look at the position of a follower. This is the least demanding position. The business uses technology but is not greatly impacted by it. Some examples might be florists, attorneys, realtors, and taxicab companies. They all need various types of communication tools: phones, radios, Internet, etc. Taxis might even use GPS positioning technology. Florists need refrigeration. All could use computers one way or another. Realtors use computer-based applications, including the Internet, to analyze, sell, and search for real estate.

But in general, none of these followers would typically be considered the avant-garde of technology users. They simply need to keep up with their competitors' level of service, using technology provided by technology firms. They are users of technology, not developers.

Requirements of this first category are to casually monitor any developments in technology that might affect them. If these followers get a little behind in technology, then no big deal.

Heavy User: Second, there are those who use technology more heavily and are more dependent upon it. It is not unusual for this category of business to pitch technology as a part of the service it provides. The medical industry is heavily dependent upon technology. They use technical devices to diagnose and treat patients. Airlines use computers and communications to schedule and track planes, passengers, flight attendants, and pilots. Call centers are heavily dependent upon computer applications, phone switches, and communication lines. A large number of companies fall within the category of heavy users.

The businesses in this group can be both users and developers, or, at least, key partners in the development of technology. All of them buy or develop computer applications, for example. All make demands upon vendors to keep them up to date with modern technology tools: diagnostic devices, communication switching devices, fast communication lines, responsive computers, the latest repair devices, etc. At a minimum, they encourage suppliers, such as aircraft manufacturers, to develop new technology to help them in their business. Competition is fierce for players in this category of business.

This second group of businesses must keep their ears to the ground in regard to technological developments. Since technology is integral with their business, they cannot afford to be ignorant of technological developments. If competitors beat them to the punch in implementing technology, then market share or whole market segments can be lost. Technology experts must be on staff. These experts must keep their skills and knowledge up to date. They must keep management informed of developments in their respective fields of specialization.

Developer: Third and final is the category of businesses in which technology embodies the core product or service that is provided. Research and development organizations might fall into this group. Computer manufacturers, aircraft manufacturers, communications providers, cable TV companies, database software companies, R&D labs, and the like are developers and sellers of technology. Technology is everything to them. It is what sets them apart from their competitors. Technology makes or breaks them.

This category of businesses must be on the bleeding edge of technology. They must continually push the envelope in the search of new technology. They must be the leaders in technology. If this type of business entity does not develop and implement new technology, it will eventually die. Except for staff support functions, everyone in the company must stay deeply immersed in technology. It is the employee's life.

Going back to an earlier statement in this section, it is essential that a company define itself and then recognize the role technology plays in business operations. For the technology-dependent company to take a lackadaisical approach to technology is to become suicidal. The company must assign the appropriate resources to technological pursuits, which includes spending bucks on technology—even expenditures that turn out to be dead ends. All pertinent avenues must be explored. Ignorance is unacceptable.

THE INFORMATION EXPLOSION CONTINUES

Communication links have grown. The use of computers has become ubiquitous. The Internet is continuing to expand and redefine the communications network. Anyone with a browser and an Internet connection has access to the world. With communication reaching out so much farther than before, the richness of information available has itself improved greatly. Benefits continue to grow for those who use it.

> "The quest for knowledge and the application of that knowledge for man's benefit will not be denied."
> —Roger M. Blough

Not only does the ordinary citizen have access to more information of higher caliber, but so do businesses. Better connectivity makes virtual corporations a reality. A company's need for physical and organizational connectivity does not exert the same overpowering influence it had in the past; therefore, traditional vertical and horizontal integration within the same corporate organization is less important today. Communication is more interactive. Information can be readily and securely exchanged in real-time. Information is much more current—or it can be.

As always, information and its access are a competitive advantage. The increased information connectivity means less need for intermediaries. Incumbent businesses are no longer so securely anchored. Insurgent businesses can reach the customer easily these days. Incumbents and insurgents must both learn to navigate the changing landscape.

E-BUSINESS

Separation: As use of the Internet became more pervasive in the late 1990s, established brick-and-mortar companies wanted a piece of the action. They would spin off an independent subsidiary to concentrate on e-commerce—another arm of the business housed in an online store. This was somewhat analogous to throwing a kid into the water to force him or her to learn how to swim. The problem was that some of the kids drowned, many of them, in fact.

The reasoning at the time—and maybe rightly so—was that the dot.com entity would not be allowed to thrive within the regular corporate walls. Too many room dividers would have to be torn down and rebuilt. Existing corporate culture would strangle the fledgling business. Executives saw the dot.com subsidiary as an answer to resistant bureaucracy. The passionate Internet people were allowed to lock arms and go forward without repressive shackles. Now the pendulum has swung in the other direction.

Revelation: Even if the separate e-commerce entity managed to survive the meltdown, the whole Internet strategy of the company was re-examined. In some cases, the entity was divested. In others, it was merged back into the parent company. Still, some were allowed to continue as separate, but subsidiary entities.

Restoration: The Monday morning quarterbacks have finally concluded that the Internet can be just another tool for the parent company to use—and without making a separate entity to handle it. You did not need to set up a separate company to deploy computers when they first became practical, just a new department. Therefore, the Internet is not necessarily a new vision for the company; rather, it is typically just an additional conduit for implementing the existing company vision.

Now, it is usually better to think of a business as engaging in *e-commerce*, i.e., electronic commerce. As a result, the modern company becomes an *e-business*, a company that uses the Internet as an integral part of the business model. That does not take away from the fact that some businesses are e-businesses at their core; e-business is THE function. But the present discussion is centered on those businesses where web-based systems are an important piece of the pie, but not the whole pie.

Hard Lessons: We have made mistakes with the Internet. It has often been said that technology moves a lot faster than people learn how to use it. That was certainly the case with the Internet. It was like a new hemline, everyone wanted to wear the new style of dress, without regard to whether is was appropriate for the person wearing it. Now people realize the Internet is just another accessory that can enhance, rather than replace.

Properly applied, the web-based systems and their associated telecommunication functions offer a great way to improve business operation efficiency. They do not replace fax machines, email, package delivery, snail mail, telephones, or even standard computer applications. They simply provide a new interface and alternative processing mechanisms to carry out functions in ways that weren't possible before. The same basic business functions still need to take place: manufacturing, distribution, sales, delivery, and billing, for example. One of the big benefits of the Internet is that it facilitates faster and more comprehensive communication, at more convenient times, from almost anywhere. It is a new facilitator.

IT PARTNERSHIP

At one time, the information technology (IT) department concentrated on being an accounting machine. Give them the numbers and they would create transaction registers, organize and summarize the data, and spit out the reports. (The paper industry was the big winner.)

The evolution of IT puts it into a different role today. First, the department is now often a division or a wholly owned subsidiary. Information technology is increasingly a strategic resource. Going even further, IT is becoming a strategic partner within the business. It is a delivery vehicle for product and service.

Which brings up a question? Is IT a core function that should be retained within the corporate structure, or can IT be outsourced? HP and IBM are pushing to offload a company's computer processing to on-demand computing power. It offers less expensive and more flexible resource utilization. Less money is tied up in computer hardware—fixed assets.

Outsourcing, or Not: There are several possibilities: (1) keep all IT functions within the company, (2) outsource all of IT except for liaison personnel, or (3) outsource portions of IT and keep the rest in-house.

Start by analyzing whether a particular IT function can be outsourced. Outsourcing makes sense if the function performed by IT is not strategic in nature, meaning it is simply required for a commonplace support role. An example would be payroll processing.

Payroll is definitely a requirement for the operation of a business. Without payroll you are unlikely have any employees. However, there are plenty of payroll service companies. Why waste valuable people on running and maintaining the payroll system? These personnel resources could be applied more profitably elsewhere, like to the core business.

Unless a department or function is very unimportant to the operation of the business—in the eyes of the executive team—upper management is going to have to devote time and energy to running the department. Competent personnel will have to be provided to staff the department or function. They must be managed. Management requires managers.

But does the function you are devoting time and energy to, provide a product or service that distinguishes you from your competition? Continuing with the payroll function, as an example, does it provide a unique function?

Certainly not, unless payroll is THE core function of the company. Every company has to provide payroll functionality.

It gets a little more complicated when you look at an IT function such as the one that provides web-hosting services. There are three possibilities here:

First, if the company is in the business of providing web-hosting capabilities to any and all customers, this IT function is core business. It should not be outsourced unless the company is simply in the business of being a broker between buyers and sellers of web-hosting services.

Second, if web hosting is just a vehicle for delivering the product or service, then it could be outsourced. Providing online real estate listings might be an example. If selling real estate is the true core business, then web hosting is not, in and of itself, core business. Web hosting could be outsourced here.

Third, it could be that web hosting is not a core business but the nature of the business is such that it is essential to keep it in house. For example, suppose the business must maintain such a high level of security that having the web-hosting service provided by a third party is out of the question. An intelligence organization certainly cannot afford to outsource the computer systems and applications that house intelligence data.

In any case, it is unlikely that every IT function needs to be kept in-house. Nor is it likely that none of the IT functions can be outsourced. Rather, the most likely scenario is to outsource the IT functions where it makes business sense, where you wish to limit the use of valuable resources to core functionality. Keep core functionality in-house.

That does not mean you would not use your limited IT resources to provide advice on IT outsourcing. IT people are certainly needed to help validate and evaluate the outsourcing effort. You need competent watchdogs.

First bottom line: Look at the individual functions provided by IT and determine which ones can be effectively outsourced to third-party IT organizations where the IT function is a core business to them.

Now let's turn to the partnership aspect.

Partnership: Since information technology is such an all-pervasive force, particularly since it deals with critical business information; IT has become a line function. The fact that information is the coin of the realm, so to speak, and since knowledge is power; there is no justification for treating IT as just a support function. IT should be treated as a full-fledged partner in the business. The IT division head should report directly to the CEO, as all major divisions of the company should.

IT is about voice and data communications, meaning information exchange. It is about gathering data and making it useful to the executives in all divisions of the company. Depending on the nature of the business, IT also provides an interface to customers and suppliers. IT is typically woven into the very fabric of the business. Phones, computers, and the Internet have all revolutionized business <u>and</u> private life. Strip away all the functions provided by IT, and most businesses would be out of business.

Therefore, IT should be a party to the deliberations leading to all major decisions of the company. IT is just as important as marketing, sales, manufacturing, customer service, human resources, finance, etc. IT provides solutions to business problems and alternatives for ways of doing business.

<u>Second bottom line</u>: The Chief Technology Officer (CTO) or Chief Information Officer (CIO), whichever title you prefer, should be an accepted member of the executive team, in full standing.

51

The Internet

In spite of the recent dot.com meltdown, the Internet is here to say. The dot.coms ignored basic business principles. They went for the glitter. "Damn the expense. Don't worry about profits. Just join the parade." Business 101 caught up with them.

The Internet is a terrific medium, a revolutionary way to communicate—plus improve business efficiency. Businesses just need to figure out how to use it. There are many uses, from e-commerce to intra-company communications.

IMPACT OF THE INTERNET

The Internet has made geography meaningless in many cases. At one time—in the distant past of our fast moving age—it was said that the Internet was as revolutionary as the advent of the PC. Wrong! The Internet has brought an exponential change, not a geometric one.

> "The Net is a 10.5 on the Richter scale of economic change."
> —Nicholas Negroponte

There have been early and costly losses in the dot.com world, but everything that happened has led to a solidifying of position. The Internet might have been wounded by all the dot.com shakeout, but the result is a stronger entity. Many lessons have been learned. Business reality just needs to be applied in the new revolutionary context.

The Internet, as we know it today, has been created by little worker bees, not the behemoths of industry, the titans of the corporations, nor the overpowering influence of government. The Internet has come of age in spite of the controlling powers. There have been many contributors, often the unfettered minds of creative individuals outside the chains of established organizations. Of course, big business has helped, but most of the basic innovative concepts came from the little people.

Being a part of the Internet wave is not enough. Witness the debacle of many Internet companies—and their venture capitalists—all of whom forgot common business sense. In short spans of time, much can be overlooked and ignored; but the longer-range lens of history has a different perspective, a more balanced viewpoint. Time does march on. Events do ultimately have their impact. The slow leak can be ignored only so long before the submarine sinks and implodes. Deficits cannot continue indefinitely.

Therefore, it is not enough to be a participant in the Internet world. The executive had better be a savvy businessperson, too.

INTERNET COMPETITION

Because the Internet strips away speed and distance constraints and because it increases potential exposure, it has had an impact on competition. The initial dot.coms held sway at first, and they did not worry about costs. Their prices ignored the expense of the product or service delivered. Get market share at all costs. Now that reality has come back into play, the big boys—the old-line established companies—are making their presence known.

But the way business is conducted has changed. The advent of phones changed business and so has the Web. Barriers to competition have been pushed aside that were standing in the way before. There has been a leveling of the playing field that big and small companies cannot ignore. Dot.coms can still come up out of nowhere—and they are going to be smarter this time! But brick-and-mortar companies are branching out—and they have deep pockets.

Supply and demand work on a much faster timeline than ever before. Supply is enhanced through Internet capabilities, such as search engines. Demand is just a click away. The consumer has more options. A business has more options. Competitors can react faster. A business must be more flexible and be able to respond more quickly. The astute executive needs to stay wide-awake. Complacency is unacceptable. Internet competition is a factor that cannot be ignored.

INTERNET CUSTOMERS

Acceptance of the Internet is much different than it was several years ago. More people have access, and more people want access that do not presently have it. The reasons for people wanting to use the Internet vary all over the map. Demographics do not present a true picture of potential web users. People with an identical demographic makeup can have different dispositions toward online shopping and web surfing. Their attitudes can be very different.

One of the first questions to ask is how are they disposed to technology, how do they feel about it. Although there are plenty of exceptions, older people are less interested in technology. They feel less comfortable with it. Younger people, on the other hand, are very comfortable with technology and readily embrace it. To them it is a natural part of their lives. The people in the middle might go either way, depending upon their background and exposure.

From a marketing standpoint, a family's income may be the determinate of whether or not a potential consumer will go online to buy a product or service. The high-income family will likely have a computer and Internet access, unless their attitude toward technology overrides the income factor. But remember the caveat: older people often have higher incomes than younger groups.

Low-income families can have a very positive attitude toward technology—in fact, they may crave it—but their income level may prevent them from acquiring a home PC to get online. But there is often an out. If the low-income person has access to the Internet at work, and if he or she can afford a particular product, then that person may go on the Internet to buy the product. Remember, low-income consumers can always go to a public library to get Internet access. A company should not discount low-income families for website use, especially if the product is something the family would buy anyway.

Deeply held attitudes about technology can change over time, depending upon circumstances. The motivation to use technology, in general, and the Internet, in particular, can change.

Peer pressure (family, friends, fellow workers, etc.) can motivate a person who would not otherwise use the Web to do so. Job pressures, like being forced to use a computer for normal work responsibilities, can make the technology laggard learn to use the Internet and be comfortable in doing so. An overriding desire to have fun can lead a person to start searching for entertainment on the Web. That could include either interactive fun (games) or just access to fun (airline reservations).

Keep remembering that circumstances can change. Life-changing events and new daily distractions can even take a person off the Internet. Society's attitude toward things changes as time passes. Therefore, continually retest your assumptions. Never assume you have a customer for life—for many different reasons.

In short, discard your notions about population graphics. A person's disposition toward technology and his or her motivation to use the Internet are the driving forces. But those driving forces can change. Stay alert.

52

Website Considerations

WEB COLLABORATION

Advances on the Web bring many opportunities for collaboration. Software tools are available on intranets to create draft documents that are stored as web pages, which, in turn, can be used to collect feedback from selected reviewers. Comments are stored, plus reactions to the comments. The person acting as the overall editor can then include or exclude the suggested revisions before publishing the final document, an HR policy, for example. Everyone will have had his or her say.

Company intranets can also be used to bring together all departments involved in a deal, say, a reply to an RFP. Bid response time can be accelerated when up-to-date RFP information is shared freely and promptly. Intranets can also be used to share operational problems and reach solutions quickly. A company can turn on a dime in response to a competitor's threat. Timely information exchange is key to business success.

Extranets reach out beyond the internal intranets and set the stage for effective communication with people external to the company. Extranets can be used, for example, to speedily exchange information with suppliers. Inventories can be minimized and on-time shipments can be maximized in response to manufacturing needs. Web services technology can facilitate the interchange of information and instructions.

But extranets can also be used to improve information flow between you and your customers. The customer can check account information, enter new orders, track purchase order fulfillment, revise orders, or just communicate with account executives. Customer relations can get a real boost from a properly designed extranet.

The virtual corporation that intertwines business partners can get an assist from an effective extranet. Critical information can be shared quickly. The virtual group can effectively function as one unit. Timely information is king—a competitive advantage.

Web collaboration brings improved efficiency. Time and distance are erased. Don't miss the opportunity.

COMPANY WEBSITE

A company website should be directed toward satisfying business and customer needs. The type of site will depend upon the audience, who could be customers (or clients), suppliers (or other business partners), investors, or employees. The website needs to be tailored to the needs of the audience.

User-Driven Design: There are some basic rules in website design that should be followed, but an executive should not fall into the ego-driven trap of thinking he or she should be the chief web page designer. The website owner should not be directing web page design. Rather, the needs of the target audience need to be determined and the website designed accordingly.

A lesson learned long ago in software application development still applies: The computer user should determine the functionality supported and the nature of the user interface design. A programmer or web developer is never the primary user of the website. The end-user is. Ask the user what he or she wants. Listen to what the user says. The website developer is just the implementer of the end-user's requirements.

If the website tries to do everything for everyone, it will fail miserably. As an analogy, there is no such thing as an automobile that suits everyone. People are different. Different car models target different buyers. Therefore, website developers must decide on specific target audiences and then design accordingly.

Simple Usability: Usability is an issue. Unless the targeted website user is a techno-geek, there is no real advantage to cluttering the site with a lot of technology for technology's sake. If there is an overabundance of bells and whistles on the site, the IT group has probably had an undue influence on web page design. The purpose of a website is not to impress other website developers. A good website is probably boring to most developers—which is perfectly OK.

Speedy Response: Users want speedy access to the functions or information they need. Never lose sight of the fact that website developers have access to high-speed networks in most cases. On the other hand, the typical user—except someone in a corporate setting or in a private residence with broadband access—is more likely to have a dial-up connection, which is SLOW, SLOW, SLOW! If the user has a choice between a fast site and a slow site, which do you think the user will frequent? More and more people are moving to broadband access, but not everyone is there yet. Don't run your users off.

Unnecessary Clutter: Take a lesson from TV. When you have recorded something on a VCR, say, a movie; what do you do with the commercials that were recorded throughout the movie? You fast forward through them to get to the next part of the movie. Along a similar vein, if you are watching TV and a commercial comes on, what do you do? You get up and get a snack or go to the bathroom, or you talk to your companion. Unless you are really starved for entertainment or are deep into marketing, you do your best to ignore the majority of commercials. They are dead time. So, don't swamp the website user with extraneous information.

But, let's take this even further. A website opens up tremendous possibilities for the marketing people in other respects. Marketing people are loaded with brochures and presentations. What a chance to get it all out for the whole world to see. What a sales opportunity. All of a sudden, you have thousands of web pages. Even if the potential customer did care, how is he or she going to successfully navigate the maze? A website user wants to get to the desired function or information in just a few web page clicks.

Marketers can fall into another trap: virtual malls, online theme parks, virtual villages, online trade shows, etc. Like the developers in IT, the marketing types have a glorious opportunity to impress other marketing people—overwhelm the competition. But who does the buying? Is it the competitor's marketing department or your customers?

Organizational Considerations: If the target audience is internal to the organization, it is sometimes OK for the website to be designed along organizational lines. However, there are even some limits to this. If an employee is seeking information or help on some matter, he or she may not know all the details of a company's organizational structure. The user simply wants to find the appropriate function or piece of information. Make it easy for him or her to get there. Don't force the user to know who reports to whom. A simple keyword search engine may be the ticket in this case.

A customer is typically uninterested in organizational structure. The customer seeks a product or service from the company. How the company is organized is immaterial. The customer just wants to be linked with the proper product or service that solves a problem, a need. People do not normally buy just because buying is great fun. They want to solve a problem, and they need your company to help them. If you make it difficult for them to get your help, they will go someplace where help is more easily obtained.

So, ask your potential users what they need. Quit making assumptions that result in misguided efforts—a waste of time, talent, resources, and money. Provide a service. Serve the user instead of website developers and marketers.

WEB PAGE DESIGN

Since the Internet is such an integral part of business today and since the executive should have some rudimentary knowledge about website design, some basics are presented here. In many cases, you are betting the farm on your website.

There is no single right way to design a website. It depends on the functions provided, and, most importantly, on the intended users of the site. This section will discuss only very basic design principles. The executive can use these principles to draw some broad conclusions about how a web page should function and how it should be designed.

The executive, though, is reminded that web pages should not be designed by executives or IT web professionals. Control of web page design should rest with the users. What the end-user wants in usability is the deciding factor. The web development person should counsel the end-user about design but leave the final say to the end-user.

Try to determine what is important to the user and how he or she thinks about it. If you can't learn how the user thinks, your competitor will. Use every opportunity you can to talk to the user and find out how the site is used—or would be used, if given the chance.

Intuitiveness: The foremost rule for usability is to make sure the web page functions in a self-evident manner. The web page user should not have to think any more than necessary. Remember that a competitor's website is just a few clicks away. Don't drive the user to another site.

Some web designers expect users to read everything on a web page. They don't. Instead, the user scans the page until he or she sees something that is interesting or helpful. The user doesn't always make the best choice; more often, it is a best guess. People are in a hurry and won't take time to thoroughly analyze the page. If a wrong choice is made, it is easy to use the Back button to get to the previous page and start over.

When the user first looks at a page, there should be a clear visual hierarchy. If something is more important, it should stand out—large print, nested, or bolded, for example. Links to other pages should be obvious.

Consistency: The structure of the page should follow recognized conventions. Titles and repetitive functions should appear at the top of the page. Submenus, if applicable, should appear on the left. Miscellaneous information, such as copyright notices, Top buttons, and privacy information links belong at the bottom. The main body of the page should be centered on the right.

Consistency should reign supreme throughout the website. Don't change the rules of the game in midstream. This is not the time for individual departments or divisions within a company to express their individuality. It is a time for standards. Users don't like surprises. Once he or she learns how to do something or how to navigate the site, don't introduce the same function under a different name. Use a consistent color scheme and font style.

Conciseness: Clutter is an enemy of good web page design. The sin of many web developers is trying to place too much on one page. When a page looks cluttered to a user, he or she will likely escape to a simpler page (and site)—unless forced to use the page.

Being concise in wording is key. The busy user does not want to spend a lot of time reading a page. The web page developer should get the point across quickly and concisely. This is not a place for literary diarrhea. If there is too much to read, it won't be read.

Simple Navigation: Navigation should be straightforward, which also means that website hierarchies should follow a functional or categorical pattern easily understood by the user. This is not the place to mirror the company's organizational structure. The user doesn't care. He or she just wants to locate a product, a service, a function, or some information. Throw company ego out the door.

Web navigation conventions should be used. This is no time to re-invent the wheel. For example, when you get into a car, you expect the steering wheel, gear selector, brake pedal, and accelerator pedal to be in certain places. You want the dashboard in front of you, not in the door. Learn from car designers. Be conventional.

When the user is cruising around the Web, he or she wants to know where he or she is at any given moment. The page should indicate (upper left) the name of the site or company. If the major sections of the site are shown at the top of the page, the current section should be highlighted.

Varying User Sophistication: Forget any myth about there being a typical user. People are different. They will interpret things differently. Besides having different tastes and tendencies, users have different levels of sophistication in regard to web browser use. You will have beginners and experts. Regardless, every new user of your website is a beginner on your site. He or she may figure it out quicker or slower than someone else. This all points to the fact you need to allow for different levels of users. Have easy paths for the beginner and fast paths for the sophisticated, repeat user.

Avoiding Fancy: Avoid the black hole of trying to incorporate fancy graphics and the latest technology into the website—unless they are unavoidable. Users are more impressed with getting their job done in the fastest possible time than being entertained. If you get too fancy, the user of an older browser version will be left out in the cold. Forget bells and whistles. You should be more interested in serving the user than impressing techno geeks.

Testing: Force the developers to put the site through usability testing—meaning testing by typical users, preferably people who do not have preconceived notions about how the site should function. Remember, we are looking for intuitive operation. Developers are always surprised when something obvious to them is a total mystery to the uninitiated user.

Fully test both the functionality and the usability of a site before it goes live. Then retest the site when any changes are made to it. Periodically review the whole site. You have probably seen those houses that ramble all over the hillside after new additions have been added in a seemingly haphazard manner. Make sure your website does not do the same over time.

Simple and Fast: Finally, let simplicity and speed of operation prevail. Simple means simple to understand and simple to operate. Speed means fast operation on a dial-up modem connection. Fast corporate networks are no test at all. The faster, simpler website wins in the end. Be a winner.

WEBSITE USERS

Website users come in three basic flavors, and website design must allow for all three. The three types are beginners, intermediates, and experts. The categorization is in reference to your site, not necessarily the Web, meaning the users of your site could be anyone from new users to veteran users. You need to cater to all three.

A point worth mentioning before proceeding: Less informed ad agencies try to take the same approach used for TV and apply it to websites. But TV watchers are more passive than web surfers. Every hour or so, the TV watchers switch to a different channel to get a different program.

People using the Web are more active and involved. They are constantly interacting with their web browser. You have to provide them the right doors and hope they open them. Old style marketing approaches don't work on the Web. Banner ads, for example, have been much less effective than originally expected. Pop-ups can be blocked. There has been a rude awakening on how to advertise on the Web. Now, back to the original topic.

Beginners: Beginners are new to your site. They are first-time or near first-time visitors. Their initial experience with the site can be pivotal. There are a lot of sites out there. At the first sign of trouble, they hit the exit doors. Make sure the home page makes a good impression and gives the new user an intuitive access to new-user functions, such as explanations and overviews. A few seconds with the home page should give the new user a clear indication of where to go next. Make it easy and comfortable to stay on the site.

Intermediates: Intermediate users have been on the site before and are satisfied enough to come back. They are starting to bond with the site and the company—if they weren't already bonded with the company before the website. Having concluded the site has something to offer, the intermediate user gradually uses the site in more sophisticated ways. Therefore, the site had better be able to handle the increased demands. Ideally, the intermediate user begins to integrate the site into his or her daily routine. You can still lose this type of user, but the risk of doing so is less. Stay vigilant, though, because a new site may preempt your place in the intermediate user's life.

Experts: Expert users know the site inside and out. They spend a lot of time on the site. They go directly to the function they need. The experts want fast and efficient execution—they can be quite impatient and demanding. They want support for their needs. They often are contributors to the site and its operations. Consequently, they need effective ways to communicate with the website owners. Their input is invaluable—because they care and because they are knowledgeable about the site. Let them communicate. Listen to them. Respond to their input. Change the site in deference to their needs, if necessary.

So, a website must be versatile, able to accommodate different levels of users.

WEBSITE SUCCESS

When trying to come up with measurements for website success, there are no easy answers. Knowing the number of hits made against the site, for example, is not particularly helpful. Hits do not equate to sales. This is a case where you probably need to continually think outside the box and reevaluate what you are trying to accomplish.

If you are running the site as an *e-business*, meaning a relatively stand-alone business, the factors to measure will be one thing. If you are running the site as an integral part of the whole business, i.e., you are engaged in *e-commerce*, there are other things to measure. The context of the latter is different than the former.

The *e-business* site is looking for indicators of how people are attracted to the website and how you can get them to come back for repeat business. In the context of your company, the site is the only game in town. Your competitors are other websites, not other parts of your company.

In a complementary *e-commerce* context, the customer has access to the company's brick-and-mortar facility and its website. The customer could use both, either of the two, or primarily one, but not exclusively. At any given time, it will depend upon whether the customer would prefer to go to the brick-and-mortar facility—to get more personal attention or to "touch" the products—or whether the customer is so pressed for time that the website is best answer.

For a particular sale, the initiating action could occur at the physical site; but follow-up activity—like checking order status—could occur on the website. On the other hand, an order could be placed on the phone, then tracked later on the website—or even on another website like UPS, if UPS were doing the delivery.

So, the problem is still the same long-standing need to track a business's success at acquiring, retaining, and satisfying customers—the right customers. There are just new metrics to master, those provided by the web activity. But there are new opportunities for gathering information. You can track different things and look for their causative factors. Revise the metrics gathering process as you learn more about what is meaningful.

See which web pages are being used the most or the least; and try to determine why. Find out what the customers like about the site and what they don't. What causes visitors to stay with the site and use it for repeat business? What turns them away? The hard part is finding out why people stick their head in for a second and never return. To determine this may require pulling in testers who are representative of users in general and who are complete strangers to the site. What information is helpful to users of the site? Which functions are helpful? Which functions are needed but are missing from the site?

An active site, one that is really used, will change over time as new features are added and old ones are modified. Usability testing is not a one-time affair. It needs to be revisited regularly. When changes are made to the site, the resultant site needs to be re-evaluated before and after implementation.

Reliability of the site is very important. If a site is not reliable, people will not use it. How often does the site go down, and for how long? What happens when the site goes down? How long can the site stay down without any long-term negative impact?

What type of users are the most profitable? Where should you be concentrating your energies? In the end, you need to concentrate on the customer and how a website can enhance the customer experience.

53

IT Projects

COMPUTER PROJECTS

Computer software applications are essential to the operation of most modern businesses, as are computer-based hardware and associated technology. Larger businesses must set up and operate computer networks (LANs and WANs). Communication networks, such as phone systems, can also be a necessity. Installing or updating these technology-based systems is, thus, a fact of life.

As a rule, the biggest project management problems are going to come from software applications. Hardware system projects give less grief. Either they work or they do not, and you know it quickly. Software is a different story, whether relatively independent of or tightly interfaced with the hardware.

Buy, Build, or Customize: Software applications can be bought off the shelf or developed using custom programming—or somewhere in between. If bought off the shelf, there can still be problems of compatibility, i.e., interfacing with hardware or other software applications.

The simplest case is to buy some common software application, such as a word processor or spreadsheet. On the other end of the off-the-shelf spectrum is some predefined, large application such as accounting or payroll. To complicate matters, some vendors bundle accounting, payroll, purchasing, human resources, fixed assets, project accounting, and so on, into an even larger application suite. This can ease compatibility problems since the whole suite is coming from one vendor. The different parts can already talk to each other.

But interfacing with hardware and other applications is the Achilles heel. The software vendor is unlikely to be the same company as the hardware vendor. And the database vendor might be some altogether different vendor. If interfacing with several software vendors is needed, the water gets muddier. There are more things to go wrong.

Realize that even when you buy a pre-existing application, custom programming may be required for the interfaces to hardware or other software. The larger software vendors with a large stable of products will often have a large consulting staff to help you install and implement the new system, plus continually keep it up to date. That ought to tell you something—the system has complexities.

The larger and more pervasive the new system, the more likely that business operations will be impacted by the new software and that they will have to be changed. Procedures and even policies may have to change. The before and after of any impacted business processes must be studied, and the potential impact needs to be gauged. Disruption of operations is the norm. The changes will probably impact employees and customers. This is where the consulting arm of the vendor comes in, with their experts—for a price, of course. "We are from the vendor. We are here to help." Your staff had better be prepared for this.

Normally, the most adventuresome route to take is that of developing a new application from scratch, a custom-programmed system. One school of thought is that if you can buy a solution that is close to what you need, do so and change your operations to match the new software. The other side of the coin is to buy software and modify it. This is risky because future releases of the underlying base package can severely impact the customizations already done. Once you buy the application and customize it, you are committed. Thoroughly analyze the situation before making a decision. Lean toward applications that more nearly match your intended flavor of operations.

Software is very complex. To develop a system properly necessitates determining user requirements, developing a good system design, coordinating application development, and thoroughly testing the resultant system. As you are painfully aware, just a small glitch in a program can wreak enormous havoc, even at the cost of life and limb.

"To err is human, but to really foul up requires a computer."
—Paul Ehrlich

Project Management: The overwhelming majority of software projects come in late, over budget, and incomplete. Effective project management and commitment by all involved people can help alleviate most problems; but unreasonable expectations and demands from upper management and users can undermine the whole effort. Reasonable demands and pragmatic approaches to the project can save the day.

The more complex or ambitious the project, the more likely it will fail or be cancelled outright. Many projects are started but never finished. The old practice of doing a feasibility study before launch is a good one. In modern terms, the "due diligence" analysis is very beneficial and can avoid wasted money.

Ill-Advised Estimates: One of the biggest failures of management is expecting or demanding accurate estimates on costs and schedules for a complex software development project before it is even started. Developers want to please their leaders and more than likely will be overly optimistic about how quickly a new system can be developed. It is not enough that the developers come up with and commit to their own schedules; the input for schedules must also be valid and based on sound judgment and experience. You need to figure out—in detail—where you are going and how you are going to get there.

However, at the start of a software project, you normally have not determined the detailed application requirements from the user. Trying to estimate the project before you have done application design is like trying to estimate the cost and schedule for building a custom house before the architect has worked with the buyers and the builder to come up with a house drawing.

If a project gets into trouble, management's solution is often to throw more bodies into the effort in order to meet deadlines. Sometimes that can help. It is more likely that more people mean worse communication and more chaos. More bodies can actually make the project drag out even longer. There is the old but valid proverb that applies to system development, "Nine women cannot have a baby in one month."

Re-Estimating: So, you must be more practical in approaching a software development project. Demands of the marketplace may dictate crash projects, but the more rational approach is to break complex projects into multiple phases, with phased-in implementations of system functions. Develop and implement a piece at a time.

Further, make it a part of accepted practice that costs and schedules are to be re-estimated at the end of each phase. Estimates should change as development proceeds—for the simple fact that knowledge of the project grows the further you get into the project.

Put on your logical thinking hat. At the start of a typical project, the requirements of the new system are only known in broad terms. Users typically do not have a full understanding of what they want in the finished system. After doing a good job of requirements gathering, the development team has a better idea of the effort involved in completing the project. Upon completion of the next stage, design, they have an even better idea of the effort remaining in the outstanding phases. The more phases that have been completed, the greater is the knowledge. Re-estimate. Re-estimate. As the project progresses, you will get better estimates and more accurate schedules.

Changes in Requirements: Another fact of life is that as the project proceeds, system requirements can change. The more the new application is explored, along with all its implications, the more likely that initial system requirements will change. Also, accept it as a hard and fast rule that once a new system is installed, it will need to be changed. Either the users will come up with requests for changes and enhancements, or the marketplace will change. If few requests come in for change after implementation, it is a good bet the new system is not being used very much. A dynamic, responsive system will require changes over time. Users will demand the changes be made. Have a change management process in place to deal with changes in requirements, both before and after implementation.

COMPUTER APPLICATION RESPONSIBILITIES

The ownership of computer application systems should not rest with the Information Technology division. Systems are normally developed for users, not IT. Systems serve their users, not the reverse. The IT department is a service department, not an end in and of itself.

This requires a special breed of people to interface between users and technology. These people should be technology savvy but user centered. They must have good systems sense and have a dedication to usability and usefulness. Good business sense is definitely needed. Further, they must be able to communicate well, which requires the ability to listen well. Communication is a two-way street. Hence, they must have great interpersonal skills.

With very few exceptions, most users do not really know what they want in a new system. They have general concepts and broad requirements in mind, maybe even a bunch of detailed requirements; but building an effective system requires much more. The requirements must be transformed into a workable and practical set of functions that can be developed and implemented in a cost-effective manner. This requires a team effort.

The end-user is responsible for the system requirements, and the point person for the technology side is responsible for the technical solution. But there must be cooperation and compromise between the players. One makes demands and the other, acting as an advisor, tries to figure out an acceptable way to satisfy the demands. Cost (budget), time, resources, and end purpose of the system are the driving forces behind a given project. They represent its constraints. Therefore, any solution must be practical and reasonable.

Once a system has been implemented, all bets are off. After the end-users start interacting with and using the system in the real world, shortcomings will turn up. Modifications will be needed. Enhancements will be required. A perfect computer application is a figment of the imagination. Regardless of which side of the fence they stand on, user or IT, the developers cannot anticipate all the needs of the system or the situations that will be encountered.

The world changes. The business environment changes. Competitors come up with threats you never dreamed of. Customers make new demands. In short, a system, if it is used at all, will require changes and enhancements. Accept it, budget for it, and get on with it. It should raise some eyebrows if no one is asking for revisions to the system after it has been implemented. As stated earlier, this is a good indication it is not being used as intended, or is being used only sparingly.

Part XII

FINANCES AND EXPENDITURES

54

Financial Reporting

TIMELY FINANCIAL REPORTING

We have modern computers. We have interactive computers. We have fast databases. We have or can develop great reporting tools. Why do companies continue to think in terms of 30-day reporting periods? In the modern day world, data that is 30-40 days old is "ancient history" and not very proactive in a fast-paced business world. Long monthly closings should be a thing of the past.

> "You can absolutely go broke being successful."
> —Jerry White

Operational data can certainly be reported and consolidated more often than once a month. If nothing else, the old concept of standard costing can be used to get near real-time accounting figures. Chief financial officers do not wait until monthly bank statement time to keep a handle on cash balances. Why not keep up with revenue and expenses?

Near real-time project accounting is possible today. Hours worked (with extended cost figures), non-payroll expenses, and revenue can be entered and the results reported with close-enough accuracy for timely business decisions.

Timely financial reporting should be just that—timely. Its main purpose should not just be to support the generation of monthly, quarterly, and annual reports. Why can't it be upgraded to help support the daily operations of the business? Executives need timely reporting to make timely decisions.

P&L STATEMENT ORIENTATION

Finance and accounting people seem to concentrate too much on current earnings, perhaps to the detriment of long-term earnings. This reflects an orientation to the Profit and Loss Statement that is, perhaps, more appropriate to a mature organization in a mature market in times past. Start-ups know better. You have to spend in the present in order to achieve future earnings.

Remember that shareholders look to the future, but they want the best of both worlds. They want to see good current earnings and good future earnings. A venture capitalist, by definition, looks to future earnings and future returns on investment, and is not overly concerned about current earnings for a new company.

The CFO, on the other hand, typically concentrates on current and past earnings. Month-over-month, quarter-over-quarter, and year-over-year performance figures are the areas of concern. As to the future, they think of the past as providing the clue to future performance. They make projections of revenue and expenditures using historical figures and projected sales. Using these figures, they also make projections about cash flow, since it must be managed closely.

In a fast-paced market, one in which disruptive technologies are the norm, too much concentration on earnings per share can be a bit misguided. You must spend now for future earnings. You must act now for the future. You may not be able to plan far into the future, but you must take a balanced approach to present and future earnings.

If current earnings are down because of investments in the future, tell the gurus on Wall Street what is going on. Cash cows are still cows. They do provide a steady stream of milk. But you should breed for future racehorses, winning racehorses. If you play your cards right and tell the proper story in regard to down payments (current expenditures) on the future, any dip in stock price will be temporary since the earnings dip is itself temporary.

However, you must tell the truth about future expectations—based on well-founded beliefs. If not, the shareholders will eventually find out and your stock will pay dearly. Don't over-estimate future revenues and earnings.

In summary, it is OK to sacrifice current earnings for the benefit of long-term performance. No pain, no gain. Don't concentrate too much on current earnings, and then fail to allow for the future. To make money in the future, you need to spend money now.

PRICE-TO-EARNINGS (P/E) RATIO

The P/E ratio is calculated by dividing market price per share by the company's earnings per share. When the ratio is dropping, it is a sign that investors may be losing their confidence in the expected profitability or growth of a company. If the figure is rising, investors' expectations about a company are growing more optimistic as time passes. For fast-growing companies, the P/E ratio is typically higher in relative terms. More mature companies are likely to have a lower P/E.

The denominator of the fraction, or earnings, is a key figure in determining company performance. If two companies are otherwise comparable, but one has a higher level of earnings per share; the one with the greater profits is doing better, at least on the surface. However, earnings are more applicable to mature companies as compared to emerging companies. Earnings can be deferred by incurring expenses in the present in order to secure company growth in the future.

Remember that first-to-market is a prime factor in market leadership. Getting that leadership will normally require upfront expenditures. Thus, earnings may be low or even nonexistent in a growth situation. Expenses can rightfully outpace revenue.

All this means that both management and investors must take into account future earnings potential. Low or even negative earnings can be a very positive sign for a company in growth mode. Expenditures are being made now with the expectation of huge returns in the future. But again, if two comparable growth-oriented companies have radically different profits, earnings can be a valid indicator of management effectiveness.

In any case, do not be as tied to P/E ratios as you might have been in the past. Earnings do count in the long run, but not necessarily in the short run. Keep things in perspective. The market's judgment will ultimately prevail.

55

Expenditures

COST CUTTING

When market conditions turn bad or a company runs into trouble, the simple solution, the no-brainer that executives always turn to, is cutting expenditures. Although there may be an overwhelming need to cut costs, the way it is done can be a crime and often is.

Cost cutting is typically done without much in-depth thought. It is simply implemented as an order from on high. Across-the-board cuts are sold as a democratic solution and are forced down through all levels in the organization without due consideration to the consequences of cutting away both the essential and the nonessential.

Instead, when cash flow and cash on hand dictate lowered expenditures, then reduce costs with surgical precision. Making every department cut its expenditures by some common percentage is an abdication of executive responsibility. If the executives have been doing their job all along and have been monitoring the effectiveness of ongoing operations and have been taking note of future opportunities, the answers about where to cut are already pretty well known. Pare costs with intelligence and objective reasoning. Mindless cuts can bite back with a vengeance later.

If you can cut costs without laying off people, do so; otherwise, you will be seen as breaking the contract of trust and support between management and the employees. Morale and company loyalty can evaporate overnight. Laying off people might easily result in your best people getting defensive and heading for the exits because of a feeling of uncertainty. They are marketable and can easily find another position. Therefore, you cut costs now but pay for it dearly on down the road.

If laying off people becomes unavoidable, the mistake companies often make is laying off the people with long seniority and high salaries. The reasoning goes something to the effect that younger people can do the same job for less money; therefore, you should force early retirement and get rid of the high-dollar people. However, the senior people may be the ones giving the highest payback. They just might be the most dependable in times of crisis. In any case, laying off a disproportionate share of the older people will get the Feds on your back.

So, forcing early retirement can be counterproductive. You can eliminate the wheat with the chaff. The older employee, because of experience and judgment, can be worth much more to company success than the younger, less experienced worker. Those gray hairs may have been deservedly earned—and at your expense.

Therefore, be careful when engaging in cost cutting. Make sure you are not cutting off your nose to spite your face. Be logical and rational in your thinking. Analyze the alternatives and look to your company's long-term health. Use surgical cuts, ones that hurt the least.

RAINY DAY EXPENDITURES

Downturns in business will occur. Changes will happen that are totally beyond your control—a general recession, for example. While your competitors are pulling in their horns, might it not be a good time to extend yours out a little further. What is suggested here is that the bad times can conceivably be used to your advantage—especially if you play your cards right. This means cutting in other areas so you can invest in your future and thereby jump way ahead of your competitor while he or she is treading water.

One possibility is to pour more money into research and product development than you might otherwise have thought about doing. While others are sitting back and licking their wounds, you could be doing something to advance your business and open up new opportunities. Move ahead while your competitor's motor is idling. Upgrade your technology. Update your processes. Improve your people's skills.

Compared to other companies, NOT reducing R&D may, relatively speaking, mean you are moving ahead at full speed while your competitors are at reduced RPMs. Try to be smarter than they are.

Take a hard look at expenditures. Divert nonessential funds into development efforts. Assign people that would otherwise be engaged in normal operations to work on potential contributions to future business. It might make sense, if you can finance it, to avoid the normally inevitable layoffs. If you have a cash hoard, use some of it to work on the future. Think out of the box. Let your competitors hide inside the perceived comfort and security of their own boxes with the lid pulled down.

You have heard of rainy day funds. How many businesses have you ever known that actually set aside funds in the good times as a hedge against the bad times? If times are exceptionally good, you know they cannot last forever, even with the best of companies.

Have you ever told your kids to save for the future? Why not practice what you preach? The result could be that you blast out of the business trough and into the clouds while others are still trying to figure out what happened.

56

Managing Shareholder Value

SHAREHOLDER VALUE

Shareholder value is the value of stock in a company from the investor's point of view. An investor will buy stock at a certain price with an expectation that the future return (sale price plus any dividends) will be greater than the amount invested, hopefully by an appreciable sum.

In the long term, stock price is the ultimate indicator of the value of a company. In the short term, this may not be the case. Investment flows to the place of best returns over the long haul, meaning the companies with the best performance in their respective markets. Collective judgment determines stock price.

> "Do not argue with the market, for it is like the weather: Though not always kind, it is always right."
> —Kenneth E. Walden

Executives should pay attention to stock price. It tracks performance over time from two perspectives. In one case, it tracks past performance; stock prices in the past are historical indicators. Today's stock price is not so much an indicator of current value as it is an indicator of future expectations. You do not buy a stock today expecting it to remain the same. If the stock price is advancing on increased volume, the buyers are expecting the stock to rise. If the stock price is falling on increased volume, the sellers are expecting the stock price to decline even more.

Expectations can get a reality check, though, as the past dot.com debacle has shown. Greenspan's "irrational exuberance" was a valid call. It is somewhat reminiscent of the old saying that you can fool some of the people all the time and all of the people some of the time, but you can't fool all the people all the time. In the dot.com arena, the artificially elevated stock prices eventually felt the prick of negative earnings. The chickens came home to roost. Investors got tired of throwing good money after bad. Results do count after all!

Eventually the company's management must give account for their performance. If they do not deliver on investor expectations, the investors will vote the company out of favor by selling their stock. When hope is extinguished, so is stock price.

Therefore, executives must manage well and lead their company into profitable market leadership, including shareholder profitability. Decisions cannot ignore stock price. If nothing else, remember any stock options you might have.

STOCK BUYBACKS

Consider for a moment what you are really accomplishing when you use corporate stock buybacks to increase the price of a stock. This is just stock price manipulation without any change in business. It often indicates the executive team is bankrupt in ideas. Put on your entrepreneurial hat instead. Use the funds in new pursuits with a longer-term potential.

Stock buybacks are just quick fixes with no long-term impact. Studies have shown they do little to raise stock prices in the long run. Spend the money more wisely on future opportunities.

Closing Comments

This book has covered a lot of ground. The details of carrying out just some of the suggestions could easily take whole books. But the objective of the book was not to present all the gory details, just nudge the business leader into thinking about ideas that may have been ignored or forgotten.

After reading the book, the perceptive leader should start paying more attention to what is going on around him or her and think outside the box more often. The concepts reviewed in the book are designed to help the company leader seek a more successful approach to professional life and business endeavors. The leader will likely agree with some of the ideas and reject others. That is a leader's prerogative.

If some of the ideas have piqued your interest and you want to explore them in more depth; look at the list of recommended books and tapes, or go to your bookstore or local library. There are just thousands of good ideas waiting for you to harvest and reap their bountiful benefits.

But it is not enough to know what to do; you must act on the ideas!

Recommended Books and Tapes

There are many books and tapes with great ideas, but these are my favorites from those read and listened to in recent years. Many of the thoughts and ideas had significant impact on what is found in this book. Most are recent publications.

BOOKS

Bedbury, Scott, with Stephen Fenichell. *A New Brand World: 8 Principles for Achieving Brand Leadership in the 21st Century.* New York: Penguin Group—Penguin Putnam Inc., 2002.

Blanchard, Ken, and Sheldon Bowles. *Gung Ho!.* New York: William Morrow and Company, Inc., 1998. (also available on tape)

Boone, Louis E. *Quotable Business: Over 2,800 Funny, Irreverent, and Insightful Quotations about Corporate Life.* 2nd ed. New York: Random House, Inc., 1999.

Buckingham, Marcus, and Curt Coffman. *First, Break all the Rules: What the World's Greatest Managers Do Differently.* New York: Simon & Schuster, 1999. (also available on tape)

Collins, James C., and Jerry I. Porras. *Built to Last: Successful Habits of Visionary Companies.* New York: HarperBusiness—HarperCollins Publishers, 1994. (also available on tape)

Dauten, Dale. *The Gifted Boss: How to Find, Create and Keep Great Employees.* New York: William Morrow and Company, Inc., 1999.

Davis, Stan, and Christopher Meyer. *Blur: The Speed of Change in the Connected Economy.* New York: Warner Books, Inc., 1998. (also available on tape)

Dawson, Roger. *Secrets of Power Negotiating: Inside Secrets from a Master Negotiator.* 2nd ed. Franklin Lakes, NJ: The Career Press, Inc., 1999.

Deep, Sam, and Lyle Sussman. *Yes, You Can: 1,200 Inspiring Ideas for Work, Home, and Happiness.* Reading, MA: Addison-Wesley Publishing Company, 1996.

Drucker, Peter F. *Management Challenges for the 21st Century.* New York: HarperBusiness—HarperCollins Publishers Inc., 1999. (also available on tape)

Farson, Richard, and Ralph Keyes. *The Innovation Paradox: The Success of Failure, The Failure of Success.* New York: Free Press—Simon & Schuster, Inc., 2002. (also available on tape)

Fox, Jeffrey J. *How to Become a Rainmaker: The People Who Get and Keep Customers.* New York: Hyperion, 2000. (also available on tape)

Frank, Leonard Roy, ed. *Random House Webster's Wit & Humor Quotationary.* New York: Random House, 2000.

Gladwell, Malcolm. *The Tipping Point: How Little Things Can Make a Big Difference.* New York: Little, Brown and Company, 2000. (also available on tape)

Goleman, Daniel. *Working with Emotional Intelligence.* New York: Bantam Books—Bantam Doubleday Dell Publishing Group, Inc., 1998. (also available on tape)

Hamel, Gary. *Leading the Revolution.* Boston: Harvard Business School Press, 2000. (also available on tape)

Johnson, Spencer. M.D. *Who Moved My Cheese?: An A-Mazing Way to Deal with Change in Your Work and in Your Life.* New York: G. P. Putnam's Sons—Penguin Putnam Inc., 1998. (also available on tape)

Koch, Richard. *The 80/20 Individual: How to Accomplish More by Doing Less—The Nine Essentials of 80/20 Success at Work.* New York: Currency—Doubleday, Random House, Inc., 2003.

Krug, Steve. *Don't Make Me Think: A Common Sense Approach to Web Usability.* Indianapolis: Que—Macmillan USA, 2000.

Larson, Alan. *Demystifying Six Sigma: A Company-Wide Approach to Continuous Improvement.* New York: AMACOM—American Management Association, 2003.

Lencioni, Patrick. *The Five Dysfunctions of a Team: A Leadership Fable.* San Francisco: Jossey-Bass—John Wiley & Sons, Inc., 2002.

Levinson, Jay Conrad, Rick Frishman, and Jill Lublin, with Mark Steisel. *Guerrilla Publicity: Hundreds of Sure-Fire Tactics to Get Maximum Sales for Minimum Dollars.* Avon, MA: Adams Media Corporation, 2002.

Lundin, Stephen C., Harry Paul, and John Christensen. *Fish!: A Remarkable Way to Boost Morale and Improve Results.* New York: Hyperion, 2000.

Miller, Lawrence M. *Barbarians to Bureaucrats: Corporate Life Cycle Strategies.* New York: A Fawcett Columbine Book, Ballantine Books—Random House, Inc., 1989.

Modahl, Mary. *Now or Never: How Companies Must Change Today to Win the Battle for Internet Consumers.* New York: HarperBusiness—HarperCollins Publishers, 2000. (also available on tape)

Moore, Geoffrey A. *Living on the Fault Line: Managing for Shareholder Value in the Age of the Internet.* New York: HarperBusiness—HarperCollins Publishers Inc., 2000. (also available on tape)

Neff, Thomas J., and James M. Citrin. *Lessons from the Top: The Search for America's Best Business Leaders.* New York: A Currency Book, Doubleday—Random House, Inc., 1999.

O'Shea, James, and Charles Madigan. *Dangerous Company: Management Consultants and the Businesses They Save and Ruin.* New York: Penguin Books—Penguin Group, Penguin Putnam Inc., 1998.

Pfeffer, Jeffrey, and Robert I. Sutton. *The Knowing-Doing Gap: How Smart Companies Turn Knowledge into Action*. Boston: Harvard Business School Press, 2000.

Robbins, Anthony. *Awaken the Giant Within: How to Take Immediate Control of Your Mental, Emotional, Physical & Financial Destiny*. New York: A Fireside Book, Simon & Schuster, 1991. (also available on tape)

Siegel, David. *Futurize Your Enterprise: Business Strategy in the Age of the E-Customer*. New York: John Wiley & Sons, Inc., 1999.

Smart, Bradford D., Ph.D. *Topgrading: How Leading Companies Win by Hiring, Coaching and Keeping the Best People*. Paramus, NJ: Prentice Hall Press—Simon & Schuster Company, 1999.

AUDIO TAPES

Blanchard, Ken, and Sheldon Bowles. *Raving Fans: A Revolutionary Approach to Customer Service*. Canada: Random House AudioBooks, 1993. (also available in book form)

Bronson, Po. *What Should I Do with My Life? The True Story of People Who Answered the Ultimate Question [Abridged]*. New York: Audioworks—Simon & Schuster Audio Division, Simon & Schuster, Inc., 2003. (also available in book form)

Brown, Les. *Live Your Dreams*. New York: Harper Audio—HarperCollins Publishers, 1992. (also available in book form)

Freund, James C. *Smart Negotiating: How to Make Good Deals in the Real World*. New York: Sound Ideas—Simon & Schuster Audio Division, Simon & Schuster, Inc., 1995. (also available in book form)

Jennings, Jason, and Laurence Haughton. *It's Not the BIG That Eat the SMALL...It's the FAST That Eat the SLOW: How to Use Speed as a Competitive Tool in Business*. Beverly Hills, CA: New Millennium Audio—NMWorldMedia, Inc., 2001. (also available in book form)

Mackay, Harvey. *How to Build a Network of Power Relationships.* New York: Sound Ideas—Simon & Schuster Audio Division, Simon & Schuster, Inc., 1995.

Roberts, Wess, Ph.D. *Leadership Secrets of Attila the Hun.* New York: Sound Ideas—Simon & Schuster Audio Division, Simon & Schuster, Inc., 1995. (also available in book form)

Senge, Peter M., et al. *The Fifth Discipline Fieldbook: Strategies and Tools for Building a Learning Organization.* New York: Bantam Doubleday Dell Audio Publishing—Random House, Inc., 1999. (also available in book form)

Index

abuse of power, 154
accepting change, 95
accidents at work, 280
accountability, 8
accounting, project, 369
acquisitions, 16, 64
action, not talk, 3
active listening, 156
activities, leisure, 29
adaptability, employee, 216
adapters to change, 99
adjustments, corrections, 35
advantage, competitive, 289, 310
advice, consultants, 295
advice, trusted, 149
advice, uniqueness, consultants, 297
advisor, 248
advisor, trusted, 149
advocate, employee, 277
agenda, meeting, 269
agent, negotiator, 188
agents, change, 99
agreement, 161
agreement, formal, negotiations, 197
agreement, mediation, 199
alienation, retailer, 322
allegiance, company, 102
alternatives, 151
alternatives to firing, 265
alternatives to outsourcing, 24
ambition, employee, 216

analysis, business functions, 24
analyze yourself, 123
analyzing training needs, 253
applications, computer, buy vs. build, 362
aristocratic corporation, 12, 17
assessment, employee, 64
assessment, self, 111
assets, capital, 55
assistant, your, 158
assumptions, basic, 1
assumptions, business, 6
assumptions, challenging, 150
assumptions, technology, innovation, 21
attitude, positive, employee, 215
attitudes and emotions, 93
attitudes toward Internet, customers, 351
attitudes, work, 102
avoiding responsibility, executives, 295
awareness, emotional, 108
beginning users, website, 359
beliefs, 29
beliefs vs. fear, 117
beliefs, limiting, personal, 124
benefits, selling, 318
best bosses, 211
best employees, 211
best employees, concentrating on, 246
best people, 211
best practices, 293
blended offer, 287
board of directors, 271

body language, 156
books, recommended, 379
boss, best, 212
brainstorming, modern, 166
brand loyalty, 309
briefing, new hire, 235
buffer in plans, 209
bureaucracy, excessive, 135
bureaucracy, 291
bureaucratic corporation, 12, 17
business and information technology, 341
business assumptions, 6
business efficiency and the Internet, 349
business focus, 283
business functions, analysis of, 24
business operations model, 19
business success, 33
buybacks, stock, 376
buyer vs. seller, 45
buzz marketing, 311
calmness, 165
candidate screening, employee, 225
candidness, 150
capital ownership, 55
cause, mission, 47
CEO, international, 91
challenging work, 82
champions of change, 97
change, 95
change agents, 99
change champions, 97
change factors, 96
change, accepting, 95
change, implementing, 61
change, structural, 64
changes in direction, 57
changes in requirements, IT projects, 365
channel conflict, Internet, 322
character, good, 107
characteristics, employee, 215

charismatic culture, 88
charting a course, 36
Chief Information Officer, 348
Chief Technology Officer, 348
choosing a course, 36
choosing markets, 311
choosing the best, or not, 278
closings, monthly, 369
closure, 159
closure, lack of, 139
clutter, unnecessary, website, 355
coaching, 246
collaboration, group, 162
collaboration, web, 353
collaborative culture, 87
collapse, time and distance, 9
command and control culture, 87
commitment, 102
common sense, 150
communication, 171, 173
communication basics, 173
communication, commitment, 103
communication, email, 273
communication, organizational, 178, 185
communication, team, 181
communication, written, 177
communications gone amok, 139
communications, company, 157
communications, corporate, 292
communicator, good, employee, 215
company allegiance, 102
company cultures, 86
company direction, 31
company operations, 281
company website, 354
competence in management, 209
competencies, core, 54
competency, core, prototyping, 44
competition from Internet, 350
competitive advantage, 289, 310

competitive pressures, negotiations, 194
competitors vs. consultants, 298
competitors, communication, 176
competitors, voice of, 60
complacency, 104
completion dates, 160
compromise, 165
compromise, mediation, 199
computer application responsibilities, 365
computer applications, buy vs. build, 362
computer projects, 362
concessions, negotiations, 190
conciseness, web page, 357
concluding negotiations, 196
confidence, self, 112
confidentiality, 178
conflict resolution, 164
connectivity in business, 289
consensus, 110, 161
considerations, organizational, website, 355
considerations, website, 353
consistency with customers, 332
consistency, negotiations, 192
consistency, web page, 357
consistent message, 309
consultants, 295
consultants, too many, 296
consulting engagement parameters, 301
consulting firms, 224
contact, human, 335
contact, personal, customers, 338
contagion, fear, 116
contagious emotions, 109
contract, formal, negotiations, 197
control mechanisms, 205
control, delegation, 292
controlling time, 133
cooperation, 165
coordination of players vs. customers, 334
core beliefs, ideologies, 49

core competencies, 54
core competency, prototyping, 44
core values, 147
core vs. support functions, 53
corporate life cycle, 10
corporate life cycle, overview, 11
corporate revolutionaries, 60
corporate staff, size, 291
corrections, adjustments, 35
cost, 285
cost cutting, 372
courage, employee, 216
course objectives, 256
course of action, personal, 128
course, choosing, 36
credibility, negotiations, 191
criticism, disagreement, 151
CRM, 333
cross-selling, 320
cultures, company, 86
cultures, merging, 65
cushion in plans, 209
customer experience, 335
customer identification, 330
customer information, 288
customer issues, 336
customer lock-in, 335
customer loyalty, 334
customer needs, 288
customer needs vs. website, 354
customer questionnaires, 337
customer relationship management, 333
customer satisfaction, 284, 317
customer satisfaction, website, 360
customers, 327
customers, communication, 176
customers, enthusiastic, 329
customers, Internet, 351
customers, managing, 333
customers, not always first, 20

customers, wrong, 330
customization, product or service, 288
cutting costs, 372
dashboard, executive, 184
data, operational, 369
dates, completion, 160
deadlines, 205
debriefings, 182
decisions about technology, 342
decisions, being party to, IT, 348
decisions, timely business, 369
decisive leader, 73
defense against problems, 337
deference to outsiders, 296
delegate control, 292
delegate downward, 239
delegate planning, 292
delegating authority, responsibility, 82
delegation, non, 135
delivery of product, 306
delivery vs. promise, customers, 331
delivery, product or service, 286
deniers of change, 100
departmental service, 292
deployment of resources, 52
design, user-driven, website, 354
design, web page, 356
desire, negotiations, 195
developing subordinates, 244
diagonal promotions, 249
differences, diversity, 259
difficulties, customer, 337
direction, company, 31
directors, board of, 271
disagreement, criticism, 151
discipline, 146
dislikes, likes, 29
dispositions toward Internet, customers, 351
dissatisfied customer, 336

distance, collapse, 9
distractions and stress, 113
diversification, 66
diversity of background, 61
diversity training, 259
dot.com meltdown, 349
downturns, business, 373
drive for success, persistent, 144
due diligence, 64
dying company, 13, 18
dynamic pricing, 319
early growth company, 11, 15
early retirement, 373
earnings, 370
earnings potential, 371
e-business, 344
e-business site, 360
e-commerce site, 360
education, basic, professional, 27
efficiency, 293
ego, 78, 175
email, 273
email, lost time, 139
emotional awareness, 108
emotional influence, 109
emotional intelligence growth, 28
emotions, 108, 131, 165
emotions and attitudes, 93
emotions, controlling, 113
emotions, customer, 289
employee assessment, 64
employee characteristics, 215
employee exits, 262
employee hiring, 222
employee interdepartmental moves, 250
employee losses, good, 266
employee loyalty vs. customer, 334
employee mis-hires, 220
employee motivation, 80
employee pay, 240

employee reviews, 263
employee stock ownership, 241
employee talent, 217
employee vs. consultant, 299
employee, best, 214
employee-driven company, 239
employees and investors, 219
employees vs. customers, 332
employees, communication, 176
employees, good, 34
employees, hoarding, 276
employees, keeping them, 237
employees, more valuable, 257
employees, new, 61
employees, older, 266
employer loyalty, 238
encounters and emotions, 109
encounters with employees, 84
encounters, team members, 181
encouragement, 83
end-user responsibilities, computer, 365
enthusiastic customers, 329
entrepreneur, 89
entrepreneur, transition from, 90
entrepreneurial executives, 90
environment, supportive, 238
equipment hoarding, 277
equipment outsourcing, 55
estimates, ill-advised IT project, 364
ethics, 106
evaluate hiring process, 229
execution, 143, 148
executive dashboard, 184
executive firings, 265
executive learning path, 252
executive position, new, 147
executive responsibilities, consultants, 298
executive training, 255
executives, entrepreneurial, 90
expectations, customer, 332, 333

expectations, managing, 208
expenditures, 370, 372
expenditures and finances, 367
expenditures, rainy day, 373
experience, customer, 335
experiences vs. fear, 116
experimentation, 44
expert users, website, 359
expertise, consultant, 300
extranet collaboration, 353
factors in marketing, 307
factors, change, 96
factors, market, 21
factors, success, new, 35
failed negotiations, 197
failings, employee, 263
failures, debriefed, 182
family and friends time, lost, 136
family, friends, 29
fast response, website, 358
fear, 115
fear as a motivator, 117
fear's existence, 115
feedback, 83
feedback, fellow workers, 27
finances and expenditures, 367
finances, personal, 132
financial reporting, 369
financial reporting, timely, 369
firing people, 262
firing, employee, 262
firings, 213
first to market, 307
fixing the problem, 168
flexibility, 40
flexibility, negotiations, 193
focus, 143
focus groups, 309
focus, business, 283
focus, failure to, 135

focusing on strengths, 9
friends and family time, lost, 136
friends, family, 29
fun at work, 104
funds, rainy day, 374
game plan for negotiations, 189
generate ideas, 38
goal setting, 81, 144
goals, 148
goals, attainable, 208
goals, lofty, 35
goals, personal, 125, 126
going with the flow, 278
good steward, 72
group collaboration, 162
group lists, 273
group skills, 275
growth of workers, 82
gut feelings, 146
happiness at work, 104
health, physical, 130
hires, reviewing previous, 221
hiring employees, 222
hiring process, 220
hiring process, evaluation, 229
historical precedence, 4
hoarding, 276
human contact, 335
idea stage of company, 11, 14
ideas, generate, 38
ideas, great, 3
ideas, sharing, 293
ideas, test them, 44
identifying customers, 330
ideologies, core, 49
impact of Internet, 349
improvements, making, 182
improvements, making, in products, 332
inattention, 311
incentives, consultants, 300

incompatibilities, employee, 264
individualism culture, 88
influence, 153
influence and power, 153
influence of technology, 341
influence of training schools, 314
influence, emotional, 109
influences, success, new, 35
information explosion, 344
information hoarding, 277
information sharing, 83, 178, 185, 293
information sharing, consultants, 299
information technology, 339
information technology and business, 341
information, customer, 288
information, incomplete, 164
information, not inventory, 179
initiative, 78
inner peace, 114
innovation, 39, 145
innovation roadblocks, 43
innovation, embracing, 45
innovation, stimulating, 58
insincerity, 157
intangible factors vs. product or service, 289
integration team, mergers, 65
integrity, negotiations, 191
intelligence, emotional, 28
interactions, team, 180
interdepartmental moves, 250
intermediate users, website, 359
internal functions, 291
internal staff promotions, 248
international CEO, 91
Internet, 349
Internet access, employee, 274
Internet channel conflict, 322
Internet competition, 350
Internet customers, 351

Internet lessons, 345
Internet prices, 319
Internet sales, 324
Internet vs. customer issues, 336
Internet, impact of, 349
interpersonal skills, 157
interpersonal skills, employee, 215
interrupting, 157
interruptions, unnecessary, 137
interview, structured, 230
interviews, employee, 226
interviews, new executive position, 147
intranet collaboration, 353
intuitiveness, web page, 356
inventory, 179
investment, executive, 241
investors, 375
investors and employees, 219
investors, communication, 176
issues, customer, 336
issues, problems, 148
IT partnership, 346
IT projects, 362
jargon, too much, consultants, 298
job postings, 223
judgment, negotiations, 192
junior people, consultants, 298
keeping employees, 237
kill the product, 306
knowing, but not doing, 3
knowledge, 251
knowledge of organization, 7
laggards in change, 100
lawsuits, avoiding, 278
layoffs, 372
leader, decisive, 73
leader, passionate, 75
leader, pragmatic, 72
leader, respected, 76
leader, supportive, 74

leader, vacillating, 74
leader, visionary, 77
leader, what is a, 71
leaders of change, companies, 98
leaders, not clones of each other, 203
leadership, 69
leadership in action, 77
leadership results, 76
leadership, closing remarks, 377
leadership, good, 34
leadership, market, 371
leadership, product or service, 45
learning paths, best, 251
leisure activities, 29
lessons from Internet, 345
lessons of dot.com meltdown, 349
leverage, applying, negotiations, 193
life cycle, corporate, 10
likes, dislikes, 29
listening, 175
listening to advisors, 152
listening to customers, 338
listening, active, 156
litigation vs. mediation, 199
lock-in, customer, 335
long-term ties, employees, 214
losses, employee, 262
losses, employee, good, 266
loyalty and trust, 106
loyalty to brand, 309
loyalty to organization, 8
loyalty, customer, 334
loyalty, employee, vs. customer, 334
loyalty, employer, 238
making things happen, 159
management, 201
management competence, 209
management fundamentals, 203
management notes, miscellaneous, 273
management, good, 34

management, project, IT, 363
managers as trainers, 258
managing customer relationships, 333
managing customers, 333
managing expectations, 208
managing people, 7
managing shareholder value, 375
market factors, 21
market leadership, 371
marketing and sales, 303
marketing basics, 307
marketing factors, 307
marketing the product, 305
marketing, buzz, 311
markets, choosing, 311
mastery, personal, 121
mature corporation, 12, 16
meaningful results, 204
meaningful work, 239
measurement of results, 3, 204
measurement process, review, 205
mediation, 198
mediation vs. litigation, 199
meetings, 268
meetings, idea exchange, 61
meetings, ineffective, 134
meltdown, dot.com, 349
mentoring, 248
mergers, 64
message, consistent, 309
messengers of buzz marketing, 312
mingling with employees, 84
mis-hires, 220
mission, company, 47
mistakes, inevitability, 4
mistakes, risks, 35
model, business operations, 19
model, new, implementation, 61
model, personal operations, 26
moderator, meetings, 269

modern brainstorming, 166
monetary incentives, other, employee, 238
money vs. time, 140
monitoring progress, 205
monthly closings, 369
motivation, employee, 80
motivation, fear, 117
motivations, employee, 238
navigation, website, 357
necessity, weakness, negotiations, 194
needs, customer, 288
negotiating, power, 187
negotiations, 187
net price, selling, 318
networking, 154
networking, professional, 28
new employees, 61
new executive position, 147
new hire productivity, 235
objectivity, 40, 150
objectivity, consultants, 296
offer, blended, 287
offer, employment, 228
older employees, 266
ombudsman position, 277
operational data, 369
operations model, personal, 26
operations, company, 281
opportunities, watching for, 39
opportunity knocking, 144
opportunity, windows of, 40
optimism, 79
organizational communication, 178
organizational considerations, website, 355
organizational knowledge, 7
orientation, new hire, 235
orientation, P&L statement, 370
outsiders, deference to, 296
outsourcing, 23
outsourcing equipment, 55

outsourcing, alternatives to, 24
outsourcing, or not, IT, 346
outstanding tasks, 161
ownership, computer applications, 365
P&L statement orientation, 370
parameters, consulting engagement, 301
partnership arrangements, 24
partnership with IT, 347
passionate leader, 75
pay, employee, 240
peace, inner, 114
peers coaching, 247
people, employees, 285
people, good, 34
people, junior, consultants, 298
perfection in efficiency, 293
performance vs. stock price, 375
performance, employee, 263
performance, long-term, 370
persistence, personal, 129
persistent drive for success, 144
personal contact, customers, 338
personal mastery, 121
personal operations model, 26
personal stability, 111
personal time, lost, 136
perspective, negotiations, 192
perspective, personal, 130
planning, daily, 140
planning, delegation, 292
planning, lack of, 136
planning, strategy, 58
politics, 155
politics vs. consultants, 299
pools, talent, 217
position definition, employee, 223
position, employee, right vs. wrong, 245
positive attitude, employee, 215
potential, earnings, 371
power, 153

power and influence, 153
power negotiating, 187
powerbrokers, 155
practices, best, 293
pragmatic leader, 72
preeminence, fleeting, 336
previous employees, 267
price-to-earnings ratio, 371
pricing benefits, selling, 318
pricing, dynamic, 319
pricing, real-time, 319
pride, 78
priorities, 79
priorities in training, 254
prioritization, failure in, 134
problem determination, 149
problem resolution, 164
problem solving, 168
problem solving, sales, 316
problems, 160
problems, issues, 148
product delivery, 286, 306
product development, 305
product enhancement, 306
product leadership, 45
product marketing, 305
product or service, 284
product rejection, 308
product training schools, 313
productive output, 83
productivity, new hire, 235
products and marketing, 307
professional training, 255
profit goal, 9
project accounting, 369
project management, IT, 363
projects, computer, 362
projects, IT, 362
promise vs. delivery, customers, 331
promises, commitment, 103

promoting from within, 248
promotions, diagonal, 249
prototypes, building, 43
public awareness, 309
purpose, cause, mission, 47
pursuit of success, 142
qualifications of advisor, 149
quality, 285
questionnaires, customer, 337
R&D, 42
rainy day expenditures, 373
raise the bar, 208
rapport, 110
reacting to change, 97
real-time pricing, 319
receiving vs. transmitting, 175
recommended books and tapes, 379
recreational time, lost, 136
recruiting efforts, 223
re-estimating IT projects, 364
reference checks, employee, 228
rejection, product, 308
rejects, hiring, 229
relationship management, customer, 333
relationship, interactive, 289
relationships, personal, 131
relationships, productive, 156
reliability, website, 361
repeat sales, 317
report, consulting final, 302
reporting, financial, 369
reporting, timely financial, 369
requirements, changes in, IT projects, 365
research and development, 42, 373
resolution, conflict, 164
resolution, problem, 164
resolution, speedy, 160
resources, deployment, 52
resources, supplying, 82
resources, wise use, 293

respect, 83
respect for authority, 8
respected leader, 76
response time, website, 355
response, fast, website, 358
response, speed of, to customer, 289
responsibilities, 160
responsibilities, computer application, 365
responsibility for completion, 205
responsibility, avoiding, executives, 295
responsiveness, 157
results via measurement, 204
results, evaluate training, 254
results, good, 35
results, leadership, 76
results, reviewing, 183
retailer alienation, 322
retirement, 29
retirement, early, 373
return on assets, 56
revenue, three types, 310
reviewing results, 183
reviews, employee, 263
revolutionaries, corporate, 38, 60
reward ideas, 293
risk vs. fear, 116
risks of buzz marketing, 313
risks, mistakes, 35
risks, taking small, 44
roadblocks, innovation, 43
romance at work, 279
safety concerns, 280
salaries, 237
sales and marketing, 303
sales cycle, 305
sales, Internet vs. retail, 324
satisfaction, customer, website, 360
savings, selling, 318
schedule slippage, 205
schools of technology, 313

scope of consulting engagement, 301
screening candidates, employee, 225
search firms, 224
self analysis, 123
self-assessment, 111
self-confidence, 112
self-control, 112
self-discipline, training, 252
self-evaluation, 28
self-worth, employee, 216
seller vs. buyer, 45
selling, 316
selling a solution, 316
selling dollars, 318
serenity, 113
service delivery, 286
service leadership, 45
service or product, 284
service upgrades, 287
service, departmental, 292
serving the corporation, 292
settlement, mediation, 199
shareholder value, 375
shareholder value, managing, 375
sharing ideas, 293
sharing information, 178, 293
sharing information, consultants, 299
signposts, 143
silence of customer, 331
simplicity, 4, 146
simplicity vs. consultants, 300
simplicity, web page, 358
skill building, employee, 245
skills development, 28
skills, team, 275
slippage of schedules, 205
slippage, causes, solutions, 206
solution, selling, 316
solutions, selling them, 308
solutions, uniqueness, consultants, 297

solving the problem, 167
sophistication, user, website, 358
speedy resolution, 160
spin-offs, 67
spirituality, lost, 136
spotlight, executive in the, 9
stability, personal, 111
staff size, corporate, 291
stages of corporate life cycle, 11
standards, personal, 125, 127
star player culture, 87
start-up company, 11, 14
state of mind, power, 154
statement, P&L, orientation, 370
status quo, 104
staying current, not, 138
staying power, 45
steward, good, 72
stock buybacks, 376
stock options, 241
stock ownership, employee, 241
stock price, 375
stock purchase plans, 243
strategy planning, 58
strengths, dwelling on, 213
strengths, focusing on, 9
strengths, personal, 123
strengths, subordinates, 244
stress and distractions, 113
structural change, 64
structured interview, 230
subordinates opinion, competence, 210
subordinates, developing, 244
success, 119
success, business, 33
success, debriefed, 182
success, exploiting, 79
success, pursuit of, 142
success, website, 360
successful, being, 142

supervision, excessive, 135
supervisor, 8
suppliers, communication, 176
supplies hoarding, 277
support functions, 53
support, emotional, 109
supportive environment, 238
supportive leader, 74
survival, 115
system requirements, changes, 365
system requirements, computer, 365
taking action, personal, 128
talent, employee, 217
tapes, recommended, 379
task assignment, 205
team, 148
team interactions, 180
team skills, 275
teams and supervision, 8
technology influence, 341
technology schools, 313
technology, decisions, 342
technology, developer, 343
technology, follower, 342
technology, information, 339
technology, user, 342
technology, using, 341
terrorists, management, 38
testing, website, 358
threats, negotiations, 195
time and timing, 40
time management, personal, 130
time pressures, negotiations, 194
time theft, 133
time vs. money, 140
time, collapse, 9
time, controlling, 133
timely financial reporting, 369
to-do list, 140
tolerance, diversity, 261

tools, improper, lost time, 137
tracking stocks, 67
trainer training, 256
training, 251
training by managers, 258
training for changes, 63
training needs, 252
training needs, analyzing, 253
training objectives, 256
training, diversity, 259
training, priorities, 254
training, product, 313
training, professional, 255
transition from entrepreneur, 90
transmitting vs. receiving, 175
trust, 83
trust, 105
trust in the organization, 105
trusted advice, 149
trustworthiness, 106
truth vs. customer, 336
tyrant vs. fear, 118
underground marketing avenues, 312
understanding, 165
understanding others, 156
uniqueness of advice, consultants, 297
upbeat work environment, 239
usability, website, 354
user sophistication, website, 358
user-driven design, website, 354
users, website, 359
value system, 81
values, 29
values, core, 147
victory over self, 132
virtual corporation, 6
virtual corporation, 20, 22, 354
vision management, 48
vision statement, 48
vision, developing company, 329

visionary leader, 77
weakness, necessity, negotiations, 194
weaknesses, not dwelling on, 213
weaknesses, personal, 123
weaknesses, subordinates, 244
web access, employee, 274
web collaboration, 353
web communities, 309
web page design, 356
web surfing, 274
web surfing, lost time, 137
website considerations, 353
website success, 360
website users, 359
website, company, 354
websites, retailer vs. company, 323
windows of opportunity, 40
win-win resolution, 165
wisdom, conventional, ignoring, 38
word of mouth, 175
work and fun, 104
work attitudes, 102
work environment, upbeat, 239
work performance, improved, 257
worth of consultants, 300
writing it down, 177
wrong customers, 330
wrong, right to be, 145

0-595-31053-2